HIS KINGDOM COME

His Kingdom Come

Orthodox Pastorship and Social Activism
in Revolutionary Russia

JENNIFER HEDDA

NORTHERN
ILLINOIS
UNIVERSITY
PRESS

© 2008 by Northern Illinois University Press

Published by the Northern Illinois University Press, DeKalb, Illinois   60115

Manufactured in the United States using recycled, acid-free paper

All Rights Reserved

Design by Julia Fauci

Library of Congress Cataloging-in-Publication Data

Hedda, Jennifer.

His kingdom come : Orthodox pastorship and social activism in revolutionary Russia
/ Jennifer Hedda.

    p.   cm.

Includes bibliographical references and index.

ISBN 978-0-87580-382-1 (clothbound : alk. paper)

1. Russia—Church history—20th century. 2. Russkaia pravoslavnaia tserkov'—
Clergy—Political activity. 3. Church and social problems—Russkaia pravoslavnaia
tserkov'. 4. Church and state—Russia. 5. Russkaia pravoslavnaia tserkov'—History—
20th century. 6. Gapon, Georgii Apollonovich, 1870-1906. I. Title.

BX491.H43 2008

281.9'4709041—dc22

2007034872

CONTENTS

PREFACE

Social commentators and critics in the West have been predicting the demise of the Christian church since the late eighteenth century, when the Enlightenment, the French Revolution, and the Industrial Age began to transform western society. The church was intimately associated with the other institutions of the old order—divine right monarchy, feudalism, the noble estate, serfdom—all of which were extinct by the end of World War I. Furthermore, it was founded upon beliefs, customs, and values that dated back hundreds of years; these traditions constituted a core element of its identity. Could such ancient traditions be reconciled with modernity? Many secular thinkers predicted that they could not, and anticipated that modernity would win out over the faith. Certainly many Christians have feared the same, from the nineteenth century into the present day. Yet, thus far Christianity has withstood the onslaught of modernity: it persists while other ancient institutions have disappeared. Believers may take its survival for granted, but a quick glance at the ongoing struggle between tradition and modernity in many Muslim societies today reminds us how difficult—and how important—this struggle is.

The church has survived because Christians have found ways to *combine* tradition and modernity, rather than simply rejecting one and embracing the other. During the nineteenth century, when sweeping social and cultural changes were undermining the church's historic claims to preeminence and authority, many Christian thinkers in Europe and the United States began to develop a more socially oriented interpretation of Christianity that was responsive to the needs and hopes of believers living in an industrialized, urbanized society in which technology and science were increasingly influential. This social Christianity found many expressions: in the writings of Alfred Ritschl, Adolf Harnack, and Walter Rauschenbusch; in the ministry of Félicité de Lamennais; in the papal encyclical *Rerum Novarum* of Leo XIII; and in the activities of the Salvation Army. The "social gospel" movement that developed in the United States in the late nineteenth and early twentieth centuries had an especially far-reaching impact on American society, inspiring key leaders in the American civil rights movement. This case is but one example of how Christians willing to reinterpret the church's mission and goals discovered new opportunities for leadership and the exercise of influence, making it possible for Christianity not only to survive the transition to modernity but to grow and develop further.

Modernity arrived in the eastern parts of Europe somewhat later than it did in the West, but the challenge it posed to the church there was no less serious, though the story of how the Christians of the Eastern Orthodox church responded has not yet been studied in any great detail. This book examines the case of tsarist Russia, which experienced a whirlwind of socioeconomic and cultural changes during the six decades that preceded the Bolshevik Revolution of 1917. The officially established and culturally dominant Russian Orthodox Church criticized and resisted many of the changes that were transforming Russian society, but both clergy and lay believers also found ways to adapt their religious beliefs and practices to meet the new demands thrown up by modern life. The church's surprising resilience enabled it to weather not only the stresses of Russia's late imperial period, but also to ride out the waves of revolution that washed over the country in the twentieth century. Today the Russian Orthodox Church is again confronted by rapid and unpredictable change. Perhaps it can draw strength from knowing that its history, like the history of the church in the West, has been shaped by innovation as well as tradition.

I would like to acknowledge and thank some of those who supported, encouraged, and challenged me while I was working on this project. I am thankful to Professor Richard Pipes, who allowed me the independence I needed to pursue a topic of research that differed from his own interests. My warmest appreciation goes to Pat Herlihy, James Flynn, and Paul Valliere for their unfailing interest in and enthusiasm for my work over the course of many years. I also must gratefully acknowledge the unflagging patience and support of Greg Freeze for this work and, in particular, his willingness to act promptly and generously as a mentor.

Although I may not have always shown it, I appreciated the questions and criticisms raised by all those who discussed my ideas with me or read this work at various stages, including Edward Keenan, Cemal Kafadar, John LeDonne, Adele Lindenmeyr, Laura Engelstein, Valerie Kivelson, Greg Gaut, Nadia Kizenko, Chris Ely, David Brandenberger, Eric Lohr, Laurie Manchester, and Emily Gottreich. Thanks are also due to those fellow graduate students who befriended and assisted me during my semester of research in Russia: Heather Coleman, Gabriella Safran, Nick Breyfogle, John Strickland, Steve Dukes, Joseph Alfred, and David Schimmelpenninck van der Oye. My thanks are also due to the anonymous reviewers who submitted detailed comments and suggestions for revisions to me through Northern Illinois University Press; their comments influenced my revisions significantly.

As I worked on rewriting the manuscript, I received invaluable advice, support, and encouragement from my friend and colleague at Simpson College, Nancy St. Clair. I also appreciated the interest in my work that many other colleagues demonstrated, particularly Nicolas Proctor, Bill Friedricks, Owen Duncan, Amy Doling, Erin Reser, and Alison Wolf.

I would like also to acknowledge with gratitude the assistance of the professional librarians and archivists whose knowledge and helpfulness greatly assisted me in my work at the Russian National Library in St. Petersburg, the library of the St. Petersburg Seminary and Academy, the Russian State Historical Archive and its excellent library, the State Museum for the History of Religion, the libraries of Harvard and Columbia universities, and the New York Public Library. Special thanks go to Edward Kasinec of the Slavic Reading Room at NYPL for his interest in my subject and his generous bibliographic assistance. I am also grateful to Kristi Ellingson at Dunn Library of Simpson College; her assistance in procuring interlibrary loans for me while I was revising the manuscript was invaluable.

Finally, my thanks to those institutions and organizations that provided me with the funds necessary for study, travel, and research: the Department of History at Harvard University, the Graduate School of Arts and Sciences at Harvard University, and the Mellon Fellowship Office at the Woodrow Wilson National Fellowship Foundation. Research for this work was also supported in part by grants from the International Research and Exchanges Board and the Foreign Language and Area Studies Fellowship program.

None of these individuals or institutions is to be held responsible for the opinions and ideas expressed in this work or for any errors of fact or interpretation. These are my responsibility alone.

HIS KINGDOM COME

INTRODUCTION

Early in the year 1905, a revolution against Europe's last autocratic government erupted in Russia. On 9 January, tens of thousands of workers gathered at meeting points throughout the working-class districts of St. Petersburg, the imperial capital, and prepared to march en masse to the Winter Palace in order to present a petition to the tsar and emperor, Nicholas II. The petition called on the tsar to fulfill his duty as a Christian ruler to render justice to his people by granting them political freedoms and social reforms. Although the marchers were unarmed and proceeded through the streets of the city singing hymns and bearing religious icons, church banners, and portraits of the tsar, some of the soldiers who blocked the main roads and bridges leading to the Palace Square shot at them, while cavalry units on horseback dispersed the crowds around the palace with sabers, swords, and whips. Dozens of marchers were killed and several hundred were wounded, including women and children who had been among the marchers. The massacre of these humble petitioners shocked the country, provoking strikes and riots in the capital and across the empire in the days that followed. The events of that "Bloody Sunday" triggered the revolution of 1905.

The man who wrote the petition to the tsar and organized the workers' march seemed a most unlikely revolutionary. His name was Father Georgii Gapon, and he was a priest of the Russian Orthodox Church, Russia's oldest and most well-established institution. The Orthodox church had been closely associated with the rulers of the country ever since the legendary day in the ninth century when Prince Vladimir of Kiev converted to Orthodox Christianity and ordered his subjects to do the same. Although there had been times during Russia's pre-modern era when the church enjoyed a significant degree of autonomy and even a few famous occasions when members of its clergy dared to criticize the country's powerful rulers, in general the church's history was characterized by cooperation with and support for the government. Moreover, since the early eighteenth century, Peter the Great (1682–1725) and his successors on the Russian throne had worked to bind the church even more closely to the state in the belief that this would strengthen the state's popular influence and enhance its legitimacy. The formula "Orthodoxy, Autocracy, and Nationality" that Count Sergei Uvarov articulated during the reign of Nicholas I (1825–1855) highlighted the importance of the church in the political system and the close connection the rulers perceived between the church and the state. This intimate relation between the church and state had a profound effect upon the Orthodox clergy, whose lives were shaped and delimited not only by church canons but also by numerous state decrees that regulated their education, their service, and many of their personal choices.[1] Little wonder that many nineteenth-century Russians, especially those who were educated, regarded the Orthodox clergy as servants of the state.[2] Even as the contours of a revolutionary situation began to take shape at the end of the nineteenth century, few observers in Russia would have thought there was any potential for revolutionary leadership among the clergy. In fact, Russian radicals (and liberals as well) excoriated the clergy as blindly loyal upholders of the ancien régime, branding them with a reputation that persists to this day.[3]

Given such a context, Father Georgii's role in the events of Bloody Sunday seems difficult to explain. If the Orthodox church was a pillar of the autocracy, how did a clergyman come to lead a mass demonstration that sparked a popular revolution? Most accounts of 1905 sidestep this question and simply identify Gapon either as a loyal stooge used by the secret police in a bungled effort to try to undermine revolutionary organizations among the urban workers or as a rogue priest employed by the regime's opponents to appeal to the simple folk who still took religion seriously. Both views reflect the thorough politicization of the commonly accepted interpretations of Bloody Sunday, in which the participants are viewed as actors motivated primarily by political views and objectives to act for or against the regime. If we accept this assumption of the primacy of politics, however, we develop a kind of tunnel vision and see only those individuals whose actions and ideas have a political significance, and often only while they are active. Thus, in histories of the 1905 revolution Father Georgii usually appears abruptly on the scene only a few months before the march to the Winter Palace as the leader of a rapidly growing workers' organization and exits immediately after the march is violently suppressed. The questions of how and why Gapon became involved in that organization and how it related to his life and career before his moment in the spotlight are rarely raised. When they are, political issues remain paramount, despite the fact that Father Georgii's career in the church suggests we at least entertain the possibility his decisions were motivated by ideas or beliefs grounded in religion. Considering the history of the church's relations with the state, questions about how Father Georgii's status as a clergyman related to his involvement in activities that the state viewed as challenging its authority are particularly relevant and important: Was he the only clergyman involved in this kind of work? Were his ideas and activities unusual for an Orthodox priest? Did his peers and superiors approve of his work and his ideas or not, and why?

In attempting to address such questions we soon realize how much we are hindered by the general politicization of the church's history during this period. Because the Orthodox church was so closely associated with the tsarist regime, it was regularly invoked by the regime's defenders and attacked by its opponents. The detractors' scathing criticisms in particular have left a deep impression on the historiography of the period in which the church is frequently depicted as its harshest critics saw it—reactionary, repressive, intolerant, sycophantic, apathetic, ineffective, weak, obsolescent, irrelevant. This one-sided and unfair portrayal has been further distorted by the tendency to reduce the church to a political player, of interest (or not) only insofar as the ideas or activities of the Synod, the bishops, or the clergy related to the fierce political struggle of the late imperial period. Such a narrowly focused concern with politics has obscured and distorted the study of the Russian Orthodox Church. Until very recently, it has discouraged scholars from asking a basic question: setting aside the high politics of church-state relations, what do we know about how the Russian Orthodox Church actually functioned in the life of Russian society? We lack the information to determine whether it was usual for Russian Orthodox clergymen to be involved in any community organizations or to be responsible for any activities outside of performing the liturgy and requested religious rites and ceremonies. We do not know whether members of the Russian Orthodox clergy had any thoughts or opinions regarding the church's mission, its relation to society, or their role in fulfilling its work. A glance at the history of the Christian churches in Europe and the United States at this time reminds us that in those places the clergy, armed with a new emphasis on the social aspects of Christian teaching referred to as the "social gospel," significantly expanded their social outreach in response to new challenges raised by the enormous economic, social, and cultural changes of the nineteenth century.[4] Did the social gospel movement have any influence in Russia, or was there any parallel in the Russian Orthodox Church stimulated by similar developments? This question highlights our ignorance of how the Orthodox clergy viewed the challenges the church faced as Russia experienced its own wrenching social and economic changes in the late nineteenth and early twentieth centuries.

This study addresses our lack of knowledge about how the church functioned in late imperial Russian society by focusing on the parish clergy of St. Petersburg from the time of the Great Reforms in the middle of the nineteenth century to the eve of World War I. Throughout Russia, the parish clergy were the ones who carried out the church's daily work, interacting with the lay population as well as with each other and the members of the church hierarchy to carry out their responsibilities as priests, teachers, counselors, and administrators; in St. Petersburg, the parish clergy were Father Georgii's peers, the men among whom he served in the years before the 1905 revolution, whose work and ideas provide the most immediate context in which to understand the origins of Gapon's activities. Looking at these individuals, the first half of this book poses three basic questions. First of all, who were they? Given that the majority of the parish clergy in the capital came from the clerical estate, even after the reforms of the mid-nineteenth century allowed the sons of the clergy to choose other professions, this question is not so much about social origins as about environment and education (addressed in chapters 2 and 3, respectively). These two key factors shaped the experience and outlook of the city's parish clergy, distinguishing them from the provincial clergy and from the city's lay population. The unique ecclesiastical environment of the capital presented the local clergy with serious challenges while also affording them unusual opportunities to experiment with new ideas and activities. The education that nearly all of the capital's clergymen received at the St. Petersburg Ecclesiastical Academy, one of the church's four schools for higher learning, prepared them to take advantage of those opportunities both intellectually, through the challenging courses it offered, and practically, through the range of activities and associations it supported for students and faculty alike.

The second question concerns the parish clergy's ideas about their work in the church. What did the clergy of the capital think about the church's mission in the world, and how did they conceive of their role in fulfilling that mission? Chapter 4 examines how the St. Petersburg parish clergy came to emphasize a "this-worldly" interpretation of the church's purpose in the world during the reform era of the mid-nineteenth century, as a result of developments in the intellectual life of the church and the changes occurring in Russian society. New views on the church's purpose evolved, and they shaped the ways in which the parish clergy defined themselves, their relationship to the laity, and their responsibilities to the church community. This shift was reflected in the changing language that the clergy used to refer to themselves: not only as priests divinely empowered to perform the liturgy and the sacraments but pastors as well, inspired by the example of the Good Shepherd to foster in themselves and among their fellow clergymen deep feelings of love, compassion, and mercy toward their humble flock. These feelings often moved individual clergymen to action, which leads us to the third question: how did the clergy's conception of the church's mission and their own role influence their activities? During the reform era, the St. Petersburg parish clergy began to expand the church's charitable work, traditionally centered in the monasteries, by organizing parish-based charities. As chapter 5 explains, these parish-based charities grew in number throughout the remainder of the nineteenth century, expanding the scope of their work and the number of people involved both as donors and recipients, thus bringing clergy and laity together into an active Christian community outside the boundaries of church services. In the last two decades of the century, the clergy's outreach was significantly expanded through the work of two extra-parochial organizations, one focused on popular religious enlightenment and the second on temperance. These organizations, examined in chapter 6, operated throughout the city, actively involving scores of clergymen and hundreds (eventually thousands) of lay people in religiously inspired meetings, discussions, and activities on a weekly basis in the years immediately before the 1905 revolution. These enormously successful extra-parochial organizations shaped the environment in which Father Georgii developed his own outreach activities.

The second half of the book focuses on how the post-reform generation of clergymen—born during the reform years and trained during the very period when the ideas and activities described in the first half of the book were evolving—responded to the revolutionary upsurge of the early twentieth century. It looks closely at those individuals and groups within the St. Petersburg pastorate whose religious ideals inspired them to challenge the regime. One of the best-known clergymen of that time was Father Grigorii Petrov, whose numerous writings and lectures were hugely popular among both common folk and educated Russians. Father Grigorii was deeply admired among the St. Petersburg clergy, especially those of his generation, who were still under the age of forty in 1905. Although today he is unknown to all but a few specialists, his work (discussed here in chapter 7) was especially significant because it progressed from an emphasis on individual action within the community as a means of building the Kingdom of God in the world to an embrace of communal action through politics to effect the transformation of society and government in accordance with the principles of the Gospels. Father Georgii Gapon, in establishing the program for his workers' organization and guiding its development through the revolutionary buildup of 1904, was inspired by the same ideals that suffused Father Grigorii's work, which as chapter 8 shows, were embedded by that time in the culture of the educated clergy: a fervent commitment to public service, a belief in the necessity of speaking out and taking action, a willingness to sacrifice oneself for the sake of others, a vision of a new community transformed by Christian love and justice. These ideals continued to exert a powerful influence on the clergy of the capital even after the tragedy of Bloody Sunday, inspiring several dozen younger clergymen who defended Father Georgii in the days following the massacre to organize a group to articulate and promote a new vision of Christian politics that would renovate the church and empower it to lead the transformation of Russian society, as discussed in chapter 9. The Renovationists did not succeed in building up much popular support for their program. As the authorities worked to restore order following the upheavals of 1905 and 1906, these clergymen, along with Father Grigorii Petrov and others whose interpretation of the church's mission had led them to act or speak out in favor of changing the existing order, were increasingly subject to strong administrative pressures. In the final chapter of the book, we see how some of the parish clergy in the capital attempted to maintain their social outreach work under the more restrictive conditions of the inter-revolutionary period, and how the difficult conditions of these years variously influenced particular clergymen, leading some to abandon the clerical profession and others to seek alternatives to the established church, while still others—some in relief and some in bitter frustration—retreated to the safe haven of locally focused charitable and educational work. Thus, on the eve of the Great War the church in St. Petersburg appeared to be a center of calm and order once again, though beneath its frozen surface the controversies raised by the clergy's role in the 1905 revolution still swirled, ready to rise to the top when the 1917 revolution shattered the immobilizing ice that had built up around the church during the preceding decade.

This study of the St. Petersburg parish clergy challenges familiar stereotypes of the clergy and the Orthodox church. Ilya Repin's famous painting *Easter Morning* portrayed the parish clergy as their critics often described them: ill-educated, drunk, and greedy cynics who exploited the piety of the people by carrying out the traditional rites of the church while neglecting their parishioners' poverty and ignorance. This representation and others like it are well known because the old regime's many critics often attacked the church as a part of the system that they wanted to change. The intensive study of these critical works in the post-1917 period by scholars seeking to explain the collapse of the old regime and the success of the revolution made their common views of the church and its clergy both familiar and accepted, not as part of the political discourse of the late imperial period but as descriptions of reality. My work proceeds from a different basis, beginning instead with the sources produced by the parish clergy themselves about their lives and their work: their published memoirs; their sermons, lectures, articles, and books; the records of the organizations that they established and maintained over many years and the official annual reports that the diocese recorded about their activities. These sources provide an opportunity to see the clergy as they publicly represented themselves, emphasizing the virtues they aspired to, the beliefs that inspired them, the goals they pursued, and the accomplishments they attained. By looking at such sources over a period of several decades, we can also see how the clergy's ideas and activities evolved during the late imperial period in response both to developments internal to the church and events in Russian society more broadly, leading to an appreciation that the Orthodox church was not a static institution, for its clergy were an integral part of Russian life, shaped by the same challenges and opportunities that influenced other groups in Russia.

The idea of approaching the subject of the church's place in society from within by looking at what religious ideas, beliefs, and practices meant to the parish clergy and seeking to understand how the clergy's conception of Orthodoxy evolved in response to changing times proceeds from the new perspective that other scholars of religious history have developed during the last twenty years. The fact that organized religion not only survived the processes of modernization, but has even grown stronger in many post-industrial societies (as well as in developing countries) challenges the secularization thesis, the long-dominant belief that religion would decrease in influence and importance as societies evolved toward an Enlightenment ideal of universal reason and scientifically based knowledge. The failure of the secularization thesis has prompted many historians to look at the subject of religion in the modern period with new eyes: instead of asking how religion was weakening in the face of modernization, scholars now ask how religion adapted and persisted despite the many dramatic changes of the modern world. This question has been of particular importance to the study of Russia, given the widely shared assumptions that in the imperial period, religion in this largely peasant country was "traditional," defined by the hierarchy, and largely resistant to change. A number of historians of Russian religion have challenged these assumptions by looking at how different individuals or groups actually practiced and discussed their religious beliefs. Vera Shevzov and Nadieszda Kizenko show how lay people and clergymen integrated practices and beliefs associated with icons, the celebration of the liturgy, participation in the sacraments, and reverence for saints into their world views and their daily lives, infusing them with personal and communal meanings that changed over time, reflecting changes in the culture, the economy, and society.[5] Chris Chulos adds another dimension to this work by investigating how Orthodoxy fit into the daily lives of the peasantry in the post-reform period; as the countryside experienced the changes that signaled modernization, peasants found new ways of integrating their existing religious practices and beliefs with the demands of modern life.[6] Page Herrlinger, building on the work of Reginald Zelnik and Mark Steinberg, shows that while popular urban Orthodoxy differed in significant ways from village Orthodoxy, it remained a vital and active element in the lives of most factory workers in the late imperial period.[7] The work of

Laurie Manchester, Catherine Evtuhov, Brenda Meehan-Waters, and Nadieszda Kizenko demonstrates that Orthodoxy also continued to be important in the lives of Russia's educated elite, who drew on both religious and secular sources in formulating their values, their ethics, and their view of the world.[8] Laura Engelstein argues that, indeed, this ongoing effort to craft an enlightened Orthodoxy true to the traditions of the church but responsive to the needs of people in the modern world has been a prominent characteristic of Russian religion throughout the modern period.[9]

Two common themes emerge from the studies of these historians: first, Orthodoxy was a lived religion that people changed and adapted to the needs of their lives and times; second, the non-elite members of the church played a creative, active role in defining what Orthodoxy was and applying its teachings to their own lives and to the needs of their communities. In contrast to the stereotype of the church as staunchly resistant to change, new scholarship portrays the church as a dynamic and creative institution that was strongly integrated into Russian society, both aware of and capable of responding to the changing needs presented by the modern world. Even in the late imperial period, Orthodoxy continued to be a living faith that had active meaning in the way that Russians of all social conditions—laity *and* clergy—thought about and lived their lives. While the parish clergy indeed suffered many constraints and disadvantages as a result of the economic, social, and political conditions the state imposed on their estate, as Gregory Freeze's masterful studies demonstrate, many still evinced a strong and persistent commitment to serving the church and the faith. In this, they were motivated in large part by their shared ideal of bringing the Kingdom of God into reality through preaching and acting on an ethic of Christ-like love and service to others. This ideal resonated with the laity, whose response to the clergy's outreach was reflected in their own use of the language of service, love, and community and their participation in the activities established under the clergy's leadership.

While other scholars have been interested in Russia's religious philosophers and in religious beliefs and ideals among the laity, the subject of religion among the clergy has not yet received much attention, perhaps because it seems obvious that men who served in the clergy had some sort of ideas about their faith and that these, in all likelihood, were connected with their work. My interest has been in trying to understand what religious ideals motivated the more educated and conscious members of the parish clergy, particularly in their interactions with the society in which they lived, and in how these ideals and the goals associated with them changed as Russian society developed in the late imperial period. Because I have been particularly concerned to understand those ideas and activities that made the work of Father Georgii Gapon possible, I have focused on the clergy who believed that the church had to change with the times if it wanted to maintain its influence, and who were willing to advocate for new ideas both within the life of the church and in society more broadly. Many of these clergy were influenced by the writings of the handful of Russian theologians and philosophers, such as Vladimir Solov'ev, who were striving to develop a new interpretation of Orthodoxy consonant with modernity, an endeavor Paul Valliere has described as "liberal Orthodoxy."[10] The term can be somewhat misleading in the broader context of Russian history, for not all those who were willing to countenance the creative development of the church in response to the demands of modernity upheld what is commonly recognized as a liberal agenda with regard to politics or social reform; it was possible then (as now) to be theologically liberal and yet politically or socially conservative. For a noteworthy proportion of the St. Petersburg pastorate, however, new views of Orthodoxy did both inspire and justify a change in attitude toward their role in the church and their relation to secular society. These ideas also provided a common frame of reference for the clergy and laity alike to share as they worked together in their communities to bring about social change. Finally, the religious ideas that stimulated the clergy's increasing outreach to society and expanding cooperation with the laity led some clergymen to enter the political arena during the 1905 revolution as advocates for radical change in the church, the political system, and society. In this sense, the religious ideas developed and acted upon by the St. Petersburg clergy were *transformative*. They constituted a program—or perhaps it is better to say a vision—for the construction of a Russia different from that represented by either the autocracy or the secular political parties. That vision remained unrealized, but its power and influence should not be forgotten.

This book demonstrates that religion, society, and politics were intimately interconnected in tsarist Russia. The clergy and laity, who shared similar values and beliefs about the world based on their common religion, interacted with each other in their efforts to identify and address the problems Russia faced as its economy, society, and culture changed rapidly and dramatically in the second half of the nineteenth century. The laity were often critical of the clergy and the clergy were frequently frustrated by the laity, but both were partners in building a modern society in Russia. That project was often hindered by state authorities, who resisted the growing autonomy of Russian society and attempted to retain command and control over all aspects of Russian life. Resistance to the state came not only from radical intellectuals inspired by secular ideologies; it came also from Orthodox believers, both clerical and lay, whose criticisms of the state were grounded in concepts about the purpose of the government, the nature of society, and the meaning of human existence that ultimately derived from Orthodoxy. Without an appreciation for these elements of late imperial Russian culture, we cannot fully understand Russian society and politics. The study of religion and the church are not matters of interest only to specialists in those fields, but should concern all who study the history of the country.

CHAPTER ONE

FOUNDATIONS OF

THE MODERN RUSSIAN

ORTHODOX CHURCH

The history of the Russian Orthodox Church in the modern period has been marked by change and struggle, despite the persistent stereotype of the church that associates it with a quiescent stagnation. A modernizing state imposed change from without, as a succession of rulers from Peter the Great onward tried to centralize power in the hands of the state administration while strengthening their influence over a large, diverse, and widely scattered population. The state's reforms had mixed effects for the church, reducing its administrative and financial independence in relation to the government and diminishing the rights and status of the parish clergy, while at the same time significantly expanding the reach and enhancing the authority of the hierarchy. The church was not merely acted upon by the state, however, but was itself engaged in efforts to improve in order to pursue its own historic mission more effectively. To some degree, the church's agenda overlapped with that of the state, particularly in the area of clerical education, which both state and church authorities promoted vigorously throughout the eighteenth and nineteenth centuries. Inevitably, however, there were tensions as well, most often played out in the competition between the hierarchy and the tsar's appointed overseers for dominance in the church. This competition was frequently on display in St. Petersburg, where the central organs of the church and state administration resided. Yet, church life in the capital did not suffer despite being in the midst of this conflict; indeed, it flourished, thanks to an unusual combination of local features that enabled the St. Petersburg church to thrive in the midst of the competition and change that marked life in the imperial capital.

The Petrine Reforms and Their Legacy

Although the history of the Orthodox church in Russia dates back to the late ninth century, the chief institutions of the modern church were established in the eighteenth century. It was then that the administration of the church and its relation with the state, the organization of the clerical estate, and the system of ecclesiastical education were fundamentally altered by Peter the Great and his successors. Foremost among Peter's reforms was the abolition of the office of patriarch and the establishment of the Holy Synod in its place. Since 1589, when the Russian Orthodox Church had been granted the status of an autocephalous body by the patriarch of Constantinople, the Russian patriarchs had served as the heads of the national church. However, when Patriarch Adrian, one of Peter's early critics, died in 1700, Peter delayed the appointment of a successor, leaving the position vacant for twenty years. He finally abolished the post in 1721, when he issued the *Dukhovnyi reglament* (Ecclesiastical Regulation), which placed the church under the supervision of an ecclesiastical college similar to those that oversaw other areas of government administration, such as the navy, agriculture, or mining affairs. The tsar himself appointed the first members of this ecclesiastical college from among the ranks of the clergy. Nevertheless, the arrangement did not ensure the clergy's complete compliance. When the first group of appointees met to discuss the new body and the tsar's proposed regulations for it, they objected to being designated a college ranked among the other government ministries. They requested instead that the tsar grant their college the lofty name of "Most Holy Governing Synod" and establish it as both distinct from and superior to the other administrative boards that constituted the government. Peter agreed to both requests, elevating the Synod to the level of the Senate and making the two bodies equal and equivalent in their status and function within the government.[1]

Despite the Synod's early assertion of symbolic privilege, however, Peter the Great's laws still brought the church's central administration more firmly under government control and supervision than it had been before. Whereas the patriarchate had been separate and distinct from the state administration, the Synod was an integral element of it, as both its structure as a collegial body and its functional and physical links to the Senate

demonstrated. The tsar appointed the Synod's members and the state issued the laws that bound the Synod's actions. Moreover, after Peter introduced yet another administrative reform in 1722, the Synod found itself
under the watchful eye of the tsar's personal representative: the director
general of the Synod.[2] Although the director general did not have the authority to participate in the Synod's discussions and decisions, his position
as the tsar's "eye" on the Synod and his responsibility to serve as a liaison
between the Synod and the government gave this position a potentially
large influence, a position often exploited by its holders in the nineteenth
century. In the time of Peter and his successors, however, the clergymen
who constituted the Synod had greater influence, which they employed to
expand the authority of the hierarchy throughout the church, to carry out
their own program of internal reform, and to defend the church against the
state's often ineffectual efforts to establish greater control over it.[3]

Although Peter the Great's restructuring of the church's central administration is the most well known of his ecclesiastical reforms, he and his successors enacted other important changes to the church as well.[4] At the
diocesan level, the government instituted reforms that increased the number of dioceses, diminished their size, and centralized their administration,
all of which had the effect of increasing the number of bishops and aug-
menting their status and power within the church. These changes seriously
aggravated the division between the hierarchy and the parish clergy, a conflict usually described as pitting the "black," or monastic clergy, against the
"white," or married, clergy. Only the black clergy were eligible for appointment to the higher-level administrative positions in the church; the white
clergy served in the parishes without much hope of advancing any further
within the church unless they were widowed and took monastic vows. The
considerable differences in status, income, privileges, and duties that separated the hierarchy from the parish clergy caused much friction between
the two groups. Members of the hierarchy frequently expressed a harsh
contempt for the poorer, less-educated, and less-powerful white clergy who
served under them, while members of the white clergy voiced bitter resentment toward the worldly and privileged hierarchs of the black clergy.

Peter the Great's reforms worsened the position of the white clergy
within the church and within Russian society by curtailing their liberties
and imposing greater state regulation on them. The new obtrusiveness of
the state was especially evident in determining who could become a member of the clergy. To keep members of the other legal estates from shirking
their increasingly onerous obligations (such as taxes and military service)
by seeking entry into the clergy, Peter decreed that only those born into
clerical families were eligible to become priests; thus, the possibility for pursuing a vocation as a clergyman was closed to anyone who was not from a
family of priests.[5] Furthermore, to prevent the sons of clergymen from flee-
ing their clerical duties, he forbade members of the clerical estate to enter
other professions, thus forcing even those who had no interest in or talent

for the service of the church to enter into the clergy. In order to prepare for their eventual service in the church, the law required sons of the clergy to attend church schools founded by the state, run by the bishops, and maintained separately from secular educational institutions. The result of these decrees was that the clergy became a closed estate defined primarily by its members' obligations to the state rather than their vocation for the church. The separation between the members of the clergy and other groups in Russian society was reinforced by the practice of intermarriage between clerical families. Because of these laws and practices, critics of the clergy in the nineteenth century frequently labeled them a "caste."[6]

The state not only determined who could become a clergyman, but also which members of the clerical estate could be appointed as a parish priest. Peter established a register (shtat) of all the available positions in the church's parishes and their corresponding ranks and duties. He decreed that only those who met the state's basic requirements concerning origins, education, and character could be considered by the Synod for a position. Competition could be fierce, since the birthrate among the clergy produced more candidates than there were available positions; those who did not win appointments faced the threat of conscription for life-long service in the army and exclusion of their descendants from the clerical estate. Once awarded a position, the humble parish priest continued to be subject to state regulations governing his service. The state expected him to fulfill certain police and administrative duties, the most notorious of which was the requirement to report any complaints or plans against the government heard in confession to secular authorities. The priest was also to record and report births, marriages, and deaths in his parish for state records.

Beyond these state-imposed duties, however, the clergyman had no authority to intervene in secular matters, even on the government's behalf. Catherine the Great imposed this restriction after a large number of parish priests took part in the massive Pugachev rebellion of 1773–1775. She decreed that the clergy were no longer to take any part in noble-serf relations. Under Catherine and her successor, the clergy were in effect prohibited from all independent expression of political and social views (whether critical or supportive of the state), a prohibition enforced through the censorship of sermons and publications. Clergymen were also prohibited from holding positions in secular organizations, whether state-organized or (after 1855) private. As Gregory Freeze has pointed out, these *legal* exclusions from involvement in secular matters, and "not a theology of submission, [were] the principal reason for the clergy's failure to play a more active role in secular affairs" in the era before the Great Reforms.[7]

Despite the clergy's obligations to the secular government, the rewards for their service were meager. Peter the Great had abolished many of the clergy's privileges—such as exemptions from taxes, conscription, and recruitment to the bureaucracy—to limit entrance into the profession. His successors were extremely reluctant to restore those privileges or to give others, such as exemption from public corporal punishment, granted by Tsar Paul I only at the end of the eighteenth century. Thus, the white clergy suffered a low status within the church in comparison with the hierarchy, and also in society in comparison with the nobility. Their duties and lack of privileges made them closer to the peasants and petty townspeople than to the upper class. Neither did the government compensate the clergy for their services with money. The state did not pay the members of the parish clergy a salary. Instead, the clergy depended on two scanty resources: the income or produce generated by the small plots attached to the parish church and the money voluntarily given by parishioners for the perform-ance of religious rites and services. In both instances, the clergy shared the same poverty that afflicted the peasants who constituted the majority of the Russian population. Their income was often barely enough to support the priest and his frequently large family, so that the stigma of poverty was added to the shame of low legal status and social dependence.

The reforms of the eighteenth century produced long-lasting effects, both positive and negative, for the church. In the spheres of administration and finance, the state made considerable encroachments on the church's power and autonomy. The church's central administrative organs became more vulnerable to the state's interference, and the church suffered finan-cially from the state's creeping usurpation of its independent sources of rev-enue and wealth, first under Peter the Great, who appropriated the prop-erty and revenues of the patriarchate, and then under Catherine the Great (1762–1796), who secularized the church's lands. While the state granted the church a regular budget that remained under the Synod's control, it was sufficient only for the institution's most basic needs. Yet while the state's eighteenth-century reforms compromised the church's independence in some respects, they also strengthened its effectiveness in other areas. The hierarchs saw their power significantly enhanced both at the diocesan level, where their authority was almost unchecked, and at the central level, where they controlled the Synod.[8] Even the strong directors general of the later nine-teenth century found it difficult to impose their will consistently on the Synod when the body as a whole or even one influential member resisted. For the white clergy, however, many of Peter the Great's reforms were detrimental to their status and rights. The priesthood became a regulated legal estate with more duties than privileges; its members had many causes for resentment against both the hierarchy and the state.

CHANGE AND ITS CHALLENGES IN THE NINETEENTH CENTURY

Most surveys of Russian history give little attention to developments in the Orthodox church after their discussion of Peter the Great's ecclesiastical reforms, leaving the impression that the church did not change signifi-cantly between the 1720s and the 1920s, when the Bolshevik regime set out to destroy once and for all an institution long since rendered weak and defenseless by the modernizing state. The commonly held view of the Orthodox church as particularly conservative, traditional, and resistant to change has only reinforced the tendency to overlook its history in the imperial period. Nevertheless, the Orthodox church did change in the eighteenth and especially the nineteenth centuries. Although for reasons of space that history cannot be fully discussed in this work, two particular developments that emerged in the period cannot be overlooked if one is to understand the character and position of the parish clergy in St. Petersburg in the late imperial era. The first was the impact of the church's sustained effort to educate the members of the clergy and the clerical estate; the second was the way in which the education of the clergy influenced its views of the church, the state, and Russian society. Although the authorities of both the church and the state supported the education of the clergy, neither anticipated how a more educated clergy might challenge the assumptions and operations of the imperial establishment.

The number of clergy with at least some basic education slowly increased throughout the imperial period, while the opportunities for a small but growing number of clergy to attain an advanced education expanded as more teachers were trained and the church's school system matured. The improvement of the church school system during the nineteenth century was focused on expanding the higher levels of the system, strengthening the connections between the higher and lower levels, and integrating the school system with both church and society by extending the schools' contacts with the clergy and the laity. The ideas for these reforms were first discussed during the short reign of Paul I (1796–1801) but implemented only during the reign of Alexander I (1801–1825). Alexander was committed to improving the educational system of Russia generally. Among his early reforms were the reorganization of the secular schools and the founding of the imperial universities, begun in 1802.[9] A similar, though less well known, effort to reform the church school system followed. It aimed to make the church's schools parallel and equal to the state's at all levels, including the highest. Its most notable achievement was the establishment of four ecclesiastical academies at St. Petersburg, Moscow, Kiev, and Kharkov between 1808 and 1819.[10] These academies were intended as counterparts to the six imperial universities.[11]

As the new and highest level in the church school system, the academies' fundamental mission was to provide advanced theological training to clergymen who would serve in the most important administrative and missionary positions in major cities and in Russian churches abroad. The academies also had additional responsibilities that broadened their mandate considerably. They were to supervise the curricula and books used at the lower levels of the church school system and to promote religious enlightenment among the clergy through the establishment of libraries and publications. They were also instructed to foster a greater appreciation of Orthodoxy among the general population through educational activities, including publishing, preaching, and the establishment of religious organizations. Because their responsibilities extended beyond the education of their own students to the religious enlightenment of the whole clergy and Orthodox society, the academies fostered the emergence of a new self-consciousness within the church in the nineteenth century. They also contributed to the multiplication of connections between the church and educated society.

The spread of the academies' influence was gradual at first, even within the church. The classes of the first two decades of the nineteenth century rarely had more than a few dozen members, and many of the early graduates went into government service instead of church employment. Of those who stayed in the church, more became teachers in the lower levels of the church school system than ordained clergymen. Even so, the schools helped to improve the teaching provided to the offspring of the clerical estate at the lower levels of the system, both through direct supervision of the schools and their training of the schools' teachers.[12] The academy graduates who became priests were given immediate preferment for the church's most demanding and prominent positions—the parishes of the capitals and other urban centers, the Orthodox churches of the western provinces (Poland, Ukraine, and Belarus), the missions in the eastern parts of the growing empire, and the embassies and missions abroad. In time, the number of academy graduates in these critical areas increased as new men replaced the older generations of priests. The accumulation of educated and well-traveled clergymen in these areas came to serve as a leavening agent, raising the level of religious consciousness both in the local churches and in society more generally.

Beyond the influence they exercised indirectly through the work and ideas of their graduates, the academies had a direct impact on the development of a more definite sense of historical and theological consciousness within the church in the first part of the nineteenth century. Taking seriously the idea that they had a public educational mission, the academies, from the early 1820s, expended a considerable portion of their limited resources on the development of their libraries and the publication of the church's first periodicals. Intended for both clergymen and lay people, the periodicals contained spiritual readings, sermons, teachings, excerpts from the church fathers, and essays on church history. These pioneering efforts soon inspired the growing number of professional scholars at the academies to pursue more ambitious projects, such as the translation and publication of the writings of the Eastern Church fathers, with commentaries, in the 1830s and 1840s. Such work in turn stimulated the development of a significant body of Russian Orthodox historical and theological scholarship in the 1840s and 1850s: the catechism of Filaret (Drozdov), which became the standard confession for the Russian Orthodox Church, was published in 1839, and the Russian translation of the complete works of the church fathers was begun in 1843. Antonii (Amfiteatrov) published his foundational treatise on dogmatic theology in 1848, while at the same time Filaret (Gumilevskii) was publishing his multi-volume history of the church. Gumilevskii also published a treatise on the church fathers, a work of dogmatic theology, and a twelve-volume work on the Orthodox saints. His contributions were complemented by the work of Makarii (Bulgakov), also the author of a multi-volume church history and a leading theologian whose introduction to theology and five-volume work on dogmatic theology became standards in the field.[13] This work provided the basis for the numerous and significant works of theological and historical scholarship of the later nineteenth century, which helped to inform and inspire the expansion of the church's mission to society during the reform period and after.

The quickening of the church's intellectual life in the early nineteenth century and the newly awakened sense of purpose that it encouraged among the educated clergy complicated the church's relations with the government, which was also undergoing important changes. The educated clergy were slowly expanding their view of the church's mission to include more active outreach to society at the same time that the government was reviving the view that the church was essential to the maintenance of social and political order. In a sense, both the hierarchy and the bureaucracy wanted the church to do more work in the world, but they did not necessarily agree on the type of work, how it should be carried out, or why. Sometimes their agendas coincided, though often they did not. Occasionally an apparent compatibility of goals turned out to be superficial, as when the church embraced a policy the government initiated only to use it to pursue its own agenda. One might think of the relations between the church and state as comparable to the point-counterpoint of a fugue: each institution followed a different pattern that interwove and overlapped with the other: harmonious in some places, dissonant in others; separate and yet interdependent.

One theme that emerged from this fugue in the first half of the nineteenth century was the struggle between the director general of the Synod and the church's ranking bishops for the dominant role in the church's central administration. In the eighteenth century, the director general had not been an important figure in either the church or the government. The office had little visibility or prestige, and its occupants' vaguely defined powers were interpreted in a limited fashion. However, beginning in the reign of Alexander I, the director general of the Synod acquired a broader influence over church affairs as a result of the administrative restructuring that replaced Peter the Great's colleges with ministries.[14] The government established the Main Administration of the Orthodox Confession and assigned the Synod to its supervision in 1802. The Synod acquired the status of a ministry, which allowed the director general the right of direct address to the tsar (1803). This was a highly coveted privilege that not even the most preeminent of the bishops enjoyed. In 1810, the Main Administration was augmented by the addition of the Administration of Foreign Confessions. It was further elevated in the years 1816–1817, after Prince Alexander

N. Golitsyn, who had been the director general since 1803, was appointed to serve simultaneously as the minister of education. The two ministries were combined and named the Ministry of Spiritual Affairs and Education (1817–1824). This "dual ministry" elevated the position of the director general of the Synod in the secular government and greatly increased his leverage against the bishops of the Synod.

Although the combined ministry did not outlast Golitsyn, the trend toward increasing the power of the director general's office continued into the reign of Alexander I's successor, Nicholas I (1825–1855). In 1836, Nicholas appointed as director general a man notorious in the history of the church for his heavy-handed rule: Count Nikolai A. Protasov, who held the position until 1855. During his nearly two decades in office, Protasov carried out a thorough administrative reorganization of the administration that resulted in a considerable increase of the director general's authority at the expense of the Synod's. Protasov used his right of direct report to the tsar to gain prior approval for his initiatives, which were then presented as *faits accomplis* to the Synod. Thus, Protasov seized control of the church's properties and finances from the Synod and appropriated authority over the church school system. Subsequently, he undertook a reform of the seminaries and academies that imposed an almost military discipline on students and teachers alike, modeling the schools after the martial institutions so admired by the tsar. This reform extended the power of the director general beyond the central offices of the church administration. At nearly the same time, Protasov also undertook a revision of the statute on diocesan consistories in order to increase the number of positions in the church bureaucracy that were directly responsible to the director general, and to enhance the power of those offices whose personnel he controlled.[15]

The expansion of the powers of the director general under Alexander I and Nicholas I reflected the shared conviction of the rulers as well as their appointees that the Orthodox church was a key element in the social and political order and that the government should support, encourage, and, when necessary, assert control over. For the Orthodox clergy, the increased attention of the secular government to the church's place in society in the early nineteenth century was a mixed blessing. The ruler's power might be used to support the church to develop along lines the clergy endorsed or to compel the church to follow a path the clergy did not want it to take. The tensions between the government's expectations of the church and the clergy's agenda were particularly acute in the imperial capital, where the church faced unusual challenges but also enjoyed unparalleled freedoms, thanks to the strong position of the local hierarch, the underdevelopment of the city's ecclesiastical institutions, and the exceptional characteristics of the St. Petersburg parish clergy. By looking more carefully at these specific features of church life in the capital, one can see both how the general features of the church's experience during the imperial period were expressed and how local variations manifested their influence as well.

THE METROPOLITANATE OF ST. PETERSBURG—
Defying the Directors General

The development of the diocese of St. Petersburg during the nineteenth century was shaped by continual struggle between the directors general of the Synod, who sought to expand their control over the church with the tacit support of the emperors, and the local hierarchs, who employed the enhanced authority they acquired during the eighteenth century to shelter the personnel and institutions of the local church from the central administration while also attempting to strengthen the church's overall autonomy. The position of the local hierarch within the church administration, as well as some of the particular features of the diocese itself, enabled the diocese to assert an unexpected degree of self-government despite its location at the very heart of the imperial administrative system.

When Peter the Great established the city of St. Petersburg, its churches were placed under the authority of the ancient diocese of Novgorod, which continued to overshadow the new diocese of St. Petersburg in both size and prestige even after a new diocese for the capital and its surrounding region was created in 1742. Finally, in 1770 an administrative reorganization of the church incorporated most of the old diocese of Novgorod into the diocese of St. Petersburg, enlarging the latter and reducing the status of its most serious local rival. At the same time, the archbishop of St. Petersburg was raised to the rank of metropolitan, making him the equal of the hierarchs of Moscow and Kiev and superior in rank to all other members of the episcopate. Even more significantly, the metropolitan of St. Petersburg was granted a position as a permanent member of the Synod, thus guaranteeing the continued importance of the diocese regardless of future changes to its size.[16] Over time, the metropolitan of St. Petersburg came to be recognized as the body's "first member"; he routinely served as the group's chairperson, both in terms of the role he played during the Synod's meetings and in representing the Synod's opinions and decisions to the government and the public. Throughout the nineteenth century, the metropolitan of St. Petersburg was the highest ranking, most prominent clergyman in the church, the individual closest to being the "head" of the institution in its dealings with the imperial government and Russian society.

The metropolitan of St. Petersburg was selected for his position by the Synod, which had authority over all episcopal appointments. Having selected a candidate for the position, the Synod submitted the name for the approval of both the director general and the emperor. In general, the Synod's decision prevailed, with the acquiescence of the emperor and sometimes over the objections of the director general. This had been the case in 1821, for example, when Prince Golitsyn, despite his official positions as director general and minister of education and his personal influence with the emperor Alexander I, failed to prevent the Synod's appointment of Serafim (Glagolevskii, served 1821–1843) to the St. Petersburg metropolitanate. Neither Golitsyn nor his successor as director general, Count Protasov, was able to remove Metropolitan Serafim from his position; even though Serafim was sharply critical of both men, his position was secure. Similarly, later in the century Director General Konstantin Pobedonostsev was not able to remove Metropolitan Isidor (Nikol'skii, served 1860–1892) from his position, despite the well-known antipathy between the two men.[17] However, on a few occasions the director general was able to impose his choice for the St. Petersburg metropolitanate on the Synod. This was the case in 1892, when Pobedonostsev overrode the Synod's preference for Antonii (Vadkovskii), the first archbishop of Finland, a distinguished scholar of homiletics much beloved by the clergy of the capital. Instead, Pobedonostsev imposed on the Synod his own candidate, Palladii (Raev), exarch of Georgia and former archbishop of Kazan, a much older and more conservative hierarch of no particular intellectual distinction.

In that case, however, the director general's triumph was only temporary, for in 1898 the Synod at last succeeded in obtaining the appointment of Archbishop Antonii to the metropolitanate. Antonii held on to the position until his death in 1912, despite the fact that by 1903 he and Pobedonostsev were deeply embroiled in an intense conflict over the issue of church reform. Although he faced exceptionally hostile criticism from the far right during and after the 1905 revolution, Antonii maintained his official position; many supporters even regarded him unofficially as the church's primary leader during the crisis and considered him the most likely candidate for the position of patriarch of the Russian Orthodox Church in the event the position was restored.[18] Pobedonostsev resented Metropolitan Antonii's clear preeminence in church affairs, but there was little he could do to diminish it; the practice of transferring uncooperative bishops to distant and undesirable parts of the empire that Pobedonostsev had used to assert his control over less influential hierarchs could not be applied in the case of such a prominent church leader.[19] Despite the fact that Pobedonstsev and his successors (of whom there were five between Pobedonostsev's resignation in 1905 and Metropolitan Antonii's death in 1912) all opposed the capital's influential hierarch, none could remove him from his position or eradicate his influence over the local church. Only in the very last years of the empire did the Synod lose its influence over episcopal appointments. This was not because of any increase in the power of the directors general, but rather the result of the baneful influence of Grigorii Rasputin, who came to exercise an unwarranted authority over most high-level appointments in the state and ecclesiastical administrations as a result of his hypnotic power over Emperor Nicholas II's wife.[20]

The metropolitan, like other diocesan bishops, was responsible for overseeing the administrative, judicial, and financial affairs of the eparchy. He supervised all the clergy in the diocese, both parish and monastic, and all the monasteries (male and female), church-related schools, parish-based primary schools, and classes for religious education in the state schools as well.[21] In order to assist the metropolitan with this heavy administrative burden, the Synod elevated several of the sees in the metropolitanate to vicarates, assigning to the vicar bishops various tasks related to the administration of the diocese, such as supervision of the schools.[22] Most aspects of the metropolitanate's daily administration were handled by the consistory, an administrative board headed by a secretary assisted by two vicar bishops, several members of the clergy (both monastic and parish), and a number of lay clerks. In many dioceses, there was conflict between the local hierarch and the secretary of the consistory chancellery, who was appointed by and answered to the director general of the Synod as a result of Protasov's 1841 reform of the consistory statute, which removed the secretary from the authority of the local bishop.[23] In the case of St. Petersburg, however, such conflicts were rare because most consistory personnel, including the secretaries, were graduates of the St. Petersburg Ecclesiastical Academy, an institution with strong historical ties to the metropolitanate. These graduates' ties were continually reinforced by the metropolitan's residence at the Alexander Nevskii monastery, which also housed the diocesan seminary and the St. Petersburg Ecclesiastical Academy.[24] Academy graduates who worked at the consistory tended to feel more loyalty to the metropolitan than to the director general, a sympathy especially pronounced under Antonii (Vadkovskii), who had served first as inspector (1885–1887) and then as rector of the academy (1887–1892) before becoming metropolitan of St. Petersburg in 1898.[25] Thus, both local institutions and the metropolitan's role within the Orthodox church generally helped strengthen the bishop of St. Petersburg against the encroachments threatened by the director general's expanding power during the later imperial period.

The Churches of the Capital—

The Advantages of Underdevelopment

The local circumstances of the church in the capital also influenced other aspects of its development. Given the proximity of the offices of the metropolitan, the Synod, and the director general, one might expect the local church of the capital to have been a highly developed and strongly supervised body, a model for the rest of the country to observe and imitate. In fact, however, the local church was overshadowed and often overlooked by the central authorities of both the church and the state. Although this neglect stunted the institutional development of the local church, it offered the city's clergy and laity an unusual latitude to experiment with informal organizations and practices in order to discover those that suited their changing religious and social needs. As a result, the church communities of the capital were freer and thus more responsive to their members' initiatives than were churches further removed from the imperial center.

Because of its later establishment, its peripheral location in one of the less-populated regions of the empire, and the dominant role of the capital city, the diocese of St. Petersburg had a number of distinctive characteristics. To begin with, it was small. Of the fifty-seven dioceses listed in the director general's annual report for 1891, the St. Petersburg diocese ranked only forty-third in the number of Orthodox inhabitants. While the Moscow diocese had more than one and a half million Orthodox inhabitants and the Kiev diocese had nearly 2.5 million, St. Petersburg had a total of 865,278.[26] Most other dioceses had between 1–2 million inhabitants, with the average being about 1.2 million.

Despite its small size, statistics suggest that believers living in the St. Petersburg diocese lacked sufficient buildings for regular worship. In 1840, there were only 367 churches serving the half-million believers of the diocese. Over the next fifty years, the number of churches grew significantly, nearly doubling to 601 in 1890. However, since the population of the diocese grew more quickly, the problem of having too few churches to serve the needs of the inhabitants persisted and even worsened.[27] Whereas in 1840, there had been an average of 1,400 worshippers for each church, by 1890 that average had increased to nearly 1,800. Although there were a few dioceses with higher ratios, most were considerably lower. In 1880, when St. Petersburg had nearly 1,500 worshippers per church, Moscow had barely 800.[28]

The number of clergy serving in the diocese of St. Petersburg was also small. In 1898, the diocese had a total of 1,351 people serving in the church. Of these, 904 were ordained: 304 of these were deacons, 480 were priests, and 120 were archpriests.[29] At a time when the Orthodox population of the diocese stood at nearly one million people, this meant that each priest was responsible for an average of 1,660 individuals. If one looks at the number for the city of St. Petersburg alone, the ratio is more distorted. In 1900, when the total population of the city was about 1.2 million, there were only 277 Orthodox priests serving in 246 churches. Figuring the Orthodox population of the city at just over one million, this meant that each city priest was responsible for 3,682 souls. The difficulties that priests faced in serving this population became painfully evident during the major church holidays. One observer noted that by 1900 some churches in the capital had four or five thousand worshippers crammed into their Easter vigil services; in a number of parishes, the clergy were faced with confessing as many as fourteen thousand people in the week before Easter.[30]

Of course, raw numbers alone cannot accurately characterize the quality of church life in the capital. But during the last quarter of the nineteenth century, the diocesan administration worried ceaselessly about the inadequate number of churches in the diocese, especially in the city. The annual reports of the consistory regularly remarked that there was a dire need for more churches, even though a spate of church building in the 1880s increased the number of churches in the diocese from 494 to 601; by 1913 that number had increased to 809.[31] The chief obstacle to the building of an adequate number of churches was financial.[32] The money for repairing and renovating old churches and for building new ones came primarily from lay donations. Since the areas that most needed new churches were usually the poorest in the diocese, funds from the local population were scarce. The diocese could contribute some funds, but its budget was neither large nor flexible. The Synod also provided money from time to time, but its resources were restricted as well; it had no independent financial means, and its part of the state budget was far smaller than the allotments given to the secular ministries. The difficulties of the St. Petersburg diocese reflected one of the general weaknesses of the church: its lack of financial independence and its reliance on the resources of a poor population and a miserly central government. The capital also suffered, as did other urban centers, from the effects of too-rapid growth and the transience of the population.

The churches located in the diocese were organized in several different administrative categories, an arrangement that helped determine who had the authority to collect dues and make clerical appointments. Most churches in St. Petersburg diocese belonged to the diocesan administration, though there were also churches belonging to the court administration and to the military administration.[33] There were five main types of diocesan churches: cathedral, parish, cemetery, monastery, and institutional. Several of these types will be unfamiliar to most readers or different from what might be expected and thus require a brief description. The *cathedral churches* were little different from the parish churches in function, since in most cases they had parishes attached to them. They were usually larger and more elaborate (though not to the degree of the great medieval cathedrals of Europe) with a greater number of clergy assigned to them. There were several cathedrals in the city; no particular one was considered the home or the seat of the metropolitan, who lived in the Alexander Nevskii monastery. However, some cathedrals—Kazan, St. Isaac's, St. Andrew's, and the Smolnyi—had special ceremonial or administrative functions. *Cemetery churches* were located near or in graveyards and were concerned primarily with burial rites and services for the dead. They did not have parishes, though they did have regular clergy and services. *Institutional churches (domovye tserkvi)* were attached to government offices, schools, hospitals, prisons, and charitable institutions.[34] They did not have a parish in the traditional territorial sense, but rather in a functional sense, for they were intended to serve those belonging to a particular institution (though sometimes believers from the surrounding neighborhood attended services as well). In addition to these categories of churches, there were also hundreds of chapels and prayer houses, which lacked a consecrated altar and a resident clergy.[35]

Ordinarily, the *parish churches* were the most numerous and well-known churches in the diocesan administration. Such was not the case in the capital. St. Petersburg had extraordinarily few parish churches, and those it did have were territorially ill defined. This became painfully evident in 1891, when the Synod requested the diocese provide it with a list of its parishes and their boundaries. The request was prompted by the repeal in 1885 of a law passed during the reform era that had strictly limited the establishment of new parishes in order to prevent the multiplication of parish communities in poorer areas that could not afford to sustain them from local dues. The law was extraordinarily unpopular and when it was repealed there was a flood of requests for new parishes, which led the Synod to ask that all dioceses submit a list of their existing parishes. The diocesan authorities of the capital found that they did not have such a list at hand, or even the information necessary to produce an approximation. In fact, they did not manage to compile the requested register of parishes until 1900. At that time, they identified 32 diocesan parishes within city bounds and 15 outside of them, making a grand total of 47 parish churches, for an Orthodox population of approximately one million people.[36] The number shocked even the consistory bureaucrats, who usually counted several hundred parishes within the diocese's boundaries. In 1898, for example, these officials had reported that 302 of the 655 churches in the diocese were parish churches.[37] Even this was not a large number, considering that Moscow had 1,150 parish churches, nearly four times as many parishes for an Orthodox population a little less than twice as large.[38]

The official list of parishes recognized only those parishes whose establishment and boundaries had been formally approved and registered by church authorities. Officially establishing a parish was expensive and involved a cumbersome bureaucratic process that discouraged attempts to create new parishes when old ones became overcrowded. Local communities responded pragmatically to such constraints. For example, the Mother of God church in the Kolomenskaia district (known informally as Bolshaia Kolomenskaia) was a medium-sized city parish with a population of 7,874 in 1899. As the population in the district soared, this parish community simply rebuilt its church on a larger scale every dozen years or so, rather than request a subdivision of the parish to create new, smaller units. The parishioners had to pay the building costs, but over the years their parish dues went down as they came to be spread over a larger population.[39] Another pragmatic response was the appropriation of conveniently located churches for use as parish churches regardless of their official registration. Over time, many churches that functioned as parish churches were naturally considered as such by the local population, the clergy, and even diocesan bureaucrats. A significant number of these were actually institutional churches, of which St. Petersburg had an unusually large number, counting 174 institutional churches in the official register of 1901. This meant that there were nearly four times as many institutional churches in the city as there were officially recorded parish churches; the institutional churches actually constituted about half of what were normally regarded as parish churches. This was a highly unusual circumstance: in the whole empire, there were only 1,870 institutional churches in 1898 as compared to 35,561 parish churches, so that there were 19 parish churches for every one institutional church. Moscow was the only other diocese with a significant concentration of institutional churches: it had 133 institutional churches in addition to its 1,150 parish churches, meaning that even in that city, there were more than 8 parish churches for each institutional church. By contrast, in St. Petersburg there were 5 *institutional* churches for every one *parish* church.[40]

From the 1860s onward, lay commentators and diocesan bureaucrats worried about "the parish problem," not only in St. Petersburg but in the empire overall. Many church reform projects were proposed in the last decades of the imperial regime and all included some discussion of parish reform.[41] The central government, pragmatic and thrifty, wanted the parishes to take up some of the responsibility (and cost) of maintaining local charities and schools. More idealistically inclined advocates hoped the revival of the parishes would foster lay religiosity, improve popular moral standards, and ease social tensions. Given how much depended on the parish in the minds of reformers, it is not surprising that the lack of clearly defined and widely recognized parishes in the capital was alarming. This concern was already reflected in the remarks made by the committee that put together a history and statistical survey of the diocese of St. Petersburg in the early 1870s. The committee noted the small number of parishes, their slow growth, and their shifting populations with distress. It suggested that the competition from the institutional churches kept the parish churches impoverished and disrupted the formation of parish communities that could support local schools and charities.[42] Thirty years later, the former consistory bureaucrat Alexander Geno expressed similar concerns. He pointed out that the average number of people to each city parish had risen to more than 22,000, which meant that each parish priest was responsible for an average of more than 8,000 souls. He argued that if the diocese did not increase the number of parishes immediately, the city's population would become indifferent to Orthodoxy and ultimately abandon it altogether.[43] He declared that relying on the institutional churches to fill in as parish churches was unwise because they were not under the control of the diocesan authorities and could not be relied upon to act in the interests of the whole church; they would seek to protect their own interests instead, as was demonstrated, for example, in the efforts that many institutional churches made to avoid paying taxes and dues to the diocese.[44]

However, not everyone within the church was convinced that St. Petersburg's underdeveloped parish system posed a problem. The clergy who actually served in the city churches generally considered the parish question illusory. Institutional churches could and did take on the functions of parish churches, supporting local schools, charities, and community organizations just as the official parishes did. Their activities disproved the assumption that church communities could not or would not form around the non-parish churches and that believers unmoored from the traditional parish system would be lost to the church forever. In fact, it seems that the very weakness of the parish system in St. Petersburg spurred the organization and growth of both community-oriented services at institutional churches and the citywide, extra-parochial church associations that were uniquely characteristic of the capital at the end of the nineteenth century. Unfettered by the constraints of the existing parish system, these associations demonstrated and promoted the vitality of church life in St. Petersburg.[45] They allowed both the parish clergy and Orthodox believers the flexibility they needed to develop largely autonomous religious-social organizations that met the needs of the community, rather than the state.

THE PARISH CLERGY OF ST. PETERSBURG—

An Unusual Asset

The dynamism of church life in the capital was in large part the result of the leadership exercised by the city's parish priests, who defied the common Russian stereotype that depicted the typical parish clergyman as a greedy, corrupt, uneducated, and often drunk time-server without any sense of a spiritual vocation. By the end of the nineteenth century, the clergy of the capital demonstrated more than any other group in the church the success of the one-hundred-and-fifty-year campaign initiated by Peter the Great and carried on by several generations of bishops to raise the educational standards of the church. In 1900, one observer estimated that nearly 90 percent of the St. Petersburg diocesan clergy had completed the six-year seminary course.[46] Moreover, more than two-thirds had also attained some level of higher education at one of the ecclesiastical academies. Since these numbers are for the whole diocese and not just the city, and since they include the lower ranks of the clergy (deacons and psalmists) and not just the priests, they are actually on the low side. If one were to consider only the priests who served in the city itself, the proportion of those who had an academy degree in addition to their seminary diploma would have been well over 90 percent. Even most deacons in the city had academy degrees, and it was not unusual to find recent graduates of the St. Petersburg Ecclesiastical Academy serving as lowly psalmists (readers) in the churches of the capital. By way of comparison, outside of St. Petersburg only 5.7 percent of the priests and none of the lower-ranking members of the clergy had an academy education.[47] In the capital, the dream of the church's modernizing reformers had been realized: all members of the clergy were literate, and the vast majority had studied theology, Scripture, ancient and modern languages, history and philosophy at the secondary or even tertiary level. Not only were the clergy of the capital among the best-educated groups in the church, they were considerably better educated than the average resident of the capital.

Most of those who had an advanced degree had studied at the St. Petersburg Ecclesiastical Academy. Their academic program offered a general theological education that required four years of study, with students expected to pass oral and written examinations on an annual basis in order to advance to the next year. In the final year, students wrote a candidate's thesis, a piece of original scholarship that had to be approved by the faculty before the student was allowed to graduate. The course of study was demanding, the equivalent of the university program, and those who completed it thereby demonstrated their intelligence, talent, self-discipline, and diligence. Not only did the school offer them this rigorous academic training, but from the late 1880s it also encouraged future clergymen to begin developing their pastoral skills through service in the Society for the Dissemination of Moral-Religious Enlightenment in the Spirit of the Orthodox Church (Obshchestvo rasprostraneniia religiozno-nravstvennago prosveshcheniia v dukhe pravoslavnoi tserkvi; hereafter referred to either as ORRP or as the Society for Moral-Religious Enlightenment). Both the challenging work of the society and the demanding course of study at the academy brought the small classes of seventy to eighty students together and cemented personal bonds that could last for decades.

The clergy of the capital were a remarkably cohesive group. In part, this was because so many of them shared the same background: most came from clerical families, were natives of the diocese, and had attended the St. Petersburg seminary before entering the academy. The intensity and importance of their common educational experience combined with the conditions of service in the capital brought the clergy together professionally as well as socially throughout their careers. The small number of ordained clergy in the city was one factor that facilitated this contact; in 1900, there were only 277 priests and 188 deacons serving in the city of St. Petersburg.[48] Another factor was the unimportance of the distinctions between their positions: a few churches in the city were distinguished by their wealth and prestige, but the clergy who served in these churches did not presume themselves better than those who served in the city's other churches, perhaps because all who served in St. Petersburg were far more privileged economically and socially than the mass of ordinary clergymen who served in the provinces. Unlike the provincial clergy, the clergy of St. Petersburg enjoyed sufficient and secure incomes and regular contact with diverse types of educated, well-traveled, sophisticated people of importance in lay society and the church. These contacts helped to equalize relations among the clergy who served in St. Petersburg at the same time as they differentiated them from the clergy elsewhere.[49] Compared to other members of the white clergy, the parish priests of St. Petersburg enjoyed an unusual degree of material security and social status, both within the church and in society generally, giving them an exceptional level of confidence as individuals and as a group, and enhancing their influence in the late imperial period.

The clergy of St. Petersburg were also brought together by the city's extra-parochial church organizations, which counteracted the isolation that the clergy often experienced when their work was confined to their own churches. The most important of these extra-parochial organizations was the Society for Moral-Religious Enlightenment, which mobilized clergymen from all over the city to work in groups to provide moral-religious education to the laity through lectures and discussions organized outside of church services at halls and churches throughout the city. The society's members met annually at first, but as their numbers grew and their work expanded they began to organize more frequent meetings. From the early 1890s, the society sponsored regular meetings at which *all* the clergy of the city were welcomed: one monthly series was concerned with improving preaching, another with more general pastoral concerns. By 1905, these were operating essentially as clerical conventions at which a wide range of ecclesiastical, social, and even political issues were discussed. The society also produced a number of publications for its members. Its newspaper, founded in 1895, served in lieu of the gazette that was commonly published by the local church administration in other dioceses. The society thus helped to articulate a sense of common purpose among the St. Petersburg clergy while both promoting and benefiting from the cohesion that already existed among members of that group. This cohesion in turn enabled the clergy of the capital to exert an unusual degree of influence on the development of ecclesiastical and religious life in St. Petersburg in the second half of the nineteenth century.

During the synodal period, the development of church life in the capital was influenced both by trends that shaped the history of the whole church and by unusual conditions particular to the capital itself. The position of the local hierarch was greatly enhanced during the course of the eighteenth century, which saw a general trend toward increasing the authority of the hierarchy within the church in relation to the parish clergy. When the directors general of the Synod tried to expand their own authority over the church in the nineteenth century, they encountered staunch resistance from the metropolitans of St. Petersburg, whose role of leadership in the Synod enabled them to protect the local church community of the capital from excessive administrative interference even while they stood up for the rights of the entire church. The parish clergy of the capital also benefited significantly from one of the most notable developments in the church during the imperial period—the expansion of clerical education and the accompanying emphasis on educational achievement as the key criterion in preferment to the church's most important positions, among which were included the parishes of St. Petersburg. The city's priests were distinguished by their advanced level of education and training, for which they were awarded positions that gave them a greater degree of material security and social respect than was generally enjoyed by the poor village priests often taken as representative of the church during the imperial period. As a result, the priests of St. Petersburg were well prepared to take advantage of the relative autonomy of the local church and its institutional underdevelopment to expand and diversify their efforts to respond to the religious-social needs of their community in the second half of the nineteenth century.

BRIDGING THE GREAT DIVIDE

The St. Petersburg Ecclesiastical Academy

and the Church's Mission to Society

During the course of the nineteenth century, the St. Petersburg Ecclesiastical Academy became one of the key institutions of ecclesiastical life in the capital. As one of the church's four schools providing higher education for the youth of the clerical estate, the academy graduated hundreds of students who went on to serve in some of the church's most important and prominent positions: as ordained clergy in the empire's major cities and missions abroad; as high-level bureaucrats in the monastic, diocesan, and synodal administrations; as seminary teachers, academy professors, scholars, church publicists, canon lawyers, and church intellectuals. Other alumni of the academy found positions in the secular world as teachers, university professors, journalists, writers, and government bureaucrats. However, while the academy undoubtedly played an important role in the empire's system of higher education, the school's greater significance with relation to the history of the church was the result of its vigorous program of religious education and outreach to lay society, which contributed greatly to the local clergy's reconceptualization of the church's

purpose and goals in relation to the modern world. The school also provided an intellectual bridge between the clergy and the laity of the imperial
capital, helping to span the divide that many observers of the middle and
later decades of the nineteenth century, both clerical and lay, feared had
developed between the church and society.

MOVING IN FROM THE MARGINS—
The Academy's Early Evolution

During the eighteenth century, those leaders of the imperial government
and the Orthodox church who had received a western education began to
promote an understanding of religion that emphasized the necessity of believers (both lay and clerical) acquiring a conscious, articulate understanding of Christian teachings and practices.[1] This cognitive religion contrasted
sharply with what its enlightened adherents denounced as the blind, un-
comprehending devotion of illiterate believers to the customs of their an-
cestors, many of which were deemed unnecessary or even harmful by those
whose education had separated them from such "traditional" beliefs and
practices.[2] Believing that religious enlightenment would provide the foundation for the establishment of an orderly and efficient modern polity, the
emperor Peter the Great (1689–1725) and his successors, along with an increasing number of bishops, labored to establish a network of primary and
secondary schools for the education of the parish clergy in the hope that
these clergymen, in turn, would enlighten the benighted peasantry. Although the number of schools and students enrolled in them increased during the century, the absence of an educational system, the lack of a common
program of instruction, the incoherence of the schools' mission, the lack of
funds and leadership, and the resistance of many members of the parish
clergy as well as the episcopate to the new approach to ecclesiastical training
greatly hindered the development of the church's schools, thus limiting their
influence on the parish clergy, the church, and the laity in this early period.[3]

The true beginnings of the church's educational system are to be found
in the reigns of the emperors Paul I (1796–1801) and Alexander I (1801–1825).
In a decree of 1797, Paul designated four schools in the empire as ecclesiastical academies, elevating the seminaries in St. Petersburg and Kazan to the
same rank already enjoyed by the schools located in Kiev (since 1701) and
Moscow (since 1721). In the decree, Paul summed up the assumptions and
goals that had motivated the state's view of the church's schools since Peter
the Great's time. According to that view, the improvement of society depended on the education of the clergy, who were the natural leaders of society. Through the clergy, the state hoped to promote the enlightenment of
the people, which in turn would contribute to the stability of the state and
the maintenance of peace and social order.[4] The most talented students
from the seminaries were to be recruited to the academies for a program of

advanced study, which included theology, rhetoric, philosophy, natural sciences, and both ancient and modern languages.[5] Graduates would be prepared to serve in the church's front-line positions: censoring secular and religious publications, composing tracts against the non-Orthodox, and preaching to the educated public. Emperor Paul hoped that as defenders of the Orthodox faith, religious instructors, and role models, this academy-educated clerical elite would improve Russian society (and thus fortify both church and state) by spreading religious enlightenment.[6]

Paul's successor, Alexander I, significantly expanded and improved the church's schools, establishing a ladder system of education that paralleled that of the state-run schools with the best students from the diocesan seminaries continuing their education at the regional academies.[7] Under the new academy statute of 1808—written in large part by Bishop Filaret (Drozdov), later to become the metropolitan of Moscow but at this time serving as the rector of the St. Petersburg Ecclesiastical Academy—the definition of the academy's mission was significantly broadened. Previously, the school's mission had been to educate a comparatively small group of elite students who would then be appointed to positions of leadership in church and state institutions from which they would exercise a beneficial influence over the rest of society. The new statute expanded the academies' mission by charging the schools with supporting the education and enlightenment of *every* member of the clerical estate.[8] The academy faculty were given responsibility for reviewing all instructional materials used in the church schools of their educational region and conducting periodic inspections of these schools.[9] The academies were also granted additional state funds to improve their library collections, which were to be made generally available to local members of the clerical estate.[10] Additionally, the 1808 statute assigned the academies important responsibilities related to the preservation and promotion of enlightened Orthodox belief among the laity. The academy faculty were to review and approve the books used in secular schools' courses on history, philosophy, or religion. The academy faculty were also given the thankless task of censoring both Russian and foreign publications.[11] Beyond these duties assigned to them by the imperial government, the faculty of the St. Petersburg academy sought other opportunities to extend their influence over the local clergy and the lay public. In 1821, several young professors of the academy, encouraged by St. Petersburg metropolitan Mikhail (Desnitskii), founded the church's first "thick journal," *Khristianskoe chtenie (Christian Reading)*, in 1821.[12] The monthly journal was aimed at a general educated audience, offering a mixture of spiritual readings, reflective essays on the Christian life, and sermons.[13] The number of subscriptions to the journal grew steadily over the next twenty-five years, enabling the academy to translate and publish many original sources, commentaries, and interpretations of Christian teaching, all of which furnished further religious enlightenment for their readers while also encouraging the growth of professional scholarship in the theological sciences.

During the reign of Nicholas I (1825–1855), the academies continued to fulfill the tasks assigned to them by the statute of 1808. However, the role played by the church's educated elite in supervising important sectors of the country's intellectual life came under increasingly strong criticism from the intelligentsia, who emerged in this period to challenge many aspects of the established order. Although the government of Nicholas I emphasized the importance of the church to the political order both in its rhetoric and its policies, it maintained strict control over the church's activities and prevented the clergy from undertaking any initiatives of their own to expand the church's work beyond those matters the state had already assigned to the ecclesiastical realm. Thus, the schools evolved very little during Nicholas's long reign, even as Russia and the rest of the world were beginning to change dramatically. When Alexander II came to the throne at last in 1855, the academies (along with most other institutions in the church and in Russia generally) were ready for change.

Throughout the pre-reform period, the academies' mission had been shaped primarily by the needs and demands of "official Russia" as rulers worked together with reforming bishops and bureaucrats to create schools that would help to strengthen and stabilize the established political order in which both the state and the church were rooted; changes were conceived, formulated, and implemented from the top down. In contrast, during the reform period of the late 1850s through the 1860s the demand for changes in the church often came from below, from members of the parish clergy and educated lay people who wanted such changes to reflect their own values and priorities.[14] And while a few radical members of the intelligentsia wanted to reduce or eliminate the role of religion and the church in public life, many more members of the educated laity wanted the church to broaden its mission and embrace a wider array of responsibilities in society. In the capital, this desire for the church to engage the concerns and interests of society was demonstrated with unusual clarity in an event that occurred in 1858, when Father Jean Soyard, a charismatic Dominican monk from France, was allowed to preach to the general public at the city's Catholic church. To the surprise of local authorities, he attracted large audiences of curious Orthodox believers, some of whom expressed interest in attending a comparable series of talks on Orthodoxy.[15] Metropolitan Grigorii (Postnikov) called on the city's clergy to respond to the challenge Soyard's success seemed to represent, authorizing those priests with master's degrees from an academy to deliver sermons without first submitting them for prior censorship and instructing the clergy of Kazan cathedral to schedule their preaching at the same time as Soyard's lectures. Archpriest V. Polisadov, who taught catechism classes at St. Petersburg University, was also given permission to open a series of public lectures and informal discussions at the university chapel. These ad hoc responses failed to satisfy the public, however; they wanted authoritative answers to their questions about religion and the Orthodox church, as the author of a comprehensive history of the school—himself a former student and professor—recalled:

> Those who spoke from the church pulpit could not answer all the inquiries touching on learned theological subjects and the interests of the church and the discipline of theology. At this time in St. Petersburg . . . the deciding word on such subjects belonged to the highest institution of ecclesiastical scholarship [that is, the academy].[16]

Recognizing that the public's apparent thirst for religious knowledge offered the St. Petersburg academy a unique opportunity to expand its modest mission of educational outreach to lay society, the school's rector turned to Aleksei P. Tolstoi, director general of the Synod, with a request to open the academy's lectures to the public or to establish a series of lectures on theological topics for the public. The director general was sympathetic to the request, for in 1855 he had proposed that the academy try to improve the laity's knowledge of Orthodoxy by publishing a series of popular religious works, financed by a grant of 50,000 rubles from the Synod. When Tolstoi turned to the respected leader of the church, Metropolitan Filaret (Drozdov) of Moscow, for advice on the academy rector's request, however, Filaret discouraged both alternatives. He argued that allowing the public to attend lectures at the school would be a distraction for the faculty and students. He also warned that the church would suffer great harm if the academy's proposed series of lectures failed, either as a result of the audience's indifference or due to hostile criticism from the enemies of Orthodoxy. Agreeing with Metropolitan Grigorii that the city's clergy should be the ones to respond to Soyard, Filaret suggested that sermons addressing lay misconceptions of Orthodoxy for educated audiences should be delivered at the chapel of St. Petersburg University on Sundays and holidays. The members of the academy were thus compelled to forego this first opportunity to respond to public demands to broaden their engagement with society. Nevertheless, both the educated public of the city and the students and faculty of the academy retained the conviction that the school could be an important liaison between the church and the lay public.[17]

The belief that the church had a responsibility for addressing the needs and concerns of society influenced the reforms inaugurated in the late 1860s, when the tide of reforms introduced by Alexander II's government finally lapped at the foundations of the church. Reform of the church school system had been under discussion since 1860, when the emperor first appointed a committee to examine the issue.[18] The committee's proposals for reform had then been reviewed by members of the hierarchy and even discussed publicly in the press, allowing the educated public to express their opinions and exercise some influence on the reform process. That process was energized by the appointment of the archpriest Ioann L. Ianyshev to the rectorship of the St. Petersburg Ecclesiastical Academy. Father Ioann was the first member of the parish clergy to be given a high-level administrative position in one of the academies; all previous administrators had come from the monastic clergy, the same group from which members of the hierarchy were drawn. During the reform period, members of both the laity and the parish clergy had criticized this practice, attributing the academies' isolation from society to the fact that the schools were headed by monks, who were accused of being estranged from the concerns of the world both as a result of their ascetic ideology and lifestyle. The appointment of a non-monastic priest to the administration of the St. Petersburg academy was intended to provide the school with a leader familiar with the concerns of educated society in the capital and capable of addressing them effectively without compromising the church's teachings.[19] Father Ioann's record was impressive: he had a doctoral degree from the St. Petersburg academy in moral theology, a comparatively new area of academic study in Russia, in which he was a pioneer. He had served at the Orthodox church attached to the Russian embassy in Prussia; he had taught at St. Petersburg University and served as the catechism instructor for the empress Maria Fedorovna. In addition, he was considered to be a preacher of exceptional talent.[20] He was well known and widely respected not only by the clergy of the capital but also by members of educated society. He was exactly the sort of leader the academy—and the church—needed to help bridge the gap between the church and society.

After the new director general of the Synod, Count Dmitrii A. Tolstoi, convened representatives from the four academies to discuss the reforms proposed for the schools in 1867, Father Ioann took charge of the daunting task of translating the recommendations accumulated over the previous seven years into a new academy statute.[21] The resulting legislation, enacted in 1869, reflected the historical mission of the schools while also responding to the demands of the reform era. The main purpose of the academies continued to be defined as the provision of higher education in the theological sciences to qualified students who expected to go into the service of the church, primarily as seminary teachers and parish clergymen. In order to improve the schools' ability to provide their students with a good education, the schools' annual budgets were greatly increased, allowing them to expand their libraries, increase faculty salaries, raise student stipends, and hire new professors.[22] The expansion of the schools' resources was also intended to enable them to increase their interaction with the world outside their walls. Many changes, both large and small, were incorporated into the 1869 statute with the clear intention of breaking down the barriers between the academies and the outside world. The schools were permitted to admit qualified students regardless of their social background, thus opening the school to students who did not come from the clerical estate. Auditors were to be allowed in all courses, essentially opening the halls of the school to the public. Not only was the outside world being allowed into the schools, but the school's students were encouraged to familiarize themselves with the world beyond the academy. Whereas students of previous generations had been kept in strict isolation from the surrounding world, those who attended the schools in the 1870s were allowed to go into the city and have non-clerical visitors on the school grounds; some students were even allowed to live in apartments outside of school grounds. Students were also given permission to subscribe to secular newspapers such as *Sovremennik (The Contemporary)* and *Syn otechestva (Son of the Fatherland)* and to organize their own reading room, which included works of contemporary Russian literature and German philosophy.[23] Father Ioann justified these liberties, which stood in stark contrast to the harsh discipline that had been imposed upon students under previous administrators, by saying, "The student is preparing himself to be a public activist. For this reason he must be familiar with public life, with social currents."[24] Such a statement clearly demonstrated the desire to promote a greater understanding between the educated elite of the church and Russian society by fostering more interaction between the church's higher schools and the lay public.

The students and faculty of the St. Petersburg academy responded enthusiastically to the school's new openness. Academy students, like the university students of the early 1860s, became interested in working to improve the lives of the people. For them, the role model was Father Alexander V. Gumilevskii, a St. Petersburg priest who frequently visited the school to talk about his work organizing the city's first parish charities.[25] Many students also became enthusiastically involved in the Sunday school movement, volunteering to provide instruction in literacy and other basic skills for working-class adults. As one former student recalled: "We genuinely sympathized with the emergence and wide development in our days of the so-called Sunday schools. . . . Many of us took an active and lively part in these [schools]. Whole groups of students . . . would go out to those sectors of the city where those adults who wished to study would gather."[26]

The professors' engagement with society was more intellectually oriented. They participated in the establishment of the church's first newspaper, *Dukhovnaia beseda (Spiritual Conversation)*, in 1858. In 1861, the faculty initiated the revamping of the monthly journal *Khristianskoe chtenie*, replacing the spiritual and moral readings with news and commentary on religion, the church and society, and reports on faculty research.[27] Finally, in 1875 the academy opened a weekly periodical, *Tserkovnyi vestnik (The Church Herald)*, for reporting on current events of importance to the church, the government, and Russian society generally.[28] Abandoning the moral didacticism of earlier publications, these periodicals demonstrated serious interest in contemporary issues and a desire to participate in the public discussions of them.

Under the vigorous rectorship of Father Ioann, the St. Petersburg academy enjoyed both an active internal life and more extensive relations with the outside world than had previously been permitted. The school flourished. The number of students grew, doubling between 1872 and 1880.[29] The student body also became slightly more diverse, including not only seminary graduates but also a few students from secular schools.[30] The faculty increased their interactions with the outside world as well, joining

local and national scholarly societies and participating in the meetings of
the St. Petersburg division of the Society for Lovers of Spiritual Enlightenment. Father Ioann played a leading role in this organization, which attracted both clerical and lay listeners to its public discussions of Orthodoxy,
the Old Belief, and the Old Catholics. This was but one of the ways in
which Father Ioann acted as an energetic liaison between the school and
the educated society of St. Petersburg. Well known for his oratorical talents,
the academy rector drew large audiences to his weekly sermons at the academy chapel. He also sponsored the public preaching of the academy students and promoted the interest of patrons in the most promising fledgling
clergymen. He maintained a wide acquaintance outside the academy and
encouraged other faculty members to do the same.[31] By these means, the St.
Petersburg academy fostered in its members a sense that their service to the
church was closely connected with their ability to understand and interact
with lay society. As a result, in the reform era the St. Petersburg academy
moved from the margins to the center of the church's efforts to respond to
the changing needs and expectations of the city's Orthodox community.

LIGHTING THE WAY—
The Academy during the Counterreform Era

The era of progressive reforms came to a quiet and gradual end during
the second decade of Alexander II's reign as the initial optimism that had
greeted the elegant young emperor's ascension to the throne soured in response to the ruler's personal failings and the government's political difficulties. By the end of the 1870s, the government faced a crisis of growing
proportions as underground revolutionary groups multiplied and became
increasingly bold in carrying out terrorist acts against public officials; members of educated society, while rejecting revolutionary violence as a means
of changing the government, nevertheless demonstrated an alarming degree of sympathy for the revolutionaries' criticisms of the government. In
this period of uncertainty and discontent, the assassination of Emperor
Alexander II on 1 March 1881 was an event of enormous political significance. The ruler's violent death shocked both the government and society,
seeming to confirm the suspicion already harbored by many that the government had been proceeding down an increasingly dark and dangerous
path that had to be abandoned immediately before it pitched them all into
the abyss. Accordingly, the new emperor, Alexander III (1881–1894), came
to the throne determined to reverse what he saw as the misguided and
harmful policies of the previous reign, introducing an era commonly characterized as one of "counterreforms."

Although the era of counterreforms was criticized both by contemporary
liberals and many later historians, it provided unexpected benefits for the
Orthodox church. While Alexander II had demonstrated the conventional

piety expected of a Russian ruler through attendance at church services and occasional pilgrimages, the way in which he presented himself and his government—his "scenario of power"—did not especially privilege the role of the church or the clergy.[32] In contrast, Alexander III emphasized the importance of the Orthodox church in the life of the state and society very strongly. During the last decade of Alexander II's rule, the future Alexander III, under the guidance of his conservative, nationalist advisors (among whom the most influential was the future director general of the Synod, Konstantin Pobedonostsev), developed an image of himself as a "true Russian man" in contrast with his cosmopolitan, Europeanized father. The qualities that most clearly marked the heir's "Russian character" were his intense personal piety and his devotion to the Russian Orthodox Church, demonstrated by his love of prayer and gospel reading, his attendance at religious services, and his love of traditional religious art, architecture, and music.[33] When Alexander III came to power, his scenario significantly elevated the role of the Orthodox church: it became "the principal symbol of the national monarchy," the "bearer of the national spirit," and the means by which the monarchy was united to the people.[34] Consequently, throughout Alexander's reign the government demonstrated its close connections with the church through the use of religious ceremonies and services on public occasions, the celebration of significant events in the history of the church by the state, and the use of state funds to build magnificent churches in the "Russian style."[35]

For the St. Petersburg academy (as for the institutions of the church more generally), the leading role Alexander III gave to the church in the theater of imperial politics represented a mixed blessing: on the one hand, such prominence carried the threat of increased attention and possibly interference from the government; on the other hand, it also offered the opportunity for acquiring greater material and moral support and expanding the school's outreach. Initially, the threat seemed greater and more real than the potential opportunities, for the assassination of Alexander II and the accession of Alexander III to the throne resulted in the abrupt elevation of Konstantin Pobedonostsev to a position of extraordinary influence. Pobedonostsev had served as one of Alexander III's tutors and had become a most important mentor. In the dark days after the assassination, Pobedonostsev—appointed director general of the Synod only the year before—emerged as one of the strongest and most decisive voices in the government. During the decade that followed, he continued to exercise a significant degree of authority within Alexander III's administration, less as a result of his official position than his personal relation to the emperor.[36]

Convinced that Alexander II's reforms had weakened the church, Pobedonostsev initially focused on reversing the changes of the preceding era. In particular, he was determined to reform the ecclesiastical academies. Pobedonostsev had long been a critic of Father Ioann Ianyshev, rejecting both his scholarly work on moral theology and criticizing his

"lax" administration of the St. Petersburg academy, which he had personally visited for an inspection in the spring of 1880, just having been appointed to the office of director general of the Synod.[37] Shortly thereafter
Pobedonostsev organized a committee to discuss revision of the 1869 academy statute. In a deliberate snub to the rector of the St. Petersburg academy, who had led the drafting of the earlier legislation, the director general
pointedly excluded Father Ioann from the group.[38] Moreover, while the
committee was still working on drawing up new rules for the academies,
Pobedonostsev acted in advance of the law to impose some of the anticipated restrictions directly on the St. Petersburg academy, presenting Father
Ioann with an unmistakable challenge to his authority as rector. The director general revoked some of the freedoms that Father Ioann had allowed
the students to enjoy, such as living off-campus, visiting the city, receiving
lay visitors on campus, sharing classes with auditors, and administering
their own reading room.[39] Father Ioann protested these changes, but in
vain. After two years of resistance he finally gave up what seemed to be a
hopeless struggle, resigning his position as rector in 1883.[40] Pobedonostsev
quickly replaced him with his own candidate, the bishop of Ladoga Arsenii
(Briantsev), who openly declared that his main purpose was to eliminate
the spirit of Ianyshev's "liberalism" at the academy.[41]

These changes alarmed many observers at the school and among the
city's clergy. They feared Pobedonostsev would impose so many rules and
restrictions on the academy that it would be impossible for it to continue
with its public mission. In fact, while the new statute approved in 1884 did
strengthen administrative discipline over students and faculty, it did not
compel the academy to give up its work of developing and promoting public knowledge about Orthodoxy. As it turned out, in the long term the revision of the academy statute actually improved the school's ability to fulfill
its mission by broadening its curriculum and raising its academic standards.
As a result, students who attended the school between 1884 and 1905 received an excellent education in Orthodox studies that prepared them for addressing many of the intellectual and religious challenges of adapting the life
of the church to the changing needs of society in the decades that followed.

Under the 1869 statute, one of the most important functions of the
academies was the training of teachers for the church's schools, particularly
the diocesan seminaries.[42] The three-year program, which led to a candidate's degree, included a required course on pedagogy and focused on specialized areas of study rather than general theological education.[43] In contrast, the 1884 statute defined the school's mission more broadly, declaring
that its goal was "to provide higher theological education in the spirit of
Orthodoxy for the enlightened service of the Church in the pastoral, educational and other fields of activity."[44] The specialized curriculum was replaced with one that was both more general and more demanding. The
number of required courses was increased from five to twelve, with a heavy
emphasis on theology.[45] To accommodate the new requirements, the num-

ber of classroom hours per semester was increased slightly and the course of study for a candidate's degree was lengthened to four years. A master's degree required one to two additional years of study.[46]

For the St. Petersburg academy, these changes to the school's mission and curriculum resulted in the institution becoming much more focused on establishing and maintaining rigorous academic standards for students and faculty alike.[47] While the academies had always been elite institutions, the emphasis on admitting students primarily on the basis of academic merit increased in the 1880s as the admissions process became demanding. The rectors of the diocesan seminaries in the northwestern region sent the academic records of their best students to the academy each year. After reviewing the records, the faculty council of the academy invited qualified candidates to the capital to sit for the competitive exams that determined entrance into the academy and the award of scholarships. Under the 1884 statute, a significantly smaller percentage of this highly qualified pool of applicants was admitted to the school than before: whereas in 1881, the academy admitted 93 percent of its applicants, after 1884 the percentage dropped to an average of 62 percent.[48]

It is possible that the change also reflected the increasing number of applicants to the school after a law of 1879 prohibited seminary graduates from entering the state universities, thus making the academies the only option for young men from the clerical estate who sought a higher education. The St. Petersburg academy reached its peak enrollment in 1882, when it had 399 students; in his annual report to the metropolitan, Father Ioann noted the school's resources were stretched beyond their limits: as a result of the high student numbers, faculty and administration were overworked, the classrooms and library were overcrowded, and there were not enough scholarships to help all the needy students.[49] From 1884 to 1888, the enrollment was firmly capped at 250, but after that the number rose inexorably, hitting 298 in 1902 and hovering around that level until the outbreak of the first world war. Annual reports from this period occasionally noted with regret that highly qualified and desirable students had to be turned away because the school simply could not accommodate them.[50] The school was not only filled but even overcrowded; in fact, it became a regular practice to house overflow students in the school's sick ward, a practice apparently considered preferable to allowing students to find off-campus rooms![51]

Once admitted to the academy, students entered into a course of study and a general intellectual environment that stressed the importance of analytical thinking and strong communication skills. Students were required to write at least one major research paper every year as well as an unspecified number of course papers and sermons. Oral exams loomed at the end of each year to determine which students could continue the course of study; students were annually ranked in their class on the basis of their performance. In the final year, each student worked for the entire year on his candidate's thesis, which had to be approved by a faculty committee for the student to graduate. At every opportunity, the students' work was subjected to careful examination by the faculty, who consistently emphasized the importance of rational argument, logical reasoning, appropriate evidence, clear organization, and effective communication in their critiques of student work, which were published in the journal *Khristianskoe chtenie* as part of the reports of the faculty council's monthly meetings. Student work of outstanding academic merit was rewarded with cash prizes, established by the faculty and presented annually. Winners saw their essays published in the prestigious pages of the academy journal. Faculty also supported student scholarship by approving the formation of two student academic societies: the Student Psychology Society (1900) and the Student Literary Society (1903). The members of these societies, which included students from other local institutions of higher education, met on a monthly basis to present their research to each other, often with several faculty members in attendance. The Student Psychology Society was especially popular among the students, and junior faculty members Alexander Kartashev and Archimandrite Mikhail (Semenov) regularly attended its meetings. The emphasis of the 1884 statute on the students' academic preparation combined with strong faculty support for student scholarship thus greatly enriched the intellectual environment at the academy.

As a result, the students who graduated from the school during the years this statute was in effect generally possessed well-honed intellectual skills and a solid academic grounding in the theological sciences. The training enabled a number of the school's graduates to become leaders in the church life of the capital, whether serving as teachers, parish clergymen, or church bureaucrats.[52] They were the ones who most often took the lead in expanding the church's social outreach work through the organization of charities, temperance societies, and missionary groups; they sustained the church's religious-educational mission through their participation in the Society for Moral-Religious Education and its affiliates and their numerous publications on a wide range of issues concerning the church, religion, and society; finally, they took on leading roles in the movement for church reform and renewal after the turn of the century.

The faculty were also affected by the statute's tendency to emphasize academic rigor and intellectual skills.[53] To stimulate the faculty's interest in research and promote public knowledge of their work, the law made several provisions for "the improvement and spread of theological knowledge."[54] It established cash prizes awarded on a competitive basis for works of original scholarship in any of the subjects taught at the academy. The statute also authorized the members of the academy to offer public lectures on their work and to found scholarly associations.[55] Within a few years of the statute's enactment, there was a noticeable shift of emphasis of the faculty's work away from teaching toward research and professional scholarship.[56] The nature of this shift is demonstrated by the approach the faculty developed in the 1880s for the selection and hiring of new faculty. New faculty were hired by the faculty council, which represented both junior and senior faculty. The council handled most aspects of the school's administration, and although their decisions on some matters had to be approved by a higher authority (the rector, the metropolitan of St. Petersburg, or the Synod), in most cases the faculty council succeeded in carrying out the professors' agenda. In the 1880s, the council experienced an unusually active period of hiring to replace retiring faculty members who had come in during the reform period. In hiring new faculty, the council placed more emphasis than previously on candidates' qualifications as scholars, focusing on the candidates' records as academy students, the quality of their theses, and their publications. Trial lectures were rarely given and candidates' teaching qualifications seem never to have been a subject of concern. What mattered most was whether the potential new faculty member would be an active scholar who could make original contributions to his field of study.[57]

By the end of the 1880s, the St. Petersburg academy had established a regular routine for acquiring new faculty. The two senior students with the highest grade point average, who had usually also won prizes for their candidates' theses, were appointed for a year of postgraduate study under the tutelage of one of the professors. After that year had passed the students were hired to the faculty, usually in the capacity of junior assistant professors, a shadow rank that was not recognized by the 1884 statute. After attaining a master's degree, these lecturers were promoted into the regular ranks of the faculty as positions became available. During their academic apprenticeship, these junior scholars were given considerable support in their further study. Since they were "extra" faculty without official status, their teaching time was not really needed and they were often able to devote themselves to research, travel, and publication. As a result, when these young scholars finally joined the faculty, they were often already established specialists with substantial experience in research and publishing. The fact that they usually had little experience inside the classroom was apparently not considered relevant to their prospects of success.

In fact, the impression one acquires in the course of perusing the many documents generated by the faculty is that teaching was not a particularly strong concern for most of the professors. Perhaps this was in part because the faculty exerted complete control over their classrooms. There were no standards given for the teaching of any subject, even by the council, and no examinations of faculty or students by any outside authorities. There was no classroom visitation by the administrators and no student reporting on their professors' lectures to the rector or inspector. The sole supervisory requirement was that at the beginning of the year the professors submit a syllabus to the rector for review; however, the rectors themselves did not demand this and few professors bothered to comply voluntarily. This did not mean the professors were indifferent toward their students' learning; they did, after all, spend a considerable amount of time evaluating student performance on entrance exams, oral finals, and the candidates' theses. It does seem, however, that their sense of professional identity was more closely associated with scholarship rather than teaching.[58]

The faculty's commitment to scholarship was clearly reflected in their publications and their participation in the activities of the community of Russian and European scholars. From the end of the 1880s, there was a remarkable increase in the number and bulk of the academy's publications. During the course of a year, about one-third of the faculty published a piece of writing. Usually these were newspaper or journal articles, but there was a regular stream of pamphlets and books that flowed from the academy's press as well. In addition to the school's printing press, the professors acquired their own press, using it to publish academic and popular religious works.[59] Most of the articles appeared in ecclesiastical publications, especially those associated with the academy.[60] The academy's journal *Khristianskoe chtenie* grew to intimidating proportions as it came to be dominated by the faculty's scholarly work.[61] Publications in journals tended to be academic, while those in newspapers were often editorials or commentary on current events. Not only did professors publish in the academy periodicals but they also ran them, rotating the editorships of *Khristianskoe chtenie* and *Tserkovnyi vestnik* among their members. *Khristianskoe chtenie* was primarily for the publication of professors' writings, though at the end of the 1890s the editor A. Lopukhin tried unsuccessfully to widen the journal's scope by including regular columns on contemporary issues in church life. *Tserkovnyi vestnik*, a weekly newspaper, was more concerned with current events and problems that affected the church and society.

The professors' other work-related activities demonstrated their interest in scholarship as well. Although the faculty was too small to support any specialized scholarly organizations at the academy itself, many professors did belong to local or national professional bodies. The annual report for 1903 listed faculty memberships in the Archaeological Institute, the Geographic Society, the Neophilological Society of St. Petersburg, and the Historical Society of St. Petersburg University. It also noted the academy had sent representatives to the Archaeological Congress and the Congress of Russian Philologists. The school maintained regular contacts with St. Petersburg University: allowing informal exchanges of lecturers and students, sharing library resources, and observing the founding day of the university each year with congratulatory telegrams. In addition, the St. Petersburg academy communicated regularly with the ecclesiastical academies in Moscow and Kiev and with Kiev University. Professors also kept up with the work of colleagues abroad through travel during their sabbatical years, correspondence with other scholars, and subscriptions to foreign theological journals.

The annual reports on the professors' activities outside of teaching emphasized further the faculty's focus on academic and scholarly work. The report for 1881 listed the faculty's main activities as editing the academy's publications, translating important church documents and treatises, serving on synodal committees, and attending academic congresses.[62] A little more than twenty years later, the report for 1903 gives a list of faculty activities that is longer, but essentially unchanged: the professors' work was focused on their publications; most participated in some sort of academic society or congress; several served on synodal committees; only two were members of any non-academic society.[63] In most of the intervening years, this section of the report does little more than give a list of the professors' publications and editorial positions.

Although the professors were strongly focused on academic work and scholarly activities, they still made important contributions to the fulfillment of the academy's mission of promoting public knowledge and understanding of Orthodoxy. First of all, they educated many of the men who became important figures in the local church. Second, their scholarly works greatly increased the volume and variety of ideas and information about a wide range of topics concerning many aspects of the life of the church. Their studies on subjects such as church-state relations in the Byzantine empire, the role of the laity in the early Christian church, or the judgments of the church fathers on the social responsibilities of the church were often considered directly relevant to contemporary discussions in the church and society about the relation of the church to the government, the rights of the laity in the organization of church life, and the obligations of the church concerning social reform. This was in part because official censorship by both state and church authorities discouraged open discussion of controversial issues. In part, however, it was also the result of the Orthodox church's reverence for tradition, which often led those who wanted to change something in the present to look for viable precedents in the past.[64]

As the scholars of the academy expanded their researches, they provided more material for such expeditions into history, thus contributing to the ways in which their contemporaries identified and framed issues for discussion and supported various arguments concerning the church's roles and responsibilities in modern society. This was possible because the professors' work was known not only among their colleagues in the ecclesiastical academies, but also by scholars not associated with the church who read the journals, attended conferences, and socialized with faculty from the academy. There were also some lay intellectuals (many from clerical backgrounds) who were interested in scholarly work on the church and helped disseminate some of the ideas and arguments made in academic works through their writings in publications of more general interest. In addition, the professors themselves helped spread their ideas beyond professional circles by writing articles, commentaries, and opinion pieces for both the religious and secular periodicals of St. Petersburg. As the movement for church reform intensified just before and during the 1905 revolution, the professors of the St. Petersburg academy played a prominent role, both in their contributions to the debates in the press and in their participation as expert consultants on the committees established to draw up proposals for change.

REVIVING RELIGION AT THE ACADEMY

Some critics of the 1884 statute feared that the strengthening of the schools' academic program, with the increased number of required classes and the emphasis on theology, would marginalize the schools by preventing the faculty and students from engaging intellectually with the modern challenges the church faced. This concern turned out to be ungrounded. During the period that the 1884 statute was in force, academy students became more actively involved in religious activities than ever before. This was not necessarily the result of the statute, despite the fact that it included many provisions intended to strengthen religious-moral discipline at the church's elite schools. Pobedonostsev believed that the failure of the 1869 statute to specify the religious duties required of the faculty and students had led to a decline in attendance at religious services and consequently a deterioration of the religious spirit of the schools, which he felt was especially evident at the St. Petersburg academy. The future metropolitan of Kiev, Antonii (Khrapovitskii), who matriculated at the academy in the fall of 1881, shared the director general's assessment. In his memoirs, he recalled that when he began his studies at the academy he had been surprised and disappointed at the absence of religious activities and the lack of interest most of his fellow students displayed about religious matters.[65] The revised statute tried to change this attitude of indifference by requiring students to fulfill their religious duties. Students were to take turns reading aloud morning and evening prayers, prayers before and after meals, and prayers before and after each class. They were obligated to observe all church fasts and to confess and receive communion each year at Easter. On all Sundays and church holidays, they were to attend at least one service and participate in the reading and singing. The administrators and professors were also to attend and participate in these services as an example to students.[66] Some of the students and many of the faculty at the St. Petersburg academy resented these requirements, perhaps not so much because they rejected religion itself as because they did not necessarily equate the practice of religion solely or primarily with prayer, fasting, and attendance at services in the way that the pious and conservative Pobedonostsev did.

Despite complaints about the statute's emphasis on religious discipline, religious activities at the St. Petersburg academy did expand and intensify during the 1880s. This development was becoming apparent well before the implementation of the 1884 statute and was most likely influenced by changes in the broader culture. From the middle of the 1870s, the educated population of the capital had demonstrated a revived interest in religious questions, as shown by the attention that the preaching of the English evangelist Lord Radstock (Granville Waldegrade) and his Russian supporter Colonel Vasilii A. Pashkov received when they visited the capital in 1875 and again between 1877 and 1880.[67] The local clergy, fearing the emergence of a new sectarian group, responded by establishing the Society for the Dissemination of Moral-Religious Enlightenment in the Spirit of the Orthodox Church (ORRP) in the years 1880–1881. Its mission was to discourage interest in the Pashkovists by promoting a better understanding of Orthodoxy among the educated laity. In the next several years the society organized lectures, discussions, and charitable societies similar to those of the Pashkovists. The open competition for congregations between the followers of Pashkov and the local Orthodox clergy stimulated considerable public interest in questions concerning Christianity, Orthodoxy, and the church, not least among members of the St. Petersburg academy. Out of curiosity and a desire to learn more about the group, a number of academy students attended Pashkovist meetings in 1880 and 1881, indicating that members of the school were aware of and responsive to developments in local religious life.[68]

From 1881 on, a number of students at the academy became more overtly interested in religious matters. Many students responded when their fellow classmate Antonii Khrapovitskii undertook to stimulate student interest in preaching by establishing a voluntary preaching circle, whose members gave sermons in the academy chapel each week. Khrapovitskii also helped improve the appeal of the required weekly services by using his connections to invite visiting bishops and respected members of the capital's clergy to perform gorgeous and moving services at the school's church.[69] Then in 1884, one of the most well-liked and respected students in the school, Mikhail Gribanovskii, astonished everyone by becoming the first student in more than twenty years to seek tonsuring as a monk.[70] His example exerted a powerful influence, and over the next fifteen years several dozen more students followed his example.[71] Khrapovitskii received his tonsure in 1885, the year after his graduation. He and Gribanovskii were then both appointed assistant inspectors at the St. Petersburg academy, enabling them to continue exercising their considerable influence over the students. Khrapovitskii organized a study group that concerned itself primarily with religious and ecclesiastical issues; several members of this group also dedicated themselves to the monastic life while they were still students, or shortly after graduation.[72]

The intensification of student interest in religious matters deepened in the late 1880s and early 1890s, when the school came under the leadership of Antonii (Vadkovskii), the future metropolitan of St. Petersburg. Antonii spent seven years at the St. Petersburg academy, two as the inspector (1885–1887) and five as rector (1887–1892); during this time he also served as a vicar bishop to the metropolitan, holding the see of Vyborg. Bishop Antonii had a decisive influence in affirming and articulating the importance of the school as a center of the church's public religious mission. His view of the academy's purpose was deeply rooted in his belief that the fundamental practices of the Christian life were preaching and charity.[73] All Christians, not just members of the clergy, had to teach others about the faith both through words and deeds. This view led Bishop Antonii to identify two educational objectives as essential to the academy's program. First, the school was to promote Orthodox enlightenment. It was the school's "highest calling" to serve as "the bearer and the disseminator of the true light of Christ."[74] The professors were to dedicate themselves to the scholarly study of all aspects of Christianity, always remembering that their understanding did not arise solely out of their own intellectual efforts but was grounded in their faith.[75] Their studies were to serve as the basis for their instruction of the students in the beliefs and practices of the Orthodox church so that the students would have the knowledge needed to carry out their Christian duties when they left the school.

The academy's second objective was to prepare students for Christian service in the world outside the school walls. Bishop Antonii believed that true Christian learning could not be confined to the cloister or the classroom. In his sermon at the beginning of the 1888 school year he declared that everyone at the academy had a responsibility to the world outside, saying, "All of us here in this, our sanctuary of sciences and in this holy temple, prepare and train ourselves in order to be the ones who continue Christ's work on earth."[76] He considered this work to be especially important at a time when the people themselves were searching for guidance and instruction:

> At the present time in our Russian society, including among the common people, there is emerging a strong upsurge of religious feeling, which in its turn awakens the idea of studying matters of the faith and demands for this hope and adequate sustenance. . . . [T]here is no doubt that the scholarly side of this matter must receive support and direction from the academies. For this our academies must . . . equip those young people who . . . will go out into the world in the service of the Church.[77]

Bishop Antonii did not imagine that the contribution of the academy to the religious enlightenment of the people could be carried out simply through the publication of impressively thick academic journals and sophisticated monographs on the legal status of the church in the Byzantine Empire. He believed that faith and knowledge had to be expressed through action in order to have an impact on the world. For this reason, he emphasized the importance of Christian charity, by which believers demonstrated the meaning of their faith to others. This was what Bishop Antonii called "preaching by deeds." It was the way "to show people the true meaning of life, . . . to bring the good news to the destitute, to cure the sick at heart, to preach freedom to those in captivity, to give sight to the blind, and to release those who suffer into freedom."[78]

To encourage academy students to prepare themselves for bringing the Christian message into the world through both word and deed, Bishop Antonii petitioned the Synod to allow students to take part in the work of the Society for Moral-Religious Enlightenment. Specifically, he wanted the students to expand the society's audience beyond the educated and well-off elite of the capital by seeking their audiences in the factories and among the inhabitants of the poorer wards of the city. In 1887, the Synod approved the request, and with Antonii's encouragement the first group of students began to establish outreach centers in the city's factories and working-class neighborhoods. Throughout his tenure at the academy, Antonii remained a strong supporter of this work, which he regarded as essential for training students to acquire the knowledge and experience they would need to become effective teachers and clergymen.[79] He hoped they would continue the work they had begun while students even after they graduated. In his address to the graduating class of 1889, he reminded the audience that they had a special responsibility for building the Kingdom of God on earth. He charged them to preach, to care for the poor and the sick, to create love and kindness, and to teach those around them by way of word and example.[80]

Bishop Antonii did not simply lecture on the importance of preaching and service; he also provided the students with a personal example. Before taking his monastic vows, Antonii had been a professor of homiletics at the Kazan Ecclesiastical Academy, where his scholarly work had been focused on the question of what had made the preaching of the apostles so effective in winning converts to Christianity.[81] As a member of the clergy he sought to express in his own life the spirit of the apostles, both in his preaching and his quiet acts of service and charity. He preached frequently at the academy and also in the city. Despite his academic background, he eschewed difficult texts and complex rhetoric, preferring to speak from the heart, explaining essential texts from the Bible in simple and practical terms. He organized a preaching circle among the students of the academy to encourage them to practice their speaking skills. In giving the students practical advice about composing and giving sermons, he emphasized that their purpose was not to impress but to teach. The message had to be simple, true, and relevant in order for listeners to hear and understand it. He told his students, "Speak as from one heart to another and your words will be alive and living, they will touch the soul and open the heart."[82]

Bishop Antonii's pastoral leadership had an electrifying effect on the students of the St. Petersburg academy. The first flush of religious revival in the early 1880s had been strongly colored by a focus on liturgical expression and traditional ascetic practices, both typically associated with the monastic clergy. Although this interpretation of religion appealed to a few, most students were not satisfied with these practices alone. They sought to express their understanding of the religious life in a more extroverted fashion. Bishop Antonii (though a monk himself) showed those students who did not want to embrace the monastic life that through preaching and charitable work they could act on their religious feelings and at the same time make a difference in the world. One student interviewed by Antonii's contemporary biographer recalled that as a result of Antonii's teaching and example the students came to realize the value of their position and their work and were inspired to dedicate themselves to Christian service. As the biographer emphasized, while Antonii was rector "the academy began to produce church activists who strove to carry the fruits of spiritual study outside the walls of the academy to the people" through sermons and extra-liturgical lectures carried out "in churches, public halls, prisons, factories, and night shelters."[83] Among the academy students who took part in this work during the 1890s were two individuals, already introduced, who would later become influential public figures in St. Petersburg: Father Grigorii S. Petrov, first a popular author and speaker in the 1890s and then an activist for political and ecclesiastical reform during the 1905 revolution; and Father Georgii A. Gapon, best known for leading the march to the Winter Palace that ended in the Bloody Sunday massacre of January 9, 1905. The Society for Moral-Religious Enlightenment provided both of these academy graduates and many others with the opportunity to become acquainted with the challenges faced by the people of Russia and the Orthodox church and to dedicate themselves to a life of active public service.

After Antonii won permission for the students to volunteer for the Society for Moral-Religious Enlightenment, young men from the school flocked to the organization, helping it to expand rapidly throughout the city in the early 1890s. Nearly all of the outreach to the working population was carried on by students, who constituted a large percentage of the active membership of the society by the middle of the 1890s. Moreover, about one-half of the student body was involved with the ORRP: in 1899, 116 of the 235 students at the school were listed on the society's membership roster.[84] By the end of the 1890s, the contributions of the academy students to the work of the society had become so important that the Synod had begun to consider how to apply the students' example elsewhere. After the first All-Russian Missionary Congress, held in Kazan in 1897, the Synod issued a directive instructing each academy to involve its students in public religious work such as preaching in city churches, lecturing in public halls, and debating the Old Believers.[85] The developments that had transformed the place of the academy in the religious life of St. Petersburg thus became a model and inspiration for the Orthodox church in other parts of the empire.

The St. Petersburg Ecclesiastical Academy made important contributions to the development of public religious life in the capital, particularly in the last third of the nineteenth century. Despite concerns about how the counterreforms of the 1880s would affect the school, under the revised statute of 1884 the academy became an important center of scholarship in the church-related academic disciplines, producing major thinkers and scholars whose work influenced both professional debates (such as those carried out by various official committees on reform) and public discussions about Orthodoxy, the church, and Russian society in the late imperial period. With the strong support of the school's administrators and the local hierarchs, the school's faculty contributed to the vigorous intellectual life of the capital through both their academic publications and their journalistic writings, published by the academy's own presses and circulated locally and even nationally through its well-respected periodicals. Yet while the professors' contributions to the religious life of the capital tended to be of a scholarly nature, the school itself was not an ivory tower, isolated from and indifferent to the society around it. Through the ORRP—which came to be closely connected with the school during the rectorship of the future metropolitan Antonii (Vadkovskii)—many students were introduced to the challenges of bringing religious enlightenment to the city's working population. In this task, the students of the ecclesiastical academy were surprisingly successful, expanding the reach of the ORRP (and through it the church) in the sprawling working-class districts of the capital. This success reflected the coincidence of the population's desire for Orthodox enlightenment with the school's commitment to pursuing a mission of public education. At the same time this outreach work and the reasons for the academy's support of it reflected changing ideas about the broader church's mission to society and the parish clergy's contribution to that mission.

CHAPTER THREE

GOOD SHEPHERDS

Preaching and Pastoral Care in St. Petersburg

The era of the Great Reforms opened up a host of new opportunities for the development of the Orthodox church's relation to Russian society. It was a particularly important period for the expansion of the parish clergy's social and intellectual role, not only within the church but also within society more broadly. Although the goals and methods of the parish clergy's work demonstrated considerable continuity with those of the pre-reform period, in the new conditions created by the Great Reforms the clergy's opportunities to develop their work expanded significantly. At the same time, expectations about the results of this work on the part of both the clergy and the educated laity increased. Vigorous public discussion of the clergy's responsibilities in the church and in the community enlivened the church-based periodicals and secular journals that came to constitute the newly established national press. This discussion as well as the experiences that clergymen had as they carried out their daily responsibilities shaped the ongoing evolution of the clergy's ideals and activities in the reform period and afterward.

RENEWAL IN AN AGE OF REFORM—
The Church and Russian Society

Since the period of the Petrine reforms, the hierarchy of the Russian church had shared with the authorities of the central government a desire to promote a more conscious, articulate understanding of Orthodoxy among the empire's population, particularly among the parish clergy and among the common folk, the majority of whom were enserfed peasants before 1861. To that end, the hierarchy had supported the establishment and gradual expansion of ecclesiastical schools for the education of the clergy and their sons. Both state and church authorities encouraged parish priests in particular to consider their continuing self-education and the religious enlightenment of their parishioners to be essential duties of their office. The parish clergy, though initially resistant to the imposition of educational standards, eventually came to recognize the benefits of education for the profession (and the estate) and to embrace the mission of bringing religious enlightenment to the common people.[1] As already noted, in the early nineteenth century this emphasis on Orthodox knowledge and enlightenment affected the work of the church in the capital, leading to the extension of the right (and the duty) of public preaching to the academy-educated clergy of the city and to the establishment of a monthly journal, *Khristianskoe chtenie*, intended to provide serious and engaging yet accessible reading on religious topics to both clergy and laity.

Despite this emphasis on the clergy's role as educators and enlighteners of the general population, the social conditions and political concerns of the pre-reform era imposed many restrictions on the church's work.[2] For example, most parish priests were not allowed to preach publicly; those urban priests who were allowed to preach had to submit their sermons to their bishop for prior review and censorship. Likewise, the clergy's publications were also subjected to pre-publication censorship. There were many restrictions on the clergy's involvement in public life: they were not allowed to establish professional or estate-based organizations, nor were they permitted to organize charitable societies or other voluntary associations. They were not allowed to interfere in relations between landowners and their serfs, and they were forbidden from publicly expressing views on political or social issues. Of course, most of the restrictions did not apply to the clergy alone: all publications were censored; no one could establish independent voluntary associations; public discussion of social and political issues was forbidden to all subjects of the emperor.

These conditions changed during the 1850s when the government, reacting to the country's unexpected defeat in the Crimean War and responding to the leadership of a new emperor, Alexander II (1855–1881), began to allow some public discussion of the issues facing the empire through the partial liberalization of the press and the gradual expansion of the public sphere. Public discussion of the causes of Russia's military defeat led to the critical examination of the empire's fundamental institutions, including the church, leading to debates within the clergy and between clergymen and lay people concerning what was wrong with the church and how to reform it. Although the church had many critics among the intelligentsia, one of the most famous condemnations of the pre-reform church was written by a country priest, Father Ioann S. Belliustin.[3] His essay, published in 1858, was more than a description of the life of a rural priest; it was a scathing critique of the economic, social, and political conditions that he believed made it impossible for the conscientious clergyman to fulfill his sacred duties. Arguing that the parish priest should be a moral and religious leader in his community, respected and heeded by his parishioners, Belliustin claimed that instead the rural clergy were despised and ignored by the hierarchy and the laity because they were poor, dependent, and powerless. The strongly drawn contrast between what the priest should be and what he was struck many of the work's readers, lay and clerical alike, who shared Belliustin's conviction that the parish clergy should have a key role in Russian society. Both the secular and the clerical press were full of articles concerning the important role that the parish clergy would necessarily play in the reformed Russia as "educators, mentors, and leaders," particularly in relation to the emancipated peasantry, along with debates on whether the clergy would be capable of fulfilling that role.[4] Both lay commentators and clerical writers seem to have been in agreement concerning the potential importance of the parish priest as an agent of Russia's transformation, primarily by means of his work in popular enlightenment.

Some clergymen of the reform period developed a broader vision of the church's role in society. Such was the archimandrite Feodor (Bukharev), a graduate of the Moscow Ecclesiastical Academy who became a professor of theology at the Kazan Ecclesiastical Academy and then an ecclesiastical censor in St. Petersburg.[5] Between 1858 and 1861, he published several articles in the St. Petersburg press concerning the church's relation to modern society.[6] His starting point was the recognition that the church could not simply dismiss or ignore the philosophical and material challenges that modernity presented to believers. Nor was it sufficient for the church's leaders simply to fall back on tradition, hoping to find in the writings of the church fathers the exact answers to the problems of contemporary times. Instead, modern theologians had to engage with the challenges of the present day in order to understand how the teachings of the church were both true to their eternal, inner meaning and yet applicable to the problems of modern times. Feodor was critical of those who argued that the church should hold itself apart from the world so that it would not become contaminated by worldly temptations and sins, a view he characterized as ascetic. He also rejected the notion that the church should be concerned only with certain "religious" or "spiritual" aspects of the world, leaving aside all secular concerns as being outside of the church's realm. It was his position that the church should be fully engaged in the world with all aspects of human life, both individual and communal.

The archimandrite grounded this view of the church's relation to the world in his interpretation of two essential Christian doctrines: the Incarnation and the Redemption. He contended that before the coming of Christ, man was separated from God by a gulf that could not be bridged even by God's chosen people, the Israelites. As a result, the Israelites lived in a hostile world that forced them to establish a rigid separation between the secular and the sacred. However, when God became flesh through the Incarnation the gulf dividing the human from the divine was spanned. The Redemption healed the breach completely because when Jesus died on the cross and was then resurrected, he not only redeemed the sins of humankind but also cleansed the world of sin. The archimandrite contended that these two sacred events ended the separation between the worlds of man and God and laid the foundations for the Kingdom of God on earth. The purpose of the church that Christ established was to build on these foundations and bring the Kingdom of God to fruition.

But if the Kingdom of God had been established at the moment of Christ's death, it had not yet been realized in the world. Archimandrite Feodor declared that this was because human beings had not fully understood and accepted the Redemption and its consequences. Embracing the Redemption meant enacting the teachings of the gospel in *all* aspects of human life. There should be no separation of the sacred from the secular, no distinction between what the gospel required of the individual and what it required of society. Consequently, in working to actualize the Kingdom of God the church could not confine itself to selected aspects of human life, neglecting everything else. It had to involve itself in all human affairs, including social concerns and even political matters. The early church had begun the task of realizing the kingdom by going out into the world and converting the pagans to Christianity. This established the external form of the kingdom. But the more important and difficult task still remained for the modern church to carry out: teaching humankind how to fulfill the promise of the kingdom by living their lives, both individual and collective, according to the precepts of the gospel.

Archimandrite Feodor's call for the church to reexamine its attitude to the modern world was deeply informed by his knowledge of the Scriptures and the church fathers; he was not an outsider who wished to harm the church through his critique but an insider who wanted to strengthen and renew it.[7] He succeeded in constructing a theological justification for redefining the church's mission as an effort to complete God's intended transformation of the world by means of an active struggle against the wrongs of the existing order, carried on by individuals living out their Christian beliefs. Moreover, he particularly emphasized the importance of the clergy's role in the transformation, reminding those who were ordained that they walked in the footsteps of Jesus himself and should thus follow the example that he set of reaching out in love and compassion to comfort and heal the suffering world:

> We must take to heart the diseases and failures of the rest of our brethren as if they were our own diseases and failures. If we actually do this it may be that the healing of these diseases is not far off, for it is only through gracious communion in the love of the all-healing Lamb of God who takes away the sins of the world that we come to accept other people's diseases, even grave ones, as our own.[8]

The clergy thus had a particular responsibility to engage with the problems of the world in a sympathetic and understanding way; they had to know what the diseases of the modern world were in order to treat them. They had to be like the good shepherd who goes out into the wilderness to seek the lost sheep; they had to be like the doctor who goes among the mortally ill to care for his patients. Feodor thus reminded his fellow clergymen that they were leaders in the difficult, but exciting, struggle to change the world, a view that was embraced with particular eagerness by Feodor's students at the ecclesiastical academies and the younger generation of clergymen.

In the pre-reform period, the archimandrite's challenge would have fallen among the weeds, to be choked out by the political and practical restrictions that bristled up all around the edges of the church's sphere of concerns. But in the heady days of the early reform era, his words took root in the fallow minds of clerical youth. Like their counterparts at the *gimnaziia* and the universities, the students of the church's seminaries and academies welcomed criticisms of the old order and responded eagerly to calls for the building of a new Russia. In St. Petersburg, for example, students from the ecclesiastical academy took part in the Sunday school movement of 1859–1862 in the belief that engaging in practical work to improve the lives of the common people was an essential element of the church's mission.[9] In Kazan, where the archimandrite Feodor had taught from 1854 to 1857, several students of the ecclesiastical academy assisted in organizing and carrying out a requiem service for peasants killed by government troops in a local uprising in 1861. When asked by school authorities to explain their actions, they expressed compassion for the condition of the common people and a profound belief that they served the mission of the church (as well as the tsar and the people themselves) through their efforts to elevate and enlighten the masses.[10] While the archimandrite Feodor's theology was not the only influence on these youth, it was certainly an important factor in shaping their views on the church's responsibility in the world.

The youth and the clergy of the capital had a more immediate example of how ideas such as Feodor's could be applied to the church's daily work in the person of Father Alexander V. Gumilevskii. Father Alexander was somewhat younger than the archimandrite, having graduated from the St. Petersburg academy in 1855.[11] Following the vocation that he had felt since his final year at seminary, Gumilevskii took clerical orders and was assigned to an impoverished parish in the capital.[12] His parishioners were perched precariously on the lowest rungs of the middle class, quiet and respectable people living in straitened circumstances.[13] He threw himself into his work with all his energy. He viewed his parishioners' problems as his own and devoted himself to serving their needs in every way possible. He tended to the sick with his own hands and used his meager resources to pay their doctors and buy medicines for them. He was also an indefatigable teacher who regularly gave sermons during the liturgy and conducted informal discussions on religion with his parishioners.[14] In addition, he volunteered as a catechist both in a local private school and in a free people's school organized by secular philanthropists. He participated in teaching at the first Sunday schools in St. Petersburg in 1859 and established both a Sunday school and a regular day school for his own parish in 1860. He also sought to extend his teaching by means of the printed word. He founded the journal *Dukh khristianina (Christian Spirit)* in 1860 and co-founded the journal *Strannik (The Pilgrim)* in 1861. Finally, he became involved in the first efforts to organize private charity initiatives. From 1860 to 1862, he acted as the spiritual advisor to the Sisters of Mercy, a group of laywomen involved in charitable work. In 1863, he founded the first parish fraternity in St. Petersburg as a means of coordinating and financing charity at the parish level. His energy and enthusiasm seemed unbounded.

Like the archimandrite Feodor, Father Alexander rejected what he viewed as the typical interpretation of the church's mission, according to which salvation depended upon praying, going to church and following the ascetic life. He argued that the Christian life demanded much more, requiring believers to take an active part in changing the world around them through self-sacrifice and service to others.[15] Father Alexander emphasized that Jesus Christ himself had provided this model for the Christian life. He had dedicated "his whole life to the service of the world" and had carried out this service among the poor and the outcasts, working "in the world and not in the desert."[16]

Father Alexander also disagreed with the view that the principles of Christianity were applicable exclusively to the lives of individuals. A large part of his work was devoted to realizing the principles of Christianity in society. He welcomed invitations to participate in the community-based schools and charitable organizations that some members of the laity were establishing in the early 1860s. For him, the main goal of these endeavors was not the perfection of the social order or the eradication of heresy and apostasy among the poor. Rather, he strove for the creation of a Christian community in which the ideals of the gospel became the basis for a society of individuals who served each other with selfless love in imitation of Christ. This resembled the archimandrite Feodor's belief that the church's mission was to convert society to the inner meaning of the gospel in order to bring the Kingdom of God into reality.[17]

Although their ideas and ideals would be admired and embraced by a later generation of clergymen, in the 1860s both Father Alexander and Archimandrite Feodor encountered disapproval, resistance, and finally repression.[18] When Feodor's views sparked criticism and a public debate in the periodical press of the capital between 1858 and 1861, they aroused the concern of church authorities. Feodor was relieved of his duties as an ecclesiastical censor and sent to a monastery in Vladimir province. After a work that he had written on the Apocalypse was denied publication and confiscated by the Synod, he asked to be released from his monastic vows. The Synod granted his petition in 1863 and Bukharev returned to lay status. He married shortly afterward and took up work as an author, publishing both monographs and articles in the secular press. His life was one of considerable financial hardship, which may have contributed to the decline of his health in the late 1860s. He died in 1871.[19]

Father Alexander was also frustrated in his efforts to articulate and act upon a new vision of the church's work. Other clergymen did not necessarily share his views about their duties and the nature of the church's mission, nor were they willing to seek out struggle, hardship, and suffering as eagerly as he did. Members of the intelligentsia welcomed his social activism, but rejected his religious motivation and goals. Some government officials initially hoped to use Father Alexander's initiatives for political purposes such as promoting respect and obedience for the government among the lower classes but abandoned this plan the moment possible signs of popular discontent appeared. Finally, church authorities found his unceasing activity and his bold outspokenness unsettling and potentially dangerous. In 1866, the metropolitan transferred Father Alexander from the capital city to the small, provincial town of Narva after the priest delivered a sermon that offended the local nobility. He tried to continue his work there but with little success. In 1869 he died an early death from typhus, which he contracted during a visit to a hospital for the poor.

Preaching the "Living Word"

Despite the difficulties that Father Feodor and Father Alexander encountered in their work, the parish clergy's responsibilities were significantly expanded during the reform period. Of particular importance was the era's new emphasis on preaching. Between the 1860s and the 1890s, parish priests—not only in the capital but throughout the empire—began to regard preaching as an essential part of their duties.[20] Not only did they begin to preach more frequently but they also began to concern themselves with how to preach well. This quest led them to study the practice and history of preaching in the church and to experiment with kinds of preaching that had previously been uncommon.

In principle, church authorities had allowed and had even encouraged at least some of the clergy to preach in the pre-reform period. At the end of the eighteenth century, the metropolitan of St. Petersburg set up a schedule for priests from the city's clergy to give sermons in the three main cathedrals of the capital: the Kazan cathedral, St. Andrew's cathedral, and the cathedral of Sts. Peter and Paul. Collections of sermons and a guide to preaching were published to assist the preachers, but these tools apparently made the irksome task no easier. The clergy regularly shirked their turns in the rota, despite reprimands and fines. This effort was clearly part of the rather one-sided attempt on the part of the hierarchy to enlighten both the parish clergy and their parishioners on the doctrines of the church.[21] In fact, the well-known preachers of the pre-reform period were not members of the parish clergy but hierarchs. They were not only better educated and more strongly motivated than the parish clergy but were also relieved of the requirement to submit their sermons to prior censorship.[22]

A combination of new challenges and relaxed restrictions in the late 1850s led to a change in the St. Petersburg clergy's attitude toward preaching. When the French Dominican priest Soyard was given permission to preach publicly at the Catholic church in downtown St. Petersburg in 1858, the Orthodox clergy, as mentioned earlier, were shocked at how many of their parishioners attended.[23] Some members of the hierarchy might have looked for ways to silence Soyard, but the newly appointed metropolitan of St. Petersburg, Grigorii (Postnikov), was more open-minded. Before being appointed to his position in the capital in 1856, he had been the archbishop of Kazan and the patron of the Kazan Ecclesiastical Academy's progressive journal *Pravoslavnyi sobesednik (The Orthodox Interlocutor)*, which had supported and promoted the ideas of the archimandrite Feodor and other innovative Orthodox thinkers. In St. Petersburg, Metropolitan Grigorii approved the founding of the journal *Dukhovnaia beseda* at the St. Petersburg seminary; he used it to communicate his opinions and ideas to the clergy of the capital.[24] A well-respected preacher himself, the metropolitan set an example for the clergy of the capital to follow. He relaxed ecclesiastical censorship, and sermons were soon being delivered on a weekly basis not only in the city's three main cathedrals but in many of the city's other churches as well. Several members of the local parish clergy became famous as preachers, among them Father Ioann L. Ianyshev, appointed to the rectorship of the St. Petersburg Ecclesiastical Academy in 1866.[25]

As sermons became more common, so did debates about how and what the clergy should preach. Lay intellectuals criticized the St. Petersburg clergy for sermons that were focused on church doctrine and written in a formal and abstract language they found dull and abstruse.[26] They wanted the clergy to address contemporary problems, moral issues, and philosophical questions, using language and references that educated lay people could understand and appreciate.[27] In response, some eminent preachers defended their approach to preaching, arguing that the purpose of the sermon was to explain the principles of the faith as taught in the Scriptures and by the church fathers and that this required the use of certain logical structures and rhetorical strategies. In their view, the church was not the place to engage in philosophical debates, literary polemics, or political discussion, and the preacher need not be concerned with satisfying the laity's intellectual whims.[28] In the meantime, younger clergymen such as Father Alexander Gumilevskii were already working out a new approach to preaching, shifting away from explanations of dogma and focusing more on discussions of morality, defined as the application of dogma to real life. Reflecting the new interest in establishing and reinforcing connections between the church and the modern society, these younger clergy emphasized the need to teach both the principles of faith and how to act on these principles in one's daily life.[29]

The debates on the proper purpose of preaching helped to stimulate new scholarship in the disciplines of theology and homiletics. For example, moral theology, concerned with using Christian theology to justify and explain which attitudes and actions were right or wrong, became established as a new field of study in the 1860s. One of the pioneers in this field was Father Ioann, the rector of the St. Petersburg academy and one of the most popular preachers in the capital.[30] Another new area of inquiry was the history of preaching, which was opened up by scholars seeking answers to current debates in the practices of the past. One of the earliest studies of the history of preaching in Russia, published in St. Petersburg in 1871, was specifically concerned with the question of whether the sermon should be dogmatic or moral according to Russia's historical traditions.[31] The author, Father Iakov (Domskii), argued that in the earliest period of the church's history preachers taught both dogma and morals in short and informal talks *(besedy)* that were readily comprehensible to all believers. During the seventeenth century, however, the Russian clergy had fallen under the influence of the Catholic example and had begun to preach about complex theological issues. Sermons became more formal and less accessible to the average listener. At the same time, conditions external to the church had made it increasingly difficult for the clergy to speak freely about moral issues, which further encouraged the shift toward dogma. As a result, the effectiveness of preaching had diminished because even educated lay people could not understand dogma in the abstract. In order to make preaching effective again, Father Iakov argued that the clergy should return to Russia's original homiletic traditions and teach both morals and dogma through the use of the *beseda*.

Another scholar concerned with the history of preaching and the lessons it might hold for the reform-era generation was Professor Alexander Vadkovskii, who would later enter monastic orders and take the name Antonii, rising through the ranks to become the metropolitan of St. Petersburg in 1898. Vadkovskii graduated from the Kazan Ecclesiastical Academy with a master's degree in 1870. He remained there to teach homiletics and pastoral theology, eventually adding a new course on the history of preaching. He also served as the editor of *Pravoslavnyi sobesednik*, in which he began to publish his articles on the history of preaching in the early church.[32] One of his main concerns involved the question of what makes an effective sermon. To answer this, Vadkovskii studied the example of the apostles. He contended that people converted in response to the apostles' preaching primarily because the apostles presented Christianity as offering a solid basis for living a moral life.[33] This message was communicated by deeds as well as words, for the apostles not only spoke of Christianity but also acted upon their beliefs, becoming what Vadkovskii called "living sermons."[34] Vadkovskii argued that if the clergy of the modern church followed this example, the church would meet with far less criticism about its relevance to the contemporary world.[35] After he entered the clergy in 1883, Father Antonii took his own advice, consciously imitating the apostles and the early church fathers in his own approach to preaching. Despite his academy education and his years as a professor, he preferred to give simple sermons that often focused on temperance, charity, and mercy. He also tried to follow the example of Jesus and the disciples in his way of life. He became especially well known for his frequent visits to the prisons and hospitals of St. Petersburg, for his simple way of life, and for his immense generosity.[36]

By the 1880s, the debates on whether sermons should focus on explaining doctrine or demonstrating how it applied to real life had been resolved in favor of emphasizing morality over dogma.[37] But the problem of communicating effectively with parishioners remained. In fact, it seemed more acute than before because the clergy were more likely to judge their effectiveness as preachers by their visible impact on their parishioners' lives. A good preacher, they believed, changed the way his parishioners lived. That was simple enough to say, of course, but much harder to do. To begin with, the clergy had to overcome a number of practical obstacles. The first of these concerned clerical education and training. The seminary reform of 1839 had added one course about preaching to the curriculum; however, the course focused on the history of preaching rather than its practice. The 1884 reform of the seminary curriculum placed much more emphasis on the art of preaching and the development of students' skills as preachers: the single course in the history of preaching was jettisoned and replaced by a series of courses over three years that aimed to cultivate students' skills through analysis and imitation.[38] At the academy level, the course on homiletics and the history of preaching that had been introduced in 1869 was divided into two courses in 1884, one of which was a homiletics course focused solely on teaching students to preach effectively.[39] These changes in the curricula of the church's schools clearly reflected the ways in which expectations about the clergy's duties changed over the course of the nearly fifty years between 1839 and 1884. In 1839, it was assumed that the educated clergyman needed to know a little about the history of preaching but would not need any practical skills in the art himself. By 1884, however, there was a strong emphasis on training future clergymen how to preach, in the expectation that giving good sermons was one of the parish priest's most important responsibilities. The multiplication of practical handbooks on preaching and articles in the ecclesiastical press in the 1880s and 1890s mirrors this change as well.[40]

Even for clergy trained in the art of preaching, serious challenges to es-tablishing a regular schedule of sermons remained. First of all, finding the time during the week to compose a sermon was difficult for many clergy-men because performing the daily liturgy and visiting the inhabitants of their large parishes to provide the sacraments and carry out other prayers and rituals took up a great deal of time.[41] Then there were additional prob-lems that attended the actual delivery of the sermon. Orthodox churches generally did not (and do not) have pulpits or pews. While a preacher might stand on the slightly raised platform in front of the iconostasis (the *soleia*) to speak, in larger churches this was not sufficient to make him visi-ble and audible to a large audience. One expert on preaching asserted that on an average Sunday, not more than a third of the congregation in a city church was likely to be able to hear the sermon if given from the *soleia*. On the great holidays, when the main churches of the capital competed for the best preachers in the city to speak at their services, the proportion of listen-ers able to hear these talented speakers was even lower because the churches were so overcrowded.[42] Finally, the standard Sunday service did not have a clear place for the delivery of a sermon. The most reasonable place seemed to be after the rites of the Eucharist, but some priests felt that they were too tired by that point in the service to deliver a good sermon. Moreover, the congregation, who tended to be focused on the sacrament as the central element of the service, frequently left after its celebration, con-sidering a sermon anticlimactic and even unnecessary.[43]

Because there were such significant and persistent obstacles to delivering an effective sermon during the Sunday services, some clergymen began to experiment with alternative approaches to preaching. The most promising of these was the *beseda*, which literally means "conversation," but which also referred to the type of sermon that had been standard in the Russian Orthodox Church before the seventeenth century. The *beseda* was a simple, informal sermon delivered in a conversational tone using stories, parables, and examples from everyday life to reflect on the meaning of the Bible and the teachings of the church. As the term came to be used in the second half of the nineteenth century, it referred to lectures or discussions that clergy conducted outside of the liturgical services, often on a Sunday afternoon or a weekday evening. The younger members of the St. Petersburg clergy first began to lead these extra-liturgical discussions in the early 1860s, at the same time that uni-versity students launched the Sunday school movement, organizing evening and Sunday classes to instruct the common people in basic literacy. In St. Pe-tersburg, some students from the academy and a few members of the clergy were involved in the Sunday school movement as well as in organizing *besedy*. Their experiences with the first kind of teaching undoubtedly exerted some in-fluence on their informal preaching.

A contemporary history of the development of extra-liturgical teaching indicates that in most cases the classes were organized by newly appointed young clergymen who had a strong personal belief that they had a duty to teach the people about their faith in a way that was meaningful and inspiring.[44] The structure of the meetings was loose and informal.[45] They often included reading from the Bible, prayer, group singing, and an open-ended discussion on religious matters between the priest and his parishioners.[46] The priest might select a topic related to a reading from the Bible or an event in church life and comment briefly on it before inviting questions from the audience. A sample discussion taken from the journal of one clergyman indicates that the priest had to be well read in the Bible and quick-thinking in order to respond to the parishioners' questions and remarks about religious beliefs, popular practices, and the traditions of the church. He had to be able to give answers that accorded with church teachings and yet made sense to ordinary lay people.[47]

The *beseda* became an exceptionally popular form of preaching in the late nineteenth century, not only in the capital but in other cities and the provinces as well.[48] In St. Petersburg, *besedy* were conducted at scores of churches in the city on a weekly basis, both by clergy involved in the Society for Moral-Religious Enlightenment and by independent priests. The clergy embraced this approach to preaching, in part for professional reasons, because it enabled them to use their training and fulfill an important duty in an apparently effective manner. The style of the *beseda* had the additional appeal of seeming to resemble the preaching of Jesus and the apostles as well as the early preachers of the Russian church. In addition, many clergy found the conduct of the *besedy* personally rewarding. It satisfied their urge to engage with their parishioners, to be active leaders in their communities, and to be involved in serving the common folk, a desire that young and educated members of the clergy shared with the youth of the secular intelligentsia.[49] The focus of extra-liturgical teaching on helping believers apply the truths of Christianity to their own lives encouraged preachers to become deeply engaged with their audiences in order to understand them better and teach them more successfully.[50] The earnest tone of the discussions and the absence of ceremony helped to break down the barriers between the clergymen and lay people so that the clergy could connect with individuals. This engagement with the lives and concerns of common people aroused in some young clergymen a sense of honest compassion and a paternal urge to protect and defend these people. Such sentiments were only strengthened by the simultaneous development of a new ideal of pastorship that placed a high value on self-sacrificing service and fearless moral leadership.

From Priest to Pastor—

The "Good Shepherd" Ideal

As the clergy's interpretation of the church's mission and the conception of their own duties changed, the ways in which the clergy thought about themselves and their relation to the laity were altered. In the eighteenth

and early nineteenth centuries, texts on the duties of clergymen emphasized the clergy's spiritual authority over the laity. The service of the
clergy was directed first and foremost to God: their power to perform the
liturgy and the sacraments came to them from God, and they were responsible to God for using the sacred rites to preserve and protect the
souls of their parishioners. From the middle of the nineteenth century,
however, there was a shift in how the responsibilities of the clergy were
represented in the literature about clerical duties. More attention was
given to the nature of the clergyman's relation to his parishioners rather
than his relation to God. The emphasis on clerical authority over the laity
was eroded by a new current of thinking that stressed an attitude of love
toward parishioners, manifested in an intense dedication to identifying
and serving the needs of parishioners not only for holy rituals and dogmatic instruction but increasingly for spiritual counseling, moral guidance, and eventually even material assistance.[51]

These changes were reflected in the expansion of a previously neglected
field of study in the theological sciences, that of pastoral theology
(*pastyrskoe bogoslovie*). Although a course in pastoral theology was established at the academy level of the church's school system in the late 1840s,
the literature on the subject was initially limited to the two textbooks developed for the academy course in the 1850s.[52] Church scholars did not
turn their attention to pastoral theology in any serious way until the 1880s
and 1890s, when new monographs as well as new and expanded textbooks
on pastoral theology began to reshape conceptions of the clergyman's role
and responsibilities.[53] One of the most noteworthy changes in the pastoral
literature of those last decades of the nineteenth century was the shift in
the vocabulary used to identify and define an ordained member of the
clergy. Before the 1880s, the word most commonly used among educated
members of the clergy and laity to refer to a clergyman was *"sviashchennik,"*
or "priest," meaning a member of the clergy "having authority to pronounce absolution and administer all sacraments save that of ordination."[54]
In Russian, the nature of the *svaishchennik*'s primary function is evident
from the root *"sviat-"* with its sole meaning of "holy." Since the Russian
church emphasized the clergyman's liturgical and sacramental duties, the
word "priest" was accurate and an acceptable neutral word for an ordained
man with a certain rank in the clergy.[55] From the last decades of the nineteenth century, however, some authors of clerical handbooks and guides
began to favor a different term for clergyman: the Slavonic word *pastyr'*,
which means both priest and shepherd.[56] One of the pioneers in introducing this usage seems to have been the monk Iakov (Domskii), mentioned
earlier as the champion of the *beseda*. In 1880, he published a work entitled
*Pastyr' v otnoshenii k sebe i pastve (The Pastor in Relation to Himself and His
Flock)*. Not only did Father Iakov use the word *pastyr'* in his title, but he
also used it throughout the work, instead of *sviashchennik,* as the normal,
neutral term for referring to a member of the clergy.[57]

This shift from a preference for the word *sviashchennik* to *pastyr'* seems to be connected with the effort to articulate a new way of understanding the clergyman's role and responsibilities. Those who favored the word *pastyr'* as the general term for an ordained member of the clergy or who made a distinction between the clergyman as a *pastyr'* and the clergyman as a *sviashchennik* were trying to separate their particular conception of the clergyman's role from other notions about the priesthood, particularly ones that conceived of the priest primarily as the provider of church rituals and sacraments.[58] For authors like Father Iakov, the term *pastyr'* had unique and powerful symbolic associations that helped legitimate an expanded definition of the parish priest's responsibilities. One of the most appealing aspects of the term *pastyr'* was its clear association with the image of the shepherd, a symbol inextricably associated with both Jesus and the God of Israel. In trying to articulate what it meant to be a *pastyr'*, clergymen of the later nineteenth century often turned to passages in the New Testament in which Jesus was identified with the image of the shepherd. For example, the monk Innokentii (Pustynskii), author of a history of pastoral theology in Russia, explained in the introduction to his work that he thought the essence of what it meant to be a clergyman was best summed up in John 21:15–17.[59] After the resurrected Jesus appears for the third time to his disciples, he addresses Simon Peter three times in a row, asking him each time, "Do you love me?" Each time that Peter answers affirmatively, Jesus responds, "If you love me, then tend to my sheep."[60] The passage implies that Jesus himself was like a shepherd and that those who follow his calling must also be like shepherds, tending to the needs of the faithful. This was how Antonii (Vadkovskii) interpreted the same passage when he used it as the basis of the sermon that he delivered upon his elevation to the rank of bishop of Vyborg in 1887.[61]

The emphasis on love and service that is evident in the way both the monk Innokentii and Bishop Antonii interpreted the meaning of the passage in the Gospel of John becomes even more pronounced when one looks at an additional example of how authors of the later nineteenth century employed other images of Jesus the Shepherd. There is an earlier passage in the Gospel of John (10:1–18) in which Jesus told his disciples that he was like the good shepherd because his sheep knew his voice and followed it and because he was ready to lay down his life to protect his flock against the wild animals that threatened it. In clerical handbooks of the early nineteenth century, authors had emphasized the shepherd's authority over his flock and his duty to protect the dumb and helpless sheep from danger. The wild animals in the parable were equated with heresy, while the sheepfold that enclosed the flock represented the church. The shepherd, whose voice the sheep followed and who opened and closed the gate of the sheepfold, was a figure of knowledge and power, a model for the clergy to follow.[62]

This same text also appeared in clerical handbooks of the later nineteenth century, but with an interpretation that implied a different model of clerical leadership. Rather than focusing on the shepherd's authority, authors of the later nineteenth century emphasized the shepherd's love for his flock and his willingness to lay down his life for them. The importance of the shepherd's qualities of love and self-sacrifice was reinforced by the close association that was established between this text from the Gospel of John and the famous parable of the Good Shepherd in the Gospel of Luke (15:1–7). When the Pharisees complained about Jesus spending his time among sinners and unclean people, Jesus asked them, "Which man among you who has a hundred sheep will not leave the ninety-nine in the wilds and go after the lost one until he finds it? And when he does find it, he sets it on his shoulders, rejoicing."[63] The Good Shepherd cares so deeply for each member of his flock that he braves the dangers of the world to seek out even a single strayed sheep and return it safely to the fold. When he finds the lost one he does not punish it but rejoices that it has been found and returned to safety.[64] The way in which clerical authors of the later nineteenth century interpreted the two passages from the Gospel of John in light of the parable from the Gospel of Luke created an image of Jesus as the model *pastyr'* whose defining qualities were those of love, service, and self-sacrifice.[65] This connection between the use of the term *pastyr'* and the image of the clergyman as a Good Shepherd was strongly manifested in the way that the clergyman represented his relations to his parishioners. Authors were especially likely to refer to the clergyman as a *pastyr'* when they wanted to emphasize the clergyman's feelings of paternal love and tenderness toward his parishioners. For example, the monk Innokentii suggested in his introduction that "[t]he understanding of *pastyr'* includes the idea of the pastor's love toward his flock and his selfless devotion to their interests [and] the understanding of those he guards as a weak, powerless, lost, and defenseless flock."[66] The parishioners, often referred to in this literature as "the flock" *(pastva)* or "the tended" *(pasomykh),* were objects of the clergyman's pity and compassion; their helplessness stimulated his love and his desire to serve them and made the call to self-sacrifice seem justified. As one historian of the rural clergy concluded after reviewing the writings of many provincial priests on what it meant to be an *istinnyi pastyr',* or a true pastor: "Pastorship demanded self-repudiation. The life of a true priest is one of eternal self-sacrifice."[67] Not coincidentally, the attitude of the *pastyr'* toward his parishioners strongly resembles the attitude of many members of the secular intelligentsia toward the *narod* in this same period.[68]

The responsibility was tremendous, but so, too, were the opportunities. "Tending" to the flock could be taken broadly to mean providing for parishioners' physical and material needs as well as their spiritual requirements. Venturing into the wilderness to find the proverbial lost sheep could justify virtually any kind of activity that an activist clergyman might pursue in the name of promoting the word of God in the world, from temperance agitation to mutual credit societies to philosophical discussions about church dogma with doubters from the intelligentsia. In fact, those writers who preferred the term *pastyr'* over *sviashchennik* established a new set of priorities for the modern clergyman. While acknowledging the importance of performing the liturgy, administering the sacraments and delivering sermons, the monk Innokentii suggested that the salvation of one's parishioners depended *primarily* on the clergyman's ability to provide effective pastoral care.[69] For Father Iakov (Domskii), the clergy's chief responsibility was to serve as moral leaders for the people.[70] He argued that a good clergyman lived out the principles of the gospel in his own life, providing a "living sermon" through his active work among his parishioners.[71] The good clergyman did not confine himself to his study for prayer, study, and contemplation.[72] Like Jesus, he ventured out into the world and tried to apply the teachings of the Bible to real life. In this way, the pastor acquired an intimate knowledge of the real needs and problems of his parishioners, which enabled him to advise and assist them more effectively as well as to serve as a meaningful role model.[73]

Members of the clergy had always looked to Jesus as a model for the practice of their profession, but their interpretation of his life and work and their views on how to apply his example to the conditions of their own time evolved to reflect differing historical circumstances. Nevertheless, despite these actual changes it was still important for the clergy to connect the views and practices of their own time with the original model. In the nineteenth century, this intellectual task was taken up by Sergei Sollertinskii, a scholar and professor of pastoral theology at the St. Petersburg Ecclesiastical Academy, who published a work entitled *Pastyrstvo Khrista Spasiteli (The Pastorship of Christ the Savior)* in the late 1880s.[74] The purpose of this work was to demonstrate that the practices of modern pastorship were not actually new but had originated with Jesus himself. In Sollertinskii's view, the primary nature of Jesus's work on earth was pastoral; Jesus was thus the first pastor, whose work provided clergymen with the inspiration and the example for their own pastoral mission.[75] While acknowledging that Jesus derived his authority from his position as the Son of God, Sollertinskii argued that the power of his example for members of the clergy derived from his role as the "Son of Man." In this role, Jesus was inspired by a great love of humankind to dedicate not only his life but even his death to the service of human salvation.

Like the archimandrite Feodor (Bukharev), Sollertinskii believed that the death of Jesus on the Cross was the moment when the Kingdom of God was founded on earth. He also agreed with Father Feodor that this kingdom, though established through the Crucifixion, could not be fully realized until humans learned not only to believe in the gospel but also to live by its principles. According to Sollertinskii, the primary task of the Christian pastor was to continue the work that Jesus had begun by showing the meaning of the gospel through his deeds.[76] Like Father Iakov (Domskii),

Sollertinskii argued that the moral guidance the clergyman provided to his flock through his own example was the essence of his service as a pastor; it was even more important than the pastor's verbal instruction of his followers in the principles of the faith.[77] Sollertinskii thus focused on pastorship as the key element of the clergyman's service, emphasized moral leadership over doctrinal instruction as the purpose of pastorship, and associated the clergyman in his role as a pastor directly with the example of Jesus Christ.

In his discussion of the pastor's relation to the laity, Sollertinskii concentrated particular attention on the responsibility the pastor had for cultivating the moral consciousness of the individual, which constituted the defining essence of the individual soul. Of course, clergymen had always been deeply concerned for the fate of their parishioners' souls. One scholar of this period, who traced the changing ideas of clerical service from pagan times through the Old Testament and the New Testament, argued that the most important new idea Christianity introduced to the world was that of the individual soul; he argued that for this reason the most important concern of the clergy was the care of the individual soul.[78] Whereas in earlier times this care might have been focused on the provision of the rituals and sacraments or the teaching of correct doctrines, in the work of Sollertinskii and other authors of this period the emphasis was on cultivating the soul's moral strength so that the individual living in the world could strive consciously toward the good, working toward his own salvation and contributing to the salvation of others as well.[79]

Professor Sollertinskii's examination of the theoretical aspects of pastorship was complemented by the three-volume guide to the practical problems of pastorship published by Father Vladimir Pevnitskii, professor of pastoral theology at the Kiev Ecclesiastical Academy. Pevnitskii's course on pastorship, published between 1885 and 1890, was adopted at all the academies and became the fundamental text for advanced courses on pastoral theology and practice from the 1890s. Pevnitskii integrated the new concern for pastoral care into a broader survey of the character of the clergy and the nature of their work. This was evident from the definition of "priesthood" *(sviashchenstvo)* with which he began the first volume:

> The priesthood, or priestly—otherwise pastoral—service is a special, vitally necessary service in the church of God, taking its authority from the Founder of the church, the Lord Jesus Christ, undertaken by persons who are selected and consecrated, and consisting of the performance of the divine mysteries, the preaching of the Word of God, and the wardship of people in the spiritual life.[80]

Pevnitskii defined the priesthood as both "priestly" *(sviashchenicheskoe)* and "pastoral" *(pastyrskoe)* service in both the title of the first volume and this opening statement, indicating not only an interest in the pastoral ideal but perhaps also some confusion about how it fit in with existing ideas about the clergy and their work. Indeed, at first Pevnitskii's description of how

the clergyman was to lead his parishioners in the religious life does not differ greatly from those given in the older guides.[81] However, Pevnitskii's personal observations about how the circumstances under which the clergy
worked had changed in his own lifetime led him to a broader understanding of the clergyman's role. He observed that parishioners had become critical, demanding, and less willing to submit to the authority of the clergy; he
believed that this was in part because the secular culture had become increasingly hostile toward the church and religion.[82] He concluded that
these developments meant that the clergy had to make a heroic effort to
reawaken the love and respect of the people toward the church through
their own selfless and humble dedication to service in the community,
which included organizing parish schools, sponsoring local charities, and
initiating reading and lectures for popular religious enlightenment.[83]

As Pevnitskii presented it, this part of the clergyman's work was the most
difficult and demanding. In the second volume of his series concerning the
character and education of the clergyman, he argued that the clergy required a special education because they had so much more to do than just
perform divine services.[84] The clergyman was also a teacher of the people
and "the moral leader and cultivator *(vospitatel')* of his flock" and as such
needed the same kind of practical, professional training as a doctor, lawyer,
engineer, or agronomist.[85] Unfortunately, the training given to future clergymen at the seminary was incomplete precisely because the art of pastoral care could not be taught in the classroom but had to be acquired
through experience. Pevnitskii proposed that the seminaries establish
"spiritual teaching hospitals" so that future pastors could learn the cure of
souls in the same practical way that future doctors learned the care of the
body.[86] He also recommended that seminary graduates who planned to
enter the clergy spend the time between graduation and ordination
preparing themselves for their profession not only through reading and
further study but also through work among the people, especially by
teaching in the local schools.[87]

The entire third volume of Pevnitskii's course was devoted to the subject
of pastoral care.[88] As he noted in the introduction to the book his was a
pioneering effort, for the literature on the pastoral duty of providing
moral care and guidance to believers hardly existed in Russia, with the result that neither the clergy nor the laity was certain of what such care
consisted or how it was to be accomplished.[89] Pevnitskii's concern was
practical rather than theoretical: he reviewed the church's tradition of
pastorship only briefly, referring first to writings of the church fathers,
then to the parable of the lost sheep and finally to the example of the
apostles. Practically speaking, he believed the pastor had to have both a
general understanding of men's souls and a particular knowledge of the
individuals under his care. He had to be close to his people, involved in
their lives, and aware of their needs. Above all, he had to be motivated by
his love for them and his Christian zeal.[90]

The professor defined the goal of pastoral care as preparing people for the Kingdom of God and making the path to salvation easier for them by helping them to live according to the teaching of the gospel.[91] Since there was no established method for achieving this goal, Pevnitskii urged the clergyman to be flexible and creative in his approach. He could exercise his moral influence directly by his personal presence or his participation in the local school or charitable society, for example. He should not rely only upon his own strength, however, but also organize his parishioners to help him carry out the struggle against poverty, drunkenness, and false teaching so that they could practice for themselves the Christian virtue of helping the less fortunate.[92] More importantly, the clergyman should not restrict the field of his activities but should realize that his responsibilities included the parish's social and material needs as well as its religious ones. Pevnitskii argued that these categories of need were indistinguishable and inseparable in reality, since one of the clergyman's religious responsibilities was to promote Christian living in the family and the community, and both goals were profoundly affected by social conditions and material circumstances. For this reason, the pastor had to interest himself in the social life of the community and advise his parishioners on the organization of that life in matters such as family conduct, education, and hygiene. Pevnitskii emphasized the importance of this attention to social needs:

> [B]y virtue of his office and his calling, by virtue of his relation to the parishioners as a pastor and a father, he must promote the best organization of social conditions in his parish. Concern about this does not take the pastor away from his main purpose—the moral-religious elevation of the life of his parishioners—but on the contrary assists [him] in its attainment. Through attention to the interests and conditions of the social or civic life of his parish the priest comes into more frequent contact with the people entrusted to him and can exert on them a stronger and wider influence and can win their greater trust.[93]

Because social conditions affect the religious life of individuals and the community, the pastor must be concerned about them and try to improve them; by doing this, he also increases his influence over his parishioners and his role in the wider life of the community.

Pevnitskii was even more sensitive to the relation between material conditions and moral-religious life. He deplored the church's abandonment of its responsibilities for charitable work in modern times. He rejected out of hand the argument that was sometimes offered against the church's involvement in charity: that such material concerns were outside of the church's sphere of interest because they were of this world while the church's focus was supposed to be on the next world.[94] Pevnitskii refused to recognize what he considered to be an artificial and wrong separation between the church and the world, between the spiritual and the material. He argued that from its beginnings the Christian church had recognized the intimate relation between man's flesh and his spirit; such recognition had motivated Jesus, the apostles and the church fathers to interest themselves not only in the spiritual needs and sufferings of others but also in their bodily wants.[95] The modern pastor had to acknowledge that a person's physical condition and material needs affected his spiritual state. Physical needs could impede a person from following the path to salvation by exposing him to the temptations of vice and sin or even by burdening his heart with worry, so the pastor had to address such needs as seriously as needs that were spiritual in nature. Christian compassion should move him to help those who were sick or suffered in any way, but Christian belief should also remind him that he could not minister to the soul and neglect the body, or nurse the body without effect on the soul.

As a result of his belief in the close relation between the material and the spiritual, Pevnitskii advocated the participation of the clergy in all types of charitable work. He believed that the clergy knew the needs of the people better than the government charities and lay philanthropic organizations because of their position in the parish community and their role as mediators between the different classes. The clergy could communicate the needs of the poor to the rich and help them to organize charitable institutions that were both efficient and humane; they could also help the poor find ways to help themselves by establishing societies for education and mutual aid.[96] In addition, the pastor himself had specific charitable obligations, among them: visiting the sick, comforting the suffering, making peace, visiting prisons, and treating spiritual ills such as depression and alcoholism. Having firmly established the centrality of charitable work to pastoral care, Pevnitskii devoted the remainder of his book—more than four hundred pages—to describing how the pastor should carry out each of his obligations.

Pevnitskii's work brought together all of the important new ideas about the church and its relation to and role in society that had emerged among the educated clergy since the middle of the century and demonstrated their significance and application to the clergy's actual service. Although he incorporated elements of the older texts on clerical service (most notably on the clergyman's duties as a teacher and spiritual leader), Pevnitskii's work as a whole focused on the newer concerns related to the clergyman's responsibilities as a pastor. He considered the clergyman to be *primarily* a pastor and believed that the clergyman's first responsibility was pastoral service, which he defined broadly as the provision of moral leadership to the community of believers through the example of the clergyman's own selfless service to others. His goal was to bring people into the Kingdom of God by helping them live according to the law of the gospel, which was a law of love, service, and charity toward all. Some people required the pastor's spiritual counsel or the example of his charity work to help them fulfill this law; others who suffered from physical disease or material want needed real comfort and aid in order to live the Christian life. It was the responsibility of the pastor to provide for all these needs, imitating Christ and helping to redeem humanity.

Pevnitskii's ideal of pastoral service was based on the fundamental conviction, first expressed by the archimandrite Feodor at the end of the 1850s and widely accepted by the educated clergy, that the church was not separate from the secular world and that all aspects of men's individual and communal lives were the church's concern. Pevnitskii's emphasis on the clergyman's role as a moral leader of the community was derived from the definition of the church's mission as the total transformation of the world through the application of the moral teachings of the gospel; it also reflected the emergent awareness of the social elements of Christian teaching and a renewed emphasis on living the Christian life in addition to professing the Christian faith. His work expressed the ideal of clerical service toward which clergyman of the earlier generation, such as Alexander Gumilevskii and Ioann Belliustin, had been striving and showed how that ideal could be practically realized. The way in which he addressed the central issues of clerical service that concerned many among the church's educated elite was highly praised and widely accepted, so that during the 1880s and 1890s his definition of the nature and tasks of pastorship emerged as one of the formative influences on a new generation of clergymen.[97] These modern new pastors were distinguished by their missionary spirit, their desire to provide moral leadership to their parishioners, and their commitment to active service in the community. They infused the institutions of the church in St. Petersburg with fresh ideas and youthful vigor, contributing greatly to the rapid expansion of the church's social outreach work in the parishes and throughout the city in the years before the revolution of 1905.

CHAPTER FOUR

CHURCH CHARITY

AND THE SEARCH FOR

CHRISTIAN COMMUNITY

As the clergy of St. Petersburg reconceptualized the church's mission and their own role in fulfilling it during the second half of the nineteenth century, their activities expanded and diversified. Inspired by an ideal of pastoral leadership that emphasized love and service to others, the clergy of St. Petersburg not only applauded the expansion of private philanthropic organizations but also took part in the establishment of many church-based associations for charity, education, social service, and the promotion of temperance. These surprisingly numerous organizations were a vital part of the capital's thriving public life in the decades between 1860 and 1907, comprising a significant proportion of the total number of the charitable institutions financed by private, voluntary means in the city. Significantly, these church-based organizations flourished at the same time that many secular associations for philanthropy and popular education were also enjoying great success.[1] However, while secular philanthropic efforts have been recognized as making an important contribution to the civic life of late imperial Russia, the contribution of church-based charities to the development of the public sphere has not yet been examined. In fact, church-based organizations are generally excluded from discussions concerning the origins of the public sphere and the construction of civil society.[2] However, the distinction between secular philanthropic organizations and church-based charities is, in some ways, artificial and misleading. Members of the Orthodox clergy participated in charities established and run by private, quasi-public and public institutions, while lay persons of both genders helped to organize, support, and administer church-based charities. Both secular and church-based organizations often addressed the same types of social problems, such as poverty, illiteracy, family disintegration, and alcohol abuse, often using similar means. Religious values and beliefs provided an important source of motivation for members of both the laity and the clergy who participated in charity work.[3] Secular society was not completely estranged from the church, nor were the clergy hopelessly alienated from either the educated or the popular classes. Both the lay and clerical members of educated society in St. Petersburg often worked together to promote the development of associational life and the spirit of volunteerism that scholars today enumerate as two of the hallmarks of an emerging civil society. In this work, they were nourished by religious values as well as by civic ideals.[4]

CHARITY AND THE CREATION OF A CHRISTIAN COMMUNITY

The ideals that provided the foundation for the church-based associations of the later nineteenth century originated in the teachings of the Orthodox church, whose primers on Orthodox doctrine asserted that charity was a basic Christian duty enjoined by both the Ten Commandments and the Sermon on the Mount. The church interpreted the sixth commandment's prohibition against killing as containing an implicit injunction to give aid to others: "to feed the hungry, to clothe the naked, to visit the sick, to convert the sinner from his sin, to teach the ignorant the law, to give good counsel and to pray to the all-merciful God for the salvation of all."[5] The Long Catechism also interpreted the fifth beatitude in the Sermon on the Mount—"Blessed be the merciful"—as a call for charity as well.[6] But what did it mean to give charity? According to the teachings of the church, charity was not merely a matter of action but also of intention. True Christian charity meant more than doing good; it also meant cultivating honest feelings of love and good will toward all. Thus, in the Longer Catechism to be merciful and forgiving toward others was to manifest the spirit of charity toward them.[7] Similarly, the church's interpretation of the sixth commandment explained that it meant Christians must behave with affection, gentleness, and kindness toward all, seeking reconciliation, offering forgiveness, and making peace.[8] In both cases, the *senti-*

ment of charity toward others is emphasized as much as any *act* of charity. This was because the goal of Christian charity was not primarily material but moral and religious. The church did not promote charity in the hope of giving everyone a fair or equal share of the world's wealth or of establishing a certain standard of living for all.[9] Instead, the primary purpose of Christian charity was to bring humans closer to each other and to God. Through charity, one helped another person to attain the material or spiritual conditions necessary to focus on living a good Christian life; at the same time, one fulfilled the most important commandment in the Bible—to love one's neighbor as oneself.[10]

The ultimate purpose of Christian charity was to create a Christian community in the world.[11] As the Orthodox church saw it, charity was not a means of correcting an unjust social order but of transcending it. The church did not teach that poverty could be eliminated or that the material differences between the fortunate and the unfortunate could be erased. Rather, it taught that people should not allow such material distinctions to divide them from each other or to alienate them from God. The poor were taught to accept their misfortune without bitterness, remembering that Christ had lived among the poor and promised to them the Kingdom of Heaven.[12] The rich were cautioned that they were not the owners of their wealth but only its stewards, obligated to use their resources for the good of others.[13] The poor were to accept charity in the same spirit of love and joy that the wealthy were to give it, with the result that the differences in their material situations could be overcome by mutual Christian love. This moment of spiritual transcendence was the realization of the goal of Christian community, a glimpse of the promised Kingdom of God that would one day embrace all Christendom.[14]

The clergy of the late nineteenth century found a powerful inspiration in these ideals, which reinforced their belief that the church's mission was to bring the principles of the gospel to life in the world. Charity work allowed the clergy to show by example how a Christian could put his faith into action. Father Alexander Gumilevskii, the parish priest who led the way in organizing the capital's first parish-based charity in the early 1860s, once said that he viewed his good works as "active prayer."[15] A clergyman of the post-reform generation echoed this sentiment when he declared that an act of charity was an act of faith.[16] Moreover, charity work also offered the clergy an ideal field for the exercise of pastoral leadership. Charity work called on the clergyman to demonstrate love, compassion, pity, self-sacrifice, and service to others, much as pastorship did. Father Vladimir Pevnitskii devoted many pages to the topic of charity work in his three-volume work on pastorship, indicating that he considered it one of the pastor's most essential concerns.[17] Finally, charity work also offered to clergymen the opportunity to serve the people and contribute to improving their lives, an opportunity that they, like their counterparts in the laity, valued and actively sought out.[18]

CONFUSION COMPOUNDED—
The Curatorships and Charities of the Capital

The two main institutions for the organization of church-based charity in St Petersburg in the later nineteenth century were the parish curatorships. and the parish charities. Of these two institutions, the parish curatorships are the more familiar to students of Russian history. The results of their work were more likely to be summed up than those of the parish charities in official and unofficial publications concerning various aspects of the church's activities.[19] Because these results often seemed unimpressive on an empire-wide scale, they were also the frequent target of criticism in discussions about the failings of the parish and the need for parish reform. In contrast, the parish charities were generally overlooked in the statistical compilations concerning charity, with the result that their contributions to parish life were unappreciated by contemporaries and virtually unknown to historians.[20] In St. Petersburg, both the parish curatorships and the parish charities flourished in the late imperial period, bringing the parish clergy together with Orthodox lay people of widely varying backgrounds to work for the creation of autonomous, voluntary communities that enriched both the religious and civic life of the capital.

The parish curatorships were established during the era of the Great Reforms as part of the official effort to strengthen the influence of the church in society.[21] Reformers wanted to elevate the status of the clergy, but this required that they address the problems of clerical poverty and dependence.[22] The clergy subsisted primarily on the fees that parishioners paid them for the performance of various rituals. Naturally, most parishioners thought they paid too much while most clergymen felt they were given too little. Many clergymen wanted regular government salaries or at least subsidies, but the state strongly resisted these demands as being too costly. Instead, reformers looked for a way to organize local financial resources for the clergy's support by establishing elected councils at the parish level, beginning in 1859. Initially, these councils were given the authority to impose, collect, and administer obligatory parish dues, but many hierarchs objected to giving so much control over parish finances and the clergy to laymen.[23] In 1863, the Synod's Commission on Clerical Affairs presented an alternative form of the parish councils to the government, and in 1864 the law establishing the parish curatorships was approved. The parish curatorships differed from the councils in that the property of the parish curatorship was separated from that of the church. The collection of voluntary donations was placed under the authority of a committee that included all the clergy of the particular church, the church elder, and a few lay people elected by the general assembly of the parish.[24] The money was to be used not only to supplement the income of the parish clergy but also for maintenance of the parish church, the support of parish charities, and after 1884 the funding of parish schools.[25]

In St. Petersburg, curatorships were quickly established at the majority of those churches commonly regarded as parish churches (regardless of their official status). By 1880, there were 199 active curatorships at the 262 acting parish churches of the diocese. This number decreased temporarily during the 1880s in response to the economic downturn of that decade but stabilized at its former level in the 1890s. After 1900, the number of curatorships slowly increased, though not as quickly as the number of parishes, so that by 1908 there were 227 curatorships in the diocese.[26] Although there were other dioceses that had a greater number of active curatorships, the proportion of parish churches with curatorships was somewhat higher in St. Petersburg than for the empire generally—about 63 percent, as compared to 47 percent.[27]

The amount of money collected by the parish curatorships of St. Petersburg fluctuated from year to year, but from 1880 to the end of the 1890s, it remained in the modest range of 30,000 to 40,000 rubles a year total.[28] Between 1898 and 1905, however, the amount increased dramatically: in 1898, the curatorships collected over 64,000 rubles; in 1901 they collected more than double that amount—just over 147,000 rubles. The amount declined after that peak. After collecting almost 83,000 rubles in 1905, the curatorships did not again bring in much more than 40,000 rubles a year for their work until World War I, when donations made for soldiers' families greatly increased collections again.[29]

The curatorships of St. Petersburg were unusual in that they consistently contributed the majority of their funds to charitable and educational work. Although the curatorships had originated as an effort to supplement clerical income, in most dioceses the majority of funds collected went to the repair and improvement of parish churches.[30] In 1892, for example, the parish curatorships of the empire collected nearly two million rubles in donations but spent more than three quarters of that sum on church maintenance or improvement; only 320,000 rubles, or about 16 percent of the total, went to charities and schools. In 1898, 2.9 million out of the 3.6 million rubles collected empire-wide (more than 80 percent) went to church maintenance and improvement, while slightly more than half a million rubles (about 15 percent) was given to parish institutions.[31] During the 1890s, when the St. Petersburg diocese saw a flurry of church expansion and building, the proportion of curatorship funds earmarked for building projects increased, but even then, more than half of the curatorships' funds still went to parish charities and schools.[32] After 1900, the proportion given to charity increased rapidly, so that by 1906 virtually all of the St. Petersburg curatorships' money was being used for the parish charities and schools. Despite the fact that the curatorships of St. Petersburg collected less money than those of other dioceses, they often spent more on parish-supported institutions.[33]

By the 1880s, many observers felt that the parish curatorships had failed.[34] In the view of the bishops and the Synod, the curatorships were a failure because they had done little to improve the financial position of the parish clergy (which, of course, was their original purpose). Other commentators, often lay intellectuals with close ties to the church, criticized the curatorships for their inability to "revive" the parish as the kind of vibrant, autonomous community that many believed had once existed in some vaguely imagined time in Russia's pre-industrial past.[35] Some critics charged that many curatorships existed in name only and contributed little to the life of the church or society. Many educated people—of both lay and clerical status—thought that the money some curatorships spent in enlarging and decorating their parish churches was wasted; in their view, the money would have been better spent in efforts to alleviate popular ignorance and poverty.[36] Some of these critics blamed the local parish clergy for poor leadership because they had either failed to direct the curatorships to worthy objectives or had taken advantage of their parishioners' piety to enhance their own status through church beautification projects. In return, there were both laymen and clergymen who declared the curatorships' deficiencies were the fault of the laity, who in some cases seized control of the curatorships from the clergy and used the money for projects the clergy did not approve of, and who in other cases were completely unresponsive to the efforts of the curatorships to raise funds for worthy parish causes.[37]

The arguments concerning the parish curatorships were part of a broader discussion in Russian society in the late imperial period, one that was usually framed as a debate over the "parish problem" but that was really an effort to understand and respond to the challenges facing a society in the midst of the great transformation from agrarian to industrial community structures.[38] The periodical press of the late imperial period is filled with discussions of community, for many thoughtful people feared that Russian society was in danger of losing its cohesiveness in the midst of rapid change. Some authors regretted the passing of traditional kinds of community and sought to return to the old ways in the midst of new circumstances, while others looked for new kinds of community. For many authors, concerns about the church occupied a central place in their reflections on community. What role should the church play in society? What was the proper relation of the laity and the clergy in the community? How should the relationship between local churches and the church's central administration be defined, and by whom? Among many of those who criticized the parish curatorships, there was a common belief that charitable and educational work was an essential part of the church's mission and that laity and clergy should cooperate to accomplish this work. Although such an ambition was not always satisfied through the parish curatorships, it provided a powerful motivation for the work of the capital's parish charities.

BUILDING BROTHERHOOD—
The Work of the Parish Charities in St. Petersburg

Like the parish curatorships, the parish charities were a product of the era of Great Reforms. Whereas the curatorships were developed "from above" by reform-minded bureaucrats trying to solve a vexing financial problem, the charities were organized "from below" by members of the clergy and the laity who were inspired by the activist spirit of the 1860s to try to solve the social problems they saw around them. Although the clergy often took the initiative in organizing the charities, they were sustained by cooperation between the clergy and a wide range of lay people. Members of the royal family and the high nobility belonged to societies that also included professors, doctors, and teachers; in other societies, members of the professions worked together with military men, merchants, prosperous artisans, and successful shopkeepers. In all of these parish charities, the clergy had a central role in bringing people together, discovering what needs had to be addressed, organizing resources, and translating good intentions into effective action. They were not isolated from other elements of society but shared with many lay people a dedication to creating in the heart of a modern city thriving communities based on the ideals of fraternal love, compassion, and service.[39]

The first parish charity in St. Petersburg opened at the church of the Annunciation on Vasilievskii Island in 1862, two years before the first parish curatorships were established. In 1863, Father Alexander Gumilevskii of the church of the Nativity opened the charity for which he became famous. Many others were opened during the 1860s and 1870s, and by the end of the century parish charities had become so much a part of local religious life that it was common to organize a parish charity immediately for each new parish church.[40] The parish charities were administratively distinct from the parish curatorships. The curatorships were under the general supervision of the diocesan administration and subject to the final authority of the Synod, while the parish charities were under the authority of the Ministry of Internal Affairs, to which they submitted their charters and annual reports in accordance with the rules for secular voluntary associations. For this reason, the parish charities are mostly absent from the reports of the diocesan consistory and the director general of the Synod.

What did those who organized the parish charities hope to accomplish? What was the purpose of church-based charity? The founding charters of the different societies offer some insight into their founders' motives. These charters bear a strong resemblance to each other, reflecting in their common formulas the fact that they were written to meet the central government's requirements for official recognition and registration. Nevertheless, the ideals expressed in these charters should not be dismissed as meaningless simply because they are expressed formulaically; the language and

ideals articulated in the parish charities' charters were echoed in other publications as well and seem to have been meaningful to many involved in
church-based volunteer work. The parish charities commonly regarded
charity as beneficial both to the donor and the recipient of aid. For the
donors, giving to charity enabled them to practice an essential Christian
virtue. The charter of the church of the Annunciation, for example, declared that charity toward those in need was the duty of every Christian.
They cited the example of St. Tikhon of Zadonsk, the eighteenth-century
bishop of Voronezh who was popularly revered for his charity to all, as the
model they hoped to imitate in their own work.[41] Other charters placed
more emphasis on the impact that Christian charity would make on those
who received it. The charter of the society of St. Pantaleimon's church
(Liteinyi district) explained that the society's members wanted to release
the poor from the indignity of begging on the church porch and enable
them to go inside to pray instead. They also hoped that by institutionaliz-
ing charitable giving, they would be able to discourage false beggars from
soliciting parishioners, for as they noted, such chicanery was harmful to
the souls of these imposters.[42] In a similar moralizing tone, the charter of the
charitable society founded at the Trinity cathedral of the Left Guard of the Iz-
mailovskii Regiment said that the society wanted to alleviate poverty because
they feared it led to vice and thus endangered the souls of the Christian
poor.[43] This implicit judgment of the poor was softened in some cases, however, by compassion for their unfortunate lot. The society of the Trinity
cathedral also expressed sympathy for the difficult life faced by the poor
families of their parish and a desire to ease their hardship. The charter of
the society established at the Spasobocharinskaia church on the Vyborg
side stated, "the crying poverty and need [in the parish] aroused good people to establish a society for the care of the poor."[44]

Several of the charters emphasized that Christian charity was not merely
a mechanical redistribution of wealth by which those who had much con-
descended to give a little to those who had nothing in return for their gratitude and public praise. Instead, these charters envisioned charity as a
means of creating a community based on compassion and love. The society
of St. Pantaleimon's church stated that one of the goals of their charitable
work was to unite all members of their parish around the church in the
spirit of Christian love, expressed through good works.[45] The charter of the
church of the Annunciation's parish charity emphasized the importance of
the personal bond that charity could create between the donor and the
beneficiary by sending donors out to distribute aid personally to the poor
in their homes.[46] The society of St. Vladimir's church (Moscow district)
called members of all ranks of society, even the poorest, to join their society, emphasizing that it was not the amount of one's donation that was important but the spirit of selflessness and love in which it was given.[47] The council
of the charity at Spasobocharinskaia church felt that it had most fully accomplished its mission when it was able to say in its annual report that "all the

meetings [of the council] this year were permeated by a truly fraternal spirit of unity, love, and peace."[48] Such devotion to the spirit of community was prevalent everywhere. It explains why societies were established both in parishes so poor they could hardly support any work at all and in parishes so wealthy there were no poor people to assist: it was not the material purpose that was important to the members, but the moral one.

The formal organization of the parish charities varied. The charity was usually under the supervision of a council that included the clergy and the elder of the church along with several laymen elected by the society's membership. The president of the council was often the senior priest of the church, although some societies elected a president from among their members. The council was responsible for the administration of the society's funds and the organization of services. It met frequently, once or twice a month, while the society itself met one or two times a year. Some societies divided their parishes into sectors and designated curators who were responsible for reporting on the needs of each sector and helping to distribute aid where it was most needed. Membership was generally open to all Orthodox people living in the parish, regardless of age, sex, or attendance at the parish church. Some societies collected small dues from their members to help finance their work, but most hesitated to impose any requirements that might exclude people from the all-embracing community they wanted to form. Wealthy donors or those with respected names were welcomed, of course, but so too were persons of quite ordinary means and reputations. This inclusiveness meant that many parish charities were larger than might be expected: the average society had between fifty and a hundred members, and the society at the cathedral of St. Sergei (Liteinyi district) had four hundred and fifty members in 1898.[49]

One of the remarkable features of the parish charities was the degree to which they depended on the cooperation of both clergymen and laymen. The initiative for organizing a parish society often came from the parish clergy, sometimes with the assistance of the parish elder. There were several cases, however, in which ordinary lay people first broached the idea of a charitable society or in which clergy and laity worked together on the project from the beginning. The charity of St. Andrew's cathedral (Vasilievskii Island) was first proposed by several members of the local intelligentsia, who believed that the parish was the most natural unit for local charity. The plan was enthusiastically taken up by the senior priest and other clergy of the cathedral.[50] The Spasobocharinskaia church's society was organized on the joint initiative of the parish priest and a local writer along with several laymen from the parish.[51] Similarly, the charity at St. Pantaleimon's church was also the result of cooperation between the church's clergy and several women of high society; one of its early members was the writer Ivan Goncharov, author of the novel *Oblomov*.[52] Cooperation between the clergy and the laity manifested itself in the daily administration of the charities and their institutions. The society at Znamenskaia church (Liteinyi district) reported that the clergy ran the charity's work and the laity funded it, with both proposing ideas for new projects for the society.[53] The Kazan cathedral's charitable society was generally supervised by the clergy but its school and the soup kitchen were staffed entirely by lay volunteers, many of whom were young women of polite society.[54] At the primary school supported by the charitable society of Malokolomenskaia church (Kolomenskaia district), both clergymen and lay people volunteered their time as teachers.[55]

The services that lay people provided to the parish charities were as important as their monetary donations. The work of many societies was sustained by the members' willingness to use their time and talents for others' benefit. A number of societies included doctors who offered free medical services to the poor, pharmacists who reduced the prices of their medicines by fifty percent or more, and teachers who volunteered to teach in free primary schools or Sunday schools. The renovations in the old building that the society of St. Andrew's cathedral bought for its work were carried out by members of the society who had experience in construction and repair, and the building used by the society of the Trinity church had its floor replaced by a lay member.[56] At the building of the Malokolomenskaia parish charity, one member donated his services for cleaning the building's pipes, and another arranged for free electricity. At the charity of the Trinity church, beneficiaries enjoyed free use of the local bathhouse, free haircuts, and free apprenticeships with local tradesmen. The nature of the services offered to the charities indicates that society members came from various backgrounds and included professionals, skilled laborers, people in the service industry, and tradesmen. Charity was not a privilege of the wealthy but an obligation for all Christians. It was an essential element of a Christian community.

Money was, of course, still necessary for the charitable work of the parish societies. The available records suggest that despite their emphasis on non-monetary contributions, parish charities also enjoyed a reasonable degree of success in collecting cash donations. On average, about half of the total annual income of the parish charities of the capital came from donations.[57] A survey of 1884 indicated that the annual income of the parish charities compared favorably with that of the secular charities. Of the secular charities, 63 percent received less than 2,500 rubles a year in income and 25 percent received between 2,500 and 10,000 a year. Of the thirty-one parish societies listed, only two (slightly more than 6 percent) had an income of less than 2,500 rubles during the year, while twenty (nearly 65 percent) received between 2,500 and 10,000 rubles, and nine (29 percent) received more than 10,000 rubles.[58] The total cash income received by the official parish charities alone was almost 300,000 rubles in 1884; in 1889, it was 460,000 rubles, and by 1900 it had increased to more than 700,000 rubles a year, of which 83 percent was from donations or collections.[59] The capital of the parish charities was also impressive: only six of these thirty-one societies had less than 10,000 rubles in capital in 1884, twelve had between 10,000 and 20,000, ten had between 20,000 and 40,000, and three had more than 40,000.[60] These figures indicate that compared to the average secular charity, the average parish charity was well endowed; as late as 1901, three-quarters of all secular charities had less than 10,000 rubles in capital.[61] Already in 1884, the parish charities of St. Petersburg had more than 650,000 rubles in capital, a sum that had increased to 1.3 million by 1889 and 2.5 million by 1900.[62]

Although not much information is available about the sources and sizes of individual donations, the indications are that most societies depended on a steady stream of smaller donations (five hundred rubles or less) from a number of regular donors and only occasionally benefited from one-time donations of larger sums. While a few societies were patronized by members of the royal family or the wealthy nobility, most depended on the generosity of successful merchants, artisans, or manufacturers.[63] The society at Vvedenskaia church (on the Petersburg side) received one of its buildings from a wealthy silversmith and another from the widow of an army officer.[64] The society at Ekateringofskaia church in an impoverished factory district of the city depended on donations from local factory owners: it constructed its building on land donated by one factory with salvaged bricks donated by another factory.[65] At Spasobocharinskaia church, the building housing the society's charity work was donated by the wife of an individual having the status of "highly honored citizen," who later donated ten thousand rubles and another building.[66] The size and nature of these donations strongly suggest one important conclusion. The parish charities did not depend solely or even primarily on the wealthy nor were they the concern of the clergy alone. The church-based charities of St. Petersburg relied on the financial and personal commitment of the middle urban strata, which included professionals, businessmen, successful artisans, and retailers. Significant numbers of people from these middle groups demonstrated their commitment to the ideals of Orthodox charity by dedicating their money, time, and talents to the charities' causes in addition to or instead of the numerous charities established independently of the church. In a setting in which scores of charities competed for benefactors, the church's parish charities were surprisingly successful in attracting both volunteers and donors.

When they were first organized, most of the parish charities had rather limited means and, consequently, only limited ambitions. In their early years, the charities simply collected money and necessities from their donors and distributed them to the poor in their homes. As their resources and their familiarity with poverty in the city grew, however, the parish societies sought to establish a more stable basis for their work. They aimed at providing regular, long-term services to people in a reasonably cost-effective way. The first step was to rent an apartment that could be used as a temporary shelter for widows, orphans, the disabled, and the elderly. Given the high cost of renting, most societies focused early on collecting funds to buy or build their own building (dom). By the turn of the century, most parish charities owned some real property, with the average charity having one building at its disposal though several owned two or more.

The charities used their buildings for a variety of purposes, because by the 1890s, most of the parish charities supported two, three, or even more small institutions.[67] The most common of these were homes for the aged, most of which housed elderly widows. There were also shelters for poor, abandoned, and orphaned children, with meals and basic instruction provided, centers for children's day care, and temporary free housing, usually reserved for widows and women with young children. Outside of these common services, the charities provided a host of other activities at their buildings: Sunday classes for adults, summer dachas for sick children, medical aid, free meals, vocational training and job placement, libraries, reading rooms and bookstores, choirs, youth circles, and temperance societies. The society at Malokolomenskaia church supported a typical array of services. This society was based in a church in a modest district of low- and middle-income people. Founded in 1870, by 1900 it supported a pensioners' home, a shelter for boys, and a day-care center for girls.[68] The society at the church of the Annunciation, operating in a more comfortable middle-class area of the city, was able to construct a more extensive program. It was established in 1862 and on the occasion of its fiftieth anniversary in 1912, it reported that it maintained a shelter for girls, a pensioners' home with free housing, a day-care center, a school, a library, a bookstore, a choir, and a temperance society that claimed 14,828 members.[69] As these examples suggest, parish charities were long-lived institutions that developed gradually over a number of years, expanding their services as their resources grew. Their deep roots in the communities they served enabled them to be flexible and responsive to the social environment in which they worked.

As the nature of the institutions that the charities supported suggests, most of the beneficiaries of the church's charities belonged to the "traditional" poor, those who were unable to support themselves or who were the victims of misfortune. This included the elderly, the very young, the sick or disabled, and the widowed. In the cases of children and young widows, the charities offered not only shelter and support but also education or vocational training in order to prepare these individuals to support themselves in the future. For those who were too old or infirm to return to society as productive members, the charities provided long-term institutional care, despite its high cost.

It is difficult to gauge in numbers the contribution that the parish charities made to the total amount of aid distributed in the city or the total number of people who benefited from it because the statistics provided in the published sources are incomplete and inaccurate. The city's surveys of 1884 and 1889 indicate that the forty parish charities included in their statistics assisted more than seven thousand people a year and spent more than 300,000 rubles annually for this work.[70] However, these numbers represent only a small percentage of the total number of people assisted by all the charitable societies in the city; in 1889, the city estimated that there were 758 non-parish-based charities (including schools and hospitals) in St. Petersburg and that they spent more than eight million rubles to aid 846,801 people that year.[71] However, a closer look at these numbers reveals that for the overwhelming majority of the recipients—just over 90 percent—the charitable assistance they received was in the form of free medical care. In light of this, the contribution of the parish societies to meeting the remaining, non-medical needs of the city's poor population has greater significance.[72] It would seem that the church's charities provided a significant proportion of the total amount of charitable support given to the elderly, for example, and that many of the free temporary shelters and free meals in the city were provided through church charities.[73]

For those who worked for the parish charities, the question of how many people they gave assistance to was of little concern. They did not believe that charity could alleviate poverty and inequality simply by redistributing material goods. Ultimately, their goal was to transcend the divisions in society that material things created by bringing all Christians together in a community of brothers and sisters who were bound together by love for God and compassion for all God's children. Ideally, Christian charity respected the dignity and humanity of those who received it and ennobled the souls of those who gave it, while at the same time breaching the social barriers between the poor and the rich by calling on all to contribute what they could to the community. Many of the city's clergy welcomed the opportunity to participate in charitable work. Not only had the church traditionally been responsible for organizing charity for the needy, but the social outreach required by the work fit in well with the renewed emphasis in the reform and post-reform periods on the church's engagement with the world and the clergy's service as pastors. The appeal of the ideals was not limited to the clergy; they attracted a wide variety of lay people as well, as demonstrated by the number of those who contributed their time, talents, and financial resources to the church's charity work. The church was able to appeal to the laity and to organize them effectively under the leadership of the clergy in order to carry out work with an avowedly religious and moral purpose. This accomplishment suggests that despite the disparagements of a few alienated intellectuals, the church remained a vital cultural force that had a significant effect on the moral and social environment of St. Petersburg at the turn of the century.

CHAPTER FIVE

TEACHING, TEMPERANCE,

AND THE EXPANSION OF THE

CHURCH'S MISSION

Even as the parish-based charities of the capital were quietly multiplying during the last two decades of the nineteenth century, public attention was increasingly focused on the activities organized by a new kind of church-associated religious organization, exemplified by the Society for the Dissemination of Moral-Religious Enlightenment in the Spirit of the Orthodox Church (ORRP) and its daughter organization, the Alexander Nevskii Temperance Society (hereafter the Nevskii Society). Although both of these organizations engaged in charitable work they differed from the parish-based charities in their purpose, organization, and methods. Both the ORRP and the Nevskii Society were originally founded in order to promote specific changes in the moral-religious life of St. Petersburg society through education and exhortation. The focus of the ORRP was to improve the laity's understanding and appreciation of Orthodoxy so that lay people would not be susceptible to the appeal of non-Orthodox Christianity or sectarian religion. The Nevskii Society, which grew out of the ORRP, was established to strengthen piety, particularly among the working classes, through the promotion of sobriety. Rather than confining themselves to particular parishes, these two organizations viewed the entire city as their field of endeavor. Nor did they confine their work to the churches; both also held their functions in secular locations such as public halls, cafeterias, tearooms, and factories.

Like the parish-based charities, the ORRP and the Nevskii Society involved both lay people and clergy in their work. Unlike the charities, their work was well publicized and widely known, drawing in tens and eventually hundreds of thousands of participants each year. The extra-parochial organizations of the capital were able to capture these large audiences because their methods of outreach incorporated new initiatives that expanded the importance of religiously oriented activities in the city's popular culture.[1] They organized lectures on interesting religious topics illustrated with magic-lantern shows, people's choirs for the performance of church music, free public libraries with reading rooms and lending services, and mass pilgrimages to local holy sites. By 1904 these two organizations, led by members of the Orthodox clergy with the active support and participation of a sizable and diverse group of lay people for the purpose of promoting a religiously based vision of society, had become the capital's largest and most successful public organizations.

WINNING HEARTS AND MINDS—
The ORRP Campaign for Orthodoxy

The first extra-parochial organization to be founded in St. Petersburg was the ORRP, which was established during the crisis period of the late 1870s when the regime confronted the People's Will, a small, but violent, group of revolutionary terrorists. Beginning in 1878, the People's Will made repeated attempts to assassinate the tsar, killing many others in the process and provoking the government to take increasingly harsh measures against them. The unsettling atmosphere of confrontation led some people to think more critically about the flaws of the Great Reforms and to consider how to strengthen Russian society in the face of such a serious internal challenge.

The idea for the ORRP emerged during a series of informal meetings between prominent members of the St. Petersburg clergy and notable lay persons in the winter of 1879–1880. The meetings were initiated by the archpriest Dmitrii I. Nikitin, supervisor of the cathedral of St. Sergei, one of the most important churches in the military administration and also the church with the largest parish-based charitable society in the capital; many of St. Petersburg's most elite noble families, including members of the royal house, attended this church. Among the laymen who participated were Count N. F. Geiden, general-lieutenant A. G. Lashkarevich, the church publicist A. I. Popovitskii, and actual state councilor A. I. Maksimov. From the clergy, there were ten archpriests and nine priests, including the rector of the St. Petersburg academy, Father Ioann L. Ianyshev, the president of the Synod's Schools Committee, I. V. Vasil'ev, and the famous preachers I. N. Polisadov and I. K. Iakhontov. They had in common a wish to strengthen the relationship between clergy and laity and to develop further the church's role in public life.[2] Many of the clergy in the founding group served in the churches of the military administration, which were specifically assigned to particular units of the armed forces or to schools, offices, and bases of the military. These clergymen had extensive contact with the nobles who served as army officers and who often played important roles in the tsar's government, particularly during the late 1870s.

The immediate challenge that concerned the participants was the growing popularity of the English Christian evangelist Lord Radstock and his Russian disciple Colonel Pashkov. Radstock, who had traveled widely through Europe with his evangelical message, came to Russia in the mid-1870s.[3] He found a warm welcome in St. Petersburg, where he was allowed to preach in public halls and invited into private homes. His meetings were simple and consisted of reading and discussing the Bible, singing hymns, and praying extemporaneously. Many members of the nobility, especially women, attended these meetings with enthusiasm, finding in them a spiritual satisfaction they missed in the highly structured and formal services of the Orthodox church. Radstock's popularity alarmed many clergymen. They feared that the evangelist's Protestant rejection of church rituals and icons and his emphasis on salvation through personal faith would corrupt Orthodox believers who did not understand the teachings of their own church clearly enough to resist his criticisms of it.

Believing that a great part of Lord Radstock's appeal lay in the way he delivered his message rather than in the message itself, the founders of the ORRP decided to adopt his methods to their purpose of enlightening members of the elite about the teachings of the Orthodox church. In the charter they proposed for their new organization in 1880, the founders stated the their goal: "confirming and spreading among all classes of the Russian population a true understanding of the Orthodox faith" through the provision of lectures, discussions, and readings outside of church services at meeting halls, church buildings, and private homes. Although members of the clergy were expected to conduct many of these events, the society also allowed laymen and laywomen who had completed the secondary or tertiary levels of education in the church school system to lead meetings.[4] These meetings were to include readings from the Bible, informal discussions or exchanges of questions and answers between the lecturer and the audience, extemporaneous prayers, and the singing of religious music.[5] The society's founders hoped that this format, similar to that used by Lord Radstock, would attract his audiences to their meetings. The ORRP's charter was approved early in 1881, and the organization began to implement its program. The large number of members the society enrolled in is first year suggested that the organizers had hit upon the right formula for success. The society registered 385 dues-paying members at the end of 1881, of which 299 were from the laity.[6] The remaining 86 were members of the clergy, mostly priests or deacons. Women accounted for 79 names on the first membership list. Twenty-one members belonged to the titled nobility and there were 2 senators.[7]

Although the organization of the society was a response to the challenge presented by Lord Radstock, the motives behind the society's work were not purely defensive. The clergy who organized the ORRP and set out its agenda were also taking advantage of the opportunity presented by official concerns about Radstock's evangelism to pursue the post-reform agenda of the liberal clergy, who envisioned transforming society by applying the teachings of the Bible to all aspects of individual and communal life. Although the clergy of the St. Petersburg church had emphasized the importance of preaching since the late 1850s, many recognized that the services typically offered in Russian churches offered relatively limited opportunities for the priest to address his congregation directly through a sermon.[8] In response, the ORRP offered a program of public teaching that addressed these limitations. First of all, the society greatly expanded the times and venues in which the clergy could teach publicly. Although the Orthodox clergy had long been accustomed to visiting private homes to perform various religious services, the *public* teaching of the church up to this time had been confined to church buildings and to formal church services or (for the Orthodox youth) to school classrooms. The ORRP proposed to liberate the church from these restrictions on the time and place of its teaching and to encourage it to take its lessons out into the world, into secular locations and secular time, thus breaking down the barriers that separated the religious and secular spheres. As an ORRP publication of 1890 stated, the society's members "preached everywhere, on every occasion, on all topics, and to all people," just as Jesus Christ and the apostles had done.[9]

Second, the organization encouraged the use of a different style of teaching than that which had prevailed during the eighteenth and early nineteenth centuries, when Russian Orthodox preachers imitated the polemical, scholastic style of the Catholic clerics of the Counter Reformation in Poland. Instead, the society promoted shorter, more casual, lectures and discussions outside of formal services that allowed for a much greater degree of audience responsiveness and even participation. These sermons belonged to the category that Arkhimandrit Iakov (Domskii) labeled *besedy*, or colloquia, which he considered to be a native form of preaching especially well suited to communicating the gospel to the Russian population.[10] As the members of the society grew more experienced in public teaching, their success in appealing to popular tastes increased. By the 1890s, ORRP lectures regularly featured magic-lantern shows (the contemporary version of free movies) to illustrate such popular subjects as the lives of the prophets and saints, the history of the Holy Land, and the story of Jesus. The best lecturers were those who knew how to perform the tales of the Bible as dramatic narratives translated into the Russian vernacular in ways that illustrated the connections between the struggles and triumphs of the ordinary folk of times past and present through parables and morality tales.

The clergy who participated in the ORRP were dedicated to the belief that the central mission of the church was teaching the Word of God to the people in whatever way was possible or necessary to make that teaching meaningful. In a speech given to the ORRP in 1890, the young monk Antonii (Khrapovitskii), who had graduated from the St. Petersburg Ecclesiastical Academy just five years previously after helping to revive student interest in monasticism and Orthodox ritual, declared that preaching the Word of God was the church's "most important work."[11] A few years later the famous priest of Kronstadt, Father Ioann Sergiev, praised the society's efforts, observing that its members' devotion to teaching the gospel grew directly out of a shared consciousness that their essential pastoral duty was to teach the Christian message and lead people to the Christian life.[12] Thus, although the society was founded in response to the particular challenge of Radstock's evangelism, it reflected the cumulative influence of the previous two decades of developments within the St. Petersburg church in its agenda of reestablishing public teaching as the church's central mission.

In the first year (from 1880 to 1881), the society held meetings on a weekly basis at thirteen locations in the city's central districts. Most of the lectures were held at churches and attracted audiences of one to three hundred people each, meaning that each week, the society was attracting a total of a few thousand people to its lectures at different locations in the city. Lectures given at non-church locations had noticeably larger audiences: those held at the hall of the city council sometimes had as many as 800 auditors, while those at the hall of the Pedagogical Museum regularly had between 900 and 1,500.[13] In its second year (1881–1882), the society expanded its geographical reach beyond the city center and began to offer lectures at locations in the outer districts of the city, where there were few churches and a large working-class population. Announcements for the lectures were published in the newspaper *Tserkovnyi vestnik*, a major weekly with a national circulation that was published at the St. Petersburg Ecclesiastical Academy. In 1883, the lectures included subjects such as Orthodox confession, the liturgy, Peter's renunciation of Christ, Christ's sufferings, Christ as a saint, images of saints and iconoclasm, life after death, the church as a community of believers, and the differences between the Catholic, Orthodox, and Lutheran churches.[14] There were also lectures devoted to more philosophical subjects that particularly concerned the educated lay population, such as the nature of man, the relation of reason to faith, materialism versus spirituality, the question of the Gospels' authenticity, the significance of Jesus Christ's divine nature, the problem of biblical miracles, the relation of the moral teachings of the gospel to daily life, and the shortcomings of rationalist interpretations of Christianity.[15]

The appeal of the society's program was reflected in the size of the audiences their lectures attracted. The society's annual report for 1883 noted that the audiences were consistently large at several important locations. The lectures at the cathedral of St. Sergei drew in audiences numbering from 500 to 1,500 in that year. The institutional church attached to the Imperial Philanthropic Society, which counted many members of the capital's social elite among its members, saw 400 people a week at the first lectures of the year, increasing to as many as 1,000 later in the cycle. The lectures given at the hall of the municipal council attracted crowds of 600 to 1,000 people, which meant standing room only on some nights. The smaller hall of the Pedagogical Museum regularly had more than 1,000 people packed into a space intended for a maximum of 540.[16]

The audiences in all of these locations consisted primarily of members of St. Petersburg's *obshchestvo*, or educated society, which was the particular target of the society's work in the early years of its existence. The founders of the ORRP believed that the main reason educated people were often dissatisfied with the church and were attracted to various kinds of religious substitutes (such as Freemasonry, pietism, evangelical Protestantism, spiritualism) was that their knowledge of their native faith was shallow or even non-existent. These clergymen were certain that if the questing souls were to be given greater instruction in the teachings of the Orthodox church, they would find what they were looking for there.[17] As the lecture topics given for 1883 and 1884 indicate, the ORRP provided their educated audiences both with explanations of key elements of Orthodox doctrine and responses to some of the positivist objections raised against Christianity. The high attendance at such presentations indicates that the capital's educated elite were both interested in religious questions and willing to listen to the clergy's explanations of how the Orthodox church addressed their particular concerns. As with the case of the church-based charities, the work of the ORRP demonstrates the extent to which Orthodoxy bound together the educated laity with the educated clergy in the years before the 1905 revolution.

The reports of the society for the early 1880s indicate that the organization's leaders were fully satisfied with the development of their mission to the educated classes and the effectiveness of their response to Pashkovism. However, the director general of the Synod, Konstantin Pobedonostsev, was less sanguine about the effectiveness of the society's effort to meet Radstock's challenge merely through educational means. A series of increasingly punitive measures led to the outright suppression of Radstock's evangelical society in 1884. The organization's presses were shut down, its property was seized, its publications were interdicted, and its leaders were exiled. As a result of the official ban, public adherence to Pashkovism virtually disappeared among the upper classes of St. Petersburg society. Forced underground, the tendency developed into a distinct sect that found supporters primarily among the lower classes, where it eventually came to resemble Shtundism.

Even though the mission of the ORRP had always been broader than simply combating the influence of Radstock, the government's swift and severe action against the Pashkovists left the society somewhat at a loss, for *officially* they had justified their work with reference to the sectarian threat. For two years following the government's ban the society continued to focus most of their preaching against Pashkovism.[18] In the course of the year 1886, however, some active members of the society began to work their way toward a new conceptualization of their mission and goals. The vision was first articulated publicly by Professor Alexander P. Lopukhin, a specialist on religion in the United States who taught comparative religion at the St. Petersburg Ecclesiastical Academy. In 1886, he delivered a lecture to the society's membership in which he described the role of religion in American society in glowing terms, presenting it as a model that the church in Russia should strive to emulate. In his lecture, he described America as a deeply religious society where the strength of the churches came primarily from the commitment of the educated classes to religion and their reliance on religious principles for the solution of social problems. By contrast, he observed that in Russia the strength of the church rested almost entirely on the support of the government.[19] The implication was clear: the church in Russia should endeavor to win the support of educated society in order to strengthen the influence of the church by demonstrating how Orthodoxy related to the daily challenges that individuals faced. America truly seemed to represent a "city on a hill," which would inspire the ORRP's attempt to transform Russian society into a community suffused by the Christian spirit and responsive to the church's leadership.

The very next year, in 1887, the annual report of the society stated that it had adopted religious life in America as the model to imitate. It described American religious life as being exceptionally rich in its numerous churches, its strong religious press, and its variety of local charitable and educational institutions.[20] The implication was that the society was going to work toward building the same kind of infrastructure for public religious life in Russia. Granted that in America the numerous churches, charities, and publications arose spontaneously and not as the result of a planned campaign led by the clergy; in Russia, the ORRP hoped that building many churches, establishing charities, and promoting publications would show a religiously conscious population how to translate personal belief into community action. For them, it did not matter whether the stimulus for the activity came from the people or from the clergy. Their eyes were fixed on the final goal of creating a community in which there was no division between the religious and the secular, in which society was enfolded in the all-encompassing embrace of the church.

The society set to work immediately to begin realizing its newly articulated goal by organizing in 1887 an amateur church choir and opening a free public circulating library with 16,000 titles—the first in the city. Excitement about these new ventures ran so high that in the report for that year the society's ongoing teaching efforts were hardly mentioned; the considerable ingenuity and effort required to organize and open the library absorbed the membership's attention instead.[21] Their work paid off when the library attracted the attention of Emperor Alexander III, who visited the library with his wife in 1888 to give his approval to the project. Thereafter, the expansion of the society's work began to receive a great deal of publicity, bringing in hundreds of new members. Between 1887 and 1889, the membership—already impressive at 711 members—nearly doubled to 1,500.[22]

Donations increased as well, and in 1889 the society finally received a contribution large enough to liberate it from the financial constraints that had previously limited its work. In 1890, the society issued a call for new members to take part in the exciting new projects the organization was planning. Chief among these was the construction of a church and meeting hall for the exclusive use of the society. From this home base, the society planned to develop new activities, including the publication of a periodical, classes for children's religious education, and classes on parenting. In addition, the society hoped to expand the library and further develop their program of public lectures and discussions.[23] This extension and diversification of the society's work was given official approval in 1894 when the society revised its charter to include the added activities. Moreover, in the new charter the society outlined plans to open additional libraries and reading rooms and to organize Sunday schools and evening classes for children and adults throughout the city.[24]

The revised charter of 1894 also formalized another key element of the society's program of outreach, directed not at the city's lay population but at the clergy. Since its inception, the society had promoted a spirit of cooperation between its clerical members and clergymen who did not belong to the society.[25] The society offered advice and free literature to clergy who wanted to organize extra-liturgical lectures at their own churches. These priests were also encouraged to meet with clergy from churches where the society had opened lectures and even to attend the weekly meetings held at the society's outreach points. At these weekly meetings, the participating clergy discussed subjects for lectures and new approaches to public teaching. They also offered support and encouragement to each other. These meetings helped to strengthen the influence of the society in the city's ecclesiastical life.

The 1894 charter institutionalized these meetings and expanded both the number of participants and their agenda, declaring that the society would convene regular meetings of the city's clergy (not simply the clergy who belonged to the society) to identify and address issues concerning religious life in the capital. The pastoral conferences, as they were called, were convened once a month during the working year from September through May. The meetings drew between fifty and one hundred clergymen, mostly priests and archpriests, a significant percentage of the city's clergy. The first subject taken up in the initial meetings of 1894 was how working-class attendance at church was affected by the full-time operation of shops and businesses on Sundays. As a result of these discussions, the group drew up a petition asking the city's governor-general to prohibit trade and production in the city during the morning and evening hours on Sundays in order to allow (and encourage) workers to go to church.[26] The petition was rejected. In theory, officials approved of working people going to church but pragmatically they did not want the effort to improve the moral-religious condition of the population to compromise the city's economic development. Although the petition failed, the effort made by the city's clergy to take a direct, collective action to influence the local government to establish a new policy responsive to the church's agenda is certainly remarkable. It indicated clearly the direction that the clergy's increasing involvement in the work of moral-religious outreach to society would take in the decade that followed, as activist priests expanded their work from preaching against the ills of society to becoming involved in efforts to cure those ills through action.

After the failure of the petition against Sunday trade, the pastoral conferences did not meet for several years. They were renewed in 1899, when a full series of meetings was held to discuss several new issues facing the church. At one meeting, the clergy discussed what measures priests should employ to correct the behavior of those who failed to live according to Christian moral standards: should they punish offenders by the imposition of church discipline or should they seek to guide them to the path of righteousness through gentle admonishment and continued instruction? The majority of the participants agreed that a punitive approach would only drive weak believers away from the church; trying to correct immoral behavior through teaching was best. At another meeting, the clergy discussed the need for the church to expand its involvement in the temperance movement, in view of how intimately the abuse of alcohol was related to many other sins.

A whole series of pastoral conferences was devoted to the problem of illegal cohabitation, which the clergy believed was on the rise in St. Petersburg. They decided the cause of this problem was largely administrative: the underdeveloped parish system made it impossible for the clergy to keep track of the large and transient population and enforce the church's strict rules on marriage. They believed that many of those who cohabited illegally did so not because they were indifferent to the church's views on the practice but because they were unable to meet the requirements the church imposed on those who wanted to marry, such as presenting certificates from the priest of their home parish asserting that they were not within the forbidden degrees of consanguinity. However, rather than suggesting that the church alter the requirements for marriage, a number of clergy at the conferences argued that the city's parish system needed to be reformed so that priests would be able to have more knowledge of, and control over, the lives of the laity.[27] In general, it is evident that the pastoral conferences hosted by the ORRP encouraged the city's clergy to think critically about the moral-religious issues the church faced in contemporary society and to explore how they might take action on them. Significantly, on each of the issues discussed in 1899, the majority of the clergy who spoke advocated responses that would deepen the clergy's involvement in the world outside the church walls and enlarge the role they played in the city's day-to-day life.

In the same year that the pastoral conferences were renewed, the society also began hosting a new series of meetings for those clergy who wanted to discuss issues related to preaching and public teaching. Although the original agenda of the meetings was broad and undefined, the attention of those who attended soon came into sharp focus: how could the clergy respond to the philosophical challenges posed to them by members of the city's intelligentsia concerning issues such as the relation between Christianity and rational humanism, the nature of Christianity's teaching on the social order, and the problems of wealth and poverty?[28] Some members of the clergy were aware that there were new trends emerging among the artists, writers, and creative intellectuals of St. Petersburg in the Silver Age of the 1890s. These trends included a fascination with the occult, spiritualism, and mysticism, and the renewal of interest in philosophical questions and the philosophical approach to understanding the world. Some intellectuals affected by these developments saw themselves as participating in a quest for the ultimate answers, seeking after a higher truth that would transcend institutionalized Christianity.[29] The clergy was concerned about the implicit challenge these trends represented to the church. At the same time, they were hopeful that the intellectuals' interest in the spiritual world could provide well-prepared preachers and pastors with the opportunity to educate these "seekers" about the true nature of Christianity. The situation was reminiscent of the atmosphere at the end of the 1870s, which had originally led to the founding of the ORRP.

The meetings and discussions hosted within the Society for Moral-Religious Enlightenment throughout 1899 and 1900 prepared the ground for the clergy's participation in the meetings of the St. Petersburg Religious-Philosophical Society, which opened its first discussions in the fall of 1901. The society was established by a group of lay intellectuals led by the writer Dmitrii Merezhkovsky and his wife, the poet Zinaida Gippius.[30] These intellectuals found themselves estranged from institutionalized Christianity, for which they blamed the church and particularly the clergy. Although the stated purpose of the Religious-Philosophical Society was to provide a forum in which members of the clergy and the intelligentsia could talk about religion in the contemporary world, in truth the lay intellectuals who led the organization hoped to confront the clergy with their scathing criticisms of the church and coerce them into embracing their own unconventional views of Christianity as the basis for a renewal of Orthodoxy. The clergy who participated had their own agenda, as might be expected. They welcomed the opportunity to engage directly with the influential intellectuals who challenged the church, hoping to educate them better about Orthodoxy, to respond to their criticisms, and to persuade them of the value of the church's long-established teachings on religion and the world.

Unfortunately, the attitudes with which both the intellectuals and the clergymen approached the meetings of the Religious-Philosophical Society proved to be obstacles to real communication and understanding between the two sides. Both groups were so convinced of the correctness of their own ideas that they were unable to listen openly to the ideas of the other side or to engage their concerns seriously. The meetings resembled boxing matches more than discussions, with each side trying to defeat the other simply by hammering away at their vulnerabilities while jealously guarding their own weak points, both cheered on by crowds of supporters who only wanted to see their own side win. Since the lay intellectuals tended to dominate the public meetings of the Religious-Philosophical Society (much to the delight of critics of the church), the participating clergy decided to set up a forum that they could control by organizing a parallel series of meetings under the aegis of the ORRP, in which they discussed the role of Christianity in the contemporary world, the Christian view of war, the question of morality in literature, and modern family life.[31] In addition, the Society for Moral-Religious Enlightenment organized other activities directed at the city's secular intellectuals during the period from 1902 to 1905, including three series of lectures, a charitable society, and a periodical *Pravoslavno-Russkoe Slovo (The Orthodox Russian Word)*. As these activities demonstrate, the city's clergy were acutely aware of the challenges posed by the intelligentsia and were willing to address them directly and publicly in the years leading up to the 1905 revolution.

The resistance of some St. Petersburg intellectuals to the clergy's outreach should not necessarily be viewed as evidence of the church's failure to adapt to the demands of modern times. For even as a handful of lay intellectuals criticized the religious establishment, the activities that the Society for Moral-Religious Enlightenment organized in response to the needs of the urban masses multiplied and diversified while the number of participants increased by leaps and bounds. The lectures and discussions on religious topics that the ORRP continued to offer at locations throughout the city in the period 1890–1906 demonstrate their success in this realm. In 1890, the society had twenty-three locations with a total yearly attendance of some 300,000 people; in 1899, it had fifty-five locations staffed by 240 teachers with an annual attendance of 1.9 million people. Just four years later, the number of locations had increased to eighty-one, offering a total of six thousand lectures and drawing a total audience estimated at 2.2 million attendees.[32] In less than fifteen years, the society had nearly quadrupled its locations for lectures and multiplied its audience more than sevenfold.

The ORRP also sponsored a variety of other institutions and activities that combined an effort to meet the city population's need for wholesome pastimes with the society's mission to bring Orthodox religious education to the people.[33] For example, the society had great success with the amateur choirs it sponsored. There were three of these in the city by 1899 with a combined membership of more than two hundred singers. The choirs performed traditional songs and church music at lectures and society fundraisers as well as giving popular concerts. Another successful initiative was the establishment of public libraries. After opening the first free circulating library in the city to the public in 1887 the ORRP established two other free public libraries, one of which was at the "Warsaw" church that provided the headquarters for the ORRP. Despite the fact that the library was located in a church building under the supervision of the clergy, it offered a variety of non-religious books and periodicals to the public. In the years 1905–1906, the library's records indicate that they had 42,963 visitors, more than 800 a week. Most of these patrons came to browse in the library's cozy reading room, but more than 7,000 individuals signed books out to take home. For the most part, these avid readers were men of the lower middle class: artisans, shopkeepers, skilled factory workers. The books they took out were primarily works of secular fiction or nonfiction, but they also checked out children's books, educational works, and periodicals.

The society also extended its sponsorship of educational activities to include schools, classes, and clubs. It opened its first elementary school in 1899, adding several more in 1900 and 1901. The society also established vocational classes for teenagers and Sunday literacy classes for adults in that same period. At the same time, the ORRP made a special effort to reach out to particular segments of the population that seemed to be under-represented in their established activities, namely, educated women, college-aged youth, and members of the intelligentsia. In 1901, it organized the all-female Religious-Educational Union, whose members visited hospitals and prisons to read the Bible to the inmates and offer compassion and consolation. In 1903, it opened separate male and female youth clubs for students of the city's institutions of higher education.

The outreach of the ORRP was further extended by its active program of publishing and its commitment to church construction. In 1895, the society established a weekly newspaper, *S. Peterburgskii Dukhovnyi vestnik (The St. Petersburg Ecclesiastical Herald)*, which came to serve the same function as the diocesan gazettes published in other cities. Each year, the society printed 30,000 to 80,000 copies of various popular religious readings—sermons, saints' lives, morality tales—for distribution through their libraries and lecture points. They also helped support the much larger publication activities of the Nevskii Society, which churned out 300,000 to 700,000 copies a year of its own temperance publications.[34] The society went beyond spreading its message through the printed word, however, and undertook the challenge of building churches in the city's rapidly expanding working-class districts. Ordinarily, the costs of constructing churches fell to the diocese, which received money through the Synod from the government. But there was scarcely enough money to keep the old churches in repair let alone build new ones, so even as the population of the city swelled and the urban expanse sprawled out into the swamps, the number of churches in the capital remained stagnant. Taking the matter into their own hands, the leaders of the society decided to spend the organization's own money to build churches in the religious wilderness of the working-class districts. Work on the society's first church began in 1887, resulting in a rather modest-looking but sturdy brick church at the Warsaw Station on Obvodnyi Canal, still standing today. By 1905, the ORRP had built three permanent churches, each costing 200,000 rubles or more. They had also established half a dozen temporary churches to serve particular districts of the city until they could erect permanent structures.

All of these activities were supported and carried out by the society's members. Membership reached a peak of 1,668 in 1899, when the personal interest of Emperor Nicholas II temporarily increased the normal enroll-ment of around 1,500 members by a bit more than 10 percent.[35] Approxi-mately 65 percent of the members were considered supporters, whose con-tribution to the society was primarily financial. Another 20 percent were members of the society's choirs who didn't necessarily engage in any of the society's other outreach work. The remaining 15 percent were the "ac-tivists," those members who gave lectures, led discussions, and directed the society's many activities. Naturally, many of the society's activists were cler-gymen, but it is noteworthy that as the society diversified and expanded its activities in the 1890s more of the activists came from the laity. By 1906, 94 of the society's 229 activists (41 percent) were laymen or laywomen. Their most common roles were as teachers in the Sunday schools, choir directors, members of the Religious-Educational Union (whose membership was ex-clusively female), or participants in the youth sections; six lay people, in-cluding two women, even presented religious lectures, which was normally the preserve of the ordained clergy.

The work of these lay activists was essential to the society's mission in more than one way. Practically speaking, the lay activists were responsible for a significant proportion of the society's non-lecture activities. More im-portantly, however, their participation represented progress toward the so-ciety's most fundamental ideal: the establishment of a Christian commu-nity to bring people from all levels of society together in the work of putting their common religious beliefs into practice. The society did not want simply to revive religious life within the city's churches but to renew the religious spirit of society by bringing the church out into the world. It did not want the church to be a separate institution reserved for the clergy alone but a public institution in which clergy and laity worked together to-ward common goals. The leadership of the clergy was important but so was the commitment of lay individuals to improving themselves and helping their neighbors. Although the vision that inspired the society's work origi-nated among the capital's clergy, the success that the ORRP had in attracting lay donors, activists, and audiences suggests that this vision also had a broad appeal among the laity. As was the case with the parish charities, the successes of the Society for Moral-Religious Enlightenment demonstrate that the clergy were sensitive and responsive to the religious and social needs of Russian society at the end of the nineteenth century. They were not estranged from the laity as a result of their religious commitment, but drawn closer to them because of it.

Seeking Salvation in Sobriety—
The Temperance Societies

By far the most visible of the initiatives that the clergy of the ORRP undertook during the expansion of their outreach in the 1890s was the establishment of church-based temperance societies. These organizations demonstrated most clearly those characteristics that came to define the work of the activist clergy of the capital in the decade before the 1905 revolution: a desire to respond to the needs of the city's working classes and a willingness to work with members of the laity to accomplish a common goal. The initial impulse for the church's sponsorship of the temperance movement came from the central authorities. In 1889, the Synod sent a circular to the bishops advising them that they should encourage the parish clergy to preach temperance in their sermons.[36] More importantly, the circular gave the bishops permission to approve temperance activities in their dioceses on their own authority without having to submit requests to the Synod for approval. It was hoped that this administrative concession would encourage the clergy to organize temperance work quickly and spontaneously.[37] The clergy of St. Petersburg diocese apparently needed little urging, for the following year the consistory reported that already there were "many" parish temperance societies in the diocese, which the clergy had organized in connection with their educational and charitable work.[38] In 1891, the ORRP took up the cause as well, establishing its first temperance society at the Obukhov Steel Foundry. Interestingly enough, the initiative for this organization did not come from the ORRP activists but rather from the foundry workers.[39] Some of the workers who regularly attended the weekly lectures delivered at the foundry by a group of students from the St. Petersburg Ecclesiastical Academy approached the student-preachers and requested their help in establishing a temperance society at the foundry. The students, along with the local priest who supervised their teaching, asked permission from the governing council of the ORRP and received its approval.[40] In its first year of operation, the society enrolled a hundred members. Following this modest success, the ORRP opened similar factory-based temperance societies at the Vargunin and Stiglitz factories, each counting between one and two hundred members. The society also established a temperance society at the church of the diocesan mission, which was located in the heavily working-class district of Nevskii.[41]

The establishment of these first church-supported temperance societies coincided with the development of pro-temperance sentiment among the educated laity and the authorities of the central government.[42] The St. Petersburg

Temperance Society, the capital's first secular temperance organization, opened in 1890. Its founding members included prominent officials, doctors, nobles, intellectuals, and clergymen.[43] Secular temperance societies were also opened in other major cities of the empire around this time: Odessa in 1891, Kazan in 1892, and Moscow in 1895. The central government stumbled after the accelerating bandwagon, making its first attempt to jump on in 1894, when it established an official monopoly on the sale of vodka. Although financial motives were probably the primary motivation for establishing the monopoly, Finance Minister Sergei Witte made the ingenious argument that if the government took charge of vodka sales, it would be able to control both the quantity and quality of hard liquor sold in the country. These arguments were soon to be disproved. First, a dramatic increase in bootlegging motivated by demand for cheaper vodka *reduced* official control over the amount and type of vodka produced and sold in the country. Second, the profits gained by the government's sale of vodka mitigated efforts to reduce sales by encouraging temperance.[44] The government tried to accommodate both moral and monetary demands by establishing the Guardianship of Popular Sobriety in 1895. The goal of this official organization was to promote moderation in the use of alcohol, partly through consumer education but largely through the provision of popular entertainments that were supposed to be an alternative to the tavern. The guardianship established committees at the level of the province (*guberniia*) throughout the empire; these provincial committees then established committees at the district (*uezd*) level and for the major cities under their authority. Moscow, Kiev, Odessa, and St. Petersburg each had their own urban guardianships.[45]

For the St. Petersburg church, the key moment in the development of its temperance activities was 1898. In that year, the Guardianship of Popular Sobriety opened a special urban branch for the imperial capital.[46] This event sparked a lively discussion among the city's clergy about the issue of temperance. At a pastoral meeting convened shortly after the municipal guardianship's opening was announced, dozens of clergymen, most of them from the Society for Moral-Religious Enlightenment, met to discuss how they should respond to the government's temperance program. Over the course of two long meetings the clergymen argued about whether they should preach moderation (as the government-sponsored organizations did) or abstinence.[47] Although there was no final decision on the question, most of the clergy believed they should be supporting abstinence rather than moderation, and promoting moral and religious awareness in the place of secular distractions. Following the first meeting, one participant published an article in the diocesan newspaper (which was published by the ORRP) in which he argued that the clergy's responsibilities as the moral leaders of the people required them to go beyond the modest minimum proposed by the government and affirm their support for full abstinence. In addition, the author emphasized that education rather than entertainment was the most effective way of treating and preventing alcohol abuse. For individuals, he suggested confession and personal counseling by members of the clergy. As a means of changing the culture at large he advocated pilgrimages, moral-religious publications, discussion groups, libraries, reading rooms, and inexpensive tearooms and cafeterias.[48] This list of serious and morally uplifting activities contrasted sharply with the guardianship's programs of plays, circuses, amusement parks, and comic operas.[49]

Shortly after the guardianship opened, the clergy at two of the churches belonging to the ORRP established their own temperance organizations. The first was the Nevskii Society, headquartered at the church of the Resurrection (familiarly called the Varshavskaia or "Warsaw" church); the second was the Temperance Fraternity, organized at the society's new church of St. John the Baptist on the Vyborg side. These two temperance organizations differed from the ones established under the auspices of the ORRP at the beginning of the 1890s in that they were not focused on one particular factory but rather on two of the major working-class sectors of the city. The clergy involved in these two organizations also tended to view temperance as their primary focus: rather than approaching temperance as one of the outcomes of a morally responsible Christian life they were likely to view temperance as the path leading to the creation of such a life.[50] For this reason the clergy at these organizations focused on temperance "first" rather than "in addition to." As one would expect, these new temperance organizations of the ORRP also differed from the Guardianship for Popular Sobriety in that their leaders viewed abstinence as preferable to moderation and believed that a combination of social support, medical attention, and moral enlightenment was more likely to produce a permanent cure than the ephemeral pleasures of worldly amusements.[51]

Both of the society's new temperance organizations achieved an impressive level of success, but of the two, the Nevskii Society became larger and better known. In large part, this was due to the leadership of its founder, a charismatic young clergyman named Father Alexander Rozhdestvenskii. Father Alexander was born in 1872, the son of a priest who served in a factory village in Vladimir province. As a successful student at the Vladimir seminary, he won the right to apply to one of the ecclesiastical academies. But rather than going to the academy in Moscow, the city nearest his home province, in 1893 he chose to go to St. Petersburg. His biographer explained that the young man wanted "to become acquainted with the many thousands of poor working people in the capital," adding that the future priest was "one who grieved" *(pechal'nik)* for the plight of the working people and desired to serve them.[52] Rozhdestvenskii pursued this goal of working among the people while still a student by volunteering for the ORRP and giving lectures along with other academy students in several of the factories near the school. After his graduation in 1897, he took clerical orders and requested assignment to a position in one of the factory districts. He was appointed as the junior priest at the ORRP's Varshavskaia church. He threw himself into his work there, immediately establishing his own series of weekly extra-liturgical readings at the church and visiting all parts of the parish to become personally acquainted with the church's parishioners and their needs. After a group of his parishioners asked him to help them give up drinking, Father Alexander requested permission to open a temperance society at the church. The ORRP and the metropolitan approved the request and in August of 1898 the Alexander Nevskii Temperance Society was established.[53]

Father Alexander believed that the clergy had an essential role to play in combating drunkenness.[54] First of all, they were the ones who knew and understood the essential values of Orthodox Christianity, which provided the basis for developing a clearly defined position on alcoholism that was grounded in religious morality. Father Alexander did not hesitate to condemn drunkenness as a sin and a vice. He believed that when an individual indulged in alcohol he deliberately created a separation between himself and God.[55] This separation weakened the drinker's general sense of what was right and wrong, making him susceptible to committing even more serious sins such as fornication, adultery, robbery, and even murder. Father Alexander also argued that in addition to posing a serious danger to himself, the drinker was also a threat to the physical and moral well-being of those around him because alcohol abuse often led to poverty, the destruction of family bonds, the weakening of the health of parents and their children, and their early deaths.[56]

Father Alexander believed the clergy had to communicate their moral-religious message against the use of alcohol to the public at large. The purpose of this outreach was both to educate individuals about the dangers of alcohol and to challenge popular cultural assumptions that encouraged alcohol consumption.[57] At the same time, the clergy also had to develop practical means to help individuals who had accepted their anti-alcohol message to change their lives. Father Alexander embraced the widely used practice of the sobriety pledge. Upon joining the Nevskii Society the individual swore to avoid all alcohol for a given period—three, six, or nine months or for one year or more, up to a lifetime pledge. In many of the other temperance societies, the typical pledge was for three months, just long enough for the pledge-taker to get from one major holiday to the next. Short-term pledgers would often drink their way through the Christmas holiday, then pledge sobriety until Easter, when they would again indulge in drunken revelry. The short-term pledges helped them to stay employed and save money between the holidays without interfering with the popular traditions that accompanied the major celebrations. The practice of swearing to short-term pledges common in many temperance societies (including those run by other clergymen) generated much criticism from medical professionals as well as from clergymen, among others.[58] Consequently, although the Nevskii Society accepted short-term pledges, they encouraged members to swear to longer terms of sobriety with the result that well over three-quarters of their pledges agreed to abstain for more than a year.[59]

Adhering to a pledge of one year or longer required the pledge-taker to make a serious commitment to changing his whole way of life. Swearing off alcohol was only the first step, for in addition to committing himself to sobriety the pledge-taker also agreed to strive for moral improvement in all areas of his life.[60] The main purpose of the Nevskii Society was to provide the guidance and support necessary for this dramatic and profound transformation. The intention behind the society's work was not just to wean individuals off alcohol but to introduce them to the solid nourishment provided by a spiritually meaningful life. The new way of life that the society promoted was grounded in an "evangelical consciousness," as a result of which one maintained a constant awareness of the relevance of the gospel's teachings to one's life.[61] The leaders of the Nevskii Society fostered that consciousness through an active program of education. Members of the society met frequently: twice during the week in small groups for reading, prayer, and discussion and then again on Sundays for church services that included a sermon.[62] There were general meetings for each section of the society each month, and several times a year the entire society came together for a pilgrimage to one of the holy sites outside the city. Each individual pledge-taker was expected to be present at all meetings of the temperance society, to attend church services frequently, to support other members in maintaining their vows, and to recruit new members to the society. Outside of the group activities, the pledge-taker was encouraged to expand and deepen his understanding of the Gospels through independent reading of the Bible and works of moral edification as well as through prayer and consultation with the clergy. Members were exhorted to pay close attention to all their thoughts and actions and to try to live as "true Christians."[63]

As the society grew, it was subdivided into sections headquartered at churches around the city, each directed by a clergyman who was assisted by several dozen lay assistants. Each assistant took responsibility for a certain number of pledge-takers, making sure that they kept their promise of sobriety by checking on them regularly, bringing them to church services, suggesting books for them to read, and offering both psychological support and material assistance when necessary. By 1906, the society had ten divisions in the city staffed by more than four hundred lay assistants.[64] Not only did these lay temperance workers keep track of their pledge-takers, but they also helped to run the libraries, classes, schools, clinics, cafeterias, and day-care centers that the divisions operated as part of the Nevskii Society's network of assistance and support. A partial list of the leaders of the Nevskii Society sections in 1906 named 63 people. Slightly more than half the individuals named were lay people (34 of the 63), and 13 of these (about one-fifth) were women.[65]

The society clearly met a need felt among the population of the capital.[66] In the first three years, the society experienced strong, steady growth, registering 3,204 pledge-takers the first year, somewhat more than 4,000 the next year, and around 3,000 in the third year. They also sold thousands of

copies of their temperance brochures: more than 13,000 in the first year
and more than 20,000 in the second year.[67] By 1900, the total membership
of the Nevskii Society stood at 9,415. It was the largest of the church-based
temperance societies in the city, although the Temperance Fraternity at the
church of St. John the Baptist was also impressive in size, having a membership of 6,847 pledge-takers in 1901. Like the Nevskii Society, the fraternity did not focus its work on one parish or factory but took the working-
class region of the Vyborg side as its field of operations. It was especially
successful in attracting the support of local members of the educated society of the capital, who opened a mobile medical clinic and a pharmacy for
the treatment of alcoholics to supplement the lectures, classes, and libraries
organized by the fraternity's clergy.[68] Besides these two extra-parochial organizations, the ORRP had an additional thirteen temperance societies under its wing. Most were focused on particular parishes or factories and
numbered their membership in the hundreds rather than the thousands. The
largest of these other temperance societies were also the oldest: the temperance society that had been founded at the Stiglitz factory in 1891 had approximately 2,500 members in 1900, while the society at the Vargunin brothers'
factory, also founded in 1891, had 1,574 members.[69] This support came largely
from the industrial working class, though there were also tradespeople and
educated individuals among the ranks of the pledge-takers.[70]

Although the success that the Nevskii Society had achieved by 1900 was
noteworthy, it was modest compared to the extraordinary growth sustained
in the five years that followed. In 1901, the membership of the Nevskii Society surged from less than 10,000 to 41,262 members.[71] By 1905, the number had nearly doubled to more than 75,000.[72] In 1904, 33,575 people attended Father Alexander's temperance lectures at the Varshavskaia church
(one of the ten centers in the city for Nevskii Society lectures) and it was estimated that over one million people a year visited the modest headquarters of the Nevskii Society. In 1904, approximately 80,000 people joined the
society's annual pilgrimage to the Troitse-Sergeev Primorskii monastery.[73]
Tragically, it was after the pilgrimage organized by the society during the
turbulent summer of 1905 that Father Alexander suddenly contracted typhoid and died at the age of 33.[74] The shock of his unexpected death occasioned a great outpouring of grief. He was honored by his followers as a
martyr, one who had sacrificed his life in the service of the people and who
was to be remembered for his ability to show pity without condescension
and to give aid to others without judgment. His fellow clergymen saw him
as a role model whose willingness to take action to address one of the great
social ills of Russian society demonstrated the continuing relevance of religious teachings to modern life.

The moral vision that inspired Father Alexander was a powerful one that
had meaning not only to members of the Orthodox clergy but also to
many lay people—the working-class folk who swore pledges of sobriety, the
educated people from the urban middle class who assisted in administering

the numerous activities of the church's temperance societies, the wealthy and influential individuals from the elite who gave freely of their money to endorse the cause. Although the clergy most often initiated, organized, and directed these many and varied activities, the laity's support for this work was indispensable. The effective cooperation between the clergy and the laity in St. Petersburg suggests that these two groups were not as estranged from each other as contemporary radical critics of the establishment (and some later historians) portrayed them. The clergy *did* see the pressing problems of poverty, ignorance, intemperance, and social anomie around them and attempted to address those problems through exhortation, education, and community action. Without a doubt, they conceived of the problems they saw in moral-religious terms and proposed solutions that were of a moral-religious nature, but they did not fail to notice the influence of material conditions as well. Thus, they tried to work toward improving *both* the moral and the material ills that afflicted Russian society. During the course of the 1890s, they increasingly did so in a way that focused as much on the responsibilities of the Christian community as on those of the individual believer. Their message was not only "Help thyself" but also "Help thy brother." They did not simply preach these principles but manifested them in lives distinguished in many cases by an incredible degree of devotion to the service of others.[75]

The original motivation of the church's outreach work had been the desire to effect the moral transformation of individuals through pastoral care, preaching, and parish-based charity work. The clergy who initially took up this challenge in the 1870s and 1880s had found that theirs was truly a service of "small deeds," unrecognized by the broader public. But in the 1890s, the advent of a new generation of clergymen into service coincided with the enlargement of the church's agenda and led some individuals to begin developing a more expansive interpretation of the church's mission and goals. Going beyond the ideas that had first inspired the public work of their predecessors, these leaders proposed that the church's purpose was not simply to prepare the world for the coming of the future Kingdom of God by improving the society that already existed but to bring about the immediate realization of the kingdom on earth among humankind by building a wholly new society grounded in and suffused by the principles of the Gospels.

IN THE FOOTSTEPS OF CHRIST

The Work of Father Grigorii Petrov

By the last decade of the nineteenth century, the innovative thinking and hard work performed by the clergy of the reform generation had revitalized the ecclesiastical life of St. Petersburg. The Society for Moral-Religious Enlightenment was embarking on an ambitious new program of expansion, the temperance movement was taking off, church-based charities were flourishing, the local parish clergy preached weekly to full and sometimes overflowing churches. The local religious presses produced an increasing volume of religious literature, both academic and popular, in the form of books, newspapers, and monthly journals. The St. Petersburg Ecclesiastical Academy enjoyed a surfeit of applicants, enabling its staff to select highly qualified students while maintaining strong enrollment and high academic standards. The quality of the city's clergy continued to improve as the academy's best graduates competed for positions in the capital. There seemed many reasons to be optimistic about the church's future.

The new generation of clergy that began their careers in the 1890s epitomized this spirit of optimism. Born and raised after the emancipation of the serfs, these young men acquired their education and training during the 1870s and 1880s, when the schools and parishes of St. Petersburg were being transformed by the new emphasis on the church's engagement with modern society. For this post-reform generation, the idea that the church's mission called them to work in the world was the starting point rather than the end point of their thinking. They took for granted the notion that the church should be engaged in charity, public moral-religious teaching, and other forms of social outreach and eagerly embraced that work even while they were still students. The spirit of this new generation is exemplified by the life and work of Father Grigorii Spiridonovich Petrov, whose personal history reflects the common experiences shared by many of the younger clergymen of the capital in the years between 1890 and 1914. At the beginning of the twentieth century, Father Grigorii was arguably the most popular and well-known priest in St. Petersburg. He was especially influential among the younger clergymen and the students of the academy, who regarded him as a model pastor.[1] He had become popular through his talent for writing and speaking on the subject of how to live a Christian life in the modern world. Through his lectures, essays, and stories, he translated the ideas developed by the church's intellectual elite into terms that ordinary Orthodox believers—lay and clerical—could understand and apply to their own lives. Father Grigorii's works were appealing to a broad audience because they combined faith with optimism and common sense. He understood the challenges that contemporary believers faced and gave these believers both consolation and advice. He also celebrated the opportunities that modern life offered human beings to develop themselves intellectually and spiritually, encouraging his followers to view those opportunities as a divine gift. Above all, he emphasized the importance of putting all events and developments in the right kind of framework by relating them to the central task of humankind: the realization of the Kingdom of God.

Despite Father Grigorii's immense popularity, shortly before the 1905 revolution he was attacked by lay conservatives closely affiliated with the metropolitan of Moscow, Vladimir (Bogoiavlenskii), and the director general of the Synod, Konstantin Pobedonostsev. Over a period of four years (beginning in late 1903 and ending in 1907), Father Grigorii suffered a campaign of vilification and harassment that led to his being suspended from his position, prohibited from public writing and speaking, confined to a provincial monastery, and, finally, defrocked. This treatment at the hands of ecclesiastical authorities, endured while the country was in the midst of a revolutionary cataclysm, had a profound impact on Father Grigorii's thought. The trials he faced and his response to them came to represent the challenge confronting many of the capital's clergy during this period. Father Grigorii's sufferings inspired some of his fellow clergymen to embrace a new program of action even while his own fate served as a warning of the personal cost of failure.

Poor Widows and Good Samaritans—
Petrov's Early Views on the Kingdom of God

Grigorii Petrov was born in 1867 in the town of Iamburg in St. Petersburg province. Unlike most of those who became members of the clergy, he did not come from a clerical family. Instead, he was one of the few from outside the clerical estate who chose to enter the church's service because he felt a calling for it. Father Grigorii later explained that like many of his contemporaries, he had been inspired as a youth by an altruistic desire to dedicate himself to the improvement of the ignorant and impoverished Russian people, so recently liberated from centuries of serfdom. But while others became doctors, veterinarians, teachers, or agronomists, Petrov became a priest. For him as for many other young clergymen of this period, taking clerical orders did not represent a choice to abandon the world but to engage it in the most serious way by addressing its moral and spiritual challenges as well as its material problems.[2]

Petrov attended the St. Petersburg seminary in the mid-1880s, then entered the St. Petersburg Ecclesiastical Academy in the fall of 1887, during the first year of the rectorship of Bishop Antonii (Vadkovskii). When the Society for Moral-Religious Enlightenment began recruiting student volunteers to lead discussions at local factories, Petrov was among the first to sign up. He continued to participate in the work of the ORRP for the next seventeen years; for eight of those years, he served on the society's executive council, which was chosen by the society's members through annual elections.[3] After he graduated from the academy, he took clerical orders and was appointed to the church of the Mikhailovskii Artillery School in St. Petersburg; he also served as a catechist at the artillery school. Full of youthful energy and idealism, Petrov also found time to write numerous essays, stories, and parables on religious subjects, which he began to publish in St. Petersburg and Moscow in 1898.

Father Grigorii treated a wide range of topics in his writings, but one of his most fundamental and persistent concerns was with the Kingdom of God. This is not surprising, given the centrality of the Kingdom of God in the preaching of Jesus and the rich interpretative tradition this subject has generated. Since the beginning of the reform era in Russia, interest in the meaning of the kingdom's promise for the modern world had stimulated the reflections of several important thinkers, including the theologians Archimandrite Feodor (Bukharev) and Archpriest Pavel Svetlov, the philosopher Vladimir Solov'ev, and learned clergymen such as the archpriest Mikhail Sokolov of St. Petersburg and Metropolitan Antonii (Vadkovskii). For each of these individuals, the effort to understand the nature of the Kingdom of God was closely connected with the challenge of defining the purpose of human striving and its relation to divine action. Although there are differences in the way each author addressed this topic, they shared the conviction that the Kingdom of God had already been founded among humans by Jesus and that it would be brought into full realization at least in part through divinely guided human effort.[4] Father Grigorii shared this view and popularized it, not only among the laity but also among the city's clergy.[5]

Father Grigorii's first book, published in 1898, laid out the topics and arguments that he would develop in more detail over the next five years. The work's title, *The Gospel as the Basis of Life*, neatly encapsulated the author's essential point: that the Word of God as manifested in the teaching of Jesus should be the basis for all human thought and activity.[6] In making this assertion, Father Grigorii was arguing against those secular intellectuals who claimed that Christianity had nothing to offer the modern world and that the hope of humanity lay with science. In response, Father Grigorii pointed out that scientific thinking was quite new in the history of European civilization while Christianity had been an essential part of that civilization for many centuries. During that time Christianity had greatly enriched human life, for which it deserved recognition and respect. Even at the present time, when science seemed to be ascendant, religion was not dead; its greatest achievements still lay in the future. How could this be? Father Grigorii observed that despite all the scientific and technological progress of the present age, modern society still suffered from poverty and injustice. Not only had science failed to cure these social ills but some scientific thinkers even tried to rationalize them, claiming that competition was necessary for human progress, weeding out the weak so the strong could flourish. He rejected this application of Darwinian ideas to human society. They encouraged selfishness and egotism and thus allowed injustice to root itself deeply in each individual's heart. A society that promoted selfish competition patronized injustice as well.[7]

Looking back on the nineteenth century, Petrov questioned the claim that science, technology, and secular thought had produced unprecedented progress. If there had been so much progress, he asked, why were there so many poor people? Why were crime and violence rampant? Why did millions suffer from hunger, disease, and want? He argued that such problems, accompanied by the failure to acknowledge that they represented the persistence of injustice, demonstrated that modern society had lost any sense of purpose and direction. Society had been led to pursue the wrong ideals, and as a result it had adopted the wrong standard for judging its accomplishments. Father Grigorii argued that the solution was to return to the ideals of Christianity, which offered human beings guidance concerning their ultimate goals and a standard for judging their progress.

According to Father Grigorii, the ultimate goal of human striving was the Kingdom of God. The secular intellectual might turn away from this idea in contempt, thinking that the clerical author was reasserting the promise of the medieval church according to which believers were exhorted to live piously in the hope of seeing the rewards of Heaven after death. Although this interpretation of the Kingdom of God was common among Orthodox believers, Petrov explicitly rejected it.[8] Instead he argued, "the Kingdom of God is the righteous and morally perfect life of people on earth, [a life] awakened by Christ the Savior and constructed according to his Gospel Testament."[9] In other words, Father Grigorii believed that the Kingdom of God is not in Heaven but on earth and that it will be realized not in the future eternity of the afterlife but in the historical future of humankind. Its foundation on earth was laid by Christ, but it will be constructed by humankind according to God's plan. It is already in existence, but only as a potentiality. Petrov declared the task of realizing that potentiality and thus bringing the kingdom into full existence to be the "universal ideal of all humanity" and the purpose of human history.[10] That purpose will finally be achieved when humankind has learned to live in accordance with God's law as taught by Jesus Christ and witnessed to in the Gospel.[11]

Although Father Grigorii's conception of the Kingdom of God as a work accomplished through human endeavor was not novel or unique by the late 1890s, his explanation of it differs from that of other clergymen in one significant respect. In the sermons of Metropolitan Antonii and Archpriest Mikhail (Sokolov) of Kazan cathedral, love was the central feature of the kingdom. Antonii understood the kingdom as the rule of God's omnipresent and eternal love among men.[12] While he was rector at the academy, he taught his students (Petrov among them) that humans contributed to the realization of the kingdom by dedicating themselves to serving others out of love.[13] Father Mikhail also emphasized the centrality of selfless love in the Kingdom of God and the importance of service to others, declaring that Christian love could not be passively expressed as a mere sentiment of goodwill toward others. It had to manifest itself actively through charity. When one was inspired by the love of God to perform an act of charity for another, that moment of pure selflessness provided a glimpse of the reality of the Kingdom of God.[14] While Father Grigorii acknowledged the necessity of love he preferred to define the kingdom in terms of divine justice. In his view, love and justice were not competing virtues but complementary ones. Christian love should inspire not only charity but also justice, for if one person truly loves another he will not seek to hold that other person in bondage or oppression; he will not tolerate violence against him; he will not permit him to live in poverty.[15] Thus, in the Kingdom of God humans would live with each other "in the spirit of Gospel love and justice" without allowing a single person to suffer from oppression, violence, or poverty.[16]

Father Grigorii's first work thus argued that Christianity remained not only relevant but vitally important in the modern world because it offered human beings a worthy goal for their strivings and a standard by which to judge their progress. The goal was the Kingdom of God, which God would bring into full realization once human beings had established the principles of the Gospels as the basis of their society. The standard for success was that of justice, for the Kingdom of God would be the rule of divine justice on earth. But how was a more just society to be created? In the early works of his career, Father Grigorii focused on the moral transformation of individuals. Unlike those who argued that man was so thoroughly contaminated by evil that he was totally dependent on God for his transformation, Father Grigorii believed that human beings could change themselves for the better.[17] He did not deny that man has evil in him but he described it as an "abnormal tumor" or a "dark blemish," suggesting that evil was like a sickness that could be cured or a stain that could be removed.[18] He contended that overcoming the evil within was a human task, albeit one that required divine guidance and assistance.[19]

In the writings he published between 1898 and 1904, Father Grigorii's main purpose was to explain to individuals how to create a Christian life in the modern world.[20] According to his view, the Christian should devote himself to three concerns: seeking after truth, repenting of sin, and living according to the principles of the Gospels.[21] The Christian life must begin with the quest for truth, for an understanding of what life means, what man's purpose is and how he is to accomplish it.[22] While Father Grigorii believed that elements of God's truth could be discovered in many ways and places, he saw the Gospels as its most complete expression. For this reason, he urged his readers to prefer the Gospels before all other works.[23] This insistence that every Christian should read the Gospels for himself was unusual at the time in the Russian Orthodox Church. While Russians were not ignorant of the New Testament, private or individual reading of the Bible was not a prominent feature of Orthodox religious practice. The modern Russian translation of the Bible (as opposed to the Church Slavonic one), published between 1863 and 1875, had been available for only one generation. Many clergymen still hesitated to encourage lay people to read the Bible, fearing they would misunderstand it and challenge the church's authority.[24]

Father Grigorii, however, believed that the meaning of the Gospels was simple and could be understood by anyone who read them with a sincere desire to discover their truth.[25] He articulated this view through a number of his stories in which the Bible reveals its truth to those whose hearts are open to it. No interpretation or explanation is necessary; the person understands what he needs to by himself. For example, in the story of the teacher and student, one monk undertakes to teach a fellow monk how to read using the Bible as his text.[26] He begins with the verse, "You shall love the Lord your God with all your heart, and with all your soul, and with all your might."[27] The pupil commits this text to memory and then leaves. Although the teacher expects him to come back the next day, the monk does not. He returns only after many years. When his teacher asks him where he had gone and why he had not come back earlier, the student replies that he left to learn how to love God with all his heart. The story concludes with the observation that the student taught his teacher what it meant to read the Bible by showing him how to understand its meaning with the heart and not just the mind. Father Grigorii suggests that the simple and unlearned person who seeks truth in the Bible is more likely to find it than the educated person who reads it as if it were any other book. The person who has read only one sentence of the Bible and tried to understand its full meaning is closer to its truth than one who has read the whole Bible without understanding.

In Father Grigorii's writings, discovering truth is often associated with repentance for past errors and resolution to do better in the future. The truth a person finds in the Gospels points him in the direction he must go while the moral force of repentance provides the energy for the journey. Repentance arouses a sense of restlessness in the believer: he who repents is always watchful and alert; he is never satisfied with himself but always striving to become better; he is constantly aware that time is slipping away and that there is not a moment to be lost before death brings him to an accounting.[28] Repentance drives a person to change his ways in order to live a life more in keeping with the Gospels—a life that is characterized by patience, tolerance, good cheer, charity toward others, modesty, sobriety, and hard work.

Father Grigorii's views of what the Christian life was and how it could be attained coincided in many respects with those of the American social gospel movement. It should not be too surprising, then, that Petrov chose to translate one of the most popular and influential works of the American social gospel movement into Russian. The book titled *In His Steps: What Would Jesus Do?* was first published in 1896 and has remained continuously in print in the United States for over a century. This didactic novel tells the story of how a small town is transformed after the congregation of one church vows to follow in Christ's footsteps in their daily lives.[29] They are moved to make this vow after a poor man who comes to their town seeking charity dies because no one would help him. The man's last impassioned plea for Christian charity, made before the entire congregation and its pastor in church on a Sunday morning, is the word of truth that strikes these people to the heart and makes them realize that they are not the good Christians they thought they were. They repent of their errors and vow to realize the gospel in every part of their lives in the future. As individuals become more caring, loving, forgiving, and compassionate, the town is transformed into a Christian community of brotherly love. Although the work was written by another, the pattern of conflict and resolution here is identical to the one that Father Grigorii followed in his own didactic fiction: a decent person who thinks himself a Christian and is considered a good man by the standards of the world encounters the Word of God and is shocked out of his complacency when he suddenly realizes its true meaning. He becomes painfully aware of how his "good" life falls short of God's expectations and decides he must change it so that he can live rightly in the eyes of God.[30] Spiritual enlightenment leads to repentance and moral renewal, which are expressed through the reformed life.

As the story of *In His Steps* demonstrated and as Father Grigorii's own works affirmed, the reform of individual lives did not benefit individuals alone but also their community. The life of each reformed individual affected the lives of all those around him, serving as a model, an inspiration, and a source of support for others. In both Petrov's stories and the social gospel novel, a key element of the reformed life is service to others, through which the believer expresses his selfless love and desire to imitate Christ. Father Grigorii's favorite Bible story was the parable of the Good Samaritan, and the verses he referred to most often in his stories were from the Gospel of Matthew: "What you have done for the least of my brethren, you have done for me" and "He who would be greatest among you must be a servant."[31] His examples of loving Christian service are typically in the forms of giving charity, expressing compassion, and fostering fellowship.[32] In his stories, he emphasizes that these forms of service do not require much from the individual but repay small sacrifices with the joy that comes from sharing with others and helping to build the Kingdom of God. Even the most humble can make some contribution, Father Grigorii suggested, referring to the parable of the widow's mite. The widow's offering was small, but because it was made sincerely and with love it was of greater value than the offerings of the wealthy.[33] Thus, the Kingdom of God would emerge out of the modest works of ordinary believers whose efforts to "follow in the footsteps of Jesus" and live according to God's principles of truth, love, and justice would diminish the power of injustice in the world and help realize the Kingdom of God on earth.

THE LONELY HERO:
The Challenge of Building the Kingdom of God

Despite his early emphasis on individual transformation as the means through which the Kingdom of God would be realized, the stories Petrov wrote about the reformed life are a disappointment. The people they depict are lifeless abstractions possessing generic virtues and living their reformed lives in unreal conditions. Their acts of Christian service are singular and individual, with effects extending barely beyond the people immediately involved. Although Father Grigorii may have meant to suggest that the accumulation of such individual acts would transform society, it is hard to see exactly how this could ever happen; the gap between the smallness of the individual acts and the greatness of the kingdom that has yet to be built seems so large. Moreover, he did not write many stories concerned primarily with the reformed life, though the promise of that life was implicit in stories that focused on other themes. One story that he did write, "The Peasant Veselov," reveals a possible reason for Father Grigorii's lack of success with this subject by exposing the latent tension between the desire of the individual to change the world around him and the resistance of the world to change.[34] The story is about a peasant who leaves his home to pursue an education in the city. He builds a successful career and later returns to his village believing he will use his knowledge and money to improve the lives of the other peasants. With his inheritance, he buys a ceramics factory and revives the local economy. With the profits from the factory he organizes a school for the peasant children, provides electricity to the village, buys books and sets up a reading room, founds a hospital, and establishes a higher technical school.

The story exemplifies Father Grigorii's ideal of how the reformed individual should devote his life to serving others and making a better society by working to eliminate poverty and suffering. The story was intended to inspire readers by showing how much one committed person could change the world. What is remarkable about this story, however, is that there is *only* one person in the village working for the improvement of his fellow peasants' lives. Veselov receives no advice or support from his peasant neighbors, the village clergy, or the local members of educated society. Neither does the village respond to Veselov's efforts. The social environment of indifference and passivity in which Veselov's work takes place seems to defeat the hope that through individual efforts, society as a whole can be transfigured by repentance and love alone. At the end of this story one is left not with a Christian community regenerated by the efforts of its individual members and ripe for the realization of the Kingdom of God (as in the American novel) but with an indefatigable Christian hero laboring mightily over an impassive Russian village that hardly seems to notice his efforts.

The tension between the reforming individual and the unreformed world around him that runs like a submerged stream through the story of the peasant Veselov surges into the open in Petrov's novel, *Zateinik (The Entrepreneur).*[35] This novel was Father Grigorii's first and only attempt to present his views in a book-length work rather than in the short forms—essays, stories, and parables—that were clearly his forte. This novel follows the career of its main character, the clergyman Ivan Postnikov, through three stages: his years at seminary; his service as a junior priest in a rural parish; and finally his work as a charismatic pastor at an urban church, which is abruptly terminated by his early, heroic death.[36] At each stage in his career, the central conflict is between Postnikov's struggle to reform the world around him and the resistance of others to his changes. During the first part of the novel describing Postnikov's years at the seminary, Father Grigorii portrays his protagonist as a serious and idealistic youth confronted by a host of negative characters representing various types of corruption in the church: there are careerists and time-servers, drunks, depressives, and despotic disciplinarians, ritualists and cynical atheists, incompetents and ignoramuses. Despite the discouraging conditions Postnikov persists in his studies, following his older brother's advice to seek inspiration through prayer and Bible study.[37] While at the seminary, Postnikov discerns his vocation for pastorship. Father Grigorii's own conviction that pastorship is the highest form of service to the people is affirmed by two of Postnikov's seminary teachers.[38] At the same time, they and his older brother warn Postnikov that a pastor who is truly committed to his calling must be ready to confront many challenges. However, Postnikov declares that the Christian pastor must not be afraid of hard work, suffering, sacrifice, and opposition. His purpose is simple: to go out among the people and build the Kingdom of God.[39]

Postnikov graduates from the seminary with honors, thus becoming eligible for admission to one of the ecclesiastical academies; completion of a degree would virtually guarantee a successful career in an urban diocese or one of the well-appointed European missions. However, Postnikov decides not to continue his education but to take clerical orders and enter service immediately, thus demonstrating his commitment to his pastoral vocation and his determination to put the needs of others ahead of his own selfish interests.[40] In the impoverished and ignorant village where he is assigned as a junior priest, he acts upon his commitment to building the Kingdom of God through his selfless service to the common people. He tries to educate them both in religion and more mundane subjects and leads the way in projects for village improvement. On Sundays he preaches to them in the church; during the week he teaches them informally, singly and in small groups. He organizes a Bible study group for teenagers while his wife establishes a church choir. His wife also looks after the village children and works to improve their hygiene while Postnikov sets up an apiary and instructs the peasants in modern agricultural science. After a devastating fire, Postnikov helps the peasants to rebuild their homes and sets up a fire insurance society. When the villagers express interest in organizing a temperance society, Postnikov warmly supports their initiative.[41]

We might expect that all of this effort would be recognized and rewarded by the authorities, but it is not. Postnikov comes into frequent conflict with the village's senior priest because of his insistence on Sunday preaching, which the older priest thinks is unnecessary and potentially dangerous. Postnikov also encounters hostility from the peasants when he refuses to accept vodka as payment for his performance of private rites, as had traditionally been the practice in rural Russia (thus accounting for the stereotype of the drunken parish priest). Postnikov's bishop proves to be a critic of the priest's work as well. When Postnikov visits him to ask permission to organize a discussion group for the local clergy, the bishop reprimands him harshly, hinting that he suspects the young priest of sectarian leanings. He orders Postnikov to desist from his activities and follow the example of his betters. When Postnikov defies the bishop and continues his work in the village, his superiors label him a troublemaker. He is soon transferred to a position as a chaplain in an urban hospital, where it is hoped that his constituency will be limited.[42]

In the city, Postnikov finds new opportunities to fulfill his mission as a pastor. He organizes religious-moral discussion groups for the doctors at the hospital and volunteers at a nearby shelter. He teaches at a local school, participates in a meeting between clergymen and intellectuals, and preaches at several public gatherings. His sermons, which rely almost exclusively on the Gospels without references to the works of the church fathers or the teachings of the church, arouse suspicion among other clergymen and provoke criticism from educated lay people.[43] The growing tension culminates in a "great speech" scene, when Postnikov delivers an impassioned lecture to an audience of clergymen and intellectuals in which he declares that the world *must* be changed, that the church's mission is to lead the way in this transformation, and that the church must bring about change through love rather than fear. He is shouted down by some of the other clergy at the meeting, who had applauded an earlier speech insisting on the need to strengthen church discipline. Afterward, Postnikov is formally reprimanded by the bishop and prohibited from preaching and teaching. Nevertheless, despite the pressure to leave the clergy Postnikov persists in his pastoral work, defending the local Jews from a pogrom and helping the starving during a severe famine. He finally dies at a young age after contracting typhus from working among the poor in a city slum during an epidemic.[44]

Postnikov is not unsuccessful in his work. In the village, the peasants respond to Postnikov's efforts with gratitude and resolve to improve themselves under his guidance. The young pastor's sermons bring the whole village together "like a family" around him.[45] There are several incidents in which Postnikov has a decisive effect on the lives of individual lost believers: in the village, he turns one peasant man away from drink through kindly guidance and loving compassion; in the urban shelter, he restores a vicious criminal's faith in himself and inspires him to a heroic action in which he sacrifices his life to save that of another.[46] There is no denying that Postnikov is an admirable, and even a heroic, character. However, like the peasant Veselov, Postnikov carries out the work of building the Kingdom of God on earth almost single-handedly; the broader his field of action and the greater his challenges, the more alone he seems to be. Moreover, not only does he receive little help from others but as the novel continues he encounters increasingly stubborn opposition from precisely those people one might have expected to assist him—fellow clergymen, leaders in the church, and educated laymen.

Petrov's focus on Postnikov's great and lonely battle for the kingdom is especially striking when one compares this work with *In His Steps*. In the American novel, the work of building the Kingdom of God is carried out by the whole community under the leadership of the pastor. Individuals have their particular problems to face, but in each case, other members of the community are there to offer advice, support, and assistance. Through individual effort made in the context of mutual support, the community is slowly transformed. By contrast, in Father Grigorii's novel, there is no community of people working together to construct the Kingdom of God on earth, but only the lone reformed believer struggling to transform the world around him on his own in spite of the indifference or open hostility of others.[47] Moreover, although Petrov's hero accomplishes a great deal in his novel, by the end of the book there is no indication that Postnikov has succeeded in making any permanent changes in the world. The Kingdom of God does not seem any closer to realization than when he began. He does not overcome the opposition to his work nor does he persuade his critics to change their opinions and join him. When he dies he does not leave behind anyone who will continue his work, but only his unconverted and unrepentant opponents.

THE POWER AND THE GLORY—
A Final Vision of the Kingdom's Promise

The Entrepreneur marked a significant turning point in Father Grigorii's intellectual evolution. Up to 1904, his writings had assumed that the Kingdom of God would be realized by individuals whose efforts to live by the gospel law of love would lead to the establishment of a just society. His writings of the period 1905–1908 remained concerned with the question of how human beings were to help actualize the Kingdom of God, but his answer was quite different. In this later period, the agent of reform is no longer the individual but the Christian community, and the arena of action is not the relations between individuals but the institutions of society. The acts themselves are explicitly political. There were several reasons for the dramatic change in Father Grigorii's thought at this time. First, as the story of the peasant Veselov and *The Entrepreneur* both suggest, Father Grigorii perceived that there were inherent difficulties in his initial formulation of the relation between the individual Christian life and the common purpose of the Christian community. Second, Father Grigorii encountered opposition and criticism in his clerical career that made the tensions he explored in his literary work very real. Finally, as Father Grigorii was undergoing his personal crisis Russia was convulsed by the tremors of the 1905 revolution, an event that gave all discussions about how private ideals related to the public a new urgency.

The crisis that eventually destroyed Father Grigorii's clerical career began in the winter of 1902–1903.[48] The priest was invited to give a series of lectures about Christianity addressed to the educated classes of the city as part of the local church's efforts to assert a greater influence over the public discussions generated by the meetings of the Religious-Philosophical Society, where the contributions of the clerical participants were often strongly criticized. Father Grigorii's lectures drew large crowds of people, for he was a lively speaker who freely mixed parables, analogies, stories from the Gospels, and examples from the lives of common people. His subject was the Kingdom of God and his theme, already well established in his published work, was that individuals could assist in the realization of the Kingdom of God on earth by striving to improve their individual lives in accordance with the teachings of the Bible. Many listeners, particularly those intellectuals with liberal social or political views, welcomed his interpretation of Christianity for its spirit of optimism and humanism. He was telling them that through faith and hard work human beings could build a better society on earth and that this endeavor was a part of the divine plan for humanity that would culminate in the actualization of the Kingdom of God.

Others, however, found much to criticize about Petrov's ideas. Most of the critics were lay intellectuals associated with the conservative Orthodox publicist Vladimir Skvortsov, who had close ties with Konstantin Pobedonostsev, director general of the Synod. They published their attacks on Father

Grigorii's work (his writings as well as his lectures) in the journal *Missionary Review (Missionerskoe obozrenie)*, edited by Skvortsov, in the early months of 1903. Their criticisms were similar in many respects, focusing on three main issues: first, the meaning of the Kingdom of God; second, the significance of church tradition; and third, the correct way to teach the unenlightened. Father Grigorii's critics objected to his interpretation of the Kingdom of God as something that would be constructed on earth through the efforts of human beings. One critic who reviewed *The Gospel as the Foundation of Life* argued that Petrov's view of the kingdom was narrow, legalistic, and materialist; he believed that Father Grigorii needed to give more attention to the concept of the Kingdom of Heaven, which in his view represented a higher, more spiritual aspiration.[49] Other commentators, while not focusing as sharply on Father Grigorii's interpretation of the Kingdom of God, offered similar criticisms of the priest's view of the ability of humans to improve themselves and society through their own efforts. In the view of these commentators, individual human beings can be saved only through the grace of God, as offered by the church through the sacraments; human society as such cannot be redeemed, and moral progress is impossible.[50] For all of these critics, the only hope of humanity lay in the church; it was the church that gave humans guidance in understanding God's message correctly and attaining divine grace.[51] Father Grigorii's reliance on the Gospels alone as a guide to the Christian life aroused suspicion that he might be a sectarian. At the very least, he stood accused of *"beztserkovnost',"* an insufficient attachment to the traditions and teachings of the church, as manifested by his utter neglect of the writings of the church fathers and the works of other recognized authorities on Orthodoxy.[52] Even if this focus on the Gospels was the result of an effort to popularize the teachings of Christianity more broadly, Petrov's critics found reason to object. Some found Father Grigorii's humor inappropriate for the serious subject of religious truth; others disliked his preference for common examples or found his analogies crude, confusing, or misleading. They criticized his interpretations of some Bible verses as unconventional and believed he was careless in how he quoted Scripture. They feared his teaching misled those who were not knowledgeable about the faith or that it served some in the audience as mere entertainment. Several of them suggested that Father Grigorii's public preaching was motivated primarily by a desire for self-aggrandizement.[53]

The campaign of public criticism against Father Grigorii in an influential church journal led to his suspension from public preaching in 1904. Although he had many supporters in the church, including the metropolitan of St. Petersburg Antonii (Vadkovskii), the powerful connections enjoyed by his critics and the government's growing concern about public disorder in the midst of its war with Japan could not be denied. However, Father Grigorii continued to write and publish prolifically over the next several years. The works of this period reflect the influence of his personal experience, as a result of which he learned that a single individual could do little in the world if others with power and wealth were determined to thwart him; furthermore, he learned how defenseless the individual was before such powers. He began to see more clearly the flaws in his youthful theory that the good person was powerful enough to change the world and his belief that as individuals reformed themselves society would be reformed, too.[54] It had become clear to him that the influence of one person was limited and that the task of reforming society was more demanding than he had originally realized.

In his late essays, Father Grigorii began to explore a new approach to realizing the Kingdom of God on earth. Instead of addressing the common folk, he appealed to educated society and particularly the intelligentsia—those who saw themselves as critics of the regime and the established order. Instead of focusing on the individual's transformation of himself, he emphasized the elite's role in the reform of society. Considering the well-known history of mutual estrangement and hostility between the clergy and the intelligentsia, Father Grigorii's efforts to promote cooperation between the two groups in the name of the Kingdom of God may seem impracticable. However, they followed on the initiatives launched in 1901 by the Society for Moral-Religious Enlightenment (of which Father Grigorii was a prominent member). These initiatives were a response to the revival of interest in religious questions among the St. Petersburg intelligentsia.[55] The city's leading clergy hoped to educate the intelligentsia about Orthodoxy and to draw them back into the church's embrace, which many of them had spurned.[56] A number of activities promoted the church's new mission to the intelligentsia.[57] The professors of the St. Petersburg academy opened a series of lectures on Christian theology and morality for the educated classes in 1900.[58] The clergy welcomed the invitation to participate in the discussions of the Religious-Philosophical Society, which held its first meeting in the fall of 1901. In 1902, the ORRP arranged a series of lectures to supplement the discussions of the Religious-Philosophical Society.[59] Father Grigorii's controversial lectures were part of that series. The ORRP also organized a youth group that brought together students from the church's schools with those from the universities and higher technical schools,[60] as well as a laywomen's outreach association, the Religious-Educational Union, whose members shared the gospel with the inmates of the city's hospitals, asylums, shelters, and prisons.[61] Finally, a new journal, *The Orthodox Russian Word (Pravoslavno-russkoe slovo),* was founded under the editorship of Archpriest Peter Lakhotskii and two other prominent clergymen to address the religious interests and questions of educated society from a correct Orthodox viewpoint.[62]

Despite the initially high hopes that these efforts at outreach would reconcile the intelligentsia to the church, many of the participating clergy were deeply frustrated by the continued hostility and disrespect they encountered from the intelligentsia and soon abandoned hope that their efforts would garner any success. Father Grigorii was more optimistic than most, perhaps because his lectures had been unusually successful. Rather than turning away from the intelligentsia as some of the St. Petersburg clergy did after 1904, he sought to encourage their rapprochement with the church. He began with the argument that the basis for an alliance between the clergy and the intelligentsia was their common belief in the duty of the educated elite to use their knowledge for the people's benefit. In *The Entrepreneur*, Father Grigorii recognized that for some people service to the narod was accomplished through secular professions while for others the vocation for service came through the church. Postnikov's older brother, for example, decides to become a doctor instead of a priest, arguing to his critical uncle that he should not be expected to go into church service simply because he had attended church schools. Since he had no vocation for the church he would be doing harm to others if he became a priest just for the sake of repaying the church for the money spent on his education. His primary responsibility was not to the church but to the people: "My duty— like yours and like that of anyone, whoever he is and wherever he studied —is not a duty to the school that brought me up like part of the family, but to the family we have in the people, who have nursed all of us school-educated people and raised us up on their own shoulders."[63] Later, when Postnikov tells this brother of his plans to enter the priesthood his brother is supportive of the choice. Postnikov explains his decision in terms similar to those his brother had used, asserting that the duty of the clergy was to work among the people for the advancement of the Kingdom of God. Petrov thus sanctifies the work done by members of the educated classes and represents their work as being both comparable and complementary to the work done by the clergy. This vision is explicitly affirmed toward the end of the novel. In the climactic speech that results in his ban from public lecturing, Postnikov invites the intelligentsia to join the clergy in expressing their love for the people by dedicating their lives to the great cause of building a good society in which the people will finally be able to fulfill their God-given potential.[64]

Father Grigorii developed these ideas further in a 1906 essay entitled "The Intelligentsia and the Clergy."[65] He argued that despite their long-standing estrangement, the two groups had the same goals: to establish a society based on the principles of truth and justice and to create a better life for the Russian people. He contended that if the clergy and the intelligentsia could overcome their mutual suspicion and recognize their common purpose they could forge a powerful alliance in support of reforms that would be both practical and effective. The strengths of the two groups complemented each other: the clergy knew the true conditions of the people's lives and what they needed most, while the intelligentsia had a history of practical public service and knowledge about the process of social reform. If the compassion and experience of the clergy could be joined with the energy and ideas of the intelligentsia, they could lead society into a new era.[66] Together, they could achieve what they could not accomplish separately.

Identifying the urgent tasks that faced the educated classes, Father Grigorii pointed to the importance of education and cultural development as means of working to build a more just society.[67] He argued that the true strength of a country should be measured by the cultural level and prosperity of its average citizens. A society that educated its citizens enabled them to achieve a decent level of material life, which in turn helped to prevent gross injustices and gave the society the spiritual and material resources to develop further.[68] Comparing Russia to Germany and America, Father Grigorii criticized his country as backward. Although he knew some would accuse him of lacking patriotism, he argued that in order to improve the country, the reformers had to acknowledge that the majority of its people were ignorant and poor. Moreover, they had to understand that this deprivation was unjustifiable and inexcusable: it was an intolerable injustice. The only solution was to begin work immediately to guarantee all people a basic education.[69] Education was the key to unlocking the people's potential for creative and productive labor, which would enable them to look beyond the immediate task of survival to the project of building the Kingdom of God.[70]

Father Grigorii elaborated on the idea of an alliance between the clergy and the intelligentsia in the essays collected in *The Church and Society*. He believed that the educated classes would themselves benefit from doing practical work among the people. In this way, they could fulfill their desire to serve the people and increase their empirical knowledge of the people's lives while at the same time helping to improve how the people lived. They would gain the experience of working among the people that the clergy already had. For the clergy, however, Petrov believed the problem was not a lack of experience but a blinkered perspective. Even though many parish priests had dedicated years to working among the people, few had any understanding of social problems or politics.[71] They were surrounded by suffering and labored constantly to alleviate it, but without ever asking whence it came, why it persisted, or how it might finally be cured. Father Grigorii criticized his fellow clergymen for their resignation and passivity, their tacit belief that the problems they struggled with each day would be solved somehow by the government or by God.[72] He argued that their failure to focus on the problems humans faced in society and their refusal to concern themselves with practical, secular issues prevented them from making any real progress toward fulfilling the church's ultimate mission: "The absence of a religious-social ideal among the Church's active workers is the main reason that its true situation is so desperate . . . . [N]o improvement is possible without faith in the divinely ordained, positive value of the affairs of society."[73]

Father Grigorii published these essays in 1905 and 1906, when Russia was in the midst of a popular revolution. Many in the church cautioned the clergy to remain aloof from the tumult, arguing that the church had to be indifferent to all political parties either because it was not concerned with the transient institutions of human society or because it was obligated to uphold the divinely approved authority of the emperor. Father Grigorii, however, believed that the clergy could not be indifferent to politics and that the church had a clear standard by which to measure the claims of all those who competed for power: which group would do the most to advance the development of a just society and thus contribute to realizing the Kingdom of God? For Petrov, the choice seemed clear. He called on the clergy to support liberal intellectuals who called for reform over the radicals who demanded revolution or the reactionaries who refused to consider any changes to the system. He believed that the political goals of the liberal intelligentsia were compatible with the moral and religious ideals of the clergy.[74] He implored the clergy to look beyond the political rhetoric to see that the liberals' program was aimed at realizing the same religious principles of love, charity, truth, and justice that the clergy pursued in their work.[75]

At the same time, Petrov did not want the clergy to surrender themselves completely to the intelligentsia, for he believed the clergy had a unique obligation that required them to maintain their own distinct space in the public sphere. The clergy had to keep the ideal of the Kingdom of God constantly before the public eye and to remind the government and the intelligentsia that their ultimate aim was to create a just society for all. Petrov enjoined the clergy to speak for the people before the powers of the world: to witness publicly to the silent despair of those who were scorned and neglected, to speak for those who were gagged by fear and impotence, and to plead for those who were violated and oppressed. He charged the clergy with representing the miseries of the working class to the world and demanding justice for them in the name of Christ and the kingdom.[76] In a story published late in 1905, he offered a vivid illustration of how he perceived the clergy's special role as advocates and defenders of the people. Entitled "The Great Pastor," the story told of an event that occurred while St. John Chrysostom was serving as a deacon in Antioch in the late fourth century. Protesting a new tax the emperor had imposed, the people of the city rioted and destroyed a statue of the emperor. After the riot ended, the people began to fear the emperor's wrath. Although Father John had warned them not to riot, he went to the governor of the city and begged for mercy. Moreover, he sent the city's elderly bishop to the emperor to plead for the people, telling him that it was his duty as their pastor to intercede for them before the emperor as Christ had interceded for man before God.[77] As a result of the clergy's pleadings, the emperor relented and spared the city from punishment. This story, which was written in response to the events of Bloody Sunday, represented the clergy of the city as the people's saviors who prayed for them, preached to them, advised them, and finally, risked their own lives to beg for mercy for them before the greatest power in the world. This was the model of pastoral leadership that Father Grigorii offered for the Russian clergy to follow during the turbulent times of their own revolution. He did not think the clergy should remain removed from events; they had to be involved. It did not mean that priests should join the rioters but that they should seek to advise and warn them. This was not because the clergy were bound to uphold the power of the government in all circumstances; indeed, sometimes the clergy had to challenge the government, just as they had challenged the mob. The clergy were deeply connected to both the people and the government but also independent of both because of their constant awareness of their obligation to represent a higher power and a greater set of ideals.

Father Grigorii examined the subject of the relations between the clergy and the government further in a 1906 collection of essays entitled *The Needs of Today's Church*. The street disorders of the revolution had reached their peak in the fall of 1905, resulting in the emperor's reluctant decision to grant his subjects a constitution that allowed for the establishment of an elected legislative assembly. The first Duma was elected in the early spring of 1906. At the same time, the leaders of the church had received permission to discuss organizing an all-Russian church council, the first in more than two hundred years, to discuss reform. Father Grigorii welcomed the prospect. In his view, the main issue was to correct the relationship between the church and the government, which favored the needs and interests of the government over those of the church. Peter the Great's reforms had made the church dependent on the government, an arrangement many in the church had come to accept and defend as just and natural. But Father Grigorii thought that the original reforms were profoundly misguided when considered from the church's viewpoint. Peter the Great had not been interested in the work of the church; he thought only about the needs of the state, to which he subordinated everything else including the good of his own people. He forgot that the state itself was not an end but only a means for the attainment of a higher goal—the Kingdom of God.

> Of the fact that for all humankind . . . there is a single, overarching, eternal goal—the construction of the Kingdom of God among people, the strengthening of the justice of the Gospel and the love of Christ in human inter-relations, the promotion of the greatest expression of the spirit of the Lord in the life and activity of each person and of all—of this, Peter did not think. The idea that the government is not an end in itself, but only a means, one small part of the general human agency for the best fulfillment of the one, overarching divine concern, a means for the construction . . . of more perfect, more just conditions of life—evidently, such an idea never entered Peter's head.[78]

The church, however, could never forget that its primary purpose was constructing the Kingdom of God. In so far as the government also worked for this goal, the church should support it and work with it. But the church should not allow itself to be seduced by the power of the government into serving it for the advancement of mundane interests. Nor should the church fear that its own power in the world depended on the authority of the government. Father Grigorii argued that while the government needed the support of the church to give its power legitimacy, the church did not need any help from the government to assure its place in the hearts of men. The power of the Gospels gave the church its authority. The church had only to renew its faith in that power in order to liberate itself from the bonds of government service.[79]

The clergy themselves held the key to this renewal, for they brought the message of the Gospels into the world and made it real for believers through their teaching and their lives.[80] At a time that the church faced many challenges, the work of the clergy was more important than ever. In order for this work to be effective, however, the clergy had to remember who they were and what their purpose was. They could not allow themselves to imitate the example of others whose power and goals were of the secular world alone:

> Just as there is an artistic sensibility, a musical sensibility, so there is also a pastoral sensibility. A judge looks at life in one way. . . . A bureaucrat . . . in another way. . . . The pastor has his own pastoral path in life. He has a pastor's point of view, a pastor's problems and a pastor's influence. He has his own spirit, his own substance—a pastoral one. A pastor cannot act like a judge. Neither can a pastor act like a bureaucrat. He is a pastor.[81]

Nor could the clergy allow those who had a worldly agenda to co-opt the church for any purpose other than advancing the Kingdom of God. In particular, Father Grigorii was concerned that the clergy would allow the government to dominate the reform process, which would only result in a church that served the government's interests more effectively. It would do nothing to strengthen the church in its own mission. If the church were to be renewed, then the clergy would have to step forward to lead the way. Only those clergy who were truly pastors—called by God to bring his Word to the people—understood the needs of the church and how they could be met:

> The bureaucrat has nothing in common with the pastoral spirit. He can be an excellent human being, an obedient son of the Church who truly wishes prosperity and good things for the Church, but he cannot, he dare not, he must not use his authority to influence the operation of the Church. He has no right because he is alien to, completely deprived of, the spirit of the pastor. And the organization of the Church, the development of the Church's life, demands above all a pastor's service.[82]

On what looked to be the eve of major reform in the church, Father Grigorii thus laid out his own views very clearly. He believed the church's mission was to serve the people by leading them in the construction of the Kingdom of God on earth. Furthering this work had to be the primary concern of the church and its clergy at all times. It provided the standard by which they were to judge all else around them. In order to fulfill this work, the church had to maintain its independence from all mundane authorities: it could not subordinate itself to a secular government more concerned with its own power than the power of God, and it could not allow government authorities control over its internal affairs. The church had to claim its freedom and at the same time reassert its forgotten power over the hearts of men through the ministry of the Gospels. The parish clergy were to be the leaders in this renewal of the church, reviving the pastoral spirit while preaching the Gospels' promise of the coming kingdom among the expectant people. In short, what Father Grigorii hoped for was a revolution in the church.

Others shared Petrov's dream of a free and powerful church dedicated to the great task of building the Kingdom of God on earth. In fact, it was one individual's efforts to transform this dream into a reality that sparked the revolution of 1905, the very revolution whose suppression would soon crush not only all hope of church reform but many of those who had maintained this hope. The brief career of Father Georgii Gapon, the subject of the next chapter, was thus both the culmination and the termination of the ideal of creating the Kingdom of God on earth through the work of the Russian Orthodox clergy.

CHAPTER SEVEN

FROM RELIGION TO POLITICS

Father Gapon and the

Assembly of Russian Workers

Father Georgii Gapon is one of the well-known figures of Russia's revolutionary period, made notorious by his role in the revolution of 1905.[1] In many general surveys of modern European history and even of Russian history, Father Gapon (as he is commonly called) is depicted as a fairly typical member of the weak and corrupted Orthodox clergy, so eager to serve the interests of the autocracy that he agreed to head a workers' organization that was actually under the control of the tsarist police. According to this storyline, the bumbling priest proved to be so incompetent that the organization got out of hand and actually launched the revolution that it was supposed to prevent. A variation on this interpretation is that Father Gapon, selfishly seeking fame as a leader of the people but incapable of attaining it on his own, placed himself under the tutelage of the leaders of the liberal opposition. In this version of the story, Gapon is a puppet of the government's opponents rather than of the government's defenders, but the outcome is the same: a bungled political action leading to a revolution that destroys more than it reforms.[2]

Both of these views developed out of politically motivated interpretations of the history of the Russian revolutions: the first view was associated with radicals who advocated revolution against the tsar, particularly the Bolsheviks; and the second view was associated with the liberal reformers who came to head the Kadet party. Father Gapon plays an important part at a key moment in these revolutionary tales but ultimately he is only a minor character in a larger political narrative that is concerned primarily with the struggle for power between the revolutionaries and the tsarist government. Since that story has been of great interest to scholars as well, there has been little effort to go beyond the political narrative and look at Father Gapon in any other context. However, given the history of the clergy's ideas and activities in the capital in the pre-revolutionary decades, it should be obvious that the ecclesiastical life of the capital was bound to have a significant impact on the way Father Georgii thought about the purpose of the church, his duties as a pastor, and the relationship of his work to the development of Russian society. In this chapter, the work of Father Georgii is reexamined within such a context, placing it in a narrative focused on the efforts of the Orthodox church to define a place for itself in modern Russian society.[3]

CHRIST AND THE COSSACKS—
Heroes of Gapon's Youth

Georgii Apollonovich Gapon was born in 1870 in the Ukrainian province of Poltava, the oldest son in a peasant family of middling means. In his autobiography, Father Georgii emphasized how his family shaped the way he looked at the world. His father was well respected in their village for his wisdom and honesty. Because he was one of the few literate men in the district, he served for many years in the local village *(volost')* administration. Gapon declared that his first exposure to what he later saw as the government's oppression of the people came from his visits to the administration offices with his father and from his father's stories about unpleasant experiences with tsarist officials.[4] These stories contrasted sharply with the stories his father told about the great Cossack heroes of Ukraine's mythologized past who, according to the popular view, "fought for the liberty and welfare of the people, and stood as defenders of Christianity against the Turks and Tartars."[5] The Cossacks' exploits were also the subjects of many folktales and songs of his native village, Biliki. One epic told of the heroic feats of a Cossack alleged to be an ancestor of Gapon's family.[6] From his mother's side, Gapon was subjected to a different kind of influence. His mother was a devout woman who observed the rituals and prayers of the church meticulously and insisted that he do the same. He remembered that she loved to listen to her father read the saints' lives and that he, too, often listened to these stories, which had a strong effect on his sensitive young mind. As he later remarked: "I was deeply impressed by the holiness of all these saints and anchorites, and dreamed of the day when I should become one of them."[7] As a result of these parental influences, the Cossacks who defended the people's freedom and the saints who sacrificed themselves for God's glory became the models after which Gapon patterned his own life.

As a child Gapon tended the family's animals, but when he entered school his obvious intelligence and ambition began to open new doors. Upon the recommendation of the priest who taught at the village primary school, Gapon was advanced to pre-seminary school in the town of Poltava, after which he entered the seminary. His parents hoped that he would enter the priesthood and elevate the family's status, both materially and spiritually.[8] However, according to his published autobiography (written late in 1905 to win the support of Marxist revolutionaries for Gapon's political agenda), the teenaged Gapon was already developing a critical attitude toward the church. He disliked the ritualism typical of his mother's piety because it made the form of religion appear more important than the content. When a teacher at the seminary loaned him some of Leo Tolstoy's moral-religious works, Gapon read them with interest, finding that Tolstoy's arguments reinforced the interpretation of Christianity that Gapon had already developed as a result of his knowledge of the saints' lives. He came to agree with Tolstoy that Christianity was not supposed to be a religion of ritual and dogma but of self-sacrificing service and love for others.[9]

Tolstoy's ideas were viewed with suspicion by church authorities at that time (and later condemned).[10] Gapon believed that his embrace of the author's unconventional ideas were what led him to have trouble with local authorities. He believed that his scholarship was taken away because he had begun to question and criticize his teachers in the classroom. As a result, he had to find ways to support himself in order to continue his studies. He tutored for the families of several local priests, but the meager pay and the obvious contempt of his employers for the impoverished country boy offended the pride of a young man who was intelligent, sensitive, ambitious, and proud. Neither did Gapon get along with his classmates, most of whom were the sons and grandsons of clergymen and thus considered themselves to be superior to a peasant's son. At odds with the seminary administration, ostracized by his schoolmates, humiliated by his employers, Gapon developed a deep contempt for the Poltava clergy, whom he described as ignorant, greedy, vain, proud, and hypocritical.[11] It is not surprising that Gapon began to seek the company of those more despised and isolated than himself, passing his free time among the town's beggars and working poor. The contrast between the self-satisfied smugness of Poltava's priests and the desperation of the poor struck him: "All around me I saw misery, overwork, poverty and sickness. . . . On the other hand, I saw more clearly the contrast between the Gospel itself . . . and the ignorance and hypocrisy of the clergy."[12]

In his autobiography, Gapon declared that during his last year at the seminary he became so disillusioned with the church that he decided to abandon his plans for a clerical career and become a doctor instead. His teachers must have been disappointed, as they had recommended him highly for further study at one of the ecclesiastical academies. Unfortunately, Gapon's erratic behavior at the end of his final term resulted in a permanent black mark on his seminary record, barring him from all institutions of higher education and destroying his hopes for a medical career.[13] Gapon thus found his employment options rather limited once he had graduated from the seminary in 1893. He eventually took a job as a statistician for the zemstvo, a position that required him to journey through the villages and small towns of the province collecting information about the education, health, and welfare of the peasantry for the local government. As a result of the two years he spent in this job, Gapon became intimately familiar with the difficult conditions of the peasants' lives. His desire to dedicate himself to improving the lot of the common people was intensified. Although he said in his autobiography that he considered joining the underground revolutionary movement, he eventually returned to the idea of becoming a priest. He credited his fiancée with persuading him that the best way to fulfill his desire to serve the people was to imitate the example of Jesus Christ, "a model of sacrifice for humanity."[14]

Gapon took clerical orders immediately after his marriage and was appointed to serve as the junior priest in one of Poltava's cemetery churches in 1896. Father Georgii had hoped to serve in a rural parish, but the bishop of Poltava diocese needed the more educated clergy to serve in the town. Bishop Ilarion (Yushenov) described Father Georgii as an earnest and talented preacher with a strong interest in religious-educational work.[15] He was impressed by the young priest's ability to draw large congregations to his small, non-parish church.[16] Gapon recalled that he often preached about neighborly love and kindness to others—themes that echoed his reading of Tolstoy but that were also consonant with the tendencies of post-reform Orthodoxy. Not content with words alone, Father Georgii also sought to practice what he preached. He established a mutual aid society for the poor of Poltava that quickly became successful. He reveled in the popularity that his preaching and charity work brought, despite the jealousy he believed his success aroused among fellow clergy.[17]

Father Georgii served for only two years in Poltava before the death of his wife shattered his life. Unwilling to continue his work without her support, Gapon sought to escape his circumstances by going to St. Petersburg and applying for admission to the academy. With the help of several highly placed supporters, including Bishop Ilarion (Yushenov) and the assistant director general of the Synod, Vladimir Sabler, Father Georgii was allowed to take the entrance exams in the fall of 1898. He did extremely well and was offered both admission and a scholarship to the academy. Within a few months of starting classes, however, Father Georgii became restless and discontented. He abhorred what he perceived as the dry scholasticism of the professors and was disgusted by what he described as the worldliness and careerism of his fellow students. He soon lost interest in the lectures; his frustration with the course work was expressed in his accusation that his professors sought to suppress his originality by criticizing his essays.[18] Not surprisingly, Father Georgii did not complete his first year. Pleading illness, he withdrew during the second semester and traveled to the Crimea for a cure. While there, he considered becoming a monk, but decided against it after living at a monastery for some time. He claimed he could not endure the thought of living in idleness off the donations made by poor, ignorant peasants without doing anything to help them. Likewise, he rejected the idea of becoming a hermit after encountering one of the religious eccentrics who lived in the local caves. Such a life did not accord with his more socially oriented religious inclinations: "I could not believe in the right of a man to think only of his own salvation . . . while he left others to relieve the sufferings of his neighbors."[19]

After several months in the south, Gapon returned to St. Petersburg, certain that he did not want to take monastic orders but still unsure of his direction. With evident reluctance, he returned to the academy to repeat his first year. Friends from the Crimea urged him to consider giving up the priesthood, an idea that Father Georgii seems to have considered seriously. In November 1899, a few weeks after his return from the south, he wrote to one of his friends that he had taken to heart the advice "to take on himself, under the banner of Christ's cross, serious work with the goal of bringing good to the people and easing their suffering."[20] As a result, he had decided to pursue his old dream of studying at the university to become a doctor. However, shortly after he came to this difficult decision he received a letter from his father reminding him of his family's expectations of him. As he explained to the same correspondent in his next letter, his concern for his parents' peace of mind led him to decide finally that he would remain a priest despite his doubts. He justified his final decision in words that he would repeat again at other critical moments in his career, saying that he would find his own peace and happiness in the total sacrifice of himself and his interests for the good of others.[21] He resumed his studies but vowed to devote his energies to a more worthy cause.[22]

"AMONG THE OUTCASTS"—

Gapon's Missionary Work

One of the themes of Father Georgii's autobiography was his fierce commitment to the needs of the poor, which he connected to his own humble background and the formative experiences of his childhood and young adulthood. Those he named as his heroes all gained his admiration through their willingness to sacrifice everything for the good of others: Jesus Christ, the saints, the Cossacks, the populist revolutionaries. Likewise, his interest in Tolstoy focused on the author's argument that the essence of Christianity was self-sacrificing service to others. From his earliest days as a preacher his sermons focused on the importance of demonstrating love for one's neighbor through charity toward him. He despised his fellow clergymen precisely because he thought they seemed too concerned about their careers to care much for the needs of their parishioners. He sought to escape the bog of complacency himself by seeking out those who struggled: while at the seminary, he went out to those on the streets to hear the stories of the beggars and the outcasts and to give them comfort; at his little Poltava church, he organized his first society for the aid of the poor.

In St. Petersburg, Father Georgii quickly discovered there were many opportunities for him to pursue his charitable vocation. Already during his first year at the academy, Father Georgii was invited to give lectures at the nearby Pokrovskaia church for the diocesan missionary fraternity.[23] Although the church was located in a heavily working-class district, its focus was not on charity but Orthodox proselytism: its clergy debated sectarians, tried to convert Jews and Protestants, and explained church dogma to Orthodox believers. This was not the sort of work that Father Georgii was normally interested in, but he eagerly accepted the invitation and threw himself into the work. Soon, he was preaching passionate sermons on the importance of mutual assistance and self-improvement and lobbying the clergy of the church to organize a workers' mutual aid society. They rejected the notion out of hand. Father Georgii promptly resigned in disgust, declaring that his views of the working classes' needs were incompatible with those of the missionary fraternity.[24]

Despite this initial disappointment, Father Georgii readily accepted another invitation to participate in the church's outreach work when he returned to the academy in the fall of 1899. This time, the invitation came from the same assistant director general of the Synod, Vladimir Sabler, who had supported Gapon's application to the academy. Sabler and his superior, Konstantin Pobedonostsev, were both patrons of a small church near the commercial docks of Vasilevskii Island known as the Galernaia Gavan' (Haven) district.[25] It was a poor and shabby quarter of the city, distant from the center and undeveloped due to its vulnerability to floods. The badly paid and overworked stevedores and shipbuilders lived there, along with the vagrants and outcasts that the police periodically drove out of the city's central districts. In the Haven, Father Georgii found himself in his element. The church was old and small, served by a single priest. It had a modest parish charitable society, dominated by Pobedonostsev, Sabler, and people from their elite social circle.[26] The Society of Moral-Religious Enlightenment had just opened a section there, but Father Georgii was the first volunteer they had recruited for the area.

He met the challenges of working in this depressed little church with characteristic enthusiasm. In a letter of 31 December 1899, Gapon wrote that this "serious work" that he had undertaken had revived his flagging spirits and made him realize once again how important such service was in sustaining his faith.[27] He was glad to report that his sermons on man's duty to his fellows and the happiness to be found in serving others were drawing hundreds and even thousands of people to his church and winning him a reputation in the district.[28] Through the late winter and spring of 1900 his letters show him to be happy with his work, confident of its usefulness, and proud of his success. His church overflowed with listeners of all classes—including high-ranking members of the clergy and even Pobedonost-sev himself—who came from all over the city to hear him speak. As he explained, his theme was always that of attaining happiness through Christian service: "My main thought in all of these lectures was [to communicate] that truth, which you have observed and which I know from my own life . . . that only through serious, honest and sustained labor in the spirit of Orthodoxy is it possible to attain a conditional, but nevertheless, higher level of human happiness."[29]

Father Georgii clearly enjoyed his success, but as usual he could not be satisfied with words alone. His organizational impulse manifested itself again in his ambitious plans to establish a Christian holiday society to help the workers of the docks district pass their days off with their families in sobriety. He planned for twelve branches in the Haven area alone and hoped to expand eventually to the rest of the city as well.[30] He first mentioned the plan to his correspondent in his letter of 31 December 1899. In March of 1900, he reported that the society was on the verge of realization: two hundred members had already registered, and the priest of the Haven church and the rector of the academy (where Gapon was still a student) had already approved. He explained that the members would attend the holiday society's services and lectures and support a local choir; in these activities, Father Georgii's holiday society resembled the kind of work done by the ORRP. However, in addition, the members of his society were to pledge to help each other become better educated and to give material assistance to each other in times of need.[31] Father Georgii's optimism about the project seemed confirmed when the naval ministry granted the Haven church a substantial sum of money that spring to build a library and reading room. In spite of this, the project did not win final approval from the Synod.[32] Sabler told Gapon that the church already had a mutual aid organization for flood victims and that nothing more was necessary. Father Georgii's reaction was typical: he fumed that the project was rejected because church officials were jealous of his popularity and were trying to diminish his influence on the people.[33]

Soon after this setback, in the summer of 1900, Father Georgii left the Haven district church to serve as a chaplain in a hospital for poor children in a different part of the city.[34] In the fall of 1900, he returned to the Haven area to accept a position as the priest of the church at the Blue Cross Orphanage with responsibilities as a catechist at the Olga poorhouse. Once again, his talents as a preacher began to draw large crowds to the small church.[35] Father Georgii, however, took little interest in either the orphanage or the poorhouse. Instead, he took time away from both his duties and his studies to visit the homeless who gathered in Haven Field and to tour the city's notoriously seedy night shelters, disguised at first but then in his priestly robes.[36] Before long, he began to concoct another plan to aid the poor souls he found in the city's shelters and on the streets. Early in 1901, he wrote a proposal to rehabilitate the city's poor by sending them to workhouses in the surrounding towns of the region. He envisioned that these workhouses would enable their inmates to acquire basic education, training in a useful skill, and the attitudes and habits necessary for success. The clergy would provide moral guidance through lectures and discussions while volunteers from the laity would administer the institutions and assist in all of the practical work.[37] Father Georgii devoted a great deal and energy and thought to developing this plan.[38] He collected more than seven hundred signatures in support of it and sent copies to the highest officials in the city's administration.[39] After several prominent laywomen became interested in Father Georgii's work, he began to dream that through their connections he might gain access to the empress herself and win her support for his project.[40] However, as with his earlier proposals this plan ultimately failed to gain official approval.

By the beginning of 1902, Father Georgii had reached an impasse in his clerical career. He had seen three of his projects to improve the lives of the city's poor and working classes turned down in less than three years. His frustration must have been intense. He was immensely popular among both the common folk and the city's upper crust; his sermons drew large crowds and his projects attracted much attention and support from prominent individuals in the city government and the central administration. And yet, he was not allowed to do what he most wanted. Perhaps he began to suspect that those in power were using his passion and his talent for their own ends. Other men might have accepted this situation, but Father Georgii was not the type. From his youth he had proved himself to be both impulsive and ambitious, a man with grand visions and an overbearing confidence in his ability to fulfill them, if only lesser men would let him. He was obviously a highly intelligent person, though not intellectually inclined, but blessed with energy, charisma, and an irresistible impulse to action. He charmed those in authority even while exasperating them. He had difficulty making friends among his peers in the clergy (with whom he probably never felt comfortable due to bitter memories of his early experiences in Poltava), but among the common folk he was deeply beloved. One of his classmates recalled that although Father Georgii had few friends at the academy, the residents at the Olga poorhouse adored him for his simplicity, his good humor, his love of music, and his unstinting charity. For humble folk, Father Georgii was a man after their own hearts. He was known to give away his coat and boots in the dead of winter, though he was too poor to replace what he so quickly surrendered.[41] But his sense of charity was combined with a great pride, which aggravated his emotional impulsiveness and made him sensitive and stubborn. He would not do anything if it could not be done his way. If that proved impossible he always found someone else to blame, portraying himself as a martyr who suffered for the people, unjustly repressed and persecuted by those who resented his vision and talent.

After his plan for the workhouses was tabled by the administration Father Georgii fell back on his independent work in the Haven district, spending more and more of his time there and completely neglecting his work at the academy. He did not show up for final exams in the spring of 1902 and consequently was expelled from the school.[42] He had trouble at his place of employment as well. He accused the poorhouse's board of directors of using him for his wealthy connections, and complained about how small and poor the institution was for a man of his talents. Perhaps his complaints were an effort to salve a guilty conscience, however, for it became known in the summer of 1902 that the priest had become romantically involved with one of the orphan girls. The directors reluctantly decided to dismiss him. The meeting at which they informed Father Georgii of their decision degenerated into a heated argument. Father Georgii left in such a towering rage that the directors feared he might try to retaliate against them in some way, perhaps by burning down their building.[43] Instead, Gapon went into the streets of the Haven and aroused the working population to his defense, claiming to be a victim of the directors' jealousies and persecutions. His supporters publicly condemned the poorhouse's administration while collecting money to pay Gapon's debts.[44] For several months, Father Georgii looked in vain for another position. He found one that he wanted, but it was initially denied to him.[45] His efforts to regain admission to the academy were equally fruitless. Finally, Metropolitan Antonii (Vadkovskii) came to Gapon's rescue, intervening personally to persuade the faculty council at the academy to readmit him to the school for his final year and to obtain for him the position he sought at the Red Cross Society. Once again, Father Georgii was saved from suffering the full consequences of his hotheaded actions by the patronage of a powerful member of the church administration. Father Georgii was grateful but more determined than ever to pursue his own agenda regardless of the cautionary advice his superiors gave him. His unchecked pride and heedless ambition would soon produce consequences that even the extravagant imagination of Father Georgii could scarcely have dreamed.

STRANGE BEDFELLOWS—
Zubatov's Association and Gapon's Assembly

Some time during those difficult weeks in the fall of 1902, Father Georgii received a visit from an agent of the secret police (the Okhrana, whose mission was to discover and defuse political plots against the government). Father Georgii recalled that the agent was friendly and seemed sympathetic to his ideas. Shortly after their first meeting, the agent introduced Father Georgii to the new chief of the secret police in St. Petersburg, Sergei Mikhailovich Zubatov.[46] Zubatov catered to Father Georgii's vanity by telling him that he had heard of the influence he had over the city's working classes and that he wanted to discuss cooperating with him to establish a new kind of workers' organization, one that would be legal and under the protection of the police.[47] Its aim would be to help the workers improve their economic condition by educating them about economic matters and helping them to negotiate better working conditions with their employers. At the same time, the organization would promote workers' loyalty to the tsarist political system. Zubatov had already established a successful workers' organization of this type in Moscow and was supervising the formation of others in Vil'na and Odessa. In these other cities Zubatov had worked with a range of people: liberal intellectuals, repentant revolutionaries, and members of the clergy. The clergy had played a particularly important role in the Moscow organization.[48] Father Georgii seemed perfectly suited to take a leading role in St. Petersburg: he had experience with the working classes and he was popular among them; moreover, he was ambitious but frustrated, a man who could be manipulated if approached the right way.[49]

In his politically motivated autobiography, Father Georgii emphasized his distaste for the organs of tsarist authority. He declared that he always distrusted Zubatov and played along with him only to discover more about his plans so that he could turn them to his own purposes. As proof, Father Georgii pointed out that he criticized Zubatov's Moscow organization to I. S. Sokolov, whom Zubatov had brought up from Moscow to head the new organization in St. Petersburg.[50] Father Georgii also claimed (though it is hard to believe him) that at one of his meetings with Zubatov he disputed the need for autocracy in Russia and proposed a constitutional regime instead; he also asserted that he defended the intelligentsia against Zubatov's condemnation. After he visited Zubatov's organization in Moscow, Gapon said he concluded that the society was a sham that offered the workers nothing. In January of 1903 he submitted a report to the city prefect General N.V. Kleigels and Metropolitan Antonii critiquing Zubatov's project and advising against the church's involvement in it.[51] Although he continued to meet with Zubatov afterward he did *not* take part in the workers' association Zubatov founded toward the end of 1902. Although Gapon later suggested that his unusual reserve was the result of his qualms about working with the secret police, it is more likely that his real reasons were personal. In the previous two years Father Georgii had worked in three different missions, each of which had seemed to promise him the opportunity he badly wanted to make a real difference in the lives of the city's working people. To each, he had dedicated his energy and his considerable talent, and on each occasion he had tried to take the work one step further. But each time he had encountered opposition that proved impossible to overcome, despite his charm and his high connections. He had good reason to be wary of being recruited to yet another kind of mission that would use his charisma without letting him have any say in the program. Curbing his impulsiveness (for once), Gapon decided to wait.

By the time Gapon submitted his report on Zubatov's project, the secret police chief's men had already begun their work.[52] They organized the first meetings in November of 1902, advertising them at the factories with handbills and promoting them through Moscow workers who had St. Petersburg connections. Sokolov chaired the meetings and Zubatov himself came to speak in order to persuade the workers that the new society was legal.[53] Once they had attracted a few local workers into their circle, the group applied to the municipal authorities for permission to organize formally as a society for workers' self-improvement and mutual aid. The local department of police granted permission, explaining in its report that the society might help prevent the formation of illegal unions led by revolutionaries.[54] The group then approached Metropolitan Antonii for assistance. On his advice, the workers turned to the Society for Moral-Religious Enlightenment for help in organizing lectures for their members.[55] The ORRP welcomed the opportunity to extend its outreach to the working class further. On 2 February 1903, the society opened its large hall at the Trinity church (Moscow district) to a crowd of two thousand workers who gathered there to celebrate the opening of the St. Petersburg Workingmen's Association. The local church leaders demonstrated strong support for the new organization: there were speeches from Antonii (Vadkovskii), metropolitan of St. Petersburg; Bishop Sergii (Stragorodskii), the rector of the ecclesiastical academy; and archpriest Filosof Ornatskii, the president of the ORRP. The speakers praised the association's goals and offered to extend them whatever assistance they needed to promote the spiritual development of the workers and a spirit of brotherly love and support among all men.[56]

Although the church was supportive of the association, many other important groups and individuals in the city were not. The members of the Russian Assembly, a conservative organization of nobles closely connected with Emperor Nicholas II, had declined to support Zubatov's project when he presented it to them in December of 1902. The conservative press withheld their support as well.[57] The city prefect, the local factory inspector, and the minister of finance were all caught by surprise when the association went public, but they were quick to make their complaints once it opened.[58] Working-class activists strongly opposed the new organization, too. Hecklers repeatedly disrupted the association's first meetings; they exposed the leaders' connection to the secret police and accused them of betraying the true interests of the working class.[59] Under these pressures, the association did not attain much popular success in St. Petersburg. Moreover, in the capital it had to compete with the long-established ORRP and the Alexander Nevskii Temperance Society, which already offered similar programs of self-education, moral self-improvement, and material assistance for workers.

Father Georgii attended some of the association's meetings, but only as an observer. Still hoping to establish his own workers' organization, he began to consider ways in which he might be able to use Zubatov's group for his own purposes. A split that developed in the association in the spring of 1903 offered the opportunity he sought. A group of workers who objected to the dominant role of the police in the association formed a faction they called the "Independents." They complained about the association to the minister of finance, Sergei Witte, who had opposed Zubatov's organization. He encouraged them to boycott it. Having failed to stop Zubatov from establishing the association, Witte evidently hoped to weaken it from within by fostering a schism.[60] Although the available evidence is ambiguous, it seems that Father Georgii became associated with the Independents early in the spring of 1903. One of the archival documents published by the Bolsheviks in the 1920s is a letter dated 13 March 1903 in which a group of workers asked the rector of the academy to request the metropolitan to allow the student Father Georgii Gapon to open one of their meetings with a prayer and deliver a sermon. The request was approved.[61] Only a few weeks later in April of 1903, a group of workers petitioned the Ministry of Finance to allow them to organize a society for mutual aid and self-improvement, stating that they especially wished to study the factory laws and other subjects related to their work.[62] The petition indicated that the group had already received the approval of the city prefect for their organization; Kleigels had also opposed Zubatov's association and may well have welcomed the formation of a rival group, as Witte did. Although it is not certain that the group whose request Kleigels approved in April of 1903 was the same as the one that had asked the metropolitan's permission for Gapon's services in March of 1903, or that either was identical with the "Independents" who threatened to split the association, the timing of the groups' appearances and their connections with persons of known sympathies and antipathies toward Zubatov's project suggest that they *were* likely the same group—that is, a group of workers originally involved in Zubatov's association who came together with Father Georgii in the spring of 1903 to establish a *separate* workers' society, ostensibly for the same purposes as the association but independent of its leadership and under the protection of the association's critics in the administration.

Gapon's association with the nascent workers' group is suggested by other evidence. The socialist worker-revolutionary A. E. Karelin, who became one of the leaders of the Assembly of Russian Workers and a passionate defender of Gapon, recalled that he became acquainted with Father Georgii in the spring of 1903 at the meetings of one of the church-based temperance societies. He remembered that Father Georgii had struck him and his fellow workers as "a different sort" of clergyman because he seemed to be genuinely interested in the workers themselves and in what they really needed to improve their lives.[63] Another worker who had been personally recruited by Zubatov to the association the previous fall also stated that he had become acquainted with Gapon in April of 1903 when he visited him at the academy to find out about a new workers' group, which he believed had already been approved by Witte.[64] It is even possible that Father Georgii was the real author of the petition submitted to Witte in April 1903. In his memoirs, he said that at Zubatov's request he wrote a report about the importance of the workers' organizations that was submitted to Witte by a deputation of workers who presented the report as their own.[65] Although Gapon initially associated the report with Zubatov's response to the Odessa strike of July 1903, he followed his account of it with a description of how he came to be involved with a group of workers seeking to form an organization separate from Zubatov's in early May of 1903. This suggests that the report may have been written in the spring rather than the summer and that it may have been connected with Gapon's meeting with a group of five artisans who visited him at the academy to persuade him to join Zubatov's organization "in order to capture it for our own use."[66] Zubatov, aware that Witte was promoting a split in the association, may have hoped that he could maintain control of the splinter group through Father Georgii. Certainly, the circumstances surrounding the origins of the Assembly of Russian Workers are murky, but it is evident that the political situation was extremely delicate: Zubatov's opponents were plotting to break up the association, while at the same time some of its members were conspiring to turn the association to their own purposes; meanwhile, Zubatov was scheming to outwit both his foes and his false friends to achieve his own objectives.

After the initial meeting with the workers who visited him in April or May of 1903, Father Georgii did not immediately take any further steps to organize the workers. He finally graduated from the academy and began looking for a position in the city. During the summer months he remained in contact with Zubatov.[67] However, in late August Zubatov was summarily dismissed from his position for the role his workers' organization had played in that summer's massive strike in Odessa. Only then did Father Georgii and his associates finally move to establish their own group.[68] They began by renting a room on the Vyborg side for meetings of their "club," electing Gapon the club's president, and opening a workers' tearoom.[69] At first, they were cautious about defining the nature of the club and its purposes. Their first concern was to establish the group's financial independence: a police agent who attended one of their meetings in early September reported that the members spent most of their time discussing the club's financial matters.[70] The second concern was to work out the details of the organization, beginning with the group's name. After some discussion, the leaders settled on the Assembly of Russian Factory and Mill-workers of the City of St. Petersburg, a name that had "a very traditionalist form with Slavophile connotations [and] a nationalist coloration."[71] They also designed a seal that included the cross, despite the objections of some of the workers. Father Georgii insisted on the cross because it was personally im-

portant to him as a symbol of self-sacrifice.[72] It connected the assembly
with his earlier efforts to live out his understanding of Christianity through
loving service to others.

Father Georgii also drafted a charter for the assembly, working on the
document for several weeks in September and early October of 1903. In addition, he composed a long memo explaining the purpose of the assembly,
how it would be run and why it was needed.[73] In composing these documents, Father Georgii was confronted with a challenging task. He and his
associates had all been connected in some way to Zubatov and his association and risked being tainted by the opposition that project had engen-
dered and its ultimate failure.[74] Gapon had to demonstrate that the assembly was separate and distinct from Zubatov's association and that it posed
no threat to the establishment. Many of the statute's provisions were written expressly to allay the authorities' potential concerns. It was to be
closely supervised by the city prefect and the police; its leading members
were to be held personally responsible for any breaches of order or financial
regularity.[75] The leaders were to be members of the clergy or educated laymen, and all members of the assembly were to be both Christian and Russian.[76] Throughout both documents, Father Georgii repeatedly emphasized
that the assembly would educate its working-class members "in the spirit of
Russian national consciousness," a code expression for teaching them to be
loyal to the Orthodox church and the emperor.[77]

While distancing the assembly from its immediate predecessor, Father
Georgii also had to find a way to distinguish his group from the dozens of
church-based outreach organizations that already existed in the city. This
was difficult given that he was a clergyman whose practical experience with
the needs of urban workers had been acquired through service in such missions. Indeed, the assembly strongly resembled the city's most successful
outreach organization, the Nevskii Society, in its emphasis on the importance of teaching workers to use their free time wisely. Drinking, gambling,
and loitering were forbidden. Instead, the assembly proposed to sponsor a
choir to sing sacred and secular music, to organize a library and reading
room, to host evening concerts for workers and their families, and to
arrange religious-moral discussions and lectures.[78] What was most striking
and unusual about the assembly was not its agenda or its activities but its
approach, which was distinguished by a relentless insistence on the empowerment of the workers. Despite being supervised by members of the
clergy and educated lay persons, its purpose was to serve the needs of the
workers as *they* defined them. Although one of the purposes of the assembly was to offer the workers guidance about responsible living, the main focus was to help the members of the assembly to identify their wants and
needs and assist them in developing programs to fulfill *their* goals. The membership of the assembly was restricted to factory workers, with the exception
of a small handful of supervisors from educated society. Employers and fore-
men could donate money to the assembly but they could not participate in

it in any way. They could not even attend meetings unless given special permission. If a worker advanced to the position of foreman he had to leave the assembly.[79] The assembly's club was to be a place that fostered responsibility, independence, self-respect, and solidarity among the workers. Father Georgii argued that by giving workers the opportunity to manage their free time and their income in an atmosphere that offered both support and guidance, the assembly would enable its members to develop the values and the knowledge they needed to improve the general situation of their class through peaceful, legal means.[80] To this end, the assembly proposed to provide a forum for workers to discuss their economic needs and learn about the laws that affected them. The assembly was also to help workers learn to help themselves and each other by establishing a basic system of social welfare organized around mutual aid funds and cooperative ventures.[81]

These measures for workers' empowerment were remarkably bold, given that at this time in Russia unions were forbidden and strikes were outlawed. Nevertheless, in the dozen years before the establishment of the assembly, revolutionary groups targeting factory centers had multiplied, and the number of strikes and other industrial actions had increased. Naturally, the government was wary of any plan that proposed to allow workers to gather and talk about their grievances. The outcome of Zubatov's work—the great strike that had paralyzed Odessa in the preceding summer—seemed to confirm the authorities' fear that allowing the workers to have any kind of organization fomented public disorder and threatened to trigger a revolution. In response to this fear, Father Georgii argued that the workers could not help but be aware of their economic and legal disadvantages and that this awareness, increasing over time, would lead them to organize for the improvement of their situation regardless of efforts to prevent their doing so. He contended that instead of alienating the workers by repressing their natural and irresistible inclinations, the government should help them by allowing them to organize under the guidance of a trustworthy leader who could assist them in attaining their goals in a way that did not threaten the interests of the state.[82]

In his memorandum, Gapon asserted that only the assembly could serve the needs of both the workers and the state successfully. Other groups that claimed to assist the workers to the benefit of the state all fell short. In his view, the educated laity who talked so much about the needs of the narod did not really understand the workers or love them and were unable to devote themselves heart and soul to the "sacred cause" of educating the workers in their own interest. The state's temperance societies demonstrated contempt for the workers by providing them with cheap entertainment rather than education. The church's efforts to assist the workers were hampered by the inadequacy of the parish system and the clergy's reluctance to address economic and social problems directly. Zubatov's experiment had demonstrated that the police could not control the workers effectively either; the association had not improved the workers' situation at all and had threatened the stability of the state.[83] In contrast, Gapon argued that the assembly combined a genuine concern for the workers' spiritual and material needs under a leadership that supported the government but was not controlled by it. In conclusion, Father Georgii cautioned the authorities to heed the advice of Gamaliel, a Jewish elder who advised the leaders of Israel not to persecute the apostles for preaching in Jerusalem: "Leave these men alone! For if their purpose and activity is of human origin, it will fail. But if it is from God, then you will not be able to stop them. Be careful that you do not find yourselves opponents of God."[84] Father Georgii thus suggested that his mission was also from God and virtually demanded the authorities' approval. Surprisingly, they authorized the assembly's charter in November of 1903.[85]

SACRIFICE—
The Massacre of Bloody Sunday

From the time the assembly went public to the day its supporters marched on the Winter Palace, the organization's history has been ably recounted by others; only a brief description of the course of events in that year is necessary here.[86] The assembly held its first public meeting in early April 1904. During that spring and summer, it grew steadily. Of the 150 people who attended the first meeting, 73 became members. By the end of the first month, three hundred people were on its rolls.[87] Father Georgii was encouraged by the assembly's apparent success but hoped for further expansion.[88] Concerned that the Zubatovite taint would keep away the more skilled and educated workers who had previous experience with the revolutionary underground, Gapon formed a secret council of radical workers to articulate a hidden agenda referred to as the Program of the Five. It included measures "to eliminate the ignorance of, and arbitrariness toward, the people; to eliminate the poverty of the people; and to eliminate the oppression of labor by capital."[89] The council carefully promoted the secret program to trusted workers known to have socialist sympathies. The language and goals of this secret program echoed the radical literature of the revolutionary parties and thus won the support of workers who had suspected that the assembly was simply a revival of the association. By the end of June, the assembly had enrolled more than 700 members and established a branch location in the Narva Gates region for the workers of the giant Putilov factory.[90]

During the late summer and fall of 1904, political events strongly influenced the development of the assembly. After the minister of the interior Viacheslav K. Pleve was assassinated in July, his replacement, Prince Dmitrii Sviatopolk-Mirskii, tried to alleviate the growing political discontent by easing restrictions on freedom of speech, press, and assembly. Many of those belonging to educated society entertained high hopes for significant changes in the political order. Nourished by the atmosphere of liberation and expectation, the assembly continued to grow. A general meeting at the end of August drew over one thousand participants, and more than two thousand people attended a concert hosted by the assembly in September. By October the assembly had nine branches and about five thousand members; by the beginning of November they had added two more branches and close to two thousand new members.[91] In October and November, Father Georgii established contacts with both radical and liberal intellectuals in the capital. He met with leaders from the Social Democrats, the Socialist Revolutionaries, and the Union of Liberation to discuss the assembly's response to political developments. He also invited university students and educated laymen of different political affiliations to address the assembly's meetings, which were opened to journalists.[92] The secret council began to discuss whether the time had come to act on the Program of the Five, perhaps by writing a petition to the government similar to those sponsored by the Union of Liberation.[93] Father Georgii did begin work on such a petition, basing it on the program that he and the radical workers had drawn up the previous spring.[94] Some members of the council wanted to present it immediately, hoping to take advantage of the open struggle that was raging between the liberal opposition and the government. But Father Georgii urged caution, fearing that the time was not yet right for the workers to join the fray. He wanted to bring the workers out in support of the liberals, as his contacts at the Union of Liberation urged him to do, but he feared that the workers' own demands would be neglected in favor of the liberals' program. After all, his own past experiences had made him very cautious about letting his work be used by others to promote their own agendas. Father Georgii's caution was supported by the membership of the assembly. The leadership presented the idea of a petition to a general meeting of the assembly in late November. Despite the leaders' endorsement of the proposal, the members voted it down. However, the idea of submitting a petition and discussions about its possible content remained active in the assembly through December. The petition was finally approved by the assembly's members in citywide meetings held in the first week of January 1905.[95]

Father Georgii had always felt that words alone were not enough to bring real change. Even while discussions about the petition continued in the assembly, he looked for the opportunity to take action. In early December, two St. Petersburg factories conducted successful strikes aimed at shortening the working day and compelling changes in the factories' administrations.[96] These examples may have led Father Georgii and the members of the council to consider whether the assembly, whose members worked in many of the large factories in the city center, might use some kind of mass action as a means of bringing the Program of the Five to public attention in a dramatic way. The opportunity to act came when four workers at the Putilov factory were dismissed from their positions, allegedly because they were members of the assembly. The assembly's leaders held a series of meetings in late December to present their plan of action to the members, who finally agreed to support a strike if the fired workers were not reinstated and if the foreman who fired them was not dismissed.[97] Father Georgii and several of the council members acted as mediators but the director of the Putilov factory was intransigent. On the morning of 3 January the Putilov workers walked out, crippling one of the country's major armaments manufacturers in the midst of the war with Japan; that circumstance alone was sufficient to transform a labor dispute into a political crisis. Over the next five days the strike spread through the city as the members of the assembly working at other factories struck, convincing many of their co-workers to walk out with them. Soon all of the major industrial producers—several of which were engaged in fulfilling government war contracts—as well as many smaller concerns were forced to shut down.[98] Although the initial demands of the Putilov workers were quickly met once they struck, the workers then presented new demands that focused on reducing work hours, increasing wages, improving labor conditions, and expanding the workers' role in factory administration.[99] Negotiations on these issues went nowhere. The government found itself at an impasse—unable to impose a peaceful resolution yet reluctant to use force to break the strike.[100]

The moment had come for a decisive action. Father Georgii was ready for it. Indeed, his whole life had prepared him for the day that he would lead a great procession of the people to stand before the tsar with a petition for justice in their hands and a plea for mercy on their lips. With the Program of the Five before his eyes, Gapon worked on the final draft of his petition on 7–8 January, consulting with members of his council, representatives from the revolutionary parties, members of the Liberation movement, and journalists from the capital's liberal and radical newspapers. As he labored over the petition in feverish excitement, he was inspired by the popular image of himself as a prophet of the people, a man who stood fearless before the kings of the world to proclaim God's truth.[101] In the introduction to the petition, he called on the tsar to recognize that the divine will by which he ruled the Russian people imposed on him a moral obligation to uphold truth and justice for all.[102] He was obliged to listen to the humble requests of his subjects, who came to him seeking only what was just, trusting in him to bring salvation to the country through right action. Father Georgii thus appealed to the traditional representation of the tsar's role and his relation to the people, using an exalted language thoroughly imbued with religious phrases and images. One might suspect that this approach was merely a clever ploy, a fiction that Gapon used to disguise the thoroughly modern demands for individual freedoms and political rights contained in the petition. But as Richard Wortman has demonstrated, Nicholas II himself believed deeply in certain elements of that national myth, particularly in the idea that there existed a direct, mystical bond between himself and the narod that was expressed through their shared piety and mediated by charismatic holy men. Given this scenario, Father Georgii's approach to

the emperor seems ideal as a means of both communicating popular grievances and persuading the tsar that he had a responsibility to address them.

Moreover, Father Georgii himself seems to have succumbed to the pas-
sions that had long surged through his soul like the tides. At a meeting
with representatives from the revolutionary parties on 7 January, Gapon
shared his vision of the crucial moment in which he would personally present the petition to the tsar:

> We will go on Sunday to the palace and present our petition. If they will let us
> pass unmolested, we will enter onto the palace square and call the tsar out of
> Tsarskoe Selo. We will wait for him until evening. When he comes, I will ap-
> proach him with a deputation of several workers, give him the petition, and
> say, "Your Highness, you must give the people their freedom." And if he
> agrees, then we will demand that he give his oath there before the people.
> Only then will we return to our work.[103]

Such a scene could not possibly have been realized—the tsar responding
humbly to the people's summons, appearing before them alone in the palace
square and meekly accepting the words of the priest-prophet like an Old Testament king, agreeing instantly to swear a public oath that he would grant their
demands. Another source reports that Gapon pursued this extravagant flight of
fancy further in talking to a close colleague, saying,

> If the tsar receives our delegation, I will fall on my knees before him and con-
> vince him to sign an amnesty for all politicals before my eyes. Then the tsar
> and I will step out onto the balcony and I will read his decree to the people.
> There will be general rejoicing. From this moment I will become the first
> counselor of the tsar and practically the ruler of Russia. Then we will begin to
> build the Kingdom of God on earth.[104]

This scenario was, if possible, more unlikely than the first, but it offers insight into the way that Father Georgii thought about his actions and his
role in the historical drama of those days. He thought of himself primarily
as a religious leader, inspired to act in the name of the suffering people of
Russia by the desire to establish a society governed according to the principles of divine truth and justice, a society that would provide the foundation for the Kingdom of God on earth.

Just as success would bring about the emergence of the Kingdom of God
in Russia, so would failure would bring about apocalyptic disaster. If the
tsar did not come, if the petition were refused, if the soldiers leveled
their guns at the people—then the only response would be to declare
the tsar's authority illegitimate and prepare for revolution.[105] Balanced
between the hope of heaven and the fear of hell, Father Georgii made
his final preparations for the march that would bring the petition to the
tsar at the Winter Palace. In his autobiography, he recalled how he felt

when he visited his rooms for the last time on the evening of 7 January, the very day that he made the speeches quoted above:

> For the last time I looked at my three little rooms, through which had passed so many of the best working men and women, and also so many poor and miserable creatures, and where so many passionate speeches and discussions had taken place. I looked at the big wooden cross which I had bought and kept in my bedroom, and which I loved because it always reminded me of the sacrifice of Christ for the sake of the people. . . . It was with a heart full of grief, but also of unchangeable determination, that I left my house, not to see it again.[106]

Gapon was ready to be a hero, but if that role was denied to him he was equally ready to be a martyr, inspired as he had been throughout his life by the example of self-sacrifice he saw in Jesus Christ and the saints. That motif of salvation through sacrifice appeared again when he comforted those who worried about the risks the marchers faced, saying, "Do not grieve if there are victims. It is . . . here in the streets of the capital that blood, if it be spilt, will prepare the ground for the resurrection of Russia."[107]

Well before dawn on 9 January, tens of thousands of people gathered at the assembly's clubhouses all over the city.[108] Having listened to the petition read and explained at continuous meetings the day before, they were ready to march in support of its demands.[109] As the processions from the different quarters of the capital progressed toward the city's center, they encountered armed military units.[110] In some cases, the crowds were turned back without violence or dispersed to find less obvious ways to arrive at their destination. At several points, including on Nevskii Prospect near the Winter Palace, the crowds were fired upon with live ammunition and attacked by saber-wielding cavalry. Father Georgii himself never reached the palace. After the contingent from the Narva Gates district was stopped by imperial guards firing upon them, Gapon was forcibly seized by his own supporters and removed from the mêlée.[111] Panic and chaos spread through the capital as the short winter afternoon began to grow dark. The march to the Winter Palace had failed. The petition was never formally presented to Nicholas II, who remained holed up in his suburban palace at Tsarskoe Selo throughout the day. But the massacre of unarmed civilians by the government's armed forces outraged people throughout the country. Within a week, a massive revolution against the autocracy was under way.[112]

"AN UNWORTHY PRIEST"—
Gapon and the Russian Orthodox Church

For fifteen years—from the time he was a student at the Poltava seminary until the day that he marched on the Winter Palace—Father Georgii's clerical vocation had been shaped by his belief that the Gospels called on all humans to love and serve each other and through mutual support and cooperation to build a more just society. He had explained his view of the church's mission most clearly when he first asked the metropolitan of St. Petersburg to approve the plans for the assembly, saying,

> A servant of Christ must show the people, not by words but by deeds, that he is their guide. You cannot deny that the life of our workmen is terrible: they have no joy and therefore they take to drink. Let us give them some healthy amusement if we want them to be sober and moral. And we must also try to better their material conditions if we are to help them in a better life. In helping people to help themselves, the church also has a great task.[113]

Father Georgii's conception of the church's mission to the world was hardly unique to him. Many in the St. Petersburg clergy shared Gapon's belief that the church should work to improve the moral and material lives of the people through charity, education, and leadership on the moral-religious issues of the day. The majority of the city's clergy were personally involved in outreach work through the parish charities, the temperance societies, and the Society for Moral-Religious Enlightenment. Much of Father Georgii's practical experience in outreach had come through his own service in these church-based organizations. Although he criticized them, one must recognize his debt to them; it is unlikely that he could have attained the success he did with the assembly if the ground had not already been thoroughly prepared by the work of hundreds of other hard-working, self-denying clergymen who never became as famous as he. There *was* something that set Father Georgii apart from his fellow priests, however. One might say it was the force of his personality, which contributed to his popularity among ordinary folk, his unusual influence on people of authority, and his inability to get along with his peers. Beneath his vanity and pride, his choleric impatience and willfulness, one senses the raw, awkward peasant boy who knew what it was like to be despised and mistreated: gifted, yet always struggling to be acknowledged and respected by those who took the privileges of the comfortably born for granted. Perhaps this explains why Gapon was so touchy and difficult, why he refused to carry out his work in humble anonymity the way other priests did and why he resisted cooperating with his fellow clergymen in service to their common mission.

Regardless of the qualities of Father Georgii's personality, he could not have accomplished much if the authorities in the local government, especially those in the church, had suppressed him. In fact, from the time he was a mere child until the very eve of the Winter Palace march Father Georgii found an astonishing degree of support and encouragement from both the hierarchy and the administration: his school teachers praised his work and urged him to continue with his studies; the bishop of Poltava and the assistant director general of the Synod assisted his application to the ecclesiastical academy; the academy's rector indulged his requests for privileges and tolerated his poor academic performance; the metropolitan of St. Petersburg intervened several times to rescue him from trouble and to encourage him to continue his clerical career. Knowing the role Father Georgii played in the events that sparked the 1905 revolution, the authorities' long history of support for this difficult young priest seems surprising.[114] Yet, given the work of the church in the capital in the decades leading up to 1905, their attitude is really not difficult to explain. The men who led the St. Petersburg church around the turn of the century were the very ones who, ten to twenty years before, had developed and promoted the ideas and organizations that made Father Georgii's work possible: the practice of regular public preaching; the idea of pastoral care; the concept of a practical, "this-worldly" Christianity centered on service to others; the well-developed infrastructure of church-based charities, clerical temperance societies, and extra-liturgical instruction. They welcomed Father Georgii precisely because his talents and ambitions were so similar to their own ideas about the church and its mission.

This attitude of patient tolerance and paternal support for Father Georgii's work extended to the assembly he helped establish. The rector of the academy gave his permission for Father Georgii's initial involvement with the workers seeking to defect from Zubatov's association. Metropolitan Antonii certainly came to know something about Father Georgii's new project during the summer of 1903, but he did not interfere. In fact, the metropolitan made the work easier by giving the impoverished clergyman some money and a good job at the church of the St. Petersburg prisoner transport prison.[115] While Antonii did hesitate to approve Father Georgii's election as president of the assembly early in 1904, his objection had nothing to do with the assembly's constituency or goals. Rather, the metropolitan was offended by the idea that a priest, whom he believed had a certain dignity to maintain, could participate in a social club that allowed dancing and secular music.[116] Despite his disapproval of this aspect of the assembly's program the metropolitan did not interfere with Father Georgii's work. As the assembly's membership ballooned in the fall of 1904 and its members began to discuss first a petition and then a strike, local church authorities remained inactive, neither supporting Father Georgii nor restraining him. Even after the workers had gone out on strike and Gapon was personally involved in negotiations with the factory administration and local civil authorities, neither the metropolitan nor even the director general of the Synod offered any objections. It was only on 7 January, when the strike had paralyzed the city and plans for the march to the Winter Palace were being finalized, that the metropolitan finally summoned Gapon for an explanation.[117] When the first summons went unanswered he issued another the following day, which Gapon also refused.[118] No further actions were taken: there was no warning against the march, no condemnation of the assembly, no public censure of Father Georgii. No member of the hierarchy ventured into the streets to address the marchers, either in favor of the action or in opposition to it. This silence is striking: it seems as if the church itself was waiting with bated breath to see what the outcome of Father Georgii's extraordinary initiative would be.[119]

The awful and unexpected events of 9 January were a shock to the St. Petersburg clergy and the church administration. In the chaos that reigned for several days in the city after the Winter Palace march, the leaders of the church maintained their public silence, leaving the city's clergy to respond to the events on their own. Many individual clergymen condemned the violence and called for peace, though most hesitated to pass judgment on either the government's use of force or on the demonstration that had precipitated the clash.[120] As a group, the city's clergy had their first opportunity to discuss the events and their significance on 11 January, when they convened a pastoral convention chaired by the president of the ORRP and involving many of the city's non-monastic clergy.[121] Their first order of business was to review what was known about the developments leading up to Bloody Sunday. According to the summary of this discussion submitted to the director general of the Synod as part of the annual diocesan report for 1905, the clergy of St. Petersburg professed to know little about the assembly and the role that Father Georgii played in it. They recalled that a workers' organization had been founded at the end of 1902 (Zubatov's association) and that the Society for Moral-Religious Enlightenment had initially provided some lectures for them. Clergymen from the ORRP said that the society had stopped its lectures after a short time because the workers insisted that they address social and economic issues, which the ORRP lecturers were neither prepared nor willing to do. According to the report of the discussion, the other clergy of the city thought that Father Georgii had simply taken over the association after the ORRP stopped participating; under his leadership, they noted the group had been very successful. With regard to the events of 9 January, the clergy at the meeting agreed that Father Georgii could not have been the author of the majority of the petition. The introduction, with its strong moral-religious tone, they recognized as belonging to Gapon, but they believed the bulk of the petition's demands for political, legal, and economic reforms represented the influence of "criminal" elements, meaning the still-illegal opposition groups. The speakers whose remarks were noted in the report asserted that such political awareness was beyond the capacities of a "simple" priest and the uneducated factory workers. With a similar mixture of acknowledgment and exoneration, the clergy's discussion indicated that while they recognized Father Georgii as the leader of the march they believed that the violence had been caused by foreign political agitators who had mixed in with the crowd and inspired them to violent acts, which then provoked the authorities' strong (but perhaps justifiable) response. The official report demonstrates quite clearly the clergy's understanding of the stereotypes and assumptions that frequently shaped official conceptions of their subject population and their ability to manipulate these constructs to serve their own purposes.

It is impossible to know from this official source what the discussion at this meeting was really like or to what extent the opinions expressed represented the true thoughts of Father Georgii's fellow clergymen. The professions of ignorance about the origins of the assembly and Father Georgii's role in the events of 1904–1905 are scarcely credible, given the close-knit fabric of ecclesiastical life in the capital that is evident in so many other sources. Rather, what the official report seems to indicate is that in the days that followed the Winter Palace march, the city's clergy found themselves in a delicate situation. Father Georgii was one of their own; what he had said and done reflected on them in the eyes of the people, the nascent political organizations and the established authorities. They did not disavow his work completely, nor did they condemn him without reservation. Instead, they indicated support for the general idea of a workers' organization led by a member of the clergy. At the same time, they were careful to point out that members of the clergy were prohibited by law from discussing political issues in public or belonging to any type of political organization, a fact that was stated without endorsement. By acknowledging that a clergyman wrote the introduction to the petition, they may have been hinting at their sympathy with the introduction's claim that the government had a divinely mandated responsibility to ensure justice for the people; by rejecting the body of the petition, they indicated that they did not think the clergy should advocate specific economic and political demands. Significantly, they did not denounce the Putilov strike or the Winter Palace march or criticize the role that Father Georgii played in either event. They criticized only the violence that resulted from the march, for which they blamed neither their fellow priest nor the people but revolutionary bogeymen.

Having constructed a view of Father Georgii's work that tacitly approved some elements of it while criticizing others, the city's clergy then had to decide what their response to the events would be. Should the clergy continue developing its mission to the urban workers or give it up? After some discussion, they concluded that the clergy should pray for divine mercy for all, especially those who had died. A few thought that the clergy ought to preach on the events of Bloody Sunday, but the majority thought that the subject was too risky. This discussion naturally broadened to encompass the question of whether sermons should respond to any current events, and if so, then in what way. A few argued that sermons were most useful and interesting to listeners when they addressed the contemporary issues facing society. Others contended that the clergy's preaching should be concerned only with the exposition of the Gospels so as to avoid embroiling the clergy in the divisive political struggles that destroyed peace and order. The majority of the clergy believed that the best approach was to demonstrate the relevance of the Gospels to the present day through their own activities, as the clergy of the ORRP did. Although they did not adopt a general resolution on this issue the discussion indicates the range of views that existed on the question. When it came to deciding what the clergy might do besides preaching in the aftermath of Bloody Sunday, there was greater agreement. The majority believed that the church should not abandon its mission to the working class but instead should expand it.[122] Some advocated increasing the work of the Society for Moral-Religious Enlightenment at the factories; others proposed extending the program of the Religious-Enlightenment Union to include home visits. The participants discussed the possibility of establishing parishes with their own clergy and churches in the larger factories of the city; a special commission was formed to study the proposal.[123]

The more fundamental question underlying these particular debates concerned the church's relation to society. The group of young clergymen who had argued that current events and secular concerns should be addressed in sermons was the first to bring up the topic for debate. While they did not express open approval of Father Georgii's activities, they drew attention to his success in engaging the attention and affection of the city's workers. They believed that the number of people who followed Father Georgii's leadership "demonstrated what tremendous strength the church's claim to authority has for the majority of common workers and what a gigantic deciding force the church could be in the sphere of social-economic difficulties, if only it could discover how to participate actively in discussing such questions without contradicting its principles."[124] Father Georgii had been successful as a popular leader because he was willing to address the social and economic problems that affected the people's lives. While the outcome of the demonstration had been tragic, the basic principles of the assembly were sound. These priests urged their fellows to continue the work that Father Georgii had begun and learn from his mistakes. This assertion provoked heated debate, for while many of the other clergymen sympathized with the common people's plight they contended that the church had to remain aloof from political issues because they provoked anger and discord within the Orthodox community. Extensive discussions produced no agreement on this issue. The clergy concluded the meeting without establishing a common position on the relation of the church to current events.[125]

The day following the pastoral convention (12 January), the Synod issued its first official response to the events of 9 January: a terse decree reminding the clergy that existing laws required them to pronounce a prayer for the safety of the tsar and the eradication of sedition as well as a prayer for victory in the war as part of the daily liturgy.[126] The decree suggests that some members of the clergy were *not* adhering to the letter of the law in fulfilling the required prayers for the safety and success of the government.[127] Through this decree, the Synod expressed a position that was as close to political neutrality as possible, in that it indicated continued support for the established laws without offering approval for specific government leaders or actions. Two days later, on 14 January, the Synod issued a formal public statement.[128] After exhorting the Russian people to focus on the demands of the war with Japan, it denounced the disorders as a distraction, the work of agitators who accepted money from foreign agents to stir up the loyal but ignorant Russian folk against their divinely sanctioned leaders. Father Georgii was condemned as an "unworthy servitor of the church" who used his influence as a priest to lead his trusting flock astray. The statement concluded with the traditional counsels of the church: the people were urged to be patient and to respect the tsar and all established authorities. The clergy were instructed to teach the Word of God to all and to chastise those who fomented revolution. The government was advised to treat the people justly; the wealthy were counseled to be charitable; and the workers were told to work hard and shun wicked leaders.

On the same day the Synod issued instructions to the clergy that forbade them to offer public funeral services of any kind for those who had been killed in the Bloody Sunday massacre for fear that such services could encourage further demonstrations of political discontent. They were instructed to avoid all politics in their preaching and to urge the people to maintain peace and order.[129] The St. Petersburg clergy were convened again, this time by the authority of the metropolitan, who addressed the gathering at some length to explain his views on Father Georgii's work and its consequences.[130] The tone of this address resembled that of the discussion held during the first convention several days earlier: pity for the plight of the working people, sympathy for Father Georgii's work as a pastor, and condemnation of the "false agitators and criminal leaders" responsible for the disorders that led to bloodshed. Although the metropolitan criticized aspects of Father Georgii's character, he did not condemn the work he was doing; neither did he issue a clear statement of support for it. Instead, he pleaded ignorance and impotence: he had not really known what Gapon was doing and when he found out it was too late to stop him. The diocesan bureaucracy was already working on constructing a case against Father Georgii. On 21 January, the metropolitan submitted Gapon's service records to the consistory along with a list of the grounds on which he could be defrocked. The consistory suspended Father Georgii from his duties and summoned him to answer the charges against him before the diocesan court. Father Georgii did not appear, having already been smuggled out of the country by his supporters, so the consistory defrocked him in absentia.[131] Metropolitan Antonii approved the judgment on 4 March; the Synod confirmed it on 10 March.[132] In the meantime, the Synod issued an effusive declaration of approval for the steps the government was taking to address the workers' grievances.[133] The message signaled to the clergy that "not entering into politics" meant supporting the government uncritically while categorically denouncing its opponents.[134] This response to the political crisis did not enjoy strong support among the clergy of the capital. In fact, it aroused the outright opposition of that minority group of young priests who had encouraged their fellow clergymen to pursue Father Georgii's work more vigorously, setting the stage for the clash between the activists and the authorities that would erupt within the church in the midst of the 1905 revolution.

Father Georgii Gapon had been exactly the sort of active, popular young priest whom the church's leaders thought they needed to expand their outreach work further among the workers of the capital at the turn of the century. Despite his obvious character flaws and repeated conflicts with both peers and authority figures, he was protected and promoted throughout his short career by his superiors. Until 1904, there was little about either his ideas or his activities that seemed unusual. His interest in preaching and his dedication to social outreach work were shared both by the members of the older generation who dominated the ecclesiastical institutions of the capital and by his peers among the younger generation. The only difference was that Father Georgii's belief in the church's mission to the world was amplified by his personal desire to become a hero of the people and a martyr of the church by sacrificing himself totally to the cause that so many others served in a less dramatic fashion. The very extravagance of his action and his success in leading such large numbers of people on such a fantastic mission threw the contradictions in the church's mission into high relief and widened the cracks already developing in its edifice.

Shaken by the events of 9 January but still confident of the meaning of their mission, many of the clergy expressed their sympathy with the people and proposed to continue and even expand upon the work that they had been doing, unaware that this might now be perceived as a threat to the tottering political and social order. Others wanted to follow the path Father Georgii had blazed by engaging the church more deeply in the efforts to address critical social, economic, and political issues from a Christian viewpoint, regardless of whether that view supported the government or opposed it. The Synod declared, however, that the church was to uphold the government and avoid conflict. But conflict was unavoidable as the revolution of 1905 continued to develop, pulling the St. Petersburg clergy into its maelstrom.

RENEWING THE CHURCH

The Renovationists and Church Reform,

1905–1907

The events of 9 January 1905 precipitated the dénouement of a crisis that had been slowly developing for several decades over the question of the church's relation to modern society. As already seen, the educated clergy and devout lay people had been discussing certain aspects of this issue openly since the era of the Great Reforms. However, a critical topic had been excluded from this discussion: the church's role in the country's political system. The state had conscripted the Orthodox church to serve as one of the pillars of the autocracy, but the church itself had had little opportunity to conduct an *open, free,* and *critical* discussion of issues relating to its role in modern political life in the decades before 1905.[1] Consequently, when the revolutionary events of 1905–1906 severely rattled the framework of the system with which the structures of the church were—willingly or not—intertwined, the church suddenly found itself directly and abruptly confronted with a host of serious, difficult questions: should the church attempt to maintain its neutrality during the political struggle or should it commit itself to one side? If neutrality was undesirable or impossible, which side should the church support—the government or its opponents? If the church had to take part in the struggle, what means should it employ and how? What responsibility did the church have for bringing an end to the struggle? Should the church try to repair and strengthen what remained of the old political structures, or should it commit itself to the building of new ones? It should not be surprising that those who served in the church had different opinions on these subjects, for it was as deeply divided as any other institution in tsarist Russia. Among the clergy of the capital, a significant number of priests saw the revolution as an opportunity for a radical reform of the church based at least in part on the ideas about the church's purpose and activity that had evolved through the writing and work of the clergymen of the reform and post-reform generations. Yet these young priests' program of church renewal precipitated a bitter struggle within the church that eventually led to the ruination of some of the church's most promising young men at the same time that it seriously compromised the church's ability to respond effectively to the needs of modern Russian society.

SEEKING FREEDOM:
Church Reform and the Group of Petersburg Priests

The involvement of a St. Petersburg priest in the events that led to Bloody Sunday presented the clergy of the capital with an immediate and serious problem: should they reject Gapon's work completely and distance themselves from everything connected with him, or should they seek to affirm those elements of his mission that arose from the work that the city's clergy had been engaged in for more than a generation? Most of the clergy hesitated to condemn Father Georgii without reservation, but few were willing to endorse the ideas and activities that led to the Putilov strike and the march to the Winter Palace. However, at the first meeting of the city's clergy, convened just two days after Bloody Sunday, several young priests ventured to defend Gapon. While they regretted the results of the demonstration, they supported his basic ideas. They argued that the other clergy should imitate Father Georgii's willingness to concern himself with social, economic, and political issues because such secular concerns affected believers' religious lives.[2] However, a number of other priests disagreed strongly, and after heated discussion the meeting ended without producing any resolutions.[3]

Shortly after the pastoral convention, those who had spoken up in Gapon's favor met again to establish an informal discussion circle under the leadership of Father Peter M. Kremlevskii.[4] There were about twenty participants, mostly younger priests in their thirties (which made them about the same age as Gapon) who knew each other through the ecclesiastical academy or the Society for Moral-Religious Enlightenment.[5] After several meetings the group requested an appointment with the metropolitan of St. Petersburg.[6] As they later explained in their first publication, their primary goal was to persuade metropolitan Antonii that the church should not remain silent in the face of the repeated defeats in the war with Japan, the widespread workers' strikes, and the disorders in the streets of the capital. They argued that in such difficult times, people needed to hear the church's voice and to be guided by its leadership: "From all sides one hears demands, pleas, prayers full of spiritual suffering: they demand from us a positive and clear answer to the unavoidable questions of our society's life posed to us by our times."[7] These clergymen believed that their individual efforts as pastors to offer their parishioners moral and spiritual guidance were no longer enough; believers wanted the church as an institution to provide the leadership that Russia needed at this critical and confusing time.[8] In their view, the church's future depended on its willingness to respond seriously to these demands:

> For many, many people in this agitated and troubled time the question is now being decided, whether they will go forward under the wing of the Church or leave the Church behind as an institution that has outlived its time, connected by unbreakable threads to the old way of things. It is terrible to think that the eternal work of God is so connected with the fragile creations of men, that an incautious word might push someone away from the Church![9]

For this reason, the group believed it was of critical importance that the metropolitan work for the convening of an all-Russian church council "at which bishops together with pastors, freely elected from each diocese, and representatives of the laity can discuss all aspects of the contemporary situation of the church and resolve urgent church questions."[10] The council would enable the leaders of the church to hear the concerns of the laity and the clergy. It would also give them the opportunity to work with those groups to respond to the pressing issues facing the church in ways that would be consistent with the church's teachings and sensitive to believers' needs. The group received a sympathetic hearing. After a two-hour-long discussion with metropolitan Antonii the group received permission to continue their discussions and to communicate their conclusions to him in writing.

The Group of Petersburg Priests (as they had come to call themselves by the spring of 1905) was not the first to raise the issue of church reform. Support for the convening of an episcopal council to discuss reforms for the church had been growing rapidly among the hierarchs since the early 1890s. The subject was broached to the general public when it was introduced for debate at the meetings of the Religious-Philosophical Society in 1902, prompting a flurry of discussion in the secular press.[11] The focus of these discussions was how to strengthen local communities by building up church-related institutions at the parish level under the supervision of lay people and parish priests. Some hoped that these institutions would enjoy a degree of autonomy from the secular government, which would enable them to serve as loci for the development of civic communities as well.[12] Nicholas II became interested in the matter of reform at the beginning of 1903.[13] He instructed the metropolitan of St. Petersburg to prepare a report on church reform while at the same time he directed the Council of Ministers, under the leadership of Count Sergei Witte, to review the issue of religious tolerance. In pursuing both issues at the same time, the emperor thus returned to the apparently contradictory policies that had typified imperial religious policy before Alexander III, according to which the state promoted the strengthening of the established church while at the same time countenancing a certain degree of tolerance toward some of the empire's other religions.[14] In fact, however, this policy was driven by the state's unwavering commitment to use religion and religious institutions to serve its own ends, the primary one being the preservation of its unlimited power.[15]

Count Witte presented the results of the ministers' discussion on religious tolerance to the tsar in the fall of 1904 in the midst of the liberals' open campaign for political reform. In the middle of December 1904, Nicholas II announced that legislation granting limited religious tolerance to non-Orthodox subjects was forthcoming. This announcement aroused concern among the leaders of the Orthodox church, who feared that the other religions in the empire would benefit from rights and freedoms that the Orthodox church was denied, leading to a relative decline of Russia's traditional national religion. The events of 9 January aggravated concerns about the soundness of the church and led Witte to petition the emperor to allow the Council of Ministers to discuss internal reforms for the church in consultation with the metropolitan of St. Petersburg and the assistant director general of the Synod, Vladimir Sabler.[16] Nicholas II approved the request and shortly thereafter metropolitan Antonii submitted his memorandum on church reform to the council. Its main argument was that the church's relative weakness in Russian life was the result of the government's unwarranted regulation of the church's activities. Because the government had long restricted the church "almost wholly to worship and the conduct of ceremonies . . . the Church's voice goes almost completely unheard in both private and public life."[17] The solution was for the government to grant the church greater autonomy so that it would be free to fulfill its mission rather than denying its own calling to serve the needs of the government. Following this line of reasoning further, Antonii argued that the church did not need the government to impose reforms upon it; rather, the church should be given the freedom to reform itself, thereby reclaiming its integrity and enabling it to resume its proper role in Russian society with dignity and honor. The leading member of the state church thus denounced the government's control and manipulation of religion in the service of secular political ends because it weakened the church's ability to fulfill its own independent mission; he called on the government to grant the church the freedom to govern itself. The memo was a clear and direct challenge to the whole system of church-state relations in Russia as it had existed at least since the reign of Peter the Great.

After Witte received this memo, he requested that a group of professors from the St. Petersburg Ecclesiastical Academy draft a reform program containing specific recommendations. The professors were working on their program during the same weeks in late January and early February of 1905 that the Group of Petersburg Priests headed by Father Peter Kremlevskii was holding meetings; in all likelihood, the discussions between these two groups overlapped, given the dense network of connections between the school and the local clergy. The professors sent their report to Count Witte in mid-February, around the same time as Father Peter's group requested a first meeting with the metropolitan. The Petersburg priests and the academy professors both expressed their commitment to the vision that Antonii had already articulated in his memo to Witte, a vision of a free church allowed to reform itself so that it could carry out its mission of providing moral and religious leadership to society. The local leaders of the church in St. Petersburg, who had long been closely connected through their common fund of ideas and their shared mission, seemed largely in agreement on the church's most important and pressing needs.

Nevertheless, it soon became clear that implementing reform would not be easy. Although Witte had gone to considerable lengths to solicit opinions and recommendations on reform from the church's leaders, his own views on the matter continued to be shaped primarily by his role as the chief minister in the government. To begin with, Witte rejected the metropolitan's argument that the church should be autonomous and allowed to conduct its own reforms. Instead, he contended that the church and the state were interdependent institutions that had to work together to maintain the established order. Although he was willing to allow members of the church to participate in the reform process, he envisioned the reforms themselves as developed and implemented by the state. Second, with regard to specific reforms he sympathized with the desire of many lay people to expand and institutionalize their role in managing church affairs. His proposed changes with regard to the parish system, for example, reflected the views of activist laymen critical of the parish clergy.[18] Witte's view of the church and his program of reform were thus incompatible in several key respects with the ideas articulated by the metropolitan, the professors of the academy, and the most visible supporters of reform among the capital's clergy.

Yet, Witte was the person best able to promote the whole project of reform because of his dominance of the Council of Ministers and his role as an influential adviser to the emperor. Even he encountered difficulty, however, for when he submitted his report on church reform to the council at the end of February, the aging but still powerful director general of the Synod, Konstantin Pobedonostsev, suddenly intervened to defend Peter the

Great's system of church government against the complaints of both the clergy and lay reformers.[19] In a forceful memo submitted to the Council of Ministers on 12 March, Pobedonostsev argued that the church could not survive on its own without the assistance of the state and that any weaknesses in the church were the fault of the clergy and the bishops rather than the ecclesiastical bureaucracy.[20] He asserted that the church did not need to be reformed, but claimed that if it did it was the responsibility of the Synod and not the Council of Ministers. Pobedonostsev followed up his memo to the ministers with a complaint to the emperor himself.[21] On the following day, Nicholas II responded by transferring the matter of church reform from the Council of Ministers to the Synod, where Pobedonostsev expected to be able to quash further discussion.

The emperor's expression of approval for the proposal to call a council and implement some kind of reform in the church might have encouraged Metropolitan Antonii to resist Pobedonostsev's efforts to table the matter. On 15 March, the Synod sat down to review the materials sent to them by the Council of Ministers. At this meeting, Antonii presented his fellow bishops with a memorandum entitled, "On the Urgency of Establishing the Canonical Freedom of Our Church," submitted to him earlier that day by Kremlevskii's group and accepted by the metropolitan as compatible with his own views.[22] As had been the case with Antonii's memo to the emperor, the emphasis of this essay was on the necessity of the church's liberation from state control. First of all, the authors of the essay welcomed the proposal to establish religious toleration for the non-Orthodox peoples of the empire because it would free the church of the burden of unbelievers and increase its credibility in the eyes of non-Orthodox subjects. But they were deeply concerned by the prospect that other religions would gain freedoms that the Orthodox church did not have because of its continued subservience to the government. They warned that unless the church were freed of the restrictions the government placed upon it, it would quickly lose influence in society. Indeed, they feared that the church had already lost its ability to speak to the most thoughtful and educated individuals because for too long it had hesitated to make its voice heard in public on political and social issues. As a result, "the number of those children of the Church who do not know its voice, who do not believe it when they do happen to hear it, who do not come to it or follow after it, is ever increasing."[23] The Petersburg priests warned that as a result of this weakening of the church's influence the church's ability to fulfill its mission was in danger. In their view, the church's purpose was not simply to minister to individual believers but to lead the whole community in building the Kingdom of God.[24] For this reason they argued, "It is essential, absolutely essential, that the Church recover the strength of its fruitful influence on all aspects of human life and all the power of its voice" by reclaiming its freedom and independence from "everything that enslaves or threatens to enslave it with the external yoke of secular principles and goals."[25] They urged the church to reestablish its independence and freedom by convening a national church council empowered to institute reforms.

After introducing the memo by the Petersburg priests to the Synod, Metropolitan Antonii approved its publication in the church's national newspaper, *Tserkovnyi vestnik*, which was published at the St. Petersburg Ecclesiastical Academy. It appeared on 17 March under a more subdued title, "On the Necessity of Change in the Russian Church Administration," attributed to the Group of Thirty-two Priests. The article opened the subject of church reform to public discussion, initiating an intense debate on the church's role in society.[26] Shortly after the article appeared, the Synod formally requested that the emperor allow the convening of a church council to discuss reform.[27] Despite Nicholas's earlier demonstrations of interest, his response to the Synod's request was discouraging. While acknowledging that a church council was desirable, he declared that one could not be convened when the country was in upheaval. He stated that the council would have to be postponed to some undetermined future date after peace and stability had been restored to the empire.[28] Although that answer was disappointing, it was not an unreasonable response in the context of the spring of 1905. Many people continued to hope through the spring and summer months of that eventful year that the postponement of the council would be brief. They were encouraged by the emperor's apparent acknowledgment of the necessity of church reform and his acceptance of implementing such reform by means of a church council, despite the fact that this institution had been dormant in Russia for well over two hundred years.

Although there was significant support for church reform among the clergy and the educated laity, there were many disagreements over the reform's purpose and nature. The memo composed by the Group of Thirty-two Priests (who called themselves the Group of Petersburg Priests) focused primarily on the argument that the church had an important role to play in society, a role that it could not fulfill as long as it was on a government leash. It was not the purpose of the group to lay out a detailed program of reforms, but they did mention a few areas of particular concern: parish life, the role of the bishops, and the organization of the central ecclesiastical administration. They expressed support for replacing the Synod with a permanent council headed by a patriarch with limited powers. They also suggested several measures to reduce the power of the bishops and increase the administrative responsibilities given to the non-monastic clergy. Although these sketchy and undeveloped proposals were by no means the focus of the memo, when the paper was published they quickly became the main subject of discussion in the press. Both lay people and members of the hierarchy feared that the Thirty-two represented the desire of the parish clergy to aggrandize their own power and privileges in the church at the expense of the laity and bishops.[29] In response, lay reformers proposed reforms that would have increased the power of the laity by allowing them to elect their own clergy, participate in parish administration, and control parish finances. The bishops advocated reforms that would have enhanced their authority and placed the parish clergy more firmly under their control. Thus the memo intended to encourage support for the church and foster unity had the opposite effect: any unity concerning the purpose of the reform was obscured by conflicts over what should be reformed and how. Those conflicts likely eroded public support for the church. Moreover, the Group of Thirty-Two Priests themselves came to be viewed with much dislike, distrust, and misunderstanding, which substantially weakened their ability to exert leadership within the church and within society more generally as the revolution of 1905 continued.

FROM PUBLIC SERVICE TO POLITICS—
The Zealots for Church Renovation

Public discussion of church reform continued during the late spring and summer of 1905 but the Group of Thirty-two made only one contribution to it. They did not respond to critics who attacked their first article, nor did they publish anything to follow up on the arguments or proposals made in it. The only piece they did publish was a memorandum concerning the composition of the church council, which they submitted to the metropolitan at the end of May. This article, like the previous one, was then published as the lead article in *Tserkovnyi vestnik*, giving it a sort of unofficial approval from the church's highest-ranking leader. In that essay, the group argued that the council should include the elected representatives of the clergy and laity in addition to the bishops, whom they claimed could not represent the body of believers because they had been appointed rather than elected. While many welcomed the argument, it naturally offended some members of the hierarchy. The Group of Thirty-two acquired an ill-deserved reputation as enemies of the bishops, regardless of their obviously close relation with the metropolitan of St. Petersburg.[30] Although this article occasioned considerable commentary in the press, again the Group of Thirty-two did not respond. Throughout the summer of 1905 they remained silent, even as public hopes for progress on church reform were buoyed up by the Synod's request that the bishops submit their official opinions on the matter.[31]

It was not the progress of the reform movement but rather the rapid development of political events that prompted the group to raise its collective voice again in early October, when the country was in the midst of the general strike that had paralyzed the cities of the empire. On 8 October, the group published its first article in more than four months, entitled "The State Duma and the Pastor of the Church."[32] This article differed from the two that the group had published the previous spring in several revealing and important ways. First of all, it was not addressed to Metropolitan Antonii, but rather to the whole Orthodox church. Second, it was not published in the official newspaper of the church with the explicit approval of the metropolitan but in *Slovo (The Word),* a secular newspaper associated with the leaders of the Liberation movement and with the famous church publicist Father Grigorii Petrov. Finally, this article was not concerned with the particular issue of ecclesiastical reform but with the more general question of the church's role in the country's political life.

This was an issue that the clergy had long avoided because it was both dangerous and difficult. Historically, the Orthodox church had maintained the view that in a Christian state, the ruler and the church should work together to maintain a just and peaceful order by means of *symphonia,* according to which secular authority and ecclesiastical authority each had autonomous governance over its proper sphere. In Russia, these ideals had been manipulated by the state to its own benefit to enhance its legitimacy and power. The church's first loyalty was presumed to be to the state, whose ruler reigned by divine right and with divine approval. The church was prohibited from maintaining publicly any independent political views or activities, though it was required to serve as the government's mouthpiece whenever necessary. Thus, the government could require the clergy to report potential traitors, to read and endorse its decrees, to pray for the health and safety of its members, and in many other ways to reinforce and legitimize its authority. The government could also compel the punishment of clergy who challenged its authority by aiding opponents of the regime or discussing politics in *any* way other than those specifically approved by government authorities in sermons or in publications. As a result of this history, the Russian clergy were accustomed to viewing politics and political issues as outside of their purview.[33]

In their October essay, however, the Group of Thirty-Two challenged these historical limitations on the clergy's role in the country's political life. They were moved to do so by the proposal introduced in August for the establishment of a State Duma, an elected assembly with consultative rights.[34] For the clergy, the prospect of an elected representative body raised the question of what role the clergy should play in the elections for the Duma and in the Duma itself.[35] Should the clergy remain aloof from the whole political process? Many in the church urged this response for fear of the divisions political involvement would bring to the Christian community. Did the clergy have an obligation to uphold the government by promoting their candidates or supporting their programs, as many at the high levels of the government believed? Should the clergy take the opportunity to organize themselves independently to advocate for the interests of their estate and the needs of their institution, as some of the parish clergy claimed?

The members of the Group of Thirty-two did not agree with any of these positions. Instead, they proposed a new way of looking at the relation of the church to political life that grew out of the ideas and experiences that had been developing in the churches of the capital over the preceding quarter of a century. To begin with, they urged the clergy to become involved in preparations for the elections. As educated men, they had a special responsibility: to instruct the people about the Duma, to soothe

their fears and confusion, to overcome their caution and apathy, and to inspire everyone to take part in the elections so that the Duma would really
be an expression of the people's voice and an instrument of the people's
will.[36] Such an assembly would offer the means "for the confirmation of
God's justice on earth, for the construction of the Kingdom of God in Russia, and for the liberation of the human spirit and the human individual after centuries of oppression."[37] The Thirty-two thus considered the Duma to
be an institution of and for the common people that would be dedicated to
creating a just society to benefit the people while also realizing the will of God.
For this reason, in their preparations for participation in the Duma, the clergy
had to be conscious of their responsibilities both to the people and to God. For
the authors of the article, this meant that the clergy could not serve the interests of any particular estate, including their own. Nor could they in conscience
support any secular party or program, including any sponsored by the government. They were to remember that they were Christian pastors who served
Christ and His Church alone. Their only motivation in all their words and actions was to be the desire to uphold truth and justice.[38] They had to participate
in the political process without falling victim to politics.

The group recognized that avoiding partisanship during a time of political upheaval would be exceptionally difficult. They predicted that the
clergy would struggle with two temptations. The first was to use the Duma
to gain material benefits for the clerical estate. However, the Thirty-two argued that the Duma was not for the benefit of any particular social estate
but for the good of the whole country. Its purpose was not to win privileges
for a few but justice for all. "We must be higher, wider and deeper than our
estate," they admonished their fellow clergymen. "We must be the guardians
of the people's good, of the good of our flock."[39] The second temptation was to
succumb to the pressure to support the government without question or criticism. Those who hoped the clergy would win greater benefits from the state
through the Duma were especially vulnerable to such pressure. But, the authors asked, at what price would such privileges be bought? At the price of
complicity in a police state that denied justice to its people, a regime that
turned priests into policeman and religious services into propaganda.[40] For the
Thirty-two, this bargain was unacceptable. They rejected the belief that the
church had to uphold the established regime, describing it as the clergy's "ancient prejudice." They denounced in no uncertain terms the "blasphemous
union" between the church and the autocracy as an affront to Christian principles. When the church served the autocratic state,

> then the pastor is silent when it is criminal to be silent, when justice is flouted
> and the weak are oppressed; then he is a pastor no longer, but a mere trades-
> man, a performer of ceremonies and a servant to the powerful in this world.
> Oh Lord! How long? How long will your pastor sanctify injustice, insult and
> robbery? How long will the mouth of your pastor be closed up with the gov-
> ernment's seal?[41]

The church could not serve any government for the sake of that government alone. Its responsibility was to the greater good, the higher truth. Each government had to be judged by the light of the Gospels' teachings. Even the Duma was to be praised and supported not for political reasons but for religious ones: because these clergymen believed it would promote Christian justice, liberate the people from spiritual slavery, and offer the means of attaining truth, right, and good on earth.[42]

Clearly, the group's view of the clergy's role in politics was shaped by their conception of the church's mission to the world. The authors explicitly rejected certain views that they claimed had long been accepted in the Russian church, according to which Christianity was supposed to be unconcerned with earthly matters because the world was essentially an evil and corrupt place to be fearfully avoided by men of the church. Instead, the Thirty-two argued that while evil exists in the world, the world itself is not inherently evil. Christ himself had come into the world in order to combat its evils; he had instructed his followers to work in the world according to his example.[43] The group reasoned from this that Christians should not flee the world but work to transform it in accordance with God's plan. In support of their argument, they cited the response that Jesus gave to the Pharisees when they criticized him for eating with social outcasts: "It is not the healthy who need a doctor, but the sick."[44] Thus, the clergy should not turn away from the sinful world but should reach out to heal it:

> From the time of Adam's sin, the world has been sick; it has squeaked and wobbled along like a broken machine. We pastors, following the example of Christ, must not run away, must not turn away from this world, but go to it to reinvigorate it, to heal it with Christ's truth; we must not call others away from the world but prompt them to living in the world by Christ's truth.[45]

They concluded with another strikingly modern metaphor, declaring, "We must remember that Christianity is not a ticket from Station Earth to Station Heaven; Christianity does not despise the world, but seeks to uplift it."[46]

For several decades before the 1905 revolution, the outreach work of the parish clergy of St. Petersburg had been inspired and informed by the modern theology first articulated by the archimandrite Feodor (Bukharev), which contended that the task of the church was to transform the present world of error and evil through the application of the teachings of the Gospels in the lives of individuals and the Christian community. This theology had influenced the revival of preaching, the cultivation of the pastoral arts, the expansion of charitable organizations, and the opening up of many new avenues for the exercise of moral leadership. During this time, the clergy had studiously avoided addressing political issues of any kind directly, as indeed the laws of the empire explicitly forbade them to. But as the clergy's role in the public life of the capital expanded, it became more difficult to distinguish the line dividing moral-religious issues from political ones.[47] To be sure, most of the clergy insisted that there *was* a demarcation between those issues that concerned the church and those that did not; thus, the clergy of the ORRP had declined to continue their participation in Zubatov's association, and Father Georgii had little help from his fellow clergymen in his assembly of Russian workingmen. But for Father Georgii and the clergy who belonged to the Group of Thirty-two, the church's mission to transform the world and help realize the Kingdom of God on earth required them to erase the boundaries between the secular and religious spheres and carry their mission into the realm of politics. Perhaps, too, they recognized that in a time of revolution politics was unavoidable. Alexander Kartashev, a lay supporter of the Group of Thirty-two and a professor of church history, argued that the church *could* not avoid politics because it permeated all aspects of people's lives at that time; at the same time, he also asserted that it *should* not avoid politics because in such challenging times people needed the church's guidance. The question was not *whether* the church should be involved in politics but *how* it could bring its teachings to bear on important political questions in a meaningful and useful way.[48]

Less than two weeks after the Group of Thirty-Two published their article on the Duma, the October Manifesto was granted. Political parties were legalized and preparations for Duma elections began. Before the month was over, the Group of Thirty-two had established a political party called the Union of Zealots for Church Renovation. Although there is no complete membership list, a partial list compiled from church records and Renovationist publications indicates that there were 102 active members (listed in the appendix at the end of the book). Fifty-two were ordained clergymen, and eight were laymen who taught in the church's schools. Eighteen of the clergymen (35 percent) were also members of the Society for Moral-Religious Enlightenment, and three of them were among the ORRP's most active leaders: Peter M. Kremlevskii, director of the society's youth organization; Peter N. Lakhotskii, supervisor of the society's main church (the church of the Trinity); and Pavel A. Mirtov, the new president of the Nevskii Society. This strong connection between the ORRP and the Renovationists suggests that those who were deeply involved in the church's outreach to society were more likely than others to support the program of Christian politics. Several of the clergy were priests in the capital's most important churches, including the cathedral of St. Andrew and the cathedral of Sts. Peter and Paul. One was a diocesan missionary. Father Grigorii Petrov was a member of the Renovationists, as was the archimandrite Mikhail (Semenov), a young professor of canon law at the ecclesiastical academy who had been exceptionally active in the meetings of the Religious-Philosophical Society. Although the number of clergy enrolled in the party does not seem large in absolute terms, one must remember how small the number of priests serving the capital city was; when one considers that the Renovationists attracted the active support of about 1 of every 7 priests in the city, its importance is more evident. Clearly, the clergy who did join the union were some of the capital's most prominent pastors. The Renovationist party also gained the support of at least forty-three laymen who did not serve in the church, the best known of whom were the philosophers Nikolai Berdiaev, Sergei Bulgakov, and Vasilii Rozanov. Several of the other laymen were professors at St. Petersburg University (which had close ties with the St. Petersburg Ecclesiastical Academy); others identified themselves as publicists, authors, and philosophers. Some of them had been participants in the St. Petersburg Religious-Philosophical Society. The participation of these educated laymen in a group founded and run by clergymen indicates that there were still contacts between lay and clerical intellectuals during the revolution and that the Renovationists were not isolated by a "clericalist" program, as some Soviet authors alleged.[49]

The Renovationist program reflected the diversity of the group's membership and their desire to appeal to a broad audience that included educated lay people as well as clergymen.[50] They defined their first task as "the elaboration of those aspects of Christian truth that historically have not been fully explicated in Christian teaching or the living knowledge of which . . . has been weakened in our time," by which they meant that they wanted to explore a wider range of Christian thought than that officially sanctioned by the authorities.[51] They hoped to use the insights gained from a wide-ranging study of the historical ideas and values of Orthodoxy to support reform in many areas of church life, including the central administration, the parish, liturgical and devotional practices, and the schools. They intended to develop these reforms as part of a larger effort to discover "the ways and means of creating a Christian community," which would require the reexamination of the attitude of Christianity toward the earthly life and the role of the church in the political, social, and economic development of the country.[52] They planned to organize study circles in the diocesan and district centers that would bring lay people and clergymen together to discuss these issues. They hoped that the exchange and development of ideas would provide the basis for renewing society and renovating the church on the basis of common Christian principles.[53]

As the elections to the first Duma drew near, the Renovationists continued to focus on the issues that had concerned the Group of Thirty-two, developing their arguments about the relation of the church to the political life of Russia further. Early in 1906, they published an essay, "On the Relations of the Church and the Clergy to the Contemporary Political Life of the Community," in which they looked at how the church could help solve the country's problems. They began by repeating the argument made in the October article by the Group of Thirty-two: that the church could no longer stand apart from political events because inaction implied support for a status quo that a majority of the empire's subjects had come to agree was unacceptable.[54] The church had to become involved, if only to avoid losing its influence on society. The motivation for action was not simply defensive, however. For the Renovationists there was a positive impulse to action, embodied in the church's mission to transform existing society through the application of the Gospels in order to create a new kind of community, which would provide the opportunity for the Kingdom of God to be realized at last:

> In accordance with Christ's command and the fundamental idea of Christianity, the Kingdom of God must be revealed not only in the internal world of each Christian individual, but must infiltrate all of life; it must transform the social conditions and the objective manifestation of Christian nations' lives so that the Kingdom of God is fully manifested and incarnated in the external forms of reality.[55]

The realization of the Kingdom of God on earth justified the church's interest in all of humanity's affairs. It also set the standards by which adherents of the church should judge political developments. In the view of the Renovationists, the program most consistent with Christian principles was both liberal and democratic in nature. They supported individual rights and advocated a government of laws dedicated to serving the needs of the common people. They were especially concerned with obtaining justice for the poor and the powerless. Although they advised the clergy against joining any of the secular political parties, they supported the clergy's continued involvement in non-political organizations concerned with social issues: "[I]n the present time of sharpening class conflict, Christ's command to clothe the naked, feed the hungry and visit the imprisoned can only be fulfilled through complex social techniques, including workers' organizations, the cooperative movement, etc."[56] The specific types of organizations mentioned were not the charities through which the clergy had previously carried on the church's outreach. Rather, they were new types of organization that aimed at bringing change to the social and economic order through cooperative action by the masses, not unlike Father Georgii's assembly.

The Renovationists' arguments were developed further by one of the union's most prominent members, the archpriest Mikhail P. Chel'tsov.[57] He published two articles, "Christianity and Politics" and "Orthodox Pastorship and Social Activism," in the thick journal of the St. Petersburg Ecclesiastical Academy in the spring of 1906.[58] In the first article, Father Mikhail attacked the assumption made by many people, especially in the clergy, that Christianity had no possible relevance to politics. He argued that the opposite was true: Christianity had everything to do with politics: "The business of politics is not alien to Christianity; in fact, Christianity is obliged to Christianize politics."[59] Postulating that a good government must be based on the people's highest moral principles, Chel'tsov reasoned that in a country of Christian believers (such as Russia) this meant the government had to be dedicated to Christian principles.[60] The clergy were responsible for providing those who governed with a guiding vision based on those principles, which also expressed the aspirations of all Christians in the community. Those aspirations centered on the realization of the Kingdom of God on earth in the form of a society built upon the teachings of the Gospels.[61] This desire to help construct the Kingdom of God motivated Christians to concern themselves with what Father Mikhail called politics in general, or a politics of ends. This kind of politics, which he also called "passive politics," was directed at accomplishing a general goal that would benefit all members of society equally. It differed from partisan politics, which was concerned with solving specific problems, often with the intent of benefiting some members of society but not others. Father Mikhail also called this type of politics "active politics." In his view, clergymen should not participate in active politics; that is, they should neither join political parties nor endorse particular political programs. However, the clergy should be engaged in passive politics, evaluating all political programs from a Christian perspective and reminding those involved in active politics that their ultimate goal was to build the Kingdom of God.[62]

In his second article, Father Mikhail discussed in great detail his understanding of the clergyman's role in public affairs. He began by criticizing the ways in which lay people and clergymen alike viewed the priest's role. For some, the priest's primary purpose was the performance of the liturgy and the sacraments. Those who held this view believed that the priest's proper place was behind the altar and that he had no right to speak out on public issues. Father Mikhail acknowledged the importance of the sacraments but went on to argue that Christianity is not a religion of rites but of deeds. Thus, the clergyman should not restrict himself to performing the church's rituals but must seek to give life to the beliefs the rituals represent through actions taken outside the walls of his parish church. Others believed that the clergyman's leadership should be restricted to matters related to individual morality. For them, the priest represented a moral exemplar for individuals to imitate in private life, but he had no claim to provide leadership for the community as a whole. In response to this, Chel'tsov contended that Christianity was more than a system of individual belief. It was also a guide for the construction of a community of believers whose lives together would amount to something greater than their lives as separate individuals. Since the clergyman worked in the service of that religious community, he was naturally involved in its members' public affairs in society.[63] Unlike others, however, the clergy's view of public affairs was not distorted by partisan interests but clarified by the higher vision of the promised future represented by the Kingdom of God.[64] This same idea was expressed most clearly in another article written by Father S. Broiarskii, another Renovationist. As he argued, "Politics, the striving after earthly comforts, is not the chief thing in the Christian's life, but only the means for the realization on earth among men of the Kingdom of God, of the Lord's commandments about peace, fraternity, equality and above all, love."[65]

The Renovationists' attitude about the public role of the church was firmly rooted in a fundamentally religious understanding of human society.

They did not see religion as a personal matter restricted to the sphere of private life. They saw Christians as members of a community bound by their adherence to the teachings of Christ as recorded in the Gospels. That community had no internal borders in their eyes. The community of believers was the church at the same time that it was also the people and society. Believing the church and society to be one and the same they accepted no real division between them. A similar view had been expressed by the monk Feodor (Bukharev) fifty years before. Like Archimandrite Feodor, the Renovationists believed that the church was not only concerned with the world but also committed to changing it. The mission to realize the Kingdom of God justified the church's activity in society, providing the source of its creative dynamism and the final goal of its work in the world. Realizing the Kingdom of God required establishing a just society, an ideal compatible with a liberal democratic political program, but not limited to it. Because secular political programs alone could not encompass the full vision of humanity's goal, the clergy fulfilled an essential role. They stood at the very center of the Christian community and reached out to all parts of it, teaching the people the gospel through their sermons, showing them how to live by it through their deeds, representing the needs and aspirations of the people to the government, and inspiring the government to work toward the establishment of a just Christian society that would make possible the realization of the Kingdom of God. As their consistent use of the words "pastor" and "pastorship" made clear, the Renovationists saw the clergy not simply as priests but as the guardians and leaders of the religious community, the common people, Russian society, and, finally, the universal church.[66]

The Renovationists' views about the clergy's role in politics and the church's relation to society were summed up in the statute of the Fraternity for Zealots of Church Renovation, which was approved by the metropolitan of St. Petersburg in May of 1906. It affirmed four basic principles that the members of the organization agreed upon: (1) that as a divine and eternal institution, the church could not be subject to any temporary earthly power; (2) that all members of the church should be united by a sense of love and community, expressed in the ideal of conciliarity (sobornost'); (3) that all organizations and individuals within the church should view the world and all human activities as the field for the building of the Kingdom of God on earth; and (4) that the church should establish its relations with all other organizations on the basis of tolerance and universal love.[67] Thus, the Fraternity affirmed its support for a free church, independent from the state and governed collectively by its members, dedicated to engaging with all areas of human activity for the purpose of building the Kingdom of God. The goal of the Fraternity was to develop their views on the church's role in the modern world further and to spread these views as widely as possible among both the clergy and the laity through discussion circles, lectures, and publications.

Even before the group's statute was approved, they had opened their first periodical, a monthly journal called *The Bellringer (Zvonar')*. The name was explained in the words that appeared in the masthead: "Ring out, dear bell-ringer, ring out! And you will raise the dead from their graves." The editor, Archpriest Xenophon Belkov, wrote in the first issue that the journal's purpose was to offer the clergy a non-secular interpretation of current events, to give clergymen examples of good pastorship, and to promote church reform.[68] That cause was an issue of increasing public concern in the spring of 1906 as the pre-council convention opened to begin discussion on the organization and agenda of a future church council. The issue of church reform, which had been an issue of secondary importance to the Renovationist clergy for most of the preceding year, now became their primary concern.

A CHURCH DIVIDED AGAINST ITSELF

Intense discussions about the proposed church council and its reform agenda had continued throughout 1905 despite the emperor's March announcement that no definite date for a meeting could be established at that time. At the end of July 1905, the Synod called on the bishops to submit memoranda detailing their views on reform, encouraging them to consult with lay and clerical representatives from their dioceses. Many bishops organized diocesan conventions where academy professors, theologians, clergymen, publicists, church bureaucrats, and the bishops themselves debated vigorously.[69] Following the proclamation of the October Manifesto and Pobedonostsev's resignation from the post of director general of the Synod, Nicholas II came under increasing pressure from members of his government to issue a summons for a council.[70] Finally, on 27 December, the emperor issued a rescript affirming the need for church reform and calling on the three highest-ranking prelates (the metropolitans of St. Petersburg, Moscow, and Kiev) to recommend a time for the assembly of a church council.[71] In response, the church's leading hierarchs advised that a preparatory conference be held first to discuss procedural issues and to try to find some basis for preliminary consensus on the more contentious issues raised in the diocesan conventions. The Synod approved this recommendation on 14 January 1906. Initially, the conference's membership was to be extremely limited, consisting of only ten hierarchs, twenty-one professors, and the director general of the Synod and his assistant. However, forceful and persistent complaints compelled the Synod to appoint twenty-one additional persons—thirteen laymen and eight clergymen from the provinces—in late February and early March.[72] The proposed agenda for the conference was carefully scrutinized in the press, with some of the clergy's newspapers running long, detailed articles on the central issues and how they might be resolved.[73]

The conference met in two sessions, the first in the spring of 1906 and the second in the late fall of the same year. The mood of the participants on the conference's opening day was anxious rather than hopeful. Speakers warned that the reform effort could deepen divisions in the church and endanger the country's fragile public order. They all emphasized the tremendous importance of their work as well as its great difficulties. Some spoke of the need for haste, fearing the moment for change would pass too quickly; others urged extreme caution, worried that the church would have to live with the results of the conference for years to come.[74] However, the spring session of the conference, which ran from 8 March to 14 June, did not seem to bear out the gloomy warnings heard on the opening day. The participants worked together successfully to construct solid consensus proposals on many of the major reform issues. Discussion was serious and wide-ranging, and the records suggest that the opinions of the lay delegates and the members of the parish clergy were recognized and respected by the hierarchs. Several committees submitted minority opinions and alternate proposals for reform along with the majority report on their particular issues.[75] Altogether, the conference accomplished an enormous amount of work in a relatively short time.

Nevertheless, when the first session adjourned for the summer, the participants expressed no satisfaction with their work but only the same persistent sense of anxiety that had plagued them from the opening day. Some worried that the conference would not be allowed to reconvene in the autumn and urged Metropolitan Antonii to press for the summoning of the council before the end of the summer.[76] Indeed, the events of the summer did not bode well for the church.[77] The dissolution of the obstreperous first Duma on 9 July in the midst of growing unrest in the countryside aggravated the government's sense of besiegement. Metropolitan Antonii himself feared that the conference would not be allowed to meet again when his repeated requests for permission to reopen the conference in the early weeks of the fall were turned down by the new director general of the Synod, Peter Izvol'skii, a close ally of the new prime minister, Peter Stolypin. Not until 25 October did Izvol'skii finally give the conference permission to resume its work. Even then he warned them that they would be allowed only six weeks from that date to finish their task. The participants were reassembled in great haste, and when the conference reopened on 2 November 1906, Metropolitan Antonii greeted the members with an almost palpable sense of relief. But Izvol'skii was there, too. He bluntly reminded the participants that the conference met at the pleasure of the emperor, and its proposals were expected to strengthen not only the church but also the state.[78] Working under the elongating shadow of reaction, the conference quickly resolved the remaining issues on its agenda and adjourned on 15 December 1906, as ordered. Nicholas II began reading through the four bulky volumes of protocols produced by the conference in February of 1907, finally finishing them toward the end of April.[79] Beyond informing the Synod that he had completed the reading, he said nothing further on the subject of church reform. His silence held the church in thrall, for the conference had affirmed that the emperor would follow the precedent first set by the

Byzantine emperor Constantine at Nicaea in 325: he would summon the council, formally open the proceedings, and give final approval to all decisions.[80] And so the church awaited the emperor's call, patient as the months and then the years passed by. But the church waited in vain: the summons never came.

Not all were content to wait passively for the ruler to grant the church permission to reform. The Renovationists emerged in the years 1906–1907 as strong critics of both the reform process and the priorities of those who had become church reform experts. The original Group of Thirty-two had been established in order to give like-minded individuals from among the Petersburg clergy the opportunity to develop their views on the church's needs through discussion with each other and communication with the metropolitan of St. Petersburg. Thus, they were associated with the general subject of church reform from the time it first became a matter of intense public discussion in the spring of 1905. In fact, the group was not especially interested in the kinds of issues that preoccupied bishops, academy professors, and lay experts on Orthodoxy; they did not want to debate the details of administrative reforms, discuss legal technicalities, or deliberate over parish boundaries and church budgets. They did not view the church merely as an institution, an inert, mechanical structure that would function better after some tinkering of its separate parts, but as a dynamic living body animated by the creative spirit of divine-human effort and aspiration. What they sought was not so much external reform but renewal, rebirth, renovation *(obnovlenie)* of the inner energies of the church, in part through the reinforcement of the vital connections between the church and the world around it.

Given this high idealism, it is not surprising that the Renovationists and those who sympathized with them soon became critical of the complex, messy, and deeply politicized process of reform. Already in December of 1905, they had become involved in a heated polemic with Antonii (Khrapovitskii), archbishop of Galicia and Volhynia, over the question of whether the representatives of the laity and the lower clergy should be allowed to participate equally in the council with the bishops.[81] In January and February of 1906, the liberal newspaper of the ORRP, *Church Voice (Tserkovnyi golos)* began to carry articles criticizing the pre-conciliar conference. These prominently placed articles expressed criticisms that would come to be associated with the Renovationists: the fear that the conference was approaching the reforms in too academic a fashion, the concern that the letter of canon law would be valued over the spirit of the canons, and the desperate hope that the reformers might approach their task creatively in a way that demonstrated their recognition of the needs of the present day.[82] Once the Renovationists opened their own journals, their public criticisms of the reform process became sharper and more frequent. The criticism was characterized by two main themes. First was the claim that the legalism of the proceedings obscured the true needs of the church, in part by facilitating the exclusion of all non-expert opinions on which areas of church life needed reform and which reforms should be undertaken. The second theme was that the overwhelming attention given to administrative issues was aimed at enabling the bishops and bureaucrats to protect and expand their own power at the expense of the lower clergy and the laity to the detriment of the whole church.[83]

The Renovationists' criticisms of the reform process were deeply rooted in their alternative vision of the church and its role in society. They believed that effective reform had to be inspired by the spirit of the Gospels rather than the letter of the law, arguing that this allowed for the creativity and freedom the church needed in order to respond to the needs of the modern world. They also contended that meaningful reform would come from what they considered the heart of the church, from the clergy and laity who constituted the "true" church, not from the Synod or other bodies appointed by the government, which they viewed as being outside of and alien to the church. This definition of the church community, pointedly excluding the hierarchy as lackeys of the autocratic state rather than servants of the church, was manifested with particular consistency by the journal *Church Renewal (Tserkovnoe obnovlenie)*, published from November of 1906.[84] Many of the articles published in this journal reflected the belief that the parish clergy and the laity enjoyed a special bond uniting them in opposition to the church hierarchy and bureaucracy. One article, typical of the sort that this journal favored, argued that since a church council would likely be dominated by the bishops and focused on advancing their agenda, the clergy should forget about the church council and focus instead on strengthening their bond with the people in order to lead them in the effort to renew the church spiritually from within and below.[85] Another article contended that ultimate authority in the church belonged to the people, not the hierarchs: "The preservers of piety are the people, who are the body of the Church."[86] Thus, the clergy ought to consider the needs of the people as more pressing than the demands of the bishops. By arguing that the people were the church and that the parish clergy were more closely connected to the people than those who governed the church, the Renovationists directly challenged the hierarchy.[87]

While many of the Renovationists' contemporary critics assumed that the Renovationist animosity toward the bishops was motivated by a selfish desire to seize power in the church in order to increase their own privileges, an examination of the corpus of Renovationist writings provides a broader context for interpreting their ideas.[88] For the Renovationists, church reform was inextricably linked with the spiritual renewal of Russian society. The lead article of the first issue of *Tserkovnoe obnovlenie* was entitled "We Await a New Heaven and a New Earth." In it, the archimandrite Mikhail (Semenov) argued that renovation of the church was not about substituting new administrative forms for old ones but about infusing all aspects of church and society with the spirit of Christ in order to create a world without oppression, enslavement, violence, and poverty.[89] He contended that the renewal of the Christian spirit was not merely an individual phenomenon, privately experienced and personally expressed in the lives of isolated believers; rather, it was an experience that encompassed the community and found expression in collective, public forms. Father Mikhail and other Renovationists thus envisioned a profound change that would transform the church and all of society. This accounts for the interest the Renovationists demonstrated in social and political issues not directly connected with the church. The two Renovationist journals that opened in the fall of 1906—after the agrarian disorders of the preceding summer—carried articles urging the clergy to speak up on behalf of the impoverished and ignorant people in order to denounce the unjust capitalist system that privileged the few over the many and created intolerable suffering.[90] The clergy had a special responsibility to draw public attention to such injustice and to persist in the quest for eliminating such abuses as part of the effort to realize the Kingdom of God on earth.[91]

As elections to the second Duma approached at the beginning of 1907, the Renovationists returned to the issue of the clergy's role in politics. The Fraternity hosted a meeting to discuss how their organization would participate in the elections. Several of the younger clergymen, including Father Mikhail Chel'tsov and Father Grigorii Petrov, argued that the Renovationists should sponsor candidates for the Duma. The older clergymen, such as Father Filosof Ornatskii of the ORRP and Father Sergei Sollertinskii of the St. Petersburg academy, advised against becoming involved in the political contest, pointing out that in the realm of politics the church was inexperienced and weak.[92] The feeling of the majority of the group seems to have inclined toward supporting one of the existing secular parties rather than attempting to organize the Fraternity into a political party. An article reviewing the clergy's possible choices appeared in one of the Renovationist journals a few days after the meeting. Observing that none of the parties was perfectly in accord with the clergy's ideals, the author concluded that the clergy should support the liberal and radical parties (particularly the Kadets and the Socialist Revolutionaries), which represented the interests of the common people better than the parties of the Right. Even the moderately conservative Octobrist party was deemed unacceptable because of their staunch defense of the property rights of the comfortable classes.[93] When the Synod issued a decree that forbade the clergy from joining the Constitutional Democrats and instructed district supervisors to enroll all parish clergy in the Octobrist party, the Renovationists protested vigorously.[94] One who published his objections to the Octobrists declared that they rejected the principle in the Gospels of equality for all, opposed giving aid to the poor, and condoned the violent suppression of popular demonstrations. He argued that the clergy must not betray the people's faith by joining a party that would not give the people justice.[95] The Renovationists' journals indicated that the Renovationists generally supported the Constitutional

Democrats, though they were dissatisfied with the latter's social conservatism; occasionally, they indicated some sympathy with the Socialist Revolutionaries and the Laborite party *(Trudoviki).*[96]

The Renovationists' mixture of ecclesiastical radicalism, political liberalism, and social radicalism could be described as evangelical populism, which resembled revolutionary populism in striking ways. For example, the common people *(narod)* figured prominently in Renovationist rhetoric. The Renovationists idealized the simple folk as bearers of an authentic Christian spirit, manifested in their piety, humility, and willingness to suffer without complaint. Despite these admirable spiritual qualities, however, the *narod* were too ignorant and simple to speak up for themselves before the authorities. The Renovationists, like secular radicals, claimed that the parish clergy were in the best position to speak on the people's behalf because they knew them so intimately: they lived and worked among the people, sharing their material hardships and their moral-religious view of the world. Thus, unlike the "princes of the church," the parish clergy knew themselves what hardship and suffering were; unlike the intelligentsia, they also knew that the lives of the people were inspired by their Christian faith, which they would not surrender for a materialist and secular world view. The Renovationists insisted that Christianity offered everything that a modern society needed in order to strengthen its foundation and build a promising future. Moreover, they believed that one had only to refer to the Gospels to understand what Christianity was about. They believed that the Gospels themselves called for the recognition of human equality, the exercise of love and charity toward all, and the quest for justice for those who had been wronged by poverty, violence, and oppression. These were the principles that the Renovationists believed should guide both the church and society. It was for the sake of these principles that they themselves fought.

Despite the Renovationists' belief that they spoke for the *narod,* they never did win many supporters from among the ordinary people. And though they believed they had much in common with liberal intellectuals they also did not succeed in attracting much response from the Constitutional Democrat party, the dominant political organization of the revolutionary years. In fact, the Renovationists found their supporters almost exclusively among the educated clergy of the capital and among the small groups of neo-religious lay intellectuals in St. Petersburg and Moscow. Outside of their own circle, the Renovationists' ideas were misrepresented and misunderstood. Ordinary people knew only of the Renovationists' criticisms of the reform process, the church administration, and especially the bishops; it was apparently widely believed that the main point of the Renovationists' program was to eliminate the episcopate altogether and to increase the power of the parish clergy at the expense of the parishioners.[97] Secular intellectuals believed that the Renovationists were a clericalist party hoping to gain political power in order to advance the interests of the clerical estate and increase the power of the clergy over the lives of the laity.[98]

Naturally, the group could hardly hope to win any support from the hierarchy or the church administration in view of their harsh criticisms of the episcopate and proposals to reduce the bishops' power. Even those among the hierarchy who had initially been sympathetic to many of the Renovationists' views were eventually alienated by their scathing condemnations of the reform process.[99] Thus, the Renovationists exacerbated existing divisions in the church, making public consensus on reform impossible. They frightened those who might have supported moderate reforms into a defensive conservatism with the specter of a clerical revolt and a new schism. Although the Renovationists were not the sole cause of the failure of church reform, they certainly contributed to it. Yet one hesitates to condemn them for this, knowing how they suffered for it in the years that followed.

CHAPTER NINE

THE DECADE OF DESPAIR

1907–1917

The decade between the revolutions was a difficult time
for the Russian Orthodox Church. Even before the revolution there had
been significant tension between the state and the established church, for
although the two institutions had some common interests their ultimate
goals differed and increasingly diverged in the late imperial period.[1] The
state's focus on maintaining and strengthening Russia's position as a European great power while preserving the autocratic system of government
against internal challenges led it to enact economic, legal, and social policies
that undermined the church's influence, contradicted the church's values, or
compromised the church's agenda.[2] Of course, as long as the state continued to
see the church as an important source of political stability and strength it
would continue to provide it with some financial support and legal protection,
but this subsidization was accompanied by the expectation that the clergy
would do its part in defending the political system regardless of the cost.[3]

Despite these thick political tensions, the parish clergy of the capital
maintained the commitment to their pre-1905 mission of bringing the
church more fully into the world by extending their pastoral activities to
an ever-increasing number of fields during and after the revolution. Although for many clergymen the focus of this activity continued be reli-

gious education, moral improvement, and charitable work, some priests boldly ventured into the political arena; those who did so were often outspoken critics of the established authorities and the existing order. Such political activism posed a serious challenge for church authorities: while sometimes agreeing with the reasons for particular clergymen's actions, the hierarchy could not countenance direct challenges to their own position in the church or to the existing church-state order; they had to repress those whose words, ideas, and actions seemed to constitute a threat to the church's position. Yet even while repressing some kinds of criticism among the parish clergy, the church's leaders continued to press for reforms that would strengthen the church's position vis à vis the state and enable it to deepen its influence over society. The failure of the church reform movement, though often attributed to the church leaders even by those within the clergy, was really the fault of state authorities. However, the bitterness and mutual recriminations that this failure generated within the church—along with the atmosphere of repression created by the censorship of some church publications and the silencing of some of the most outspoken clergymen—exacerbated feelings of fear, anger, and suspicion, thus deepening the divisions within the church and weakening its authority in society in the years between the revolutions.

THE RESTORATION OF AUTHORITY

As the tide of revolution began to subside in the fall of 1906, the authorities of both the state and the church began to reassert their control over those who continued to challenge the fundamental institutions and values of the political system that was hastily put into place after the proclamation of the October Manifesto and the Fundamental Laws. The Renovationist clergy, both as individuals and as a group, found themselves especially likely to be subjected to repressive or punitive measures. This may have been because their critiques of contemporary Russia were so wide-ranging: in their sermons, lectures, and publications, they commented critically on the injustices of the socioeconomic order and on the distortions and abuses of power in the post-October political system. Not only that, but they were harsh and relentless critics of the hierarchy and the whole system of ecclesiastical administration, including the Synod and the director general's office; many articles in the Renovationist press were devoted to exposing (and in all likelihood aggravating) the often bitter struggles within the church between the members of the lower clergy and their superiors in the diocesan and synodal administrations.[4] These articles outraged both the secular and ecclesiastical authorities, but of the two it was the latter for whom the offense carried more serious consequences for members of the clergy. Imperial officials, overwhelmed by political opposition among other groups in Russian society, often turned to the bishops for assistance in disciplining the clergy.[5] In many instances when the offending clergyman's target had been a secular one, bishops protected their subordinates from serious punishments even when strongly pressured by secular authorities.[6] In cases when the dissident clergyman challenged the ecclesiastical order and in particular the authority of the hierarchy, however, the bishops were more likely to take serious action against the offender.[7] This was generally the case with Renovationist clergymen.

One of the most famous instances of repression against a member of the capital's clergy involved the archimandrite Mikhail (Semenov), an active member of the Renovationist Union, co-editor of the Renovationist newspaper *Century (Vek)* and a frequent contributor to the journal *Church Renewal (Tserkovnoe obnovlenie)*. Father Mikhail had been a prominent figure in the intellectual life of the capital since he had first arrived from Kazan in 1902 to teach canon law at the St. Petersburg Ecclesiastical Academy.[8] He had played a leading role in the meetings of the Religious-Philosophical Society and was renowned as a lecturer for the ORRP. During the 1905 revolution he became well known for his writings, in which he argued that the church had to be concerned with the problems of contemporary society because its responsibility was to work for the realization of the Kingdom of God on earth through the creation of a just social order that manifested the Christian values of humility, love, and self-sacrifice for the good of others.[9]

During the fall of 1906, the country was preparing for a new round of elections to select the membership of the second Duma, the first having been disbanded in July when its members reached an impasse with the government over the issue of land reform. The most assertive of the pro-autocracy parties, the Union of Russian People (URP), named Father Mikhail as their candidate for the town of Simbirsk (his birthplace), perhaps hoping to tarnish his reputation as an advocate of reform. Mikhail publicly denounced the URP and its ideology and instead affirmed his support of the Constitutional Democratic party, which directly violated an instruction the Synod had issued the previous spring forbidding the clergy to support that party because it did not yet have legal status. The Council of Ministers ordered the Synod to bring Father Mikhail under control immediately. The Synod fired the archimandrite from the academy and expelled him from the capital.[10] These actions seem to have clarified and confirmed some of the ideas that Mikhail had been developing during the preceding year, when he devoted himself to studying the problem of poverty in St. Petersburg firsthand by visiting the factories and the working-class districts of the capital. Deeply moved by the misery and suffering of the common people, especially the women and children, he had begun to ask himself how the church could support a political order that allowed such profound injustice. Eventually, he concluded that the church had betrayed its mission by allowing itself to become subjected to the state and by reiterating its demands for peace and calm even as it denied the people any means to attain justice.[11] Father Mikhail's open challenge to the synodal establishment led to him being charged with violating church discipline, for which the Synod sentenced him to three months' confinement in Zadonsk monastery; during his penance, he was forbidden to engage in any literary or political activity and placed on a severely ascetic regimen.[12] He appealed his case directly to the director general of the Synod, threatening to quit the established church and join the Old Believers.[13] He received no answer. In the fall of 1907, he carried out his threat, quitting the synodal church for the Old Belief immediately before he left the country.[14]

Even as the Synod was still pursuing charges against the archimandrite, it moved to repress a local priest with a national reputation, Father Grigorii Petrov.[15] Although Father Grigorii had been suspended indefinitely from his duties as a clergyman before the revolution and forbidden to speak publicly or publish his writings out of concern for the impact of some of his more unconventional ideas on simple believers, he still commanded deep respect among his fellow clergymen and considerable popular influence. During the 1905 revolution, Father Grigorii defied the Synod's ban on his publicist activities and went to Moscow to found a journal he called *God's Truth* *(Pravda Bozhiia)*, a popular publication intended to instruct the newly enfranchised masses in the responsibilities of citizenship.[16] He also resumed his public lectures, dealing with a wide variety of topics related to politics, religion, and civic life. As elections for the second Duma approached he accepted an invitation from the Constitutional Democrats to stand as one of their candidates. All of this political activity aroused the ire of the metropolitan of Moscow, Vladimir (Bogoiavlenskii), whom many dissident clergy considered to be a conservative because of his rejection of the "social gospel" interpretation of Christianity and his strong criticism of socialist ideology, which some Renovationists defended as compatible with Christian values. Metropolitan Vladimir apparently arranged to have several monks under his supervision accuse Father Grigorii of false religious teaching.[17] As a result, late in the fall of 1906 the diocesan consistory of St. Petersburg recalled Father Grigorii to the capital to face formal charges. Although the charges were dropped for lack of evidence, the consistory reprimanded Father Grigorii for violations of church discipline and ordered him imprisoned in the Cheremenets monastery for three months. The conditions of his imprisonment were not very restrictive, however, as he was allowed to receive numerous visitors from the capital.[18] Nevertheless, as a result of his confinement, Father Grigorii was unable to take the seat he had been elected to in the second Duma.[19] Some Duma members wanted to organize a protest on his behalf, but Father Grigorii requested that they refrain from such action, expressing his belief that justice would eventually win out.[20]

After his term of imprisonment was completed, however, Father Grigorii was forbidden to return to St. Petersburg. The Synod renewed its ban on his preaching and writing, extending it to include all public activity. In frustration, Father Grigorii wrote a long letter defending his work to Metropolitan Antonii.[21] Antonii had always been sympathetic to Petrov's ideas; after the consistory's first judgment against Petrov in 1907, Antonii had personally written to the director general of the Synod to praise Father Grigorii's work and to request clemency.[22] Whether his intervention had any effect is difficult to judge, but clearly it was not sufficient to restore Petrov's freedoms to him. Having already suffered from the restrictions placed on his work in the years before the revolution, Father Grigorii lashed out at this new injustice. Like the arkhimandrite Mikhail, Father Grigorii conceived of the church's mission in terms of working for justice and blamed the continued existence of injustice on the church's subordination to the powerful and wealthy. In his letter, Petrov declared that he had entered the clergy because he wanted to dedicate his life to building a society based upon the principles of justice and truth that would make possible the realization of the Kingdom of God on earth. He believed that this task was the primary mission of the church, an endeavor that all Christians were called to undertake. Yet despite the passage of nearly two thousand years since the time of Jesus, little progress had been made toward accomplishing this mission. In Russia, which boasted of its devotion to the faith and its holy mission to the world, Christianity had little impact on social conditions:

> The upper classes rule over the lower ones. By means of a small, close-knit group they hold the whole rest of the population—tens and hundreds of laboring millions—in servitude. They have seized everything from the lower classes: wealth, power, science, art, even religion. They have made the latter into their maidservant. To the mass of the people, they have left poverty and ignorance. Instead of joy, they have given them drunkenness. Instead of religion, they have given them crude superstition. And labor. Punishing, thankless labor without rest.[23]

What accounted for the failure of Christianity to make more of a difference in the world? Father Grigorii laid the blame squarely on the church. Religion had become another tool that the powerful could use to guarantee and justify their privileges. Once the church had become a part of the establishment it had allowed itself to be seduced by the blandishments of wealth and power. It had abandoned the teachings of the Gospels, which called for radical change and the transformation of the human world, in favor of a self-indulgent and comfortable hypocrisy. It had preached a meaningless religion of personal goodness and individual salvation, all the while ignoring social evil and the damnation of a society that allowed generations of people to suffer without hope and in bitter silence. The clergy witnessed this suffering; indeed, they knew it better than anyone else could:

> They stand close to the mass of the common people, close to the very heart of their life, seeing all their need and their rightless condition, hearing the ocean of groans coming up from below, nourished on the people's tears, suffocated under the oppression of a terrible nightmare created in this country by the violence of a godless power that rules without the right to do so.[24]

But the clergy were forbidden even to bear witness to the suffering of their people, for they were told that the political and social and economic problems they saw every day did not concern them. Father Grigorii argued, however, that *all* problems afflicting society concerned the clergy: "It cannot be said to the clergy that politics is a matter only for those in the government; that the workers' question, the land question, the nationalities question don't concern them. All of these questions are precisely the concern of the clergy, and the clergy before all others."[25] The clergy had to be concerned with issues related to social justice if they were to fulfill their mission of leading the community toward the realization of the Kingdom of God. For Father Grigorii, however, it had become clear that the established church as it existed in his time had become an obstacle to achieving the goals of Christianity. Expressing both anger and regret, he renounced the historical church in favor of the Church Eternal, saying: "I believe in the one, holy, catholic and apostolic church, but the servile, monastic Byzantinism, that soulless Pobedonostsevism that goes by the name of Orthodoxy, I renounce with all my reason and all my strength."[26] As a result of this letter, which was printed abroad and smuggled back into Russia for distribution, Father Grigorii was brought up before the consistory on charges of insubordination.[27] This time, the judgment was more severe. In February of 1908, the consistory ordered Petrov to be defrocked and banned from St. Petersburg and Moscow for seven years. Defrocking was a serious penalty that had repercussions for the priest's civil status as well as his clerical one: the defrocked priest could not serve in the government or in any public institution for twenty years and was deprived of his pension and any other privileges deriving from his former position. Petrov moved to Tver, but the local bishop constantly interfered with his activities as a publicist and repeatedly tried to have his books banned. He also suffered continual harassment from the parties of the Right, who attacked him mercilessly in their papers and pamphlets.[28] He remained in the provinces working as a correspondent for the liberal newspaper *The Word (Slovo)* through World War I. After the Bolshevik Revolution he emigrated to Serbia, where he gave lectures for a time before leaving for Paris. He died in exile there in 1925.

The Renovationist press regarded Father Grigorii's fate as an ominous sign of the future awaiting other members of the clerical opposition. Father Grigorii was practically an institution in his own right in the capital, given his long history of public service and his broad network of supporters at the highest levels of the church and society. While he was serving out his term of monastery confinement, hundreds of visitors made their way out to the countryside to visit him while the Synod and the St. Petersburg consistory were inundated with petitions on his behalf.[29] Liberal secular newspapers reported regularly on his case, some of them with considerable sympathy. Predictably, Father Grigorii's case was the main subject in the Renovationist press as well as in less partisan clerical publications. The process against him was widely condemned as unfair and unjust, with the blame assigned to the bishops and bureaucrats who controlled the machinery of the ecclesiastical administration.[30] Beneath this groundswell of support for Petrov, however, rumbled the first tremors of fear. If clergymen as famous, popular, and well-connected as Father Mikhail and Father Grigorii could be successfully persecuted by church authorities, was *anyone* really safe?

The students of the St. Petersburg Ecclesiastical Academy quickly discovered their vulnerability. Less than two weeks after Father Mikhail's dismissal from the school the academy students published a letter in the Renovationist journal *Vek* denouncing the church's leaders for abusing their authority to achieve political aims that were fundamentally at odds with the principles of Christianity.[31] Alarmed by the students' audacity, the faculty council of the academy convened an assembly three days after the letter appeared in order to warn students against further challenges to the Synod. The Synod itself responded a week and a half later with a stern decree forbidding all forms of student organization at the academies.[32] Barely a month later, the Synod's announcement of the consistory's first decision against Father Grigorii was accompanied by a reiteration of the prohibition against student organizations and an order to the faculty council to disband existing student organizations (apparently formed or maintained in spite of the earlier prohibition).[33] The council was slow to act, however, and within a few days of the judgment against Petrov the students had organized a meeting and composed a letter of support for him.[34] They prefaced the letter by claiming that the Synod had no authority to forbid their organizations. The Synod retaliated by ordering the expulsion of everyone who had signed the letter. When a new group of students drafted a petition demanding that Father Grigorii be allowed to take his seat in the Duma, the Synod ordered them expelled as well.[35] The swiftness and severity of the Synod's response had its desired effect. By the beginning of March, the students who remained at the academy were divided, confused, and deeply demoralized, a condition that one church publicist labeled "an invisible tragedy."[36] The Synod had demonstrated its determination to defend its authority against challenges from within the church. Further protests seemed pointless.

The students of the ecclesiastical academy may have been an especially vulnerable target for the Synod's exercise in authority but they were not the only ones to suffer for the public expression of their political opinions. Clergymen who continued to demonstrate liberal political sympathies after the dissolution of the first Duma paid a price for their convictions. At the national level, Father Nikolai Ognev, a priest who had been elected to the first Duma, was defrocked after signing the Vyborg Manifesto, which protested the Duma's dissolution by the emperor and called for mass civil disobedience. Five clerical deputies affiliated with parties on the Left in the second Duma were defrocked because they refused to obey a synodal instruction to support the parties of the Right when they took control of the floor of the Duma to issue a wide-ranging attack on liberal forces in Russian society in connection with the purported discovery of a conspiracy against the emperor's life.[37] While these official actions affected only a few clergymen, many others took them as a warning of what might happen to clerical dissidents. Moreover, these cases of political repression did not seem to be isolated. From the fall of 1906, the Renovationist newspapers of the capital regularly reported on cases from around the empire in which politically active, dissident clergy were disciplined, allegedly for their liberal or radical political views.[38] Week after week, there were new cases, mostly priests who were punished for the ideas they expressed in their sermons, lectures, or writings. Frequently, the Synod imposed censorship on those individual priests who were considered to have dangerous opinions, forbidding them from publishing or preaching. Clergymen whom bishops considered to be egregious or repeated violators of such controls were subjected to demotions, involuntary transfers, suspensions, imprisonment, and defrocking, with some clergymen suffering repeated penalties. At least one priest was reported to have committed suicide to escape the persecution he suffered at the hands of his bishop.[39] In the capital itself, the papers reported that one Father Orlov, who served at the city military prison, was dismissed from his position and threatened with defrocking after an informer accused him of giving an anti-government speech and reading revolutionary literature to the prisoners. Further investigation proved that he had simply been reading from the Gospels. Although he was not defrocked, he was also not reinstated to his former position.[40]

In addition to taking action against particular individuals among the clergy, the church administration also reasserted its control over the ecclesiastical press. A synodal decree of 25 November 1906 restored preliminary censorship for all church publications, thus bringing to an abrupt end the single year of freedom that the church's periodicals had enjoyed.[41] A month later, on 30 December, the Synod gave rectors at the ecclesiastical academies the right to exercise preliminary censorship over the publications of their institutions.[42] The following spring, church authorities began to put pressure on particular publications that were considered too critical of the post-October order. In May of 1907, Metropolitan Antonii warned the faculty council at the academy that *Tserkovnyi vestnik,* the national-circulation newspaper they had produced since 1875, was showing "anti-church" tendencies as demonstrated by its outspoken criticism of the delay in calling the church council, its support for church reform, its defense of the clergy's right to participate freely in politics, and its denunciation of the parties of the Right. The metropolitan stated that if the newspaper's editorial course were not corrected it would be closed down.[43] The warning had an immediate and noticeable impact. In mid-May, the type of subjects the newspaper covered and its editorial tone changed abruptly and dramatically. Articles in favor of church reform were replaced by articles attacking lay intellectuals who supported church reform, while editorials on political topics disappeared. The paper did not comment on either the emperor's casual dismissal of the work of the pre-council conference at the end of May or the dissolution of the second Duma in June. The tone of "neutrality" and the posture of meek compliance that the paper displayed after the warning were a stunning contrast to the earlier attitude of independent, self-confident criticism. The threat of repression alone had been enough to bring the paper into line and deprive the pro-reform clergy and laity of an important national forum for the expression and discussion of their views.

But perhaps the editors of *Tserkovnyi vestnik* were right to heed the metropolitan's warning with such alacrity, for the events of the following weeks demonstrated that the threat of closure was not an idle one. In June, authorities swiftly moved in to close down most of the publications produced by the capital's pro-reform clergy. City authorities raided the Renovationist journals *Vek* and *Tserkovnoe obnovlenie* in early June. The remaining copies of their June issues were confiscated and their presses were seized. The mildly liberal journal of the Society for Moral Religious-Enlightenment, *Tserkovnyi golos,* was handled more discreetly, but nevertheless it folded before the month was out. Only the Renovationist journal *Zvonar'* managed to stay open as a result of the grim tenacity of its editors and contributors. Between March and June of 1907 it did not appear at all because its chief editor, the archpriest Xenophon Belkov, was accused before a civil court of slandering the church for printing a letter exposing corruption in the Kharkov consistory.[44] He was acquitted of that charge but then defrocked by Metropolitan Antonii because he had violated church discipline in publicly defending Petrov after Petrov's expulsion from the clergy. Belkov was later reinstated after demonstrating on appeal that he had not violated any of the church canons, but by then the journal he had launched had been taken over by a new publisher and a new editor.[45] They remained true to Father Xenophon's vision, maintaining the journal's defiant attitude toward church authorities and its avowed belief in political and ecclesiastical reform. After a series of clashes with the censors during the fall, the journal was finally banned in December by the city prefect. Its last issue was confiscated, a crushing fine was imposed, and the editor and publisher were both arrested. The authorities were certain they had destroyed the publication, yet in January of 1908 it defiantly reappeared with a new editor, a new publisher, and a new name: *The Red Bell (Krasnyi zvon).* The new motto on the paper's masthead clearly signaled a determination to keep up its fight: "Do not put out the Spirit's fire" (1 Thess. 5:19). The journal continued to appear for two more years, despite additional fines, frequent changes of editorship, and the difficulty of finding a printer who would take on the press work. Not until the end of 1909 was the journal finally forced to close down for good after finally being bankrupted by the cost of its heroic resistance.

The stifling atmosphere of oppression that settled over the clergy of St. Petersburg in 1907 and 1908 was thickened by the Synod's attack against the St. Petersburg Ecclesiastical Academy, from which so many of the clergy had graduated and to which many still retained close ties. The dismissal of the three Renovationists among the faculty in November of 1906 and the expulsion of dozens of students supportive of Father Grigorii in February of 1907 were but the first moves in the authorities' campaign to eradicate unrest and disaffection in the church's schools.[46] In March 1908, the director general of the Synod instructed the archbishop of Kazan, Dmitrii (Koval'nitskii) to carry out a thorough investigation of every aspect of life at the academy. Publicly, the goal of the investigation was to determine the causes of student unrest during the 1905 revolution and recommend changes to the school's charter. In reality Peter Izvol'skii, the new director general of the Synod, wanted the investigator to identify all faculty who were critical of the church administration or the government so that they could be dismissed and to discover as much evidence as possible to support a radical alteration of the charter in favor of expanding the Synod's control over the school.[47] The investigation went on for months, with Archbishop Dmitrii inquiring into such matters as the names of books that students had checked out from the school library and the content of articles that professors had submitted to the school's publications, especially the suspect *Tserkovnyi vestnik*. The course of the investigation was closely followed in the one Renovationist periodical that remained open at this time.[48] When the investigation ended with the dismissal of the rector and seven professors, the expulsion of several dozen students, and the restoration of the statute of 1884 in place of the temporary rule written by the faculty council and hastily approved by the Synod in the midst of the 1905 revolution, the liberal clergy were appalled. The growing number of restrictions placed on the school in 1909, the decline of morale, and the imposition of the repressive new statute of 1910 deeply concerned those clergymen who had received their own training there. They feared that they saw in the repression of the academy the destruction of the future of the church itself.[49]

REFORM RUNS AGROUND

Even as the revolution came to an end and the authority of both state and church was restored, the St. Petersburg clergy continued to hope that church reform would soon be enacted. After the pre-council conference closed in mid-December of 1906, optimists anticipated that the council itself would be convened within a few weeks or, at most, within a couple of months.[50] As the winter passed with no further action on the part of the Synod or the emperor, the Renovationist journals grew restless. Lacking any solid information on plans for the council, the press reported rumors and indulged in speculation. The hierarchs were unjustly accused of resisting reform in the hope of maintaining their own power at the expense of the rest of the church.[51] The Synod was suspected of planning to hijack the reform process to advance its own self-serving goals while denying the wishes of the rest of the church.[52] Predictions that the council would be called after the Synod had completed preparations alternated with warnings that the Synod would never allow the council to be convened. In the meantime, petitions for particular reforms flowed to the offices of the Duma in a steady stream from clergymen and lay persons in the provinces, eventually leading the Synod to issue a decree forbidding all such petitions and asserting that it alone had the authority to carry out church reform.[53] As the months of delay turned into years, the reformist clergy continued to hope against hope that a council might yet be called.[54] Rumors that the council would soon be convened continued to appear in the Petersburg church journals in 1910 and 1911, becoming more frequent in 1912 after a new commission to study the reform question was organized.[55] At first, the liberal clerical papers of St. Petersburg welcomed the commission, believing that reform was still both necessary and possible.[56] However, disappointment soon set in when the members of the commission turned out to be the most reactionary of the hierarchs, whose clear intention was to set aside most of the modernizing and democratizing recommendations agreed upon by the comparatively balanced 1906 conference.[57] Even that work seemed to do little to bring the hope of a council closer to realization, however.[58] Though the pro-reform clergy were inclined to blame the failure to convene the council on the Synod, in truth the blame rested squarely on the shoulders of the emperor.[59] The hierarchy had demonstrated both their readiness and willingness to carry out serious reforms in the replies they had submitted to Pobedonostsev in the summer of 1905 and in the contributions they made to the pre-council conference in the spring and fall of 1906.[60] At the conference itself, however, it had been confirmed that an all-Russian church council could be convened only upon the order of the emperor. As long as Nicholas II refused to issue the summons to the council, there was little that individual hierarchs or the Synod itself could do on the matter of church reform.

Some supporters hoped that individual reforms might be enacted even without the council, either through the Synod or the Duma. One such project was that of parish reform.[61] The issue of parish reform had been a subject of discussion among the clergy and church bureaucrats since the 1870s, when the expansion of the city and the growth of the population began to put a strain on the existing parish system. Discussions on this issue had intensified in the 1890s as educated lay persons involved in church matters became interested in the subject. An article by the lay publicist A. A. Papkov published in one of the leading journals of the capital in 1902 brought the issue to the attention of the general public.[62] Thereafter, reform of the parish came to be seen as essential in any general plan for reform of the church. The Synod announced its intention to enact parish reform in November of 1905, issuing a temporary rule to serve in the meantime and encouraging the formation of parish councils to discuss the needs of the parishes. The parish question was one of the seven main areas of reform identified by the pre-council conference. A subcommittee staffed by experts on the matter worked out a detailed reform proposal that was submitted to the tsar and the Synod at the end of the conference meetings in 1906. A special committee appointed by the Synod then spent a year reviewing the proposal before accepting it. The reform plan was returned to the Synod, which submitted it to Director General Izvol'skii for approval in the spring of 1908. After Izvol'skii approved the project, it entered the labyrinth of the imperial bureaucracy. The director general sent it to the Council of Ministers, which passed it on to the Ministries of Education and Justice for review. Those ministries returned the project with recommendations for revision to the Council of Ministers, which handed it back to the director general in February of 1909. The Synod then decided to make alterations in the project based on those recommendations. The revision took more than a year and a half to work out. At the end of 1910 the revised project was finally completed and ready to undergo a second round of reviews. Before that process had been completed, however, the project was abruptly recalled to the director general's office. Izvol'skii had been replaced (in the summer of 1911) by Vladimir Sabler, who disagreed with some of the details of the project approved by his predecessor. The proposal was returned to the Synod, which continued to work on it for three more long years.[63]

Meanwhile, the Duma developed several parish reform projects of its own, which underwent a separate but equally fruitless round of revision and review between 1910 and 1914.[64] The Synod protested the Duma's interference in church affairs, but in vain, for the Duma was not alone in its impatience for reform; one of the projects it considered originated in the Ministry of the Interior. In any case, the Duma's opinions had to be acknowledged since that body's approval was required before the Synod's project could become law. The Synod finally submitted its proposal to the Duma in the summer of 1914, almost nine years after it had issued the temporary parish rule. Once the war broke out, the Duma became preoccupied by more pressing issues. It appointed a commission to review all the legal materials pertaining to the reform. The assignment took more than a year to complete and resulted in a handbook of more than a thousand pages. Another year passed before the Duma appointed a committee to consider the reform itself in 1916.[65] The file containing copies of the committee's work suggests that they were not even close to producing a final version of the reform. All of the draft projects were heavily marked with revisions but with no indication of a consensus on which would be best or how to craft a compromise between them. In 1917, time ran out and the project was left unfinished.[66]

THE WALLS CLOSE IN—
Church and Society after 1907

The years after the 1905 revolution saw an abrupt reversal of the trends that had marked relations between the church and society before 1905. The failure to reform the church had disappointed many lay people and clergymen at the same time that debates about what and how to reform had highlighted internal rivalries and exacerbated feelings of suspicion and distrust. The heavy-handed attempts made by the Synod and a number of the bishops to interfere in the Duma elections angered those members of the lower clergy who had more liberal political opinions, in addition to alienating the parties of the Left. Likewise, the Synod's angry criticisms of the Duma's activism in legislating on church-related matters and the public association of a few prominent clergymen with organizations of the Right infuriated supporters of both the Center and the Left without winning the church much credibility with any other important constituency.[67] Frustration and disappointment with the church increased at the same time that opportunities to engage in socially useful public work outside the church through the political parties, the press, and secular voluntary societies increased. The result of this combination of developments was the decline of the church's major organizations for social outreach work, as demonstrated by the post-revolutionary developments that the Society for Moral-Religious Enlightenment (ORRP) and the Nevskii Society experienced.

After 1905, the ORRP saw a large decline in its overall membership and significant changes in the origins and affiliations of its members. By 1912, its membership had declined from a pre-revolutionary peak of about 1,700 to around 900. Only about half of the 900 members belonged to the main body of the ORRP; the remainder were members of mission-specific sub-organizations, either the Religious-Educational Union or the youth group. The Religious-Educational Union, which sent members to prisons and hospitals to share the Gospels with inmates, had been an exclusively lay (and predominantly female) organization before 1905, but the decline in membership after the revolution led the society to encourage the participation of clergymen to make up for the shortfall of lay volunteers. Similarly the youth society, which had once been dominated by university students, also experienced a dramatic decline in lay members after 1907, but the decline was offset by a great influx of academy students. Of those who remained affiliated with the society's main body, barely more than 300 were donors, less than half the number that the society had once had to support its work.[68] On the bright side, there were about 250 active members involved in giving lectures and leading discussions; this represented a considerable increase in size. However, the overwhelming majority of these active members were clergymen; in 1910, there were only 17 lay people among the active members, a notable decline from the several dozen that had regularly served as lecturers in the pre-1905 period.[69] Part of this decline may have been due to the fact that there were also far fewer students from the academy taking part in the ORRP's work than there had been previously. Before the revolution there had been over 100 academy students volunteering for the society, nearly all of them of lay status; by 1910, that number was down to 48, and the majority of these students were already in clerical orders.[70]

Although the reasons for these changes are not entirely clear, it is indisputable that the society's active lay membership declined greatly after the revolution. These losses could not be made up entirely from the ranks of the clergy. As a result, the ORRP was compelled to accept certain changes in its work. Because it had fewer donors it had less money, forcing it to curtail its extensive charitable and educational activities and focus again primarily on religious teaching. The society's numerous schools, classes, libraries, and clinics were closed due both to the shortage of funds and the lack of lay volunteers needed to staff such services.[71] The society maintained its lectures for the members of educated society, but found that they were increasingly unsuccessful. As attendance dropped, the society scheduled a reduced number of lectures at a single location; even so, the number of attendees declined to ten thousand for the whole year of 1910 and to around seven thousand in 1912.[72] Moreover, many of those who attended were workers rather than educated people. This was the case in all areas of the society's work: their lectures and services drew large working-class audiences, especially on the great holidays, but fewer and fewer educated listeners.[73] Some of the society's leaders began to doubt whether the society had any further reason to exist, since it had been founded specifically to bring the church's teachings to the educated classes. At the annual meeting of 1912, the executive council of the ORRP explained to its supporters that the organization's declining numbers were the natural result of more and more local clergymen taking over the work they had once done.[74] There were no further annual reports published after that year. Thirty-two years after its founding, the ORRP seems to have simply evaporated.

Its daughter organization, the Nevskii Society, experienced a more drastic decline. By 1912, its membership had dwindled from a pre-revolutionary peak of more than 75,000 members, many committed to long-term pledges of one year or more, to only 37,765 members, mostly local working-class men who had signed on for three-month pledges.[75] Lay involvement in the activities of the Nevskii Society had fallen off precipitously; the Nevskii Society, like the ORRP, had become increasingly the domain of the clergy. In part, this decline resulted from the expansion of the secular temperance movement associated with the St. Petersburg Commission on Alcoholism. Some clergymen were active in this temperance organization as well, but the tensions that had always existed between religious and secular reformers on how and why to promote temperance increased significantly in the post-revolutionary period.[76] At a national conference organized by the St. Petersburg Commission on Alcoholism in 1910, rancorous arguments and bitter recriminations divided clerical and lay temperance supporters.[77] The clergy withdrew from the organization and called a rival conference, which met two years later in Moscow. In St. Petersburg, the rupturing of the temperance movement that occurred at the 1910 conference marked the end of an era of lay-clerical cooperation on the issue of temperance.

The estrangement between educated lay society and the progressive clergy that developed in the post-revolutionary years in St. Petersburg was manifested in other ways as well. When the St. Petersburg Religious-Philosophical Society was revived in 1908 it did not include among its members any clergymen or academy professors; the Synod expressly forbade academy professors to participate in the society. True, Alexander Kartashev, who had taken part in the meetings of the first society when he was a professor at the academy, was one of the new society's founding members, but he was no longer employed by the church; he had been dismissed in 1906 as a result of his association with the Renovationists. Without the participation of clergymen or theologians, the society tended to concern itself primarily with philosophical matters. The disgraced archimandrite Mikhail, who had been the church's star defender during the Religious-Philosophical Society meetings of 1901–1903, reported on the first meetings of the new society for the Renovationist newspaper *Vek* early in 1908. In his opinion, the discussions had become so far removed both from the real concerns of Russian society and the profound questions concerning religion in the modern world that the discussions seemed trivial and pointless.[78] Although the new society continued to meet in the capital for a number of years, its activities received no further notice from the clerical press. In part this was because after 1908, the clergy's publications ceased to make much effort to appeal to secular readers, confining themselves instead to a narrow clerical audience and to religious and ecclesiastical issues. Lay readership of the two most substantial and prominent publications of the church in St. Petersburg dropped off sharply after censorship was reimposed: by 1913, both *Tserkovnyi vestnik* and *Khristianskoe chtenie* were on the verge of bankruptcy because of the decline in their subscriptions over the previous several years. The clergy's other liberal publications did not fare much better. The several new publications that appeared after 1910 were short-lived not because they were suppressed, as the publications of the immediate post-revolutionary period had been, but because they were impoverished.[79]

The clergy of St. Petersburg, so long accustomed to being engaged in the public life of the city through their organizations and publications, felt an increasing isolation, which made them much less able to defend themselves against the authorities' repressions.[80] Clerical commentators noted that while the authorities' persecution of Father Grigorii had stirred up educated society for a brief time other cases of official harassment of other liberal clergymen had aroused little interest, let alone outrage, among lay people. In part, this was because the clergymen who suffered were not as famous; in part, it was because the church maintained an independent disciplinary system that was highly resistant to popular pressure and the intervention of local authorities. Still, the clergy of St. Petersburg were profoundly disappointed that the repression of liberals within the church went virtually unremarked by secular liberals, especially those in the Duma, who might at least have lodged some formal objection against the Synod.[81]

Worse yet was the clergy's feeling that their isolation from secular reformers further hindered the Duma's efforts to reform the church. Many members of the lower clergy were highly critical of the Synod's defensive conservatism and the inflammatory politics of some prominent churchmen, but stifled as they were by the authorities' censorship and repression they were unable to communicate their views to the general public. Their failure to communicate was not for lack of trying. Despite great difficulties, the liberal clergy of St. Petersburg managed to maintain at least one publication expressing their views for much of the inter-revolutionary period: in 1908 and 1909, they had *Krasnyi zvon;* from 1911 to 1913, *The Parish Priest (Prikhodskii sviashchennik);* from 1912 to 1915, *The Church-Social Herald (Tserkovno-obshchestvennyi vestnik);* and in 1916, the journals *Church and Society (Tserkov' i obshchestvo)* and *Church and Life (Tserkov' i zhizn').* Through these publications, they continued to explain and justify their modernist views on the relation between the church and society. But they were preaching to the converted, so to speak. Their voices were not heard beyond the thick wall the authorities of the church had erected around them.

In frustration, the St. Petersburg clergy began to turn in on themselves during the inter-revolutionary years. The repressive conditions in the church demoralized many, who became isolated not only from liberals in secular society but also from like-minded individuals within the church. The crackdown on prominent liberals among the clergy in 1907 and 1908 frightened others with similar views into retreating from the public sphere. By the late spring of 1907, the Renovationist Union was forced to close after seeing its journals shut down and its leading members dragged into court, thrown into prison, and finally cast out of the ranks of the clergy. Not surprisingly, when a few hardy survivors proposed that the organization be revived as a discussion group rather than a political party in the fall of 1908 few clergymen ventured to join.[82] The risks still seemed too great, not only to rejoin the Renovationists but to become associated with any organization in the public sphere. Many members of the clergy felt it was safest to withdraw to their local churches and forswear any further political activity.

Some clergymen reacted to this forcible deactivation by intensifying and expanding their criticisms of the church and even of Christianity itself. This was the case with Arkhimandrite Mikhail. When the controversy over his nomination as a Duma candidate for the Union of Russian People began in 1906, he had considered himself to be a supporter of the Constitutional Democrats (while also a member of the Renovationist Union). In the years that followed, however, his political and religious views became more radical as his personal experience of repression and injustice deepened the sympathy he had already expressed in his writings for the poor and working classes. This process culminated around 1910, when Mikhail (who had by that time been elevated, albeit uncanonically, to the rank of bishop in the Old Believer church) became associated with an effort to reinterpret some of the essential teachings of Christianity.[83] Mikhail characterized this

reinterpretation as the Christianity of Golgotha; its adherents called themselves "Free" Christians. The essays he wrote for their journal *The New Earth
(Novaia Zemlia)* betrayed the intellectual scars of his earlier battle with
church authorities. Most obvious was his rejection of the church as an institution necessary for the practice of Christianity. He condemned the
church as a fawning servant of earthly powers that had perverted the teachings of Christianity by using them to justify war, poverty, and injustice. As
Father Grigorii Petrov had done in his 1908 letter to Metropolitan Antonii,
Mikhail accused the church of false preaching, indifference, superstition, and
ignorance. He blamed church leaders for developing an institutional cult that
obscured the real teaching of the Bible with dogmas and sacraments and laws
made by men.[84] Mikhail's attitude led him to reject all the rituals and rules
that had come to be considered typical of the Orthodox church, as he contended that the essential Christian practices were individual prayer, private
reading of the Bible, and communal celebration of the Eucharist.[85]

Father Mikhail's rejection of the church reflected his belief that evil existed not in the hearts of individuals but in laws and institutions that per-
petuated violence and injustice.[86] During his time in the capital, Mikhail
had been profoundly affected by witnessing the poverty and misery endured by the poor and working classes, particularly by the women and children. During the revolution, prominent church leaders such as Vladimir
(Bogoiavlenskii), the metropolitan of Moscow, had tried to pacify urban
workers by explaining that their patient suffering on earth was known to
God and would be rewarded in heaven.[87] Mikhail angrily rejected this
teaching, believing that it enabled the church to tolerate what should be
intolerable: the unjust exploitation of some human beings by others in the
name of profit. In his view, the kind of suffering endured by the working
classes had no higher purpose; it was fundamentally wrong, and perpetuat-
ing it was sinful. He concluded that the church, which had long tolerated
the ills of society and had even sought to justify suffering as good and necessary for individuals, was the very embodiment of the ways in which institutions promoted evil in the world.[88] Father Mikhail further blamed the
church for failing to carry out the primary mission that Jesus had entrusted
to his followers: the establishment of the Kingdom of God on earth. In his
view, the purpose of Christianity was to eliminate human suffering by creating a just society in which there was no oppression. He did not believe
the kingdom to be internal in any sense or to have anything to do with the
afterlife, heaven, the second coming of Christ, or the end of human history.[89] It was to be created on earth in historical time by human beings. It
did not have any higher purpose but was an end in itself.[90] Furthermore, he
did not see it as the work of individuals but of all humankind. He rejected
the idea of individual salvation and embraced the concept of collective salvation instead, explaining his conviction that no one person could be
saved if others were damned.[91] Not only did he argue that salvation itself
would be collective, but also that it would be attained as a result of the sac-

rifices of the believing community. This argument was based on Father Mikhail's unorthodox interpretation of Jesus' final ordeal. Rejecting the traditional view that Jesus Christ was a divine-human being who suffered death to offer redemption for the sins of those who acclaimed him, Father Mikhail asserted that Jesus was an innocent, fully human man who voluntarily accepted the suffering wrongly inflicted on him in order to demonstrate a higher concept of justice.[92] He argued that like Jesus, each individual must take personal responsibility for the suffering of the world and undertake his own road to Golgotha—an ordeal of innocent suffering for others—in order to redeem the world.

Father Mikhail presented the main tenets of his "Golgotha Christianity" in several articles he wrote for an important Old Believer journal, *Old Believer Thought (Staroobriadcheskaia mysl')*. Not surprisingly, the articles attracted the attention of critics. In August of 1910, the Old Believer Council devoted several hours to discussing his views and his position in the church.[93] In the end the council affirmed the decision made the previous year to suspend him from serving as a priest. Instead, the bishop Mikhail made his living as a journalist, publishing both in Old Believer journals and in the secular press. In 1915, he developed a nervous disease that led indirectly to his early death in 1916.[94]

Although Father Mikhail's ideas do not seem to have exerted a noticeable influence on the clergy of St. Petersburg in the inter-revolutionary period, there were many others who shared Mikhail's feelings of bitterness, anger, and despair. During the last years of the old regime, church censorship prevented clergymen from expressing their sentiments openly, but once the first revolution of 1917 had broken the bonds of enforced silence the church had to reap the whirlwind. A number of men whom the church had repressed during the inter-revolutionary years emerged as leaders in the struggle against the church that was waged in the decade following 1917.[95] One of these individuals was B. V. Titlinov, a scholar of church history who had been hired by the St. Petersburg Ecclesiastical Academy in 1909 to replace a professor dismissed by the Synod for his liberal opinions. Titlinov's promising career had been damaged by a long and hard-fought ideological battle over the "orthodoxy" of the work he submitted for his doctoral degree. Even after he had wrested his diploma from the hands of the Synod, he had been barred from further advancements in rank, ostensibly because he was a layman. Although he was repeatedly pressured to take clerical orders, he refused to become a priest in order to advance his career. After the February revolution, he was one of the organizers of the revived Renovationist Union, which later became known as the Living Church. He became the director of propaganda and publications, setting aside his scholarly training to write a patently partisan and unscholarly work on the history of the church, a work that came to serve as a model for Soviet antireligious propaganda for decades to come.[96] Other prominent leaders of the Living Church included the archpriest Xenophon Belkov, the tenacious

publisher of the Renovationist journal *Zvonar'*, and Father Alexander Vvedenskii, who had been punished for his radical preaching during World
War I.[97] At least one member of the liberal clergy went a step further:
Mikhail V. Galkin, a young priest whose father had maintained an active
social ministry in the capital and who had himself worked as a temperance
activist and co-editor (with his father) of the liberal journal *Prikhodskii sviashchennik,* abandoned the church altogether to become an anti-religious
propagandist for the Bolsheviks.[98]

If the trying conditions of church life in the capital after 1907 left some
clergymen despairing and embittered, many others found reasons for hope
in the last years of the old regime. Among these clergymen the belief that
they remained close to the people offset the sense that they were alienated
from the hierarchy and estranged from educated society. In fact, the
clergy's connection with the common people was one of the recurring
themes in the liberal clerical press after the 1905 revolution. At first, the focus was on the importance of the clergy maintaining the role they had
claimed during the 1905 revolution as leaders of the people. In 1907,
Tserkovnyi vestnik argued that the clergy had to resist the hierarchy's efforts
to drive them out of the public sphere and to remain active, because their
selfless efforts were essential to establishing the social peace needed to carry
out reforms.[99] This idea was taken up in other clerical publications as well.
In an article complaining about the injustice of the authorities' repression
of clerical activists, *Tserkovnyi golos* argued that the clergy were the people's
natural leaders in difficult times and urged the clergy not to abandon the
people. Similarly, an article published later that year in *Zvonar'* insisted that
the clergy's work was essential for the social and moral development of the
common people.[100]

As the opportunities for political activism diminished in the years following the 1905 revolution, the clerical press turned to the question of
how the clergy could preserve and strengthen their bonds with the people
without becoming involved directly in politics. The answer most frequently
offered focused on the renewal and expansion of pastoral work, described
broadly enough to include involvement in projects—such as cooperative
societies and credit unions—that clergymen would once have considered to
be none of their concern. In a striking group of articles published in *Krasnyi
zvon* in January 1908, author after author pointed out to the clergy that
they were responsible not only for the people's religious needs but also for
their material and moral development. While encouraging the clergy to focus their attention on their parishes, the articles reminded them that they
should seek to engage themselves as deeply as possible in all aspects of the
people's lives, not just the religious but also the economic, social, and cultural.[101] One author argued that the clergy's most urgent task was to understand how the needs of their parishioners had changed and to learn how to
meet the new demands for informed leadership on a broad range of social
and moral issues at the local level.[102] Other authors pointed out that the

clergy could rely upon the religious principles of the Gospels to inform and inspire their efforts to improve the social and material conditions of their parishioners' lives.[103] Taken together, these articles indicate that the liberal clergy came to see parish-level pastoral work as providing them the opportunity they sought to work for change in the lives of the common folk.

In the later years of the inter-revolutionary period, a complementary idea developed according to which pastoral work was a means for achieving church reform. As hopes that the church would be reformed from above by a church council, the Synod, or the Duma faded, some liberal clergymen suggested that clergymen engaged in pastoral work might transform the church from below. This prospect was first identified in *Krasnyi zvon* by an author who argued that reform of the church depended on reform of the parish and that parish reform in turn depended on the leadership of the parish clergy. He concluded that as the clergy worked to change the social and religious conditions that prevailed in their own parishes the revived Christian spirit would spread throughout society and eventually bring about the renewal of the church from within.[104] For that reason, evidence of the clergy's pastoral activism was to be welcomed. When *Prikhodskii sviashchennik* surveyed the life of the church in 1912, it pointed out that the multiplication of parish-based cooperative societies, temperance clubs, libraries, missionary centers, and extra-liturgical teaching in parishes throughout the empire promised well for the church's future because it demonstrated the commitment of the clergy to their work and the support of the people for the clergy's initiatives.[105] In 1914, the journal *Tserkovno-obshchestvennyi vestnik* declared that although there was no longer any hope that the church would be reformed from above, the successes of the clergy's pastoral work demonstrated that the clergy and the people could reclaim the church for themselves and revive it from within.[106] In returning to the ideas of pastorship that had developed before the 1905 revolution, the clergy who pursued this path pointed out one of the ways by which the church might have been able to give its mission meaning in the modern world without succumbing to the seductions of secularized thought or the temptations of popular politics.

During the inter-revolutionary period, the church found itself in an extraordinarily difficult position. It remained legally and financially dependent upon the state and thus was not at liberty to act strictly according to its own interests, as the issue of church reform most clearly demonstrated. The majority of the hierarchs not only supported but strongly advocated church reform; moreover, they had carried out much of the preliminary work necessary to implement a serious, wide-ranging reform program. Yet despite the desires of the church's leaders, the parish clergy, and many among the laity (including prominent members of the central imperial administration) church reform ultimately was not enacted because Emperor Nicholas

II opposed it. Whatever degree of independence the church enjoyed in some areas of its internal life, it is clear that in this critical respect the church was ultimately dependent on the state, unable to undertake on its own initiative the reforms that it wanted and needed in order to maintain its internal cohesion and strength.

Even with regard to those areas in which church authorities had more autonomy, the church's enforced dependence on the state could have a distorting effect. This seems to have been an important factor in the hierarchy's repression of dissident clergy. Sometimes pressure from local or central government authorities compelled the hierarchy to repress particular individuals or groups from the clergy in order to prevent government intervention that would further undermine and weaken the church's authority in the eyes of the imperial bureaucracy and the populace. On other occasions, hierarchs acted to repress clergy whose outspoken criticisms of church authorities or the church-state order threatened directly to diminish respect for the church leadership among the lower clergy and/or the laity, to aggravate divisions within the church, or to tarnish the church's dignity and honor. These actions reflected the church's political weakness: in dealing with dissidents in its own ranks, it had to take into account the interests of the government and the ways in which any actions would compromise the church's relations with the government or its position in society.

And yet, the church's necessary concern for how its actions and policies would affect the state was not reciprocated by the government, whose interest in the church was largely instrumental. When it suited the government's own interests to promote particular policies related to the church, then the government took action. However, when the government believed that policies the church found inimical to its interests were politically expedient, it enacted those policies with little heed for the complaints of the church. Moreover, the government often *failed* to act in support of the church unless its own interests were affected. The position of the established church was such that it had to support the government and take into account the impact of its decisions on the government even while knowing that the government would not necessarily do anything to support the church and was likely even to implement decisions that would harm the church. Given this impossible situation, it is little wonder that the church's leadership declined to offer any expression of support to the emperor or the monarchy in the critical first days of the February revolution of 1917. Indeed the majority of the clergy—like the majority of the population generally—welcomed the overthrow of the imperial political system, which no longer seemed to benefit anyone at all.[107]

The distortions of the inter-revolutionary period were severely damaging to the church, deepening the divisions that existed within the clergy and between the clergy and the laity before 1905 to such an extent that by 1917 these divisions often seemed impossible to heal. In the case of the Renovationists, the unhealed wounds of the 1905 revolution led directly to the rupture that separated the Living Church from the Patriarchal Church in the 1920s. However, despite the many negative consequences of the inter-revolutionary period both for particular individuals and the church in general, it should not be forgotten that there were also positive developments during this period whose influence likewise extended beyond the "great break" of 1917. Foremost among these was the quiet resolution of many parish clergymen to commit themselves more deeply to outreach work that aimed at improving not only the moral but also the material condition of their parishioners. This work promoted closer relations between the parish clergy and the laity and gave both the hope that their mutually supporting labors could help to change Russian society from the ground up without engaging in the bitter political struggle that waged above them and without requiring the leadership or intervention of outside authorities. It was this work and this attitude that contributed to the church's survival at the grass roots through all the many difficult trials of the Communist period.

CONCLUSION

The rapid socioeconomic changes that transformed Russia in the late imperial period presented a towering challenge to all the institutions of the old order, not the least of which was the Russian Orthodox Church. Like the Christian churches of Europe and the United States at this time, the Russian Orthodox Church faced the challenge of demonstrating that it was still relevant and necessary to an urban-industrial society whose culture was increasingly influenced by scientific knowledge and secular culture. Certainly, there were many Orthodox believers, lay and clerical, who argued that the church should stand fast in the face of these great changes, believing that innovation was a kind of betrayal of the tradition the church guarded like a treasure against the eroding tides of human history. Yet, it has long gone unnoticed that there were other voices in the church as well, which argued that the changing times offered the church the opportunity to reexamine its traditions in a new light and rediscover elements that—though long forgotten or neglected—would enable the church to pursue its mission to the modern world with vigor and confidence.

Those from among the parish clergy who embraced modernity's challenge to the church were not simply responding to developments in the external world, however. The Orthodox church itself experienced significant change during the nineteenth century as the education of the parish clergy improved and the church's intellectual resources expanded. The effects of these developments were especially apparent in the imperial capital, where the best and brightest of the parish clergy were called to serve. These men were not the poor, ignorant, drunken priests of Russian jokes and proverbs; they were highly educated men who were dedicated to the faith and well qualified to serve as leaders in the church and society. As the world around them changed, they responded both intellectually and practically, developing an active mission of social outreach through which they sought to educate the population in the Christian faith and build a Christian community using the promotion of charity and temperance. In this endeavor, many of them were inspired by the ideal of realizing the Kingdom of God on earth through the creation of a society based on the Gospels' principles of love, charity, and justice. In emphasizing the importance of human effort and the applicability of the teachings of the Gospels to modern social problems, the St. Petersburg clergy had much in common with their counterparts in the urban churches of England and the United States who preached the idea of a "social gospel" in the later nineteenth century.

In pursuit of the ideal of the Kingdom of God on earth, some clergymen of the capital ventured into the political arena during the 1905 revolution, arguing that the church had a responsibility to provide leadership to believers in all aspects of their common life. Fathers Georgii Gapon, Grigorii Petrov, Mikhail (Semenov), and the members of the Renovationist Union all believed that the teachings of the Gospels could be translated into a political vision and a program that would bring the country both freedom and justice, a belief shared by those Europeans who belonged to the various Christian Socialist parties emerging in England, France, and elsewhere on the continent in the early twentieth century. In Russia, however, the development of Christian Socialism was stunted and distorted by the 1905 revolution, which aggravated divisions in the church and alienated the clergy from many of their former supporters in the laity while also arousing the suspicions of the state against them. The movement failed before it had really even developed, and its failure left many of its one-time supporters convinced that religion and politics should not mix.

Nevertheless, for some the idea of a Christian politics retained its appeal. When revolution erupted again in 1917, some parish clergymen (along with a few bishops) joined the Living Church group—also known as the Renovationists—whose members were brought together by their support of the revolution, their sympathy for socialist ideals, and a belief in the need for the democratization of the church. They were a small minority in the church, however, and they were unable to exert any influence over the decisions made by the All-Russian Church Council, which finally met in the years 1917–1918 to enact the church's long-planned reforms. One of these reforms was the abolition of the Synod and the office of the director general and the reestablishment of the patriarchate, a reform that the members of the Living Church fiercely opposed. In this, they found common cause with the Bolsheviks, and in the early 1920s, one faction of the Living

Church (which had divided into several competing factions early on), accepted the support of the Bolshevik government in its attempts to sideline the patriarch and gain control of the church. The leaders of the Living Church then imposed a series of reforms on the church—including a new calendar, changes to the liturgy, and the admission of married priests to the traditionally monastic hierarchy—that aroused popular outrage and resistance. After a year, the Bolsheviks withdrew their support from the Living Church and eased their repression of the patriarchal church, which recovered some, though not all, of its strength. It faced the renewed repressions that accompanied Stalin's "second revolution" of the late 1920s and the 1930s in a weakened state. Despite the fact that the patriarchal *locum tenems*, Sergii (Stragorodskii), had publicly declared the church's loyalty to the Bolshevik state and renounced all involvement in politics, the state treated the church as an enemy. Thousands of churches were destroyed, and the majority of the Orthodox clergy were executed, imprisoned, or driven out of the clergy. The patriarchal church just barely survived the assault, to be partially revived as part of Stalin's effort to rally the people to the country's defense during the Second World War. It was only then that the last remnants of the Living Church were finally eradicated, leaving behind only the bitter memory of betrayal, which even today remains closely connected in the minds of many clergymen with a visceral distrust of clerical programs for political activism, social reform, and church democratization.

Since 1988, when the reforming regime of Mikhail Gorbachev allowed the Orthodox church to celebrate the millennium of its establishment in Russia publicly with great pomp and fanfare, the church has experienced a revival. Services are once again celebrated in churches that have been restored or rebuilt, clergy are being trained in newly established classes and schools, and the patriarch and the bishops serving in his office make public statements and appear at important political events, where the country's top leaders acknowledge them with a show of respect. The Orthodox church enjoys a privileged position in relation to Russia's other religious organizations, the beneficiary of laws and officially sanctioned practices that restrict the activities of other religious groups while supporting the efforts of the Orthodox church to strengthen itself and expand its influence. The claim that the Orthodox church, the Russian nation, and the Russian state are inextricably linked has been reasserted, reminding modern-day observers of the nineteenth-century formula, "Orthodoxy, Autocracy and Nationality."

In other ways as well, the Orthodox church today remains connected to the pre-revolutionary past, despite the intervening decades of struggle and repression. Although Russia has changed dramatically since 1900, the church has not yet settled how it will answer the fundamental questions that confronted it during the late imperial period: how should the church interpret its mission in the context of the modern world, and by what methods should that mission be fulfilled? This discussion within the church, cut short by the events of 1917, has been renewed as several pre-revolutionary journals have been revived and many pre-revolutionary publications have been reprinted. Some of the divisions that fractured the church during the revolutionary years have been reopened as well. While the church's present-day leaders seem to be seeking to restore the Orthodox church to its former position of privilege by seeking a close and collaborative relation with the state, a few clergymen have come out as critics of an established church, embracing many of the arguments and ideals that motivated earlier critics of the church-state relationship.[1] One of the most well-known critics of the religious establishment today is Father Gleb Yakunin (b. 1934), whose history of principled opposition to the authorities dates back to 1965, when he wrote a public letter to Patriarch Alexei I calling for the liberation of the church from control of the Soviet state. Banned from serving in his parish by church authorities, Father Gleb continued to speak critically of the church and the state in public, focusing particularly on the authorities' repression of religion. In 1980, Father Gleb was arrested and convicted of anti-Soviet agitation, for which he was imprisoned, sent to a labor camp, and then exiled to the far northeastern corner of Siberia. After he was amnestied in 1987, he was allowed to return to Moscow and resume his duties as a priest. He sought and won election to the Supreme Soviet in 1990, becoming actively involved in the complicated politics that accompanied the end of communist rule in the years 1991–1993. As a result of his public accusations that leading members of the hierarchy had once been KGB collaborators, he was defrocked and excommunicated. He continues to be involved in politics as a critic of the Orthodox establishment and a staunch defender of human rights, especially the right to freedom of conscience.[2] Father Gleb's political activism on behalf of tolerance, religious freedom, and human rights springs from his critical views of the authorities of both the Orthodox church and the Russian state and from his understanding of the teachings of the Gospels. His writings, lectures, and activities in many ways resemble those of Father Grigorii Petrov and the Renovationists of the 1905 revolution; it is not often recognized that Father Gleb's work builds upon ideas of an Orthodox Christian politics that were first articulated by the Russian Orthodox clergy of the pre-revolutionary period. While the response of church authorities to Father Gleb today does not much differ from the response that Father Grigorii and the Renovationists received one hundred years ago, it is worth noting that Father Gleb is able to continue his work more than a decade after his defrocking, and that he enjoys recognition and support from liberal members of the educated lay public for his ongoing efforts at both the national and international levels, unlike his predecessors at the beginning of the twentieth century.

Father Gleb's political activities are well known and controversial, but they represent only one part of the pre-revolutionary clergy's legacy. Another is represented by the work of Father Gleb's mentor, the parish priest,

Father Alexander Men' (1935–1990). Father Alexander resembled the more numerous but less famous clergy whose labors sustained the outreach of the Society for Moral-Religious Enlightenment. Like them, Father Alexander dedicated his life to pastoral service, devoting particular attention to the religious enlightenment of the Soviet intelligentsia in the 1960s. He avoided politics, refraining from any public criticism of church authorities or the state. Instead, he established small circles for prayer and Bible study that attracted the interest of Moscow intellectuals. He tried to revive the practice of parish-based charity, though with little success because of the restrictions of the communist state on all types of independent activity. For decades, he wrote, lectured, and preached tirelessly on the meaning of the faith, quietly but persistently countering the propaganda of the state with the word of the Gospels. During the late 1980s, he was finally allowed to pursue his work openly and without fear of persecution. Some of those who had followed him for many years assisted him by giving lectures themselves on church history, religious philosophy, and other subjects, much as educated lay people had assisted the clergy of the ORRP in carrying their mission to hundreds of teaching points in the city every week in the early 1900s. Between 1988 and 1990, Father Alexander Men's writings and lectures reached thousands of people, most of them from the educated strata of Soviet society, who were of special concern to him, as the educated classes had been of concern to the founders of the ORRP a century before. Father Alexander's work seemed to offer hope for the revival of the Russian Orthodox intellectual tradition among the Soviet-educated elite; more than six hundred people attended Father Alexander's lecture "Christianity" on a Saturday night in Moscow in early September 1990. The next morning, Father Alexander was murdered on his way to Sunday services. The shocking murder, which was never solved, did not extinguish the spirit of his ministry, however. A number of followers continue his work of promoting religious enlightenment through publications, lectures, radio programs, and voluntary societies. Men's books are still in print, and two institutions that he founded in Moscow—the Open Orthodox University and a charity hospital for children—continue his work.[3] Father Alexander himself was canonized by the Russian Orthodox Church in 2000; his work, unlike that of Father Gleb, has won the approval of church authorities.

To many observers, the revival of the Russian Orthodox Church in the late Soviet period and its continued growth in the years since the fall of the communist government has been both a surprise and a puzzle. Given the commonly accepted belief that the Orthodox church of the pre-revolutionary period was weak, ineffective, and unpopular, how can the revival of the institution in recent decades be explained? While there are certainly many factors at work in this development, one that should not be overlooked is the progress the Orthodox church made toward addressing the challenges of modernity in the pre-revolutionary period, both intellectually and in practical terms. In the last decades of the nineteenth century, the parish clergy of St. Petersburg recognized that the rapidly occurring changes in their society required them to reexamine their notions of what the church's mission to the world was and their methods of fulfilling that mission. Returning to the sources of the Christian tradition, they found inspiration in those teachings that emphasized the importance of going out into the world to heal and to comfort, to teach and to lead, to criticize and to transform the imperfect institutions of man to be worthy of the Kingdom of God. This interpretation of the church's purpose invigorated the clergy's work and fueled the expansion and diversification of their outreach activities in the pre-revolutionary period. Although this work was all but forgotten during the communist era, obscured as it was by the violent political struggles of the revolutionary years, the legacy of Father Georgii Gapon's generation is manifest today, both in the political activism of Father Gleb Yakunin and in the pastoral mission of Father Alexander Men' and his followers. Through their work, the Russian Orthodox Church continues to adapt and respond to the changing needs of society, working for that day when, as Christians pray, "His Kingdom come, his will be done, on earth as it is in Heaven."

APPENDIX

The Union of Zealots for Church Renovation, 1906

Name*	Status	Affiliations**	Positions***
Abramovich, D. I.	Lay	*Vek*	Professor, SPB Ecclesiastical Academy
Adrianov, S. M.	Lay	*Vek*	Docent, SPB University
Ageev, K. M.	Priest	*Vek*	
Agov, V.	No info		
Akimov, V. V.	Lay	*Vek*	Professor SPB University
Aksakov, N. P.	Lay	*BV*	Professor
Aksenov, P. S.	Priest	*ORRP*	Church, Aleksandr-Nevskaia Lavra
Anichkov, E. V.	Lay	*Vek*	Professor
Askol'dov, A. S.	No info	*Vek*	
Asov, T.	No info	*TsO*	
Bazhenov, S. A.	Priest	*Vek*	
Bazhin, N. F.		*Vek*	
Belkov, E.	No info	*Zvonar'*	
Belkov, X. A.	Archpriest	*Zvonar'*	
Berdiaev, N. A.	Lay	*Vek*	Religious philosopher, writer
Bogoliubov, N. N.	Archpriest	*Vek*	Professor
Broiarskii, S. S.	Priest	*Zvonar'*	
Bulgakov, S. N.	Lay	*Vek*	Professor, Moscow University
Bukharev, Z. Ia	No info	*Vek*	
Chel'tsov, M. P.	Priest	*Vek*	Diocesan missionary; Prof. SPB University

Name*	Status	Affiliations**	Positions***
D'iakonov, A. P.	Lay	*Vek*	Professor, SPB Ecclesiastical Academy
D'iakonov, L. V.	Priest		
D'iakov, G. A.	Priest		Priest in Smolensk village, Schlusselberg
Dobronravov, I. I.	Priest		St. Andrew's cathedral
Dobronravov, N. P	Archpriest	*Vek*	Moscow
Dobrovol'skii, I. K.	Priest		Church of Gov't Paper Office
Dobrovol'skii, M. K.	Priest		Military clergy
Dokuchaev, I. I.	Priest		Church of SPB military prison
Dokuchaev, P. I.	Priest		Served at two SPB orphanages
Dolganov, E. E.	Priest	*ORRP*	Cathedral of Sts. Peter and Paul
Egorov, I. F.	Priest	*Vek*	Smolnyi Institute
El'chaninov, A. V.	No info	*Vek*	
El'tsov, A. A.	Priest		Institutional church
Ern, V. F.	Lay	*BV*	Moscow; philosopher
Faresov, A. I.	Lay	*Vek*	Writer
Filsofov, D. V.	Lay	*Vek*	Public library
Finikov, P. M.	Priest	*ORRP* ·	Krestovozdvizhenskaia church
Florenskii, P. V.	Lay	*Vek*	Writer, philosopher
Fokko, S. Ia.	Priest		Institutional church
Gassonov, S.	Priest	*Zvonar'*	
Gidaspov, D. F.	Priest	*ORRP*	Trinity cathedral of ORRP
Gorchakov, M. I.	Archpriest		Church at Post and Telegraph, Prof., SPB Univ.
Gromoglasov, I. I.	Lay	*Vek*	Professor
Gross, I. S.	Priest	*Vek*	Professor

Name*	Status	Affiliations**	Positions***
Iasov, A.	No info	*TsO*	
Il'inskii, V. I.	No info	*Vek, TsO*	
Ivanov, V.	Lay	*Vek*	
Izmailov, A. A.	Lay	*Vek*	Writer for *Birzhevaia vedomosti*
Kapralov, E. Z.	Priest	*Vek*	
Kartashev, A. V.	Lay	*BV*	Former professor, SPB Ecclesiastical Academy
Kolachev, E. Ia.	Priest	*Vek*	Cathedral of Sts. Peter and Paul
Koromaev, A. G.	Priest		Institutional church
Kremlevskii, P. M.	Priest	*ORRP*	Institutional church
Krylov, I. I.	Priest	*ORRP*	Volkovsk cemetery church
Kudriatvtsev, P. P.	Lay	*Vek*	Professor, Moscow Ecclesiastical Academy
Lakhotskii, P. N.	Archpriest	*ORRP*	Trinity cathedral of ORRP
Leontovich, K.	No info	*TsO*	
Likhnitskii, I.	Priest	*KZ*	
Lipovskii, N. V.	Priest		Institutional church
Liutserbov, D. M.	Archpriest		
Medved'ev, Ia. I.	Priest		Military administration
Mikhail	Archimandrite		No position; publicist
Mirtov, P. A.	Priest	*ORRP*	Nevskii Temperance Society Voskresenskaia church
Murin, A. G.	Priest	*ORRP*	Student, SPB Ecclesiastical Academy
Myshtsyn, V. I.	Lay	*Vek*	
Nikol'skii, V.	No info	*Vek*	
Nikol'skii, V. A.	Lay	*Vek*	Writer for journal *Sever*
Os'minskii, I. V.	Priest	*ORRP*	

Name*	Status	Affiliations**	Positions***
Ostrogorskii, I. E.	Priest	*ORRP*	Cathedral of St. Sampson
Petrov, A. I.	Priest		Church of St. Matthew
Petrov, G. S.	Priest	*ORRP*	Publicist
Pogodin, A. I.	Priest		Several SPB charities
Pokrovskii, V. A.	Priest		
Pospelov, M.	Archpriest	*Zvonar'*	
Pospelov, P. P.	Priest	*Vek*	Moscow
Presniakov, A. E.	Lay	*Vek*	Professor
Raevskii, P. V.	Priest	*ORRP*	Nevskii Temperance Society Church of St. John the Baptist
Riabkov, M. Ia.	Archpriest		Institutional church
Rovinskii, K. I.	Lay	*Vek*	Writer for *Novoe vremia*
Rozanov, V. V.	Lay	*Vek*	Writer and philosopher
Rozhdestvenskii, A. R.	Priest	*ORRP*	Professor, SPB Ecclesiastical Academy
Rudinskii, N. S.	Priest		Military administration
Sakharov, A. M.	Priest	*ORRP*	Cathedral of St. Sergei
Servishev, I.	Priest	*KZ*	
Shleev, S.	Priest		
Slobodskoi, I. P.	Priest	*ORRP*	Institutional church
Smirnov, N. P.	Priest		
Smirnov, S. I.	Lay	*Vek*	Professor
Sollertinskii, S. A.	Archpriest	*ORRP*	Professor, SPB Ecclesiastical Academy
Solov'ev, P. S.	No info	*Vek*	
Stranden, D. V.	No info	*Vek*	
Sventitskii, V. P.	Lay	*BV*	Moscow
Svetlov, Ia. M.	Priest		Institutional church

Name*	Status	Affiliations**	Positions***
Svetlov, P. Ia.	Archpriest	KZ	Professor, St. Vladimir's University
Tamarenko, L.	No info	TsO	
Tikhomirov, P. V.	Lay	Vek	Professor, Moscow Ecclesiastical Academy
Trubetskoi, E.	Lay	KZ	Writer, philosopher
Uspenskii, P. I.	Priest	ORRP	Institutional church
Uspenskii, V. V.	Lay	Vek	Professor, SPB Ecclesiastical Academy
Uspenskii, Vl.V.	Lay	Vek	Teacher, SPB seminary
Verner, I. I.	No info	Vek	
Volzhskii, A. S.	No info	Vek	
Von Geistlich, A.	No info	Zvonar'	
Voskresenskii, V.K.	Priest		Obukhov station, Nikolaev Railroad
Voznesenskii, S. A.	Deacon		Trinity church of the Izmail-ovskii regiment
Zakharov, A.	No info	KZ	

Source: This list has been compiled by gathering the names of those listed as contributors to the Renovationist journals *Vek, Biblioteka Veka, Tserkovnoe obnovlenie, Zvonar'*, and *Krasnyi zvon* and adding to them the names listed in an archival document: RGIA, f. 834, op. 4, d. 565, "Ustav 'Bratstva revnitelei tserkovnogo obnovleniia' v S. Peterburge i spisok lits sv. sana, sostoiashchikh chlenami Bratstva," ll. 3–4. The list may underrepresent laymen who belonged to the party but did not write for its journals. It also does not indicate how many supporters the party may have had among the clergy who did not risk becoming formal members.

* Names in bold type are clergymen whose participation in the party was recorded by the Synod. It is interesting to note that there seem to be several pairs of brothers in the group: the Belkovs, the Dobrovol'skiis, the Dokuchaevs, the Uspenskii laymen.

**Only those clergymen named on the Synod's list can be confidently described as party members. Others on the list are identified by the title of the Renovationist publication for which they wrote. When needed, a few abbreviations were used: *KZ* stands for *Krasnyi zvon* (which succeeded *Zvonar'* under Archpriest Belkov's continued editorship after the first journal was closed in 1907), *BV* for *Biblioteka Veka*, and *TsO* for *Tserkovnoe obnovlenie*. The names of members were also checked against the ORRP membership list for 1906–1907.

***Some information in this column was obtained by looking up names in the 1906 directories of St. Petersburg and Russia.

NOTES

ABBREVIATIONS

Archival notations

d.   delo = file

f.   fond = section (of the archive)

l., ll.   list, listy = page(s)

ob.   oborot = obverse

op.   opis' = inventory, list of files

otd.   otdelenie = division

RGIA   Rossiiskii gosudarstvennyi istoricheskii arkhiv (Russian State Historical Archive)

st.   stol = table

Bibliographical notations

ch.   chast' = part

gl.   glava = chapter

ORRP   Obshchestvo rasprostraneniia religiozno-nravstvennago prosveshcheniia v
            dukhe pravoslavnoi tserkvi

Spb.   St. Petersburg

INTRODUCTION

1. Gregory Freeze, *Russian Levites* (Cambridge, 1977) and *The Parish Clergy in Nineteenth-Century Russia* (Princeton, 1983).

2. The classic example is the work of the historian Pavel Miliukov, one of the leaders of the Constitutional Democrat party (the Kadets) after the 1905 revolution. Miliukov, *Outlines of Russian Culture*, pt. 1, *Religion and the Church* (Philadelphia, 1942).

3. See, for example, Richard Pipes, *Russia under the Old Regime* (Cambridge, 1974).

4. As a starting point, see Charles Howard Hopkins, *The Rise of the Social Gospel in American Protestantism, 1865–1915* (New Haven, 1940; reprint, New York, 1982); K. S. Inglis, *Churches and the Working Classes in Victorian England* (London, 1963).

5. Nadieszda Kizenko, *A Prodigal Saint: Father John of Kronstadt and the Russian People* (University Park, 2000) and "Ioann of Kronstadt and the Reception of Sanctity, 1850–1988," *Russian Review* 57, no. 3 (July 1998): 325–45, and "Protectors of Women and the Lower Orders: Constructing Sainthood in Modern Russia," in *Orthodox Russia: Belief and Practice under the Tsars,* ed. Valerie Kivelson and Robert Greene (University Park, 2003), 105–26; Vera Shevzov, *Russian Orthodoxy on the Eve of Revolution* (New York,

2000), "Letting the People into Church: Reflections on Orthodoxy and Community in Late Imperial Russia," in *Orthodox Russia,* ed. Kivelson and Greene, 59–80, "Chapels and the Ecclesial World of Prerevolutionary Russian Peasants," *Slavic Review* 55, no. 3 (Fall 1996): 585–613, and "Icons, Miracles, and the Ecclesial Identity of Laity in Late Imperial Russian Orthodoxy," *Church History* 69, no. 3 (September 2000): 610–32.

6. Chris Chulos, *Converging Worlds: Religion and Community in Peasant Russia, 1861–1917* (DeKalb, 2003).

7. Kimberly Page Herrlinger, "Class, Piety, and Politics: Workers, Orthodoxy, and the Problem of Religious Identity in Russia, 1881–1914" (Ph.D. diss., University of California at Berkeley, 1996) and "Raising Lazarus: Orthodoxy and the Factory Narod in St. Petersburg, 1905–1914," *Jahrbucher für Geschichte Osteuropas* 52, no. 3 (2004): 341–54; Reginald E. Zelnik, "Religion and Irreligion in the Experience of St. Petersburg Workers in the 1870s," *Russian History* 16, no. 2 (1989): 297–326, and *A Radical Worker in Tsarist Russia: The Autobiography of Semen Ivanovich Kanatchikov* (Stanford, 1986); Mark Steinberg, "Workers on the Cross: Religious Imagination in the Writings of Russian Workers, 1910–1924," *Russian Review* 53, no. 2 (1994): 213–39.

8. Laurie Manchester, "Harbingers of Modernity, Bearers of Tradition: *Popovichi* as a Model Intelligentsia Self in Revolutionary Russia," *Jahrbucher für Geschichte Osteuropas* 50, no. 3 (2002): 321–44, and "The Secularization of the Search for Salvation: The Self-Fashioning of Orthodox Clergymen's Sons in Late Imperial Russia," *Slavic Review* 57, no. 1 (1998): 50–76; Catherine Evtuhov, "Voices from the Provinces: Living and Writing in Nizhnii Novgorod, 1870–1905," *Journal of Popular Culture* 31, no. 4 (Spring 1998): 33–48, and *The Cross and the Sickle: Sergei Bulgakov and the Fate of Russian Religious Philosophy* (Ithaca, NY, 1997); Brenda Meehan, *Holy Women of Russia* (New York, 1993).

9. Laura Engelstein, "Holy Russia in Modern Times: An Essay on Orthodoxy and Cultural Change," *Past and Present* 17, no. 3 (November 2001): 129–56, and "Paradigms, Pathologies, and Other Clues to Russian Spiritual Culture: Some Post-Soviet Thoughts," *Slavic Review* 57, no. 4 (Winter 1998): 864–77.

10. Paul Valliere, *Modern Russian Theology: Bukharev, Solov'ev, Bul'gakov: Orthodox Theology in a New Key* (Grand Rapids, MI, 2000); and Valliere, "The Liberal Tradition in Russian Orthodox Theology," in *The Legacy of St. Vladimir,* ed. J. Breck, J. Meyendorff, and E. Silk (Crestwood, NY, 1990), 93–108.

1—FOUNDATIONS OF THE MODERN RUSSIAN ORTHODOX CHURCH

1. For more on the reforms, see James Cracraft, *The Church Reform of Peter the Great* (Stanford, 1971). The text of the Regulation is translated in Alexander V. Muller, *The Spiritual Regulation of Peter the Great* (Seattle, 1972).

2. The title is often given as Over-Procurator, Chief Procurator, or simply Procurator because the Russian term (borrowed from the German) is *Ober-Prokuror.* The meaning of these terms is not immediately apparent to the English-speaking reader, so I prefer the title of "director general" used in Robert F. Byrnes, *Pobedonostsev: His Life and Thought* (Bloomington, 1968).

3. Gregory Freeze, "Handmaiden of the State? The Church in Imperial Russia Reconsidered," *Journal of Ecclesiastical History* 36, no. 1 (1985), 85–92.

4. A survey of the eighteenth-century reforms with a focus on their impact on the parish clergy is given in Freeze, *Russian Levites*. This chapter draws heavily on Freeze's body of work for both facts and interpretation.

5. "Estate" is the term most often used to translate the Russian word *soslovie* (pl. *sosloviia*). However, this term designated a different kind of institution in imperial Russia than it did in western Europe. In Europe, the notion of the estates centered on the rights and privileges of their members, often defined by the groups themselves and defended against the centralizing modern state. In Russia, the *sosloviia* were defined by the state in terms of the members' duties and obligations to the state. Peter the Great gave the estate system in Russia its most definite shape in the early eighteenth century.

The forms and language of the estate system survived until 1917. For a brief discussion, s.v. *"soslovie"* in S. Pushkarev, *Dictionary of Russian Historical Terms from the Eleventh Century to 1917* (New Haven, 1970). Two interesting discussions of the estate system and the Russian social order are Gregory L. Freeze, "The Estate *(Soslovie)* Paradigm and Russian Social History," *American Historical Review* 91 (1986): 11–36; and Alfred J. Rieber, "The Sedimentary Society," in *Between Tsar and People: Educated Society and the Quest for Public Identity in Late Imperial Russia,* ed. Edith W. Clowes, Samuel D. Kassow, and James L. West (Princeton, 1991), 343–66.

6. In addition to Freeze's monographs on the parish clergy, see his translation of a famous nineteenth-century critique of the church: I. S. Belliustin, *Description of the Clergy in Rural Russia: The Memoir of a Nineteenth-Century Parish Priest,* tr. and with interpretive essay by Gregory L. Freeze (Ithaca, NY, 1985).

7. Freeze, "Handmaiden," 93; see also, Freeze, "The Orthodox Church and Serfdom in Pre-reform Russia," *Slavic Review* 48, no. 3 (Fall 1989): 361–87.

8. Freeze, "Handmaiden," 91–93.

9. See James T. Flynn, *The University Reform of Tsar Alexander I, 1802–1835* (Washington, D.C., 1988).

10. The name is sometimes given as Theological Academy or even Spiritual Academy; the Russian term is *Dukhovnaia akademiia.* I have used the term "ecclesiastical" in an attempt to convey that the schools' purpose went beyond purely theological training and included other subjects relevant to the academic disciplines of the church, including languages, history, and philosophy. A degree from one of the ecclesiastical academies would be the equivalent today of a postgraduate degree from a seminary (such as a Master of Divinity). I do not use the term seminary because that word is used for the schools in the church educational system that offered at their lower levels the equivalent of a secondary-level education and at their higher levels something comparable to an undergraduate education. The sons of the clergy were generally eligible to attend the seminaries (of which there was one in each diocese). Only the most promising seminary graduates were considered for admission to the academies, and they were subjected to an increasingly rigorous and competitive evaluation process. Academy graduates were the elite of the clergy, though not all academy graduates took clerical orders.

11. One modern scholarly study of the four academies exists: Maria Koehler-Baur, *Die geistlichen Akademien in Russland im 19. Jahrhundert* (Wiesbaden, 1997). There are two pre-revolutionary studies, both heavily influenced by the authors' contemporary political concerns: B. V. Titlinov, *Dukhovnaia shkola v Rossii v XIX stoletii,* 2 vols. (Vil'na, 1908); and F. I. Titov, *Preobrazovaniia dukhovnykh akademii v Rossii v XIX v.* (Kiev, 1906). A great deal of useful information about the academies in general during the pre-reform period is available in I. Chistovich, *Istoriia S. Peterburgskoi Dukhovnoi Akademii* (Spb, 1857).

12. The church's schools also played an important part in the development of Russia's secular education system, since they provided both teachers and students for secondary schools, the universities, and the learned professions. Robert Nichols, "Orthodoxy and Russia's Enlightenment, 1762–1825," in *Russian Orthodoxy under the Old Regime,* ed. Theophanis Stavrou and Robert Nichols (Minneapolis, 1978), 65–89.

13. George A. Maloney, *A History of Orthodox Theology since 1453* (Belmont, MA, 1976), 51–56. For a more extensive discussion, see Georges Florovsky, *Puti russkogo bogosloviia* (Paris, 1937; reprint, Ann Arbor, MI, 1971).

14. Much of the information in the following section is from Ioann (Snychev), [Mitropolit Sankt Peterburgskii i Ladozhskii] ed., *Ocherki istorii Sankt-Peterburgskoi eparkhii* (Spb, 1994), 101–15. I also used Chistovich, *Istoriia.*

15. David W. Edwards, "Orthodoxy during the Reign of Tsar Nicholas I: A Study in Church-State Relations" (Ph.D. diss., Kansas State University, 1967); and Edwards, "The System of Nicholas I in Church-State Relations" in *Russian Orthodoxy,* ed. Stavrou and Nichols, 154–65. See also Freeze, *Parish Clergy,* 1–188.

16. On the history of the diocese, see Simon Dixon, "Church, State, and Society in Late Imperial Russia: The Diocese of St. Petersburg, 1880–1914" (Ph.D. diss., University of London, 1990); Ioann (Snychev), *Ocherki;* and Vyacheslav Mukhin, *The Church Culture of St. Petersburg* (Spb, 1994). For an outline of the diocese's various administrative reorganizations, see Igor Smolitsch, *Geschichte der russischen Kirche, 1700–1917,* 1 (Leiden, 1964), 707.

17. Ioann (Snychev), *Ocherki,* 132–41. Isidor's importance to the local church is especially evident in the histories of the St. Petersburg Ecclesiastical Academy and the Society for Moral-Religious Enlightenment. See I. Chistovich, *S. Peterburgskaia Dukhovnaia Akademiia za posledniia 30 let, 1858–1888* (Spb, 1889); A. L. Katanskii, *Vospominaniia starogo professora, 1847–1913,* 2 vols. (Spb, 1914 and 1918); ORRP, *Obsheshchtvo rasprostraneniia religiozno-nravstvennogo prosveshcheniia v dukhe pravoslavnoi tserkvi, 1881–1891* (Spb, 1891).

18. The best contemporary biography is by M. V. [Galkin], *Antonii, Mitropolit S. Peterburgskii i Ladozhskii* (Spb, 1915). See also I. Korol'kov, "Pamiati vysokopreosviashchennogo Antoniia, Mitropolit Petrogradskogo i Ladozhskogo" ([n.p.], 1916); M. Vadkovskii, "Prilozhenie k Vospominaniiam o mitropolite Antonii," *Istoricheskii vestnik* 147 (1917): 162–72. For a critical assessment of Antonii's role in the church, see Gerhard Simon, *Church, State, and Opposition in the USSR,* tr. K. Matchett (London, 1974), 41–63.

19. Orthodox church tradition held that a bishop should remain with his flock for the duration of his life, but Pobedonostsev frequently violated this norm by moving bishops from one diocese to another. Sergei Firsov, *Russkaia tserkov' nakanune peremen, konets 1890–kh–1918 gg.* (Spb, 2002), 76–78.

20. On the reasons for Rasputin's influence and a critical view of its impact on the church, see Firsov, *Russkaia tserkov',* 445–85.

21. For a recent introduction to the structure and functioning of the diocesan administration in general, see V.A. Fedorov, *Russkaia pravoslavnaia tserkov' i gosudarstvo: Sinodal'nyi period, 1700–1917.* Moscow, 2003: 16–23.

22. Fedorov, *Tserkov' i gosudarstvo,* 22–23. The vicarates of the St. Petersburg metropolitanate were located at Reval (1817–1866), Vyborg (1859–1892), Ladoga (1865–1887), Narva (1887–1918), Iamburg (1897–1918), Gdov (1900–1918), and Kronstadt (1907–1918). Smolitsch, *Geschichte,* 707.

23. On the consistory, see Fedorov, *Tserkov' i gosudarstvo,* 19–21.

24. V. K. Sabler made a regular practice of appointing academy graduates to the secretarial positions while he was assistant director general of the Synod in the 1890s, as remarked in Georgii Ivanovich Shavel'skii, "Russkaia tserkov' pred revoliutsiei," 1934, TMs 157, Shavel'skii Box 4, Bakhmeteff Collection, Rare Books and Manuscripts Room, Columbia University Library, New York.

25. This sympathy is especially evident in the annual reports of the 1890s and early 1900s; for example, the reports of 1898, 1900–1902, and 1905. For more detailed discussion of the diocesan administration, see Smolitsch, *Geschichte,* 357–89, or Dixon, "Church, State, and Society," 175–235; Shavel'skii, "Russkaia tserkov'," chaps. 3–11, is especially thorough and detailed.

26. *Vsepoddaneishii otchet ober-prokurora sviateishego sinoda za 1892 i 1893 gody* (Spb, 1895), appendix No. 9, 34–35. (The table cited is labeled as being for the year 1891.) These figures refer specifically to the Orthodox population of the diocese and not the total number of inhabitants. A survey of 1885 indicated that about 86 percent of the population of St. Petersburg province were Orthodox, with Protestants being the next largest confession at 13 percent. A. M. Zolotarev, *Zapiski voennoi statistiki Rossii* (n.p., 1885).

27. On the rapid growth of the city's population in the second half of the nineteenth century, see James Bater, *St. Petersburg: Industrialization and Change* (Montreal, 1976), 309–11. Between 1870 and 1914, the city's population increased by more than 1.7 million; between 1890 and 1914, it grew at a rate of about 50,000 people a year.

28. The annual reports of the director general provided the statistics in I. Preobrazhenskii, *Otechestvennaia tserkov' po statisticheskim dannam s 1840/41–1890/91* (Spb, 1897). The statistics on the number of churches are on pp. 20–25; for the number of congregants, see pp. 40–43. Empire-wide, the diocese of Arkhangel' had the lowest number of worshippers per church, with 532; the diocese of Viatka had the highest number, with 3,785 worshippers per church. (Note that these numbers do not reflect actual attendance at church. On this issue, see Simon Dixon, "The Orthodox Church and the Workers of St. Petersburg, 1880–1914," in *European Religion in the Age of Great Cities, 1830–1930*, ed. Hugh McLeod (London, 1995), 120–21.

29. *Vsepoddaneishii otchet ober-prokurora sviateishego sinoda za 1898 god* (Spb, 1901), appendix, pp. 10–13. The designation of archpriest indicated a rank gained through education, experience, and distinguished service. Senior priests, church supervisors, and deans usually had the rank of archpriest.

30. A. Geno, "K 200–letiiu S. Peterburga. Danniia o Peterburgskoi eparkhii" (Spb, 1901), 10. This problem was not unique to the capital; in Kronstadt, Father Ioann's introduction of mass public confession was, in large part, a response to the unmanageable crowds of communicants that descended upon his church each Easter. Kizenko, *Prodigal Saint*, 51–58.

31. RGIA, f. 796, op. 442, d. 2834, "Otchet o sostoianii eparkhii za 1889 g.," l. 16. The need for more churches was monotonously reiterated in each year's diocesan report to the Synod from the 1880s on. For the numbers, see Preobrazhenskii, *Otechestvennaia tserkov'*, 20, and RGIA, f. 796, op. 442, d. 2598, "Otchet o sostoianii eparkhii za 1913 g.," l. 57.

32. The most explicit statements on the financial obstacles to church-building are in the reports for 1880 and 1883. The dependence on lay funds is also evident from the short histories of St. Petersburg churches given in V. V. Antonov and A. V. Kobak, *Sviatyni Sankt-Peterburga. Khristianskaia istoriko-tserkovnaia entsiklopediia* (Spb, 2003), which offers much valuable material (with many primary source references) on the history of church construction in the capital up to 1914.

33. The divisions between these administrations were not clear: a church might be counted as being under the court administration in one list and under the military administration in another. Additionally, diocesan bureaucrats might regard a church under either administration as being functionally a parish church.

34. A few were attached to private homes, but it is incorrect to understand the Russian phrase literally as "home churches." In this case, *dom* means something closer to "establishment." A precise description of these churches indicating the type of institution to which they were assigned is found in S. Peterburgskii eparkhial'nyi istoriko-statisticheskii komitet, *Istoriko-statisticheskiia svedeniia o S. Peterburgskoi eparkhii*, 9 (Spb, 1871). In addition, Antonov and Kobak, *Sviatyni Sankt-Peterburga*, describe dozens of these institutional churches in their encyclopedia cataloging the churches of the capital.

35. The categorization of the churches is documented and partially explained in the introductory chapter on the history of the diocese in *Istoriko-statisticheskiia svedeniia*, 9:1–69.

36. RGIA, f. 834, op. 4, d. 727, "Rospisanie gorodskikh i sel'skikh prikhodov, tserkvi, i prichtov S. Peterburgskoi eparkhii;" "Rospisanie prikhodov eparkhial'nogo vedomstva v gorode S. Peterburge" (1900). Other lists differ in the number and in the inclusion of particular churches, reflecting contemporary confusion over which churches belonged to the diocese and were officially registered as parish churches. Even the list published by the secretary of the St. Petersburg consistory wrongly included non-diocesan parishes. N. M. Kutepov, *Pamiatnaia kniga po S. Peterburgskoi eparkhii* (Spb, 1899). Other lists are in Geno, "K 200–letiiu S. Peterburga"; in RGIA, f. 796, op. 440, d. 442, "Statisticheskie vedomosti o prikhodakh Peterburgskoi eparkhii, 1908"; in T. I. Il'icheva, ed., *Khramy Peterburga. Spravochnik-Putevoditel'* (Spb, 1992); in Sergei Mikhailov, "Khramy S. Peterburga, 1912 g." (Spb, 1994); and in Antonov and Kobak, *Sviatyni Sankt-Peterburga*.

37. RGIA, f. 796, op. 442, d. 1737, "Otchet o sostoianii S. Peterburgskoi eparkhii za 1898 god," l. 41.

38. *Vsepoddaneishii otchet ober-prokurora Sv. sinoda za 1898 g.*, appendix No. 3, pp. 7–8.

39. 1899 population, as given in Kutepov, *Pamiatnaia kniga*. I. D. Turenskii, *Tserkov presviatyia Bogoroditsy, chto v Bolshoi Kolomne v S. Peterburge. Eia istoriia i opisanie* (Spb, 1912).

40. *Vsepoddaneishii otchet ober-prokurora Sv. sinoda za 1898 g.*, appendix No. 3, pp. 7–8.

41. Gregory L. Freeze, "All Power to the Parish? The Problems and Politics of Reform in Late Imperial Russia," in *Social Identities in Revolutionary Russia*, ed. Madhavan K. Palat (London, 2001), 174–208.

42. *Istoriko-statisticheskiie svedeniia*, 9: 8–10.

43. Geno, "K 200–letiiu S. Peterburga," 16–17.

44. Ibid., 7.

45. Another scholar argues that these associations could not entirely make up for the weaknesses of the parish system. Dixon, "Church, State, and Society," 303–63.

46. Geno, "K 200–letiiu S. Peterburga," 5–6.

47. Ibid.

48. Geno, "K 200–letiiu S. Peterburga," 4.

49. On the much less comfortable and secure position of clergy in the rest of the empire, see Freeze, *Parish Clergy;* also T. G. Leont'eva, "The Peasantry and the Rural Clergy in Russia, 1900–1920," *Soviet and Post-Soviet Review* 27, nos. 2–3 (2000): 143–62; and Leont'eva, "Vera i bunt. Dukhovenstvo v revoliutsionnom obshchestve Rossii nachala XX veka," *Voprosy istorii* 1 (2001): 29–43. See also, Fedorov, *Tserkov' i gosudarstvo*, 31–51.

2—Bridging the Great Divide

1. Gregory L. Freeze, "The Rechristianization of Russia: The Church and Popular Religion, 1750–1850," *Studia Slavica Finlandensia* 7 (1990): 103–7.

2. This view is clearly apparent in Peter the Great's Spiritual Regulation. See for example, the criticism of some popular religious beliefs and practices in pt. 2, points 4–5. Spiritual Regulation, 14–15. See also, point 9 on page 29.

3. For more details on the general development of the church's schools in the eighteenth century, see Fedorov, *Tserkov' i gosudarstvo*, 88–93. For the early history of the St. Petersburg academy, see Chistovich, *Istoriia;* and A. Nadezhdin, "Istoricheskaia zapiska o S. Peterburgskoi dukhovnoi seminarii," *Khristianskoe chtenie* (1884): pt. 1, 818–50. On the academies in general, see Koehler-Bauer, *Die Geistlichen Akademien.*

4. Chistovich, *Istoriia*, 102.

5. Students studied both ancient Greek and Hebrew; for modern languages they chose between German and French. Students were presumed to have mastered Latin while at seminary. Chistovich, *Istoriia*, 103–4.

6. Chistovich, *Istoriia*, 144–46. The number of students graduating from the St. Petersburg academy increased steadily under the 1797 statute: in 1799, 157 students graduated; in 1804, 243; in 1807, 277. During this time, a significant proportion of students—between 30 and 60 per year—came from social groups other than the clergy, p. 143.

7. On Alexander's reform of the state-run schools, see Flynn, *University Reform.*

8. Chistovich, *Istoriia*, 170.

9. Ibid.

10. Ibid., 325. However, since the majority of works in the St. Petersburg academy's library were in French or German, it is doubtful that many members of the clerical estate, aside from those who were faculty or students at the school, would have found the library to be of much use.

11. Chistovich, *Istoriia*, 402–6.

12. The "thick journals" *(tolstye zhurnaly)* were a feature of Russian intellectual life in the nineteenth century. Secular thick journals such as *Vestnik Evropy* have long served as important historical sources, but the church's thick journals have not yet been widely used, despite their rich and varied content. For an overview of these sources, see Robert H. Davis, "Nineteenth-Century Russian Religious-Theological Journals: Structure and Access," *St. Vladimir's Seminary Quarterly* 33, no. 3 (1989): 235–59.

13. A. Lopukhin, "Semidesiatipiatiletie Khristianskogo chteniia," *Khristianskoe chtenie* (January–February 1896): 3–25; and Chistovich, *Istoriia*, 320–22.

14. For an overview of the issues and arguments, see Belliustin, *Description*. Professor Chistovich noted the critical attitude of many articles in the secular press at this time toward the institutions of the church, not excepting the academies. Chistovich, *S. Peterburgskaia Dukhovnaia Akademiia za poslednyi 30 let (1858–1888)* [hereafter *Akademiia za poslednyi 30 let*] (Spb, 1889), 7–9. So, too, did Professor Lopukhin, who edited *Khristianskoe chtenie* in the 1870s. Lopukhin, "Semidesiatipiatiletie Khristianskogo chteniia," 3–4.

15. Chistovich, *Akademiia za poslednyi 30 let,* 15–17.

16. Ibid., 16.

17. The school did expand its outreach to the public by another means, however: in 1858, the professors of the St. Petersburg academy established a new periodical publication, *Dukhovnaia beseda (Spiritual Conversation)*. This journal published news about the church and government affairs along with occasional editorials on current events and issues. Chistovich, *Akademiia za poslednyi 30 let,* 67–68.

18. Ibid., 107.

19. Ibid., 22.

20. Ibid.; see also Ioann (Snychev), *Ocherki,* for a discussion of Father Ioann's contributions to the development of moral theology. On Father Ioann's leadership as rector of the St. Petersburg academy, see A. A. Bronzov, "Vospominaniia. Protopresviter Ioann Leont'evich Ianyshev," *Trezvye vskhody,* nos. 7–10 (1910): 1–108.

21. For a summary of the discussions of reform, see Chistovich, *Akademiia za poslednyi 30 let,* 107–18. The text of the 1869 statute is located in *Polnoe sobranie zakonov Rossiiskoi Imperii,* 2nd collection (1825–1881), May 1869, No. 47154.

22. The budgetary increases were dramatic: library funding was increased from 500 to 1,600 rubles per year, per school; professors' salaries, which had ranged from 429 to 858 rubles a year, were increased to a range of 1,200 to 3,000 rubles a year, equal to the salaries paid to university professors of equivalent ranks; student stipends were raised from 128 to 225 rubles per year. Chistovich, *Akademiia za poslednyi 30 let,* 117.

23. Grigorii Polisadov, *Iz vospominanii o vremeni prebyvaniia moego v S. Peterburgskoi Akademii (1857–1861)* (Spb, 1912), 9. Professor Katanskii, who was a student at the St. Petersburg academy during the 1870s, recalled that students also read illegal literature, and one student had a large collection that he circulated among his fellows. Katanskii, "Vospominaniia," *Khristianskoe chtenie* (1914): 787–88.

24. Bronzov, "Vospominaniia," 27.

25. Katanskii, "Vospominaniia" (1914): 763.

26. Polisadov, *Iz vospominanii,* 14–15. Katanskii and his cousin, F. G. Eleonskii, were among those who taught at the Sunday schools. Katanskii, "Vospominaniia" (1914): 763.

27. I examined sample issues of the journal for 1823, 1835, 1847, and 1860–1868. There is an index for the 1870s: *Ukazatel' k Khristianskomu chteniiu za poslednie desiat' let ego izdaniia, ot 1871 goda do 1880 vkliuchitel'no* (Spb, 1881).

28. Father Ioann first suggested the idea of a weekly paper in 1871, but none of the professors was willing to take on the editorship. Professor A. I. Predtechenskii, formerly of *Birzheviia vedomosti,* opened the new publication in 1874 when he became the editor of *Khristianskoe chtenie.* Under Predtechenskii, the paper focused on reporting national and international news; after Professor A. Katanskii became editor in 1881 the

focus turned more toward the concerns of the church and the clergy. Katanskii, "Vospominaniia," *Khristianskoe chtenie* (1916): pt. 1, 403–7.

29. Before 1872 the academy had usually had about 115 applicants a year. In 1876 this increased to 171, and by 1880 to 233. The peak year was in 1883, when the academy had 392 applicants. The increase was partly the result of the church's enforcement of canon law on the minimum ages of appointment to clerical positions, which increased the number of seminary graduates applying to all schools of higher education. The pressure on the academies was increased after 1879, when the Synod prohibited the entry of seminary graduates into the secular universities in an effort to stop the flight of the seminarians from the clerical estate. Chistovich, *Akademiia za poslednyi 30 let*, 175–77.

30. Fedorov estimates that under the 1869 statute about 8 percent of the academies' students were from non-clerical backgrounds. Fedorov, *Tserkov' i gosudarstvo*, 112.

31. The life of the St. Petersburg academy in the 1870s is well described in Katanskii, "Vospominaniia" (1916): Part 1, 57–67, 283–308, 394–419, 499–515. See also Chistovich, *Akademiia za poslednyi 30 let*, 129–96.

32. Richard Wortman, *Scenarios of Power: Myth and Ceremony in Russian Monarchy*, vol. 2, *From Alexander II to the Abdication of Nicholas II* (Princeton, 2000), 2:10–85. However, Alexander and his clerical propagandists, who included Filaret (Drozdov), the metropolitan of Moscow, did draw heavily on religious themes in their presentation of the emperor to the public.

33. Ibid., 2:178–79.

34. Ibid., 2:202–31. Wortman discusses the symbolism of Alexander III's coronation on these pages; the specific quotes are from vol. 2, pages 231 and 214, respectively.

35. Ibid., 2:236–49.

36. On the extent of Pobedonostsev's power, see A. Iu. Polunov, "Konstantin Petrovich Pobedonostsev—Man and Politician," *Russian Studies in History* 39, no. 4 (Spring 2001): 21–22.

37. Katanskii, "Vospominaniia" (1916): Part 1, 286–87. Katanskii recalled that the rector and the professors responded to the unannounced visit with undisguised hostility.

38. A. L. Katanskii, *Vospominaniia starogo professora, 1847–1913*. 2 vols. (Spb, 1914; Petrograd, 1918); 2: 111. The committee included two church bureaucrats appointed by the Synod and five professors elected by the faculty of the four academies. The archbishop of Kazan, Sergei (Liapedevskii), served as chair.

39. RGIA, f. 797, op. 53 (1883), otd. 1, stol 2, No. 62, "Ob izmeneniiakh ustava," ll. 3–4 ob. These rules were to be written into the revised statute, but they were to take effect immediately, as Pobedonostsev explained in a letter to the metropolitan of St. Petersburg (ll. 10–11).

40. His feud with Pobedonostsev notwithstanding, Father Ioann continued to have a successful and highly visible career. From 1883 to 1910 he served as the head priest *(protopresviter)* of the Church of the Holy Mother of God in the Kremlin; he was also the supervisor of the clergy of the imperial court during this time. In 1910 he served briefly as a member of the Synod before his death that same year.

41. Arsenii was disliked by professors and students alike: Katanskii, *Vospominaniia*, 2: 120–22; Bishop Nikon (Rklitskii), *Zhizneopisanie blazhneishego Antoniia, mitropolita Kievskogo i Galitskogo*, vol. 1 (New York, 1956), 76. On Arsenii's service as academy rector, see L. Tverdokhlebov, "Pamiati v boze pochivshego Vysokopreosviashchennogo Arseniia (Briantseva), Arkhiepiskopa Kharkovskogo i Akhtyrskogo" (Kharkov, 1914), 9–11.

42. "Ustav Pravoslavnykh Dukhovnykh Akademii" (1869), gl. 1, §1. The careers of graduates reflected the change of emphasis. Half of the class of 1857 (who studied under the 1814 statute) entered the clergy; fewer than 15 percent became teachers. By contrast, half of the class of 1876 (who studied under the 1869 statute) were teachers in the church schools in 1887, while slightly less than one-quarter had become priests.

About one-fifth of the academy's graduates of 1876 worked in the church bureaucracy. Information compiled from the list of academy graduates in the appendix to Chistovich, *Istoriia.*

43. Only a few general courses were required: a survey of Scripture, introductory courses in theology and philosophy, and a course in the history of philosophy. Students also had to demonstrate basic knowledge of one ancient language (Greek or Latin) and one modern language (French, German, or English). "Ustav" (1869), gl. 9, §111. After completing the introductory courses, students took courses focused on the subjects they planned to teach.

44. *Polnoe sobranie zakonov Rossiiskoi imperii,* 3rd collection (1882–1917), April 1884, No. 2160, "Ustav Pravoslavnykh Dukhovnykh Akademii" (1884), gl. 1, §1.

45. "Ustav" (1884), gl. 11, §100. The required courses were (1) introduction to the theological sciences, (2) the Scriptures and biblical history, (3) dogmatic theology, (4) moral theology, (5) homiletics and history of preaching, (6) pastoral theology and pedagogy, (7) church law, (8) history of the ecumenical church, of the Eastern and Russian Orthodox churches, (9) patristics, (10) church archaeology and liturgics, (11) logic, metaphysics, and psychology, (12) history of philosophy. Students were also still required to study two foreign languages, one ancient and one modern. "Ustav" (1884), gl. 9, §101.

46. Under the 1869 statute, a student would receive a master's degree after a fourth year of study, during which he completed a thesis and passed an exam in a single subject, generally the one he expected to teach. The 1884 statute did not specify an additional length of time of study for a master's degree, but required a book-length thesis, a public defense of the thesis, and a comprehensive exam. Graduates with master's degrees usually became academy professors; thus, raising the degree requirements also elevated the qualifications for becoming a member of the faculty. "Ustav" (1869), gl. 11, §133–139; "Ustav" (1884), gl. 11, §123–125 and §130–138.

47. Dennis Clayton has argued that the Kiev academy, which had a longer history as an institution of higher learning, evolved into an institution focused primarily on research and scholarship as early as the 1830s. Dennis R. Clayton, "Parish or Publish: Kiev Ecclesiastical Academy, 1819–1869" (Ph.D. diss., University of Minnesota, 1978), x–xi and 340–45.

48. S. Peterburgskaia Dukhovnaia Akademiia, *Zhurnaly zasedanii soveta S. Peterburgskoi dukhovnoi akademii za 1881* (Spb, 1882) 8–12.

49. "Otchet o sostoianii S. Peterburgskoi dukhovnoi akademii," *Khristianskoe chtenie* 1 (1882): pt. 1, 523–26.

50. For example, "Otchet o sostoianii S. Peterburgskoi dukhovnoi akademii," *Khristianskoe chtenie* (1889): Part 1, 523–26; "Otchet o sostoianii S. Peterburgskoi dukhovnoi akademii," *Khristianskoe chtenie* (1891): Part 1, 318–20.

51. In 1914, the academy's doctor submitted a special report warning that student living conditions were dangerously overcrowded and unsanitary. He specifically deplored the school's expedient of housing students in the school's sick ward. I. I. Kozlovskii, "Ocherk zhilishchnykh uslovii zhizni studentov Imperatorskoi S. Peterburgskoi dukhovnoi akademii," *Khristianskoe chtenie* (1914): 975–1004. The monk Iliodor (Trufanov) remembered that he had first become acquainted with Father Gapon in 1901 or 1902 during an illness that confined him to the academy's hospital, where Gapon was living due to the lack of space in the dormitories. S. M. Trufanov, *The Mad Monk of Russia* (New York, 1918), 22.

52. For a positive assessment of the contributions of the academies to Russia's cultural and intellectual life in the nineteenth century, see Fedorov, *Tserkov' i gosudarstvo,* 98–99 and 119–20.

53. This discussion of the 1884 statute does not address changes it made to the schools' administration, which were bitterly criticized by many professors as reducing the role of the faculty in favor of granting more power to the rector, the local hierarch,

and the Synod. In this respect, the academy statute was comparable to the university statute of 1884, which provoked similar complaints. Indeed, the professors at both the church's academies and the state's universities faced similar professional issues with regard to their relation to the state and to the liberal reform movement. For an excellent analysis of the universities in the late imperial period, see Samuel D. Kassow, *Students, Professors, and the State in Tsarist Russia* (Berkeley, 1989).

54. "Ustav" (1884), gl. 15.

55. Ibid., §163.

56. Some aspects of this change were apparent before 1884. One professor who taught under both the 1869 and 1884 statutes blamed the students for failing to attend class regularly and demonstrating their boredom with the lectures, which he believed led the professors to spend less time preparing lectures and more time on their scholarly work. Katanskii, *Vospominaniia*, 2:145.

57. The development of the academy professorate at this time might arguably be described in terms of "professionalization" and compared to developments that affected other groups in Russia, such as doctors or teachers in the secular schools: for comparison, see especially Christine Ruane, *Gender, Class, and the Professionalization of Russian City Teachers, 1860–1914* (Pittsburgh, 1994); Nancy Mandelker Frieden, *Russian Physicians in an Era of Reform and Revolution, 1856–1905* (Princeton, 1981); and Scott J. Seregny, *Russian Teachers and Peasant Revolution: The Politics of Education in 1905* (Bloomington, 1989).

58. Although many church scholars' research was clearly stimulated by contemporary questions, their work did not usually address such questions directly. Nor have I seen much indication in the published writings of the St. Petersburg faculty that they conceived of their scholarship as a public service in the way one historian has argued the "academic intelligentsia" at the universities often did: James C. McClelland, *Autocrats and Academics: Education, Culture, and Society in Tsarist Russia* (Chicago, 1979).

59. Katanskii, *Vospominaniia*, 2:147.

60. The majority of articles appeared in the academy's monthly, *Khristianskoe chtenie*, or its weekly, *Tserkovnyi vestnik*, and also in the monthly *Strannik*, the monthly *Pravoslavnoe obozrenie*, and the secular weekly *St. Peterburgskiia vedomosti*.

61. A. Lopukhin, "Ot redaktsiia," *Khristianskoe chtenie* (December 1902): i–iv. Issues of *Khristianskoe chtenie* in the 1890s and early 1900s regularly ran between 500 and 800 large format pages; this was true of the journals published at all of the ecclesiastical academies.

62. "Otchet o sostoianii S. Peterburgskoi Dukhovnoi Akademii za 1881," *Khristianskoe chtenie* (1882): Part 1, 548–52.

63. "Otchet o sostoianii Akademii za 1903," 20–34. Professor P. N. Zhukovich was a member of the Galician-Russian Charitable Society of St. Petersburg and archpriest E. P. Akvilonov was on the committee of one of the city's workhouses for women.

64. The role of tradition in the churches generally, but particularly in the Orthodox church, has long been a subject of debate among specialists. There is a brief introduction to the literature, along with a useful summary of the subject as it relates to Orthodoxy, in Daniel B. Clendenin, *Eastern Orthodox Christianity: A Western Perspective* (Grand Rapids, 1994), 95–116. Consult also the classic introduction provided by Timothy Ware, *The Orthodox Church* (New York, 1963; reprint, 1987), 203–15.

65. Nikon (Rklitskii), *Zhizneopisanie*, 1:66–67. Khrapovitskii's concerns focused specifically on prayer, attendance at religious services, and observance of fasts and church holidays. Unlike most of his fellow students, Antonii did not come from the clerical estate, nor had he been educated in the church school system; he was from a noble family. Contemporaries noted that the youth of the clerical estate, particularly seminary students, often demonstrated a shocking degree of irreligion, expressed in their refusal to participate in religious services or the open expression of contempt and derision for the rites and rituals of the church. According to one scholar, these displays of irreligion most likely expressed the youths' attempt to rebel against the harsh disci-

pline and material hardships of seminary life: Leont'eva, "Vera i bunt," 29–35. The difficulties of seminary life are discussed in Laurie Manchester, "Secular Ascetics: The Mentality of Orthodox Clergymen's Sons in Late Imperial Russia" (Ph.D. diss., Columbia University, 1995). The classic account of seminary life is N. G. Pomyalovsky, *Seminary Sketches* (Ithaca, NY, 1973).

66. "Ustav" (1884), gl. 12, §147–149.

67. Edmund Heier, *Religious Schism in the Russian Aristocracy, 1860–1900: Radstockism and Pashkovism* (The Hague, 1970). There is additional information about Radstock's work in the writings of two contemporary British evangelists: R. S. Latimer, *Dr. Baedecker and His Apostolic Work in Russia* (London, 1907); and W. T. Stead, *The Truth about Russia* (New York, 1888), 315–79. A recent dissertation looks at Lord Radstock's mission in the broader context of competition between Protestantism and Orthodoxy in the nineteenth century: Mark McCarthy, "Religious Conflict and Social Order in Nineteenth-Century Russia: Orthodoxy and the Protestant Challenge, 1812–1905" (Ph.D. diss., University of Notre Dame, 2004). Pashkov's challenge in the 1870s recalls that of the Dominican preacher Soyard a generation previously.

68. Bronzov, "Vospominaniia," 43.

69. Ibid.

70. Nikon (Rklitskii), *Zhizneopisanie,* 1:79.

71. The most intensive period for monastic tonsurings came while bishop Antonii (Vadkovskii) was rector. He tonsured 18 students, 12 of whom later became bishops. Simon, *Church, State, and Opposition,* 46. After the long absence of monastic conversions under Father Ioann, the tonsuring of 3 or 4 students a year struck many observers as significant. The overall number of student-monks remained small, however, never constituting more than 10 out of the average student body of 250.

72. Nikon (Rklitskii), *Zhizneopisanie,* 1:81–93. Among the members of this group was the future patriarch of the Russian Orthodox Church, Sergei Stragorodskii.

73. Antonii (Vadkovskii), *Rechi, slova, i poucheniia,* 2nd ed. (Spb, 1901), 1–7. This belief was expressed in his inaugural sermon as bishop of Vyborg in 1887. As his text, he chose Christ's exhortation to Paul: "Do you love me? Then care for my sheep."

74. Antonii (Vadkovskii), *Rechi, slova, i poucheniia,* 40–41.

75. Ibid., 226–29. This was the theme of Antonii's speech at the beginning of the 1889 school year.

76. Ibid., 224.

77. Ibid., 523–24.

78. Ibid., 225.

79. Ibid., 525. Antonii also considered the students' contributions to the society's work essential to helping sustain the upsurge of popular interest in religion. "Otchet o sostoianii S. Peterburgskoi akademii za 1891," *Khristianskoe chtenie* (March 1892): 319. Antonii gave prominent mention to the students' volunteer service in his annual reports to the Synod.

80. Antonii (Vadkovskii), *Rechi, slova, i poucheniia,* 251.

81. Antonii (Vadkovskii), *Iz istorii khristianskoi propovedi. Ocherki i issledovaniia,* 2nd ed. (Spb, 1895).

82. Antonii (Vadkovskii), *Rechi, slova, o poucheniia,* 251.

83. M. V. [Galkin], *Antonii,* 60.

84. *Otchet o deiatel'nosti Obshchestva rasprostraneniia religiozno-nravstvennago proveshcheniia v dukhe pravoslavnoi tserkvi za 1899 g.* (hereafter *Otchet o deiatel'nosti ORRP*), Spb, 1900. *Prilozhenie,* appendix 1, 306–17; and "Otchet o sostoianii S. Peterburgskoi dukhovnoi akademii za 1899 g." *Khristianskoe chtenie* (March 1899): 490. At this time, there was only one academy professor on the list of members, the archpriest S. A. Sollertinskii, who taught homiletics. When the society was founded half a dozen professors had joined, but the faculty's interest in the society rapidly faded as their attention shifted to scholarship. It is surprising to notice that the faculty had hardly

anything to say about the students' extensive and often time-consuming involvement in the society's work.

85. Referred to in *Zhurnaly zasedanii soveta S. Peterburgskoi dukhovnoi akademii za 1900* (Spb, 1901), 51–55.

3—GOOD SHEPHERDS

1. Freeze, "Rechristianization of Russia." The clergy's role as enlighteners of the people is also a major theme in A. N. Rozov, *Sviashchennik v dukhovnoi zhizni russkoi derevne* (Spb, 2003).

2. Freeze, "Orthodox Church and Serfdom;" Freeze, "Handmaiden;" Kizenko, *Prodigal Saint*, 9–11. Kizenko suggests that an additional limitation on the parish priest's influence was the infrequency of confession and communion in Russian religious practice; it was considered sufficient to perform these rites annually, a belief reinforced by the imperial law that mandated annual confession and communion for those subjects who were officially registered as Orthodox (regardless of their actual beliefs).

3. Rozov, *Sviashchennik*, 28, 83–84, and 215–16; the quote is from page 216. In the original, the terms used are *"prosvetitel', vospitatel' i rukovoditel'."* Kizenko, however, has pointed out that the reform period also saw an effort to improve the clergy's performance and the laity's understanding of the liturgy and to encourage more frequent confession and communion by instructing laity to observe these sacraments four times a year instead of just once. Kizenko, *Prodigal Saint*, 11.

4. For biographical information about Feodor, see P. V. Znamenskii, *Istoriia Kazanskoi dukhovnoi akademii*, 2 vols. (Kazan, 1891–1892), 1:124–36. Archimandrite Feodor graduated from the Moscow academy in 1846 and then taught theology, first at his alma mater from 1847 to 1853 and later at the ecclesiastical academy in Kazan (1854–1857). He served as a censor in St. Petersburg from 1858 to 1862.

5. Feodor's articles were collected and published in one volume during the 1905 revolution by the journal *Tserkovnyi golos*, which was itself published by the Society for Moral-Religious Enlightenment. Arkhimandrit Feodor (Bukharev), *O pravoslavii v otnoshenii k sovremennosti* (Spb, 1906). The following discussion draws primarily on the article "O printsipakh v delakh zhiteiskikh i grazhdanskikh" (202–12) and the series of articles sharing the title "O sovremennosti v otnoshenii k pravoslaviiu" (50–71, 259–74, 278–94, 302–9). My understanding of Feodor's theology has been shaped by Valliere's masterful work *Modern Russian Theology*, especially pp. 7–8 and 37–67.

6. Valliere favors the term "renewalist" to describe Bukharev and other Orthodox thinkers (such as Vladimir Solov'ev and Sergei Bulgakov) who were similarly concerned with the necessity of the church engaging modernity in order to renew its understanding of its mission in relation to contemporary times. At earlier stages of his work on this subject, Valliere described those who held this view as "theological liberals," including in the group both Father Grigorii Petrov and the 1905 Renovationists. See Paul R. Valliere, "Modes of Social Action in Russian Orthodoxy: The Case of Father Petrov's *Zateinik*," *Russian History* 4, no. 2 (1977): 142–58; and Valliere, "The Liberal Tradition," in *Legacy of St. Vladimir*, ed. Breck, Meyendorff, and Silk, 193–208. The latter term is probably more widely recognized in the field at the present time.

7. Arkhimandrit Feodor (Bukharev), "Evangelie, chitaemoe na blagodarstven-nykh Tsarskikh molebnakh," in *O pravoslavii v otnoshenii k sovermennosti, v raznykh stat'iakh* (Spb, 1860), 212 as quoted in Valliere, *Modern Russian Theology*, 67.

8. Polisadov, *Iz vospominanii*, 14–15; Katanskii, "Vospominaniia" (1914): 763.

9. Gregory L. Freeze, "A Social Mission for Russian Orthodoxy: The Kazan Requiem of 1861 for the Peasants in Bezdna," in *Imperial Russia, 1700–1917: State, Society, Opposition*, ed. Ezra Mendelsohn and Marshall S. Shatz (DeKalb, 1988), 123–25. Feodor's ideas, which Freeze characterizes as "this-worldly theology," were shared by other members of the school's faculty and administration, 118–21.

10. The only biography of Gumilevskii was written shortly after his death (1869) by a friend who based the work on materials Gumilevskii himself had collected especially for this purpose: N. A. Skrobotov, *Prikhodskii sviashchennik A. V. Gumilevskii. Podrobnyi biograficheskii ocherk* (Spb, 1871). The work by S. G. Runkevich, *Prikhodskaia blagotvoritel'nost' v Peterburge. Istoricheskie ocherki* (Spb, 1900) includes an extensive review of Gumilevskii's work based on materials published by Gumilevskii and the charities associated with him. Although her work generally downplays the importance of church-based charities, Adele Lindenmeyr does discuss Gumilevskii's work in *Poverty Is Not a Vice: Charity, Society, and the State in Imperial Russia* (Princeton, 1996), 132–35.

11. Skrobotov, *Prikhodskii sviashchennik A. V. Gumilevskii*, 49; Runkevich, *Prikhodskaia blagotvoritel'nost'*, 2.

12. The Church of Christ's Nativity, called "On the Sands" *(na peskakh),* was located in the Rozhdestvenskii district, off of Nevskii prospekt, on the street known in the Soviet period as *6–aia Sovetskaia ulitsa.* The church was built in 1781, expanded in 1851, rebuilt in 1886. It was closed and destroyed during the Soviet period. See the map by Sergei Mikhailov, "Khramy Sankt-Peterburga, 1912 g." (Spb, 1992) and *Khramy S. Peterburga: Spravochnik-putevoditel'*, ed. T. I. Il'icheva (Spb, 1992), 44. On the character of the district in Gumilevskii's time, see Runkevich, *Prikhodskaia blagotvoritel'nost'*, 2–3.

13. Rozov describes Father Alexander as an ideal parish priest largely because of his dedication to charity work and his willingness to address contemporary problems from an Orthodox perspective through his sermons and articles in the ecclesiastical press. Rozov, *Sviashchennik*, 46–47.

14. Runkevich, *Prikhodskaia blagotvoritel'nost'*, 6.

15. Skrobotov, *Prikhodskii sviashchennik A. V. Gumilevskii*, 118. These remarks were made in the context of a lecture that he gave to the Sestry Miloserdiia in 1860.

16. On the influence of Bukharev's new liberal theology on the clergy in Kazan, see Freeze, "Social Mission," 116–20.

17. Another priest of this generation (who had been a student at the academy at the same time as Father Alexander) later became well known for his charity work: Father Ioann Sergiev of Kronstadt. Initially, Father Ioann had been attracted to the ascetic life, despite his status as a married parish priest. However, he eventually came to admire and imitate the active life of outreach and service, believing that it more closely resembled the life of Jesus and the apostles than the monastic example did. Kizenko, *Prodigal Saint*, 40–45.

18. These details on his biography are found in Valliere, *Modern Russian Theology*, 73–78. See P. V. Znamenskii, "Pravoslavie i sovremennaia zhizn'. Polemika 60–x godov ob otnoshenii pravoslavii k sovremennoi zhizni" (Moscow, 1906) for an account of the dispute and its effects on Feodor.

19. Rozov demonstrates that preaching came to be seen as an essential part of the priest's responsibilities through his study of the provincial ecclesiastical press, which was full of articles on various aspects of preaching as well as many examples of sermons. Rozov, *Sviashchennik*, 86–90.

20. Ioann (Snychev), *Ocherki*, 109–10. On the failure of the rota system, see Belliustin, *Description*, 178–81.

21. The respected preachers of the early nineteenth century were Filaret (Drozdov), metropolitan of Moscow; Amvrosii (Kliucharev), archbishop of Kharkov; Innokentii (Borisov), archbishop of Kherson; Dmitrii (Muretov), archbishop of Kherson; and St. Feofan (Govorov), "The Recluse," bishop of Vladimir. M. A. Potorzhinskii, *Russkaia gomileticheskaia khrestomatiia, XVII–XIX vv.* (Kiev, 1887). On censorship of clergy's sermons, see David W. Edwards, "Russian Ecclesiastical Censorship during the Reign of Nicholas I," *Journal of Church and State* 19, no. 1 (1977): 83–86; and also Belliustin, *Description*, 178–81.

22. Chistovich, *Akademiia za poslednyia 30 let*, 14–15.

23. Ioann (Snychev), *Ocherki*, 130–32.

24. On Father Ioann, see Katanskii, "Vospominaniia," *Khristianskoe chtenie* (May 1916): Part 1, 500–503. One may also read his sermons in I. L. Ianyshev, *Rechi i slova* (Petrograd, 1916). The other famous preachers have long since been forgotten, but see Ioann (Snychev), *Ocherki*, 133.

25. Rozov argues that preaching was easier in rural parishes, both because the parish priest was a more central figure in village parish life and because the parishioners of the village shared a common language and common concerns, which the preacher could address, unlike in a city, where parishes could be very diverse. Rozov, *Sviashchennik,* 42–43 and 94. Rozov's analysis reflects the nineteenth-century bias that saw the village as the source of Orthodoxy's strength and the city as a threat. On this bias, see Gregory Freeze, "Going to the Intelligentsia: The Church and Its Urban Mission in Post-Reform Russia," in *Between Tsar and People: Educated Society and the Quest for Public Identity in Late Imperial Russia,* ed. Edith W. Clowes, Samuel D. Kassow, and James L. West (Princeton, 1991), 216–17; and Herrlinger, "Class, Piety, and Politics," 1–4.

26. [Arkhimandrit Iakov (Domskii)], *Russkoe propovednichestvo. Istoricheshkii ego obzor i vzgliad na sovremennoe ego napravlenie* (Spb, 1871), 403.

27. Ibid., 398–402.

28. For example, see the summary of the lecture given to the Society of Moral-Religious Enlightenment by the archimandrite Antonii (Khrapovitskii) in 1890, reported in the *Otchet o deiatel'nosti Obshchestva za 1889–1890,* 20–21, and the remarks made during a discussion of pastorship and preaching at a meeting of the preaching circle sponsored by the ORRP in 1899, reported in the *Otchet o deiatel'nosti Obshchestva za 1899,* 103.

29. In his work Father Ioann tried to distinguish between Christian morality and "natural" morality (ethics) in order to define Christian doctrines on grace, free will, and salvation more precisely. N. N. Glubokovskii, *Russkaia bogoslovskaia nauka v eia istoricheskom razvitii i noveishem sostoianii* (Warsaw, 1928), 16. See also Ioann (Snychev), *Ocherki,* 191–97.

30. [Iakov (Domskii)], *Russkoe propovednichestvo,* 5.

31. These articles were collected and published in 1892 in a small edition that quickly sold out. A second edition was published in 1895, and on the basis of this work the St. Petersburg academy awarded Antonii, then archbishop of Finland and a member of the Synod, a doctoral degree. Antonii (Vadkovskii), *Iz istorii khristianskoi propovedi. Ocherki i issledovaniia,* 2nd ed. (Spb, 1895).

32. Ibid., 13.

33. Ibid., 25.

34. Ibid., 31.

35. St. Basil of Caesarea was another source of inspiration for him. Antonii (Vadkovskii), *Iz istorii khristianskoi propovedi,* 36. It was said that despite his enormous income as metropolitan of St. Petersburg, Antonii had nothing to his name at the time of his death. An envelope that was supposed to contain money set aside for his burial was found to be empty in his desk after he died because he had given even that money away. M. V. [Galkin], *Antonii,* 244.

36. The moral object of preaching is taken for granted in the handbooks of the 1880s and 1890s: M. A. Potorzhinskii, *Obraztsy russkoi tserkovnoi propovedi XIX veka* (Kiev, 1882), 691; and V. A. Mavritskii, *Voskresenyia i prazdnichnyia vnebogosluzhebnyia sobesedovaniia kak osobyi vid tserkovno-narodnoi propovedi,* 4th ed. (Moscow, 1890), 121.

37. Potorzhinskii, *Obraztsy,* ii–iii; and Ia. I. Zarnitskii, *Sbornik propovednicheskikh obraztsov. Opyt gomileticheskoi khrestomatii* (Spb, 1891), 1. These textbooks, intended for use in the new seminary course on homiletics, began by criticizing the old course.

38. See the course outline in N. I. Barsov, *Istoriia pervobytnoi khristianskoi propovedi, do IV-go veka* (Spb, 1885); also V. F. Pevnitskii, *Iz istorii gomiletiki. Gomiletika v novoe vremia, posle reformatsii Liutera* (Kiev, 1899).

39. Rozov notes that articles related to preaching were very numerous in the provincial ecclesiastical press in the second half of the nineteenth century. Rozov, *Sviashchennik*, 86–88 and 97–117.

40. N. Barsov, "O vozmozhnykh ulushcheniiakh v sovremennoi nashei tserkovnoi propovedi," *Khristianskoe chtenie* (1894): Part 1, 174–75. Barsov was professor of homiletics at the St. Petersburg academy (1869–1889) and one of the early members of the Society for Moral-Religious Enlightenment. His ideas of effective preaching had been formed under the influence of the French preacher Soyard, whom he remembered more than forty years after he had first heard him speak. Barsov was a clergyman's son himself but did not take priestly orders.

41. Ibid., 172. For example, on Good Friday, when Barsov estimated that 18,000 worshippers packed the church at the Alexander Nevskii monastery, only the 200 people squeezed tightly into the area in front of the *soleia* could hope to hear the sermon. They had to listen to it over the noise of the restless crowd while being constantly pressed and jostled and enduring the heat and stuffiness of the overcrowded church. Barsov observed that one could hardly expect the listeners to understand the sermon under such conditions, even though they hung on every word of it.

42. Belliustin, *Description*, 179. Rozov asserts this was more common in urban churches, where he believes there was little sense of connection between the parish priest and his parishioners. In village churches, priests claimed their parishioners were eager to hear the sermons, crowding closer to the front to hear better, enforcing strict silence while the priest spoke, and asking for parts to be repeated or explained afterward. Rozov, *Sviashchennik*, 90–97.

43. Mavritskii, *Sobesedovanyia*, 139.

44. But in some cases, a highly organized program was adopted, as indicated by the series of extra-liturgical lectures published by the leading parish-based association for religious education in Moscow. Eparkhial'noe bratstvo vo imia Preosviashchennoi Bogoroditsy. *Vnebogosluzhebnyia besedy pastyria s pasomami*, 12 vols. (3 vols. bound in 1) (Spb, 1890–1894).

45. Interestingly, the format used in Marxist self-education circles at the end of the century was very similar. According to a young female medical student who studied in St. Petersburg in the late 1890s, the agenda of their meetings was as follows: 1) lecture or reading from Marx's *Capital*; 2) discussion, debate; 3) tea drinking; 4) choral singing. The structure, tone, and general purpose of the two types of meetings were similar, though the content was obviously different. See Anna Bek, *The Life of a Russian Woman Doctor: A Siberian Memoir, 1869–1954* (Bloomington, 2004), 58–59. In both cases, the opportunity for group singing exerted an especially strong appeal. Bek, *Siberian Memoirs*, 59; and Rozov, *Sviashchennik*, 84.

46. Mavritskii, *Sobesedovaniia*, 247–53; also Rozov, *Sviashchennik*, 84–92.

47. Mavritskii, *Sobesedovaniia*, 253ff for numerous examples gathered from the provincial press. Mavritskii was a priest himself and fervent supporter of the *beseda*.

48. The author of one of the standard textbooks on preaching in the 1880s saw the entire future of church preaching in extra-liturgical teaching: Potorzhinskii, *Obraztsy*, 729–30. See also the assessment offered in the Society for Moral-Religious Enlightenment's ten-year retrospective, *Obshchestvo rasprostraneniia religiozno-nravstvennogo prosveshcheniia v dukhe Pravoslavnoi tserkvi v S. Peterburge, 1881–1891* (hereafter *Obshchestvo, 1881–1891*) (Spb, 1891), 7; and the remarks by one of the founding members of the ORRP, archpriest D. Nikitin, in *Otchet o deiatel'nosti Obshchestva za 1885*, 7. The annual reports of the St. Petersburg consistory regularly described the clergy's preaching and teaching activities in detail and praised them. See, for example, RGIA, f. 796, op. 442, d. 893 (1880), l. 11; d. 1010 (1883), ll. 132 ob.-133; d. 2834 (1889), l. 19 ob; and especially d. 1948 (1890), ll. 12 and 15–16 ob.

49. A particularly important theme in Rozov, *Sviashchennik*, 30, 36–37, 47–48, 87, 218–19.

50. The work of the famous priest Father Ioann Sergiev of Kronstadt exemplified the spirit of the times. Through his charity work, sermons, performance of the liturgy, and conduct of mass confessions and communions, Father Ioann demonstrated the role of the parish priest in bringing religion to life and giving it direct, immediate meaning in the quotidian world. Kizenko, *Prodigal Saint,* 51–58.

51. Arkhimandrit Antonii (Amfiteatrov), *Pastyrskoe bogoslovie* (Kiev, 1851); Arkhimandrit Kirill (Naumov), *Pastyrskoe bogoslovie,* 2nd ed. (Spb, 1853).

52. Mieczyslaw Olezewski, "Die Pastoraltheologie in der Orthodoxen Kirche Russlands des 19 Jahrhunderts," *Ostkirchliche Studien* 38, no. 4 (1989): 315–16. Not everyone at this time embraced the development of the "new" theological discipline, as is evident in a hostile review of one of the works discussed below: N. Makkaveiskii, "Ieromonakh Innokenti. Pastyrskoe bogoslovie v Rossii na XIX v," *Trudy Kievskoi Dukhovnoi Akademii* 3 (1899): 604–6.

53. *American Heritage Dictionary of the English Language,* 1981 ed., s.v. "priest." See also *Oxford Dictionary of the Christian Churches,* 2nd ed., 1974, s.v. "priest."

54. In Russian, there is no equivalent for the neutral and non-denominational term "clergyman." There is the collective noun *"dukhovenstvo,"* but the related noun *"dukhovnik"* has the specific meaning of confessor. Individual members of the clergy were usually referred to by rank, as *psalomshchik* (reader), *diakon* (deacon), *sviashchennik* (priest), or *protoierei* (archpriest). In popular parlance, the individual clergyman was often *pop,* but the educated urban clergy considered this term derogatory and did not use it in reference to themselves.

55. The word *pastyr'* (accent on the first syllable) should not be confused with the word *pastor* (accent on the second syllable). *Pastor* referred specifically to "a priest of one of the Protestant churches"; the word was taken into Russian from the German but was Latin in origin. *Pastyr'* was defined as "spiritual shepherd; a priest" in Dal's authoritative dictionary. Vladimir Dal, *Tolkovyi slovar' zhivogo velikorusskogo iazyka,* 2nd ed. (Moscow, 1880–1882). A modern etymological dictionary traces the word *pastyr'* back to Old Church Slavonic, finding the same word in all the major Slavic languages. Max Vasmer, *Etimologicheskii slovar' russkogo iazyka,* 4 vols. (Moscow, 1986–1987).

56. The titles of the following works give some idea of the usage of *pastyr'* and its related forms: E. Popov, *Pis'ma po pravoslavno-pastyrskomu pastyrstvu,* 4 vols., 2nd ed. (Perm, 1877); P. I. Nechaev, *Uchebnik po prakticheskomu rukovodstvu dlia pastyrei,* 2 vols., 3rd ed. (Spb, 1884); S. A. Sollertinskii, *Pastyrstvo Khrista Spasitelia* (Spb, 1887); N. Raninskii, "Pastyrenachal'nik Gospod Iisus Khristos i ego sviatye apostoly" (Spb, 1891); S. Pokrovskii, *Kurs prakticheskogo rukovodstva dlia pastyrei,* 2nd ed. (Spb, 1898); N. P. Vartagav, *Istinnyi pastyr'. Sviatootecheskii ideal khristianskogo pastyria* (Simferopol, 1906); P. M. Kremlevksii, *Opravdanie pastyrstva* (Spb, 1907); V. Petrov, *Dobryi pastyr'. Pastyrskaia khrestomatiia* (Sergiev Posad, 1915); T. S. Tikhomirov, *Na prikhode. Sviashchennicheskaia entsiklopediia po vsem storonam pastyrskoi deiatel'nosti,* 2 vols. (Moscow, 1915). Not everyone accepted this shift in usage. The critic N. Makkaveiskii argued that he did not see any distinction between the kind of clergyman described as a "pastor" and the established meaning of the clergyman as a priest. He rejected the entire discipline of pastoral theology, arguing that it did not encompass anything not already included in the fields of liturgics and homiletics. Makkaveiskii, "Ieromonakh Innokentii," 604–5.

57. This distinction is neatly presented in the way one parishioner characterized a particular clergyman as a "true pastor" *(istinnyi pastyr'):* "He was not a mere performer of rites *(treboispravitel'),* but did everything for raising the moral and intellectual level, and even the material condition, of the peasants." Rozov, *Sviashchennik,* 45.

58. Innokentii (Pustynskii), *Pastyrskoe bogoslovie v Rossii na XIX v.* (Sergiev Posad, 1899), xxxi.

59. Although English-language translations of the New Testament typically render this passage as "then feed my sheep," in Russian the imperative is *pasi* (infinitive *pasti*), which means to herd or to tend. Etymologically, the imperative is clearly related

not only to the Slavonic word *pastyr'*, but also to the Russian words *pastva* (flock) and *pastukh* (shepherd). The Russian word for Easter is *Paskha*.

60. M. V. [Galkin], *Antonii*, 55–56.

61. For context, see Innokentii (Pustynskii), *Pastryskoe bogoslovie*, 84–87. The older interpretation was expressed in a work first published in 1776, *Kniga o dolzhnosti-akh presviterov prikhodskikh*, written by the archbishop of Mogilev, Georgii (Konissiskii), and the bishop of Smolensk, Parfenii (Sopkovskii). This work was the main guide on priestly duties until the middle of the nineteenth century. It was one of the texts translated in *The Doctrine of the Russian Church, Being the Primer or Spelling Book, the Shorter and Longer Catechisms, and a Treatise on the Duty of Parish Priests*, tr. R. W. Blackmore (London, 1845).

62. Luke 15:1–7. Given the textual and pictorial associations of Jesus with the Good Shepherd, it is surprising to find that the image of the shepherd and his flock is rather uncommon in the New Testament, though it appears frequently in the Old Testament, where the leaders of Israel and God himself are often described as good shepherds who love their flocks and care for them tenderly. The most well-known example is the opening line of Psalm 23: "The Lord is my shepherd, I shall not want. He leads me to green pastures, and lays me down beside cool waters." Another passage found in Isaiah 40:11 reads, "He tends his flock like a shepherd, He gathers the lambs in his arms and carries them close to his heart, he gently leads those that have young."

63. The most thorough explanation of the significance of the parable of the lost sheep is in V. F. Pevnitskii, *Sluzhenie sviashchennika v kachestve dukhovnogo rukovoditelia prikhozhan* (Kiev, 1890), 15–19. Similar treatments appear in Iakov (Domskii), *Pastyr'*, 43–45 and Innokentii (Pustynskii), *Pastyrskoe bogoslovie*, 307.

64. The shift in emphasis from leadership based on the exercise of authority to leadership based on the power of love seems to have taken place in the broader culture as well. Richard Wortman describes Alexander II's "scenario" as being based on the ideal of mutual love between the ruler and his subjects, following a pattern evident in European courts as well. Wortman, *Scenarios of Power*, 2:27, 30, 38, 61–71.

65. Innokentii (Pustynskii), *Pastyrskoe bogoslovie*, xxxi. For a critical review of this work, see Makkaveiskii, "Ieromanakh Innokentii," 604–5.

66. Rozov, *Sviashchennik*, 39. The phrase *"istinnyi pastyr'"* was used frequently in a wide range of nineteenth-century writings, including literary works and in the press. Rozov discusses this ideal with particular attention to the peasant viewpoint on pp. 43–48. (The use of the word *priest (sviashchennik)* in the quoted passage in all likelihood reflects a simple stylistic decision on the part of Rozov not to repeat the word *pastor*, given the use of the noun pastorship in the preceding sentence.)

67. Laurie Manchester has argued that the ethic of the intelligentsia was strongly influenced by clerical values, which were transposed to the secular context by clergy-men's sons who chose not to enter clerical service after the reforms of the 1860s allowed them to leave the clerical estate and pursue other professions, which they did in significant numbers.

68. Innokenti (Pustynskii), *Pastyrskoe bogoslovie*, xxxvi. Father Innokentii later became well known as a scholar, linguist, and talented preacher, serving in some of the more exotic dioceses of the church (Turkestan, Alaska). He retired in 1922 but reemerged in 1923 as a Renovationist bishop. See Manuil (Lemeshevskii), *Russkie pravoslavnye ierarkhi perioda 1893–1965 gg. Oikonomen*, ed. Martin George and M. S. Agurskij, vol. 20 (1984): 253–55.

69. Iakov (Domskii) *Pastyr'*, ii.

70. Ibid., 10–42. Olezewski argues that the distinguishing characteristic of post-reform Russian pastoral theology was its concern with the moral character of the clergyman himself, rather than the clergy's responsibility to provide moral leadership to others. Olezewski, "Die Pastoraltheologie," 311 and 327–28.

71. In her study of *popovichi* memoirs, Laurie Manchester identified two ideal types of clergyman: the ascetic scholarly type and the extroverted activist type. Both were committed to working for the salvation of their parishioners, but each had his own way of achieving that goal. Manchester, "Secularization of the Search for Salvation," 54–63. Both types are certainly evident in the later nineteenth-century literature on pastorship, but somewhat more emphasis seems to be put on the activist ideal.

72. Iakov (Domskii), *Pastyr'*, 43–81.

73. Sollertinskii, *Pastyrstvo*. Sollertinskii attended the St. Petersburg academy and became a *privat-dotsent* at the academy immediately after his graduation in 1871. He received his master's degree in 1883 and became an associate professor in 1885. He took clerical orders in 1899 and received his doctoral degree and the rank of full professor in 1901. Sollertinskii was one of the early members of the Society for Moral-Religious Enlightenment.

74. Sollertinskii, *Pastyrstvo*, 3.

75. Ibid., 231.

76. Innokentii focused particularly on this part of Sollertinskii's discussion in summarizing it for his own study. Innokentii (Pustynskii), *Pastyrskoe bogoslovie*, 346–47.

77. S. Kuliukin, "Ideia pastyrskogo dushepopecheniia," *Khristianskoe chtenie* (1901): Part 2, 341–69 and 467–81.

78. V. Uspenskii, "Izuchenie pastyrstva v protestanskom bogoslovii," *Khristianksoe chtenie* (1904): Part 1, 197–213. The Russian term that came to be used to express the essence of pastoral care was *"dushepopechenie,"* corresponding to the English care (or cure) of souls or the German *Seelsorge*. On this view of salvation, see also the work of Antonii (Khrapovitskii), *Uchenie o pastyre, pastyrstve, i ob ispovedi*, ed. Bishop Nikon [Rklitskii] (New York, 1966), 13–21. The late date of publication on this work is misleading, for Metropolitan Khrapovitskii was an active theologian in the 1890s and early 1900s, a slightly younger contemporary of Sollertinskii.

79. V. F. Pevnitskii, *Sviashchenstvo. Osnovnye punkty v uchenii o pastyrskom sluzhenie* (Kiev, 1885), 1–2.

80. Ibid., 41–78.

81. Pevnitskii thus reflects a clergyman's view of the laity's growing desire for more autonomy in local church matters. This development has attracted historians' attention: Chulos, *Converging Worlds;* Glennys Young, "'Into Church Matters:' Lay Identity, Rural Parish Life, and Popular Politics in Late Imperial and Early Soviet Russia, 1864–1928," *Russian History* 23 (1996): 367–84; Herrlinger, "Class, Piety, and Politics"; Freeze, "All Power to the Parish?"

82. Pevnitskii, *Sviashchenstvo*, 78–81.

83. V. F. Pevnitskii, *Sviashchennik. Prigotovlenie k sviashchenstvu i zhizni sviashchennika*, 2nd ed. (Kiev, 1886), 7–19.

84. Ibid., 64. Richard Stites identifies "moralism" as one of the defining features of elite secular culture in the late imperial period. Richard Stites, *Russian Popular Culture: Entertainment and Society since 1900* (Cambridge, 1992), 6. Both the educated clergy and the educated laity shared the view that as members of the elite it was their responsibility to offer moral guidance and leadership to the lower classes as a means of contributing to the improvement of society.

85. Pevnitskii, *Sviashchennik*, 70

86. Ibid., 73–101. A law of 1869 reestablished the practice of the ancient church, according to which a man could not be ordained until the age of 25 and could not become a priest until the age of 30. Since most students graduated from the seminary at the age of 22, this left them with three years before they could take clerical orders as a deacon. They were allowed to serve as readers, but seminary graduates disdained this position because of its low prestige and pay. The age limitations were waived for graduates of the academies. Freeze, *Parish Clergy*, 66–67, 161–62, 367.

87. Pevnitskii, *Sluzhenie*, 1–3. Significantly, this volume of more than six hundred pages was longer than the first two volumes together.

88. Only one author had dealt with the subject at any length: Popov, *Pis'ma*.

89. Pevnitskii, *Sluzhenie*, 18–22.

90. Ibid., 21.

91. Ibid., 57.

92. Ibid., 179.

93. Ibid., 197.

94. Ibid., 186–89.

95. Ibid., 201–24.

96. One contemporary church scholar considered Pevnitskii's contribution to be the most outstanding in the field and held it up as the standard by which he measured other works. Innokentii (Pustynskii), *Pastyrskoe bogoslovie*, 300–314. One of Sollertinskii's students, the last chief chaplain of the military clergy, Georgii I. Shavel'skii, acknowledged Pevnitskii's influence on his ideas of pastorship in the course of lectures on pastoral theology that he published in 1930. G. I. Shavel'skii, *Pravoslavnoe pastyrstvo. Osnovy, zadachi, i dukh pravoslavnogo pastyrskogo sluzheniia* (Sofiia, 1930): 3–4.

4—Church Charity and the Search for Christian Community

1. The essential work on the development of charity in imperial Russia is Adele Lindenmeyr, *Poverty Is Not a Vice*. Lindenmeyr discusses the parish charities and curatorships very briefly and without distinguishing between them (pages 129–36), but in general focuses on non-church related charities. A recent Russian survey of the development of charity in Russia also gives the impression that the church was not involved in charity work in any significant way during the synodal period: A. R. Sokolov, "Rossiskaia blagotvoritel'nost' v XVIII–XIX vekakh (K voprosu operiodizatsii i poniatom apparata)." *Otechestvennaia istoriia* 6 (2003): 147–58.

2. Lindenmeyr discusses the relation between the organization of secular charitable societies and the development of civic society in *Poverty Is Not a Vice*, 227–30; see also Lindenmeyr, "Voluntary Associations and the Russian Autocracy: The Case of Private Charity," *The Carl Beck Papers in Russian and East European Studies*, 807 (Pittsburgh, June 1990), "A Russian Experiment in Voluntarism: The Municipal Guardianships of the Poor, 1894–1914," *Jahrbucher für Geschichte Osteuropas* 30, no. 3 (1982): 429–451, and "Charity and the Problem of Unemployment: Industrial Homes in Late Imperial Russia," *The Russian Review* 45, no. 1 (1986): 1–22. A thorough review and discussion of the literature concerning the public sphere and the development of civil society in Europe and Russia is provided in Joseph Bradley, "Subjects into Citizens: Societies, Civil Society, and Autocracy in Tsarist Russia," *American Historical Review* 107, no. 4 (October, 2002): 1094–1123. Bradley explicitly excludes societies related to "churches, sects and religious associations" from his analysis, as do most other works on this issue.

3. Adele Lindenmeyr, "The Ethos of Charity in Imperial Russia," *Journal of Social History* 23, no. 4 (1990): 679–94. While recognizing the importance of religious motivations for charity work for many lay people, she does not discuss how religious motivations affected the role the clergy played in charitable organizations.

4. Gary Marker, "God of Our Mothers: Reflections on Lay Female Spirituality in the Late Eighteenth and Early Nineteenth Centuries in Russia," in *Orthodox Russia: Belief and Practice under the Tsars*, ed. Valerie Kivelson and Robert H. Greene (University Park, PA, 2003), 193–209. Marker has argued that Russians who embraced the ideals of the Enlightenment nevertheless remained committed to Orthodox values, which shaped their personal lives and the shared culture of educated society. Marker, *Days of a Russian Noblewoman: The Memories of Anna Labzina, 1758–1821* (DeKalb, 2001). Catherine Evtuhov's study of the provincial intelligentsia further demonstrates the extent to which educated individuals continued to be interested in and

deeply influenced by religious concerns and values in the later nineteenth century: Evtuhov, "Voices from the Provinces," 33–48.

5. *Doctrine of the Russian Church,* 12. This primer, developed in the seventeenth century, was adopted officially by the Synod in the late eighteenth century. The seventh edition was published in 1825. This teaching on the sixth commandment was not altered during the course of the century: a textbook on Orthodoxy published in 1892 for use in the seventh and eighth years of the *gymnaziia* featured the same interpretation. P. Gorodtsev, *Kratkie ocherki pravoslavnogo khristianskogo nravoucheniia,* 2nd ed. (Spb, 1892), 65–66.

6. *Doctrine of the Russian Church,* 113–14. The Longer Catechism was composed by the metropolitan of Moscow, Filaret (Drozdov), and adopted by the Synod for general use in the Russian Church in 1839.

7. Ibid., 114.

8. Ibid., 137.

9. Untitled article on Christianity and socialism, *Pravoslavno-russkoe slovo* 5 (March 1902), 400; I. Labutin, *Kharakter khristianskoi blagotvoritel'nosti* (Spb, 1899), 30. Labutin was a St. Petersburg priest and a member of the Society for Moral-Religious Enlightenment. He served as a priest first at the society's church at the Warsaw train station (Varshavskaia) and then at the large diocesan church at Hay Market Square (Spasosennovskaia), both located in heavily populated working-class areas. He was a popular preacher and an active organizer of local church charity work.

10. Labutin, *Kharakter,* 42.

11. For more on this idea in the context of Eastern Christianity generally, see Georges Florovsky, "The Social Problem in the Eastern Orthodox Church," *Journal of Religious Thought* 8, no. 1 (1950–1951): 41–51.

12. Episkop Vissarion, *Uteshenie i sovety liudiam zhivushchim v bednosti,* 5th ed. (Moscow, 1898). Father Ioann of Kronstadt also understood charity as a way of building community: Kizenko, *Prodigal Saint,* 68–75.

13. P. Runovskii, *Znachenie khristianstva v dukhovno-nravstvennom razvitii i otnoshenie ego k blagoustroistvu zemnoi zhizni chelovechestva* (Spb, 1889), 60–81; and M. I. Sokolov, *Pastyrskie zavety* (Spb, 1905), 144–54. The church's attitude toward wealth was discussed at a meeting of the St. Petersburg clergy hosted by the ORRP in 1899 and reported in the *Otchet o deiatel'nosti Obshchestva za 1899,* 92–98.

14. The idea that charity toward others was a means of building the Kingdom of God was a favorite idea of two preachers who became especially well known in St. Petersburg for their acts of charity—the metropolitan of St. Petersburg, Antonii (Vadkovskii), and one of the priests of Kazan cathedral, Mikhail Sokolov. See Antonii (Vadkovskii), *Rechi,* 235–41 and 249–52; Sokolov, *Pastyrskie zavety,* 96–104 and 144–54.

15. Skrobotov, *Prikhodskii sviashchennik A. V. Gumilevskii,* 17.

16. Labutin, *Kharakter,* 36.

17. Pevnitskii, *Sluzhenie,* 21 and 197–224. Similarly, see Iakov (Domskii), *Pastyr,* 118–33.

18. Among the young clergymen of the generation of the 1880s and 1890s who expressed this impulse were Father Georgii Gapon, the archimandrite Mikhail (Semenov), and Father Grigorii Petrov. "Pis'ma Gapona," *Russkaia mysl'* 5 (1907): 112; Arkhimandrit Mikhail, *Kak ia stal narodnym sotsialistom* (Moscow, 1908), 25–26; G. S. Petrov, *Pis'mo sviashchennika Grigoriia Petrova mitropolitu Antoniiu* (Berlin, n.d.), 7.

19. The annual reports of the Synod's director general were the main published source for official statistics on the church and its activities. However, these reports often contained only minimal information about the church's charity work, generally excluding the parish charities entirely (probably because they fell under the authority of the Ministry of the Interior) and often not representing the parish curatorships. For a typical example, see Sviateishii Pravitel'stvuiushchii Sinod, *Vsepoddaneishii otchet ober-prokurora sviateishego sinoda K. Pobedonostseva po vedomstvu pravoslavnogo ispovedaniia za 1898* [hereafter cited by short title] (Spb, 1901), appendix, 44–47. Although the dioce-

san report for that year counted 192 parish curatorships, the director general's report listed only 19 medical treatment centers and 42 pensioners' homes for the diocese in the appendix on church charity work. Official and unofficial surveys of charity in St. Petersburg by secular authorities or organizations contain only incomplete, contradictory, and confused statistics on parish charity: S. Peterburgskaia gorodskaia uprava po statisticheskomu otdeleniiu, *Sbornik spravochnykh i statisticheskikh svedenii o blagotvoritel'nosti v S. Peterburge za 1884 g.* (Spb, 1886) and *Sbornik svedenii o blagotvoritel'nosti v S. Peterburge za 1889 g.* (Spb, 1891); Kantseliariia po uchrezhdeniiam Imperatritsy Marii, *Sbornik svedenii o blagotvoritel'nosti v Rossii, s kratkimi ocherkami blagotvoritel'nykh uchrezhdenii v S. Peterburge i Moskve* (Spb, 1899); *S. Peterburg. Putevoditel' po stolitse s istoriko-statisticheskim ocherkom i opisaniem eia dostoprimachatel'nostei i uchrezhdenii* (Spb, 1903); P. N. Isakov, *Spravochnaia knizhka o blagotvoritel'nykh uchrezhdeniiakh i zavedeniiakh v S. Peterburge* (Spb, 1911); S. Peterburgskoe gorodskoe obshchestvennoe upravlenie, *Spravochnik o blagotvoritel'nykh uchrezhdeniiakh, deistvuiushchikh v gorode S. Peterburge* (Spb, 1913).

20. Contemporaries used the church's own statistics against it. See, for example, V. Kil'chevksii, *Bogatstvo i dokhody dukhovenstva* (Spb, 1906). The author uses numbers from the director general's annual reports to support his argument that the church had ample resources but spent very little of its wealth on charity work, thus shirking its responsibility to care for the needy and outcast.

21. On the reforms proposed during this era for the church, see Freeze, *Parish Clergy*, 298–348. Freeze argues in this work that the curatorships were a failure, 285–92. See also, Freeze, "All Power to the Parish?" 176.

22. The difficulties that many clergymen faced in the daily struggle to fulfill their duties were described in the famous expose by Belliustin, *Description of the Clergy in Rural Russia*.

23. The project was developed by Innokentii, the archbishop of Kamchatka, and Count Muravev-Amurskii, governor of the Pri-Amurskaia province. It had considerable support among the lay ministers of the government. For details on the two competing projects, see B. V. Titlinov, *Vopros o prikhodskii reforme v tsarstvovanie Imperatora Aleksandra II-ogo* (Petrograd, 1917).

24. For the rules on the curatorships, see *Pravila o pravoslavnykh tserkovnykh bratstvakh i polozhenie o prikhodskikh popechitel'stvakh pri pravoslavnykh tserkvakh* (Spb, 1881); and T. V. Barsov, *Iz sbornika deistvuiushchikh i rukovodstvennykh tserkovnykh i tserkovnograzhdanskikh postanovlenii po vedomstvu pravoslavnogo ispovedeniia*, Glava 40, *O prikhodskikh popechitel'stvakh pri pravoslavnykh tservakh* (Moscow, 1896).

25. The curatorships were not expected to organize or run either the charities or the schools but only to help finance them. Barsov emphasized that in St. Petersburg and Moscow many church-based charities were associated with a parish and partially financed by the parish curatorships but under the authority of separate charters. Barsov, *O prikhodskikh popechitel'stvakh*, 9–10.

26. The numbers are taken from the reports of the diocesan consistory to the Synod: RGIA, f. 796, op. 442, dd. 893 (1880), 1010 (1883), 1145 (1886), 2834 (1889), 1407 (1892), 1737 (1898), 1855 (1900), 1913 (1901), 2086 (1904), 2105 (1905), 2165 (1906), 2230 (1907), 2290 (1908). The consistory did not always include information on the curatorships, especially after 1908. The figures from 1893 and in part, for 1892, are taken from Sviateishii Pravitel'stvuiushchii Sinod, *Vsepoddaneishii otchet oberprokurora sviateishego sinoda K. Pobedonostseva po vedomstvu pravoslavnogo ispovedaniia za 1892 i 1893* [hereafter cited by short title] (Spb, 1895), appendix, pp. 68–72.

27. In 1898, for example, there were 36,561 parish churches in the empire, of which 17,261 had parish curatorships; in St. Petersburg diocese, there were 302 parish churches and 192 active curatorships. *Vsepoddaneishii otchet ober-prokurora sv. sinoda za 1898*, 22 and 58–62; RGIA, f. 796, op. 442, d. 1737, "Otchet o sostoianii S. Peterburgskoi eparkhii za 1898 g.," l. 42.

28. The numbers are taken from the diocesan reports listed in note 26. For comparison, see the tables in *Vsepoddaneishii otchet ober-prokurora sv. sinoda za 1892 i 1893,* appendix, pp. 68–72 and 148–52, and *Vsepoddaneishii otchet ober-prokurora sv. sinoda za 1898,* appendix, pp. 58–61. In 1892, only nine dioceses collected more than 75,000 rubles: Vologda, Viatka, Don, Ekaterinoslav, Podolia, Samara, Saratov, Tambov, and Iakut. The 329 curatorships of Kiev diocese collected a paltry 31,000 rubles, while the 74 curatorships of Moscow diocese collected only 23,000. Almost half of the dioceses reported that their curatorships collected less than 20,000 rubles that year.

29. RGIA, f. 796, op. 442, d. 2105, "Otchet o sostoianii S. Peterburgskoi eparkhii za 1905," l. 120 ob. In 1915, the parish curatorships collected almost 319,000 rubles for the families of soldiers. RGIA, f. 796, op. 442, d. 2783, "Otchet za 1915," ll. 85 ob.–86.

30. In St. Petersburg, the curatorships never gave more than 8 percent of their funds to the clergy. This proportion diminished after 1900 and was reduced to practically nothing after the 1905 revolution. Since the clergy of the city were comparatively well off and secure in their positions, they did not seek to appropriate curatorship funds for their own use.

31. *Vsepoddaneishii otchet ober-prokurora sv. sinoda za 1892 i 1893,* appendix, p. 72; *Vsepoddaneishii otchet ober-prokurora sv. sinoda za 1898,* appendix, p. 61.

32. Unfortunately, neither the figures published by the Synod nor those provided in the diocesan consistory's reports indicate how much money was spent on charity and how much on the church parish schools. The church parish schools were not dependent exclusively on the parish for their funds but received money also from the diocese, the zemstvo, and especially from the late 1890s, from the central government. Sviateishii Pravitel'stvuiushchii Sinod, Uchilishchnyi sovet, *Istoricheskii ocherk razvitiia tserkovnykh shkol za istekshee dvadtsatipiatiletie (1884–1909)* (Spb, 1909).

33. In 1892, the curatorships of St. Petersburg spent more than 21,000 rubles on charity while those of Kiev and Moscow spent only 5,000 to 6,000 each. Only three dioceses spent more on charity than St. Petersburg: Viatka spent 24,315; Samara spent 36,442; and Nizhegorod spent 56,366. *Vsepoddaneishii otchet ober-prokurora sv. sinoda za 1892 i 1893,* appendix, pp. 68–71.

34. Freeze shares this assessment, as discussed in "All Power to the Parish?" 176–78. Another historian has challenged this view, arguing the curatorships empowered the laity: Young, "Into Church Matters," 382–84.

35. The curatorships first came under fire from the zemstvo of Moscow province in 1884, when the Moscow zemstvo submitted a plan for parish reform to the Synod. A summary of the plan and Pobedonostsev's scathing rejection of it are in *Vsepoddaneishii otchet ober-prokurora sviateishago sinoda za 1884 g.,* Spb.: Sinodal'naia tipografiia, 1885: 27–36. The leading lay critic of the curatorships and the parish system in general was A. A. Papkov. See especially his *Nachalo vozrozhdeniia tserkovno-prikhodskoi zhizni v Rossii* (Moscow, 1900) and *Neobkhodymost' obnovleniia pravoslavnogo tserkovno-obshchestvennaia stroia* (Spb, 1902). The latter article, originally published in *Russkii vestnik* in June of 1902, occasioned a great deal of comment in the press, and was summarized in A. G. Boldovskii, *Vozrozhdenie tserkovnogo prikhoda* (Spb, 1903).

36. Such "traditional" expressions of religiosity as the veneration of icons, the decoration of chapels, and the dedication of beautiful items for use in the celebration of the liturgy in Orthodox life had real importance, however: Shevzov, "Icons," 610–12; Shevzov, "Chapels," 585–88; Kizenko, "Reception," 325–29.

37. I. Fudel, *Osnovy tserkovno-prikhodskoi zhizni* (Moscow, 1894) and *K reforme prikhodskikh popechitel'stv* (Moscow, 1894); and I. Lebedev, *Tserkovno-prikhodskie popechitel'stva* (Chernigov, 1902). There were also laymen working for the church who shared this opinion. See I. Berdnikov, *Chto nuzhno dlia obnovleniia pravoslavnogo russkogo prikhoda?* (Spb, 1907); and K. P. Pobedonostsev, RGIA, f. 796, op. 185 (1904), d. 1309, "Ob utverzhdenii proekta ustava 'Obshchestvo revnitel'ei razvitiia prosvetitel'noi i blagotvoritel'noi deiatel'nosti v pravoslavnykh tserkvakh.'"

38. The laity demonstrated a growing desire to play a more active role in church life in the late imperial period, often justifying their demands with references to practices that had been in use in the pre-Petrine period or during ancient times. The clergy generally opposed initiatives to give the laity more control over local church life. See particularly Chris Chulos, "Revolution and Grass-Roots Re-evaluations of Russian Orthodoxy: Parish Clergy and Peasants of Voronezh Province, 1905–1917," in *Transforming Peasants: State, Society, and the Peasantry, 1860–1930. Selected Papers from the Fifth World Congress of Central and East European Studies,* ed. Judith Pallot (New York, 1998), 113–29; Freeze, "All Power to the Parish?" 174–75 and 179–84; Young, "Into Church Matters," 377–80.

39. The clergy's central role in building up local religious communities through charity work was manifested as well in the service of Father Ioann of Kronstadt: Kizenko, *Prodigal Saint,* 67–96.

40. The diocesan reports of 1886 and 1889 stated there were charitable societies at all the parish churches of the capital. RGIA, f. 796, op. 442, d. 1145, "Otchet o sostoianii S. Peterburgskoi eparkhii za 1886," ll. 13–13ob. and d. 2834, "Otchet o sostoianii S. Peterburgskoi eparkhii za 1889," l. 17ob. It is difficult to determine from such statements exactly how many parish charities there were because of the problems in identifying which churches were being counted as parish churches in any particular source. The diocese considered there to be around two hundred parish churches in the capital, which would suggest some two hundred or more parish charities by the end of the 1880s. I have detailed information only about the forty charities that were located at churches officially registered by the Synod in the diocesan or military administrations in 1899.

41. I. D——n. *Prikhodskaia zhizn' pri Blagoveshchenskoi Vasil'eostrovskoi tserkvi s 1862 do 1912 goda* (Spb, 1912), 7. The Synod had recognized Tikhon as a saint in 1861. For Tikhon's biography, see N. Gorodetsky, *Saint Tikhon of Zadonsk: Inspirer of Dostoevsky* (Crestwood, NY, 1976).

42. [S. G. Runkevich], "Prikhodskaia blagotvoritel'nost' v Peterburge. Obshchestvo vspomoshchestvovaniia bednym Panteleimonovskaia prikhoda," *S. Peterburgskii Dukhovnyi Vestnik (SPBDV)* 8 (1898): 145–50.

43. [S. G. Runkevich], "Prikhodskaia blagotvoritel'nost' v Peterburge. Obshchestvo vspomozheniia bednym v prikhode tserkvi Sv. Troitsy leib-gvardii Izmailogo polka," *SPBDV* 14 (1899): 167–69.

44. Ibid. See also, [S. G. Runkevich], "Prikhodskaia blagotvoritel'nost' v Peterburge. Obshchestvo vspomozheniia bednym Spasobocharinskaia prikhoda," *SPBDV* 38 (1899): 445–46.

45. [S. G. Runkevich], "Prikhodskaia blagotvoritel'nost' v Peterburge. Obshchestvo vspomoshchestvovaniia bednym Panteleimonovskaia prikhoda," *SPBDV* 8 (1898): 146.

46. [S. G. Runkevich], "Prikhodskaia blagotvoritel'nost' v Peterburge. Obshchestvo vspomoshchestvovaniia prikhodskim bednym pri Blagoveshchenskoi tserkvi na Vasilievskom ostrove," *SPBDV* 17 (1897): 323–26.

47. [S. G. Runkevich], "Prikhodskaia blagotvoritel'nost' v Peterburge. Obshchestvo vspomozheniia prikhodskim bednym pri Vladimirskoi tserkvi," *SPBDV* 24 (1897): 463–64.

48. [S. G. Runkevich], "Obshchestvo Spasobocharinskaia prikhoda," *SPBDV* 38 (1899): 446.

49. The membership was comparable to secular charity societies: 58 percent of those had between ten and one hundred members. Lindenmeyr, *Poverty Is Not a Vice,* 205. The society at the cathedral of St. Sergei (in the military administration) included many military officers and high-ranking nobles, including members of the royal family, among its supporters. [S. G. Runkevich], "Prikhodskaia blagotvoritel'nost' v Peterburge. Sergeevskoe bratstvo," *SPBDV* 32 (1898): 354–55.

50. [S. G. Runkevich], "Prikhodskaia blagotvoritel'nost' v Peterburge. Obshchestvo vspomozheniia bednym pri Andreevskom sobore," *SPBDV* 34 (1898): 603.

51. [S. G. Runkevich], "Obshchestvo Spasobocharinskaia prikhoda," *SPBDV* 38 (1899): 446.

52. [S. G. Runkevich], "Obshchestvo Panteleimonovskaia prikhoda," *SPBDV* 4 (1898): 62.

53. [S. G. Runkevich], "Prikhodskaia blagotvoritel'nost' v Peterburge. Obshchestvo vspomozheniia bednym v prikhode Vkhodoierusalimskoi tserkvi," *SPBDV* 46 (1897): 914–17 and 47 (1897): 933–37.

54. [S. G. Runkevich], "Prikhodskaia blagotvoritel'nost' v Peterburge. Obshchestvo vspomozheniia bednym pri Kazanskom sobore," *SPBDV* 41 (1898): 734–38.

55. [S. G. Runkevich], "Prikhodskaia blagotvoritel'nost' v Peterburge. Obshchestvo vspomozheniia bednym v prikhode Voskreseniia Khristova v Maloi Kolomne," *SPBDV* 26 (1899): 302–4.

56. [S. G. Runkevich], "Obshchestvo pri Andreevskom sobore," *SPBDV* 35 (1898): 617–22, and "Obshchestvo v prikhode tserkvi Sv. Troitsy leib-gvardii Izmailogo polka," *SPBDV* 14 (1899): 167–69.

57. *Sbornik svedenii o blagotvoritel'nosti v Peterburge za 1889,* 282. To be exact, the societies received 48.4 percent of their income from donations, 12.5 percent from investments, 10.9 percent from collections, 9.2 percent from rents, 8.2 percent from membership dues, .6 percent from other societies, and .7 percent from fundraisers.

58. *Sbornik svedenii o blagotvoritel'nosti v Peterburge za 1884 g.,* 249–51; Lindenmeyr, *Poverty Is Not a Vice,* 239.

59. *Sbornik svedenii o blagotvoritel'nosti v Peterburge za 1884,* 253; *Sbornik svedenii o blagotvoritel'nosti v Peterburge za 1889,* 280–81; RGIA, f. 796, op. 442, d. 1855, "Otchet o sostoianii S. Peterburgskoi eparkhii za 1900 g.," l. 54. In addition to the monetary income the charities received donations of materials such as paper, firewood, building materials, land for building, and existing buildings.

60. *Sbornik svedenii o blagotvoritel'nosti v Peterburge za 1884,* 245–49.

61. Lindenmeyr, *Poverty Is Not a Vice,* 239.

62. *Sbornik svedenii o blagotvoritel'nosti v Peterburge za 1884,* 250; *Sbornik svedenii o blagotvoritel'nosti v Peterburge za 1889,* 280–81; RGIA, f. 796, op. 442, d. 1855, "Otchet o sostoianii S. Peterburgskoi eparkhii," l. 54.

63. The societies at the cathedral of St. Sergei and the cathedral of the Transfiguration, which were both part of the military administration and thus had many officers from noble families, received large donations on a regular basis, though they had neither the highest income nor the most capital in 1884. The wealthiest parish societies in 1884 were at Znamenskaia church, with 90,485 rubles in capital, and St. Samson's cathedral on the Vyborg side, with 50,009 rubles in capital. The two societies with the highest income that year were the church of the Ascension (Spasskii district) with 29,872 rubles and the church of Sts. Boris and Gleb (Rozhdestvenskii district) with 43,500 rubles.

64. [S. G. Runkevich], "Prikhodskaia blagotvoritel'nost' v Peterburge. Obshchestvo vspomozheniia bednym pri Vvedenskom prikhode," *SPBDV* 36 (1899): 423–25.

65. [S. G. Runkevich], "Prikhodskaia blagotvoritel'nost' v Peterburge. Obshchestvo vspomozheniia bednym v prikhode Ekaterinogofskoi Ekaterinskoi tserkvi," *SPBDV* 46 (1899): 541–42. This church was located in Narva district in an area dominated by big paper, resin, and beer factories with a predominantly working-class population.

66. [S. G. Runkevich], "Obshchestvo Spasobocharinskogo prikhoda," *SPBDV* 38 (1899): 445–46.

67. In 1884, 38 parish charities supported 52 institutions; in 1889, 40 parish charities supported 80 institutions; and in 1899, 38 parish charities supported 107 institutions. *Svedenii o blagotvoritel'nosti v Peterburge za 1884,* 250; *Sbornik svedenii o blagotvoritel'nosti v Peterburge za 1889,* 278–79; *Sbornik svedenii o blagotvoritel'nosti v Rossii,* 15.

68. [S. G. Runkevich], "Obshchestvo v prikhode Voskreseniia Khristova v Maloi Kolomne," *SPBDV* 26 (1899): 302–4.

69. D—n, *Prikhodskaia zhizn' pri Blagoveshchenskoi Vasileostrovskoi tserkvi*, 13. This society noted that it also funded major repairs to the parish church and collected donations for national causes.

70. *Sbornik svedenii o blagotvoritel'nosti v Peterburge za 1884*, 250; *Sbornik svedenii o blagotvoritel'nosti v Peterburge za 1889*, 280–82.

71. *Sbornik svedenii o blagotvoritel'nosti v Peterburge za 1889*, 380–82. The city's survey did not include the charities supported by the Imperial Philanthropic Society or the Chancery of the Institutions of Empress Marie, of which there were close to a hundred in the city by the end of the century. It also did not include the majority of the parish charities, so that the statistics both for the total amounts of assistance provided by the parish charities and by all other charities in the city are incomplete.

72. Ibid.

73. The church's schools were rarely included in surveys of charity in St. Petersburg. For example, the Chancery of the Institutions of Empress Marie reported in 1897 that there were 197 charity schools in the city. The diocese reported in the same year that the church had 354 parish schools with more than 16,000 students and that these were supported almost entirely by private donations to the diocese and the parish churches. *Sbornik svedenii o blagotvoritel'nosti v Rossii*, 1899, vii; "Izvlechenie iz otcheta S. Peterburgskogo eparkhial'nogo bratstva vo imia Presviatiia Bogoroditsy za 1896–1897," *SPBDV* 7 (1898): 127–31.

5—Teaching, Temperance, and the Expansion of the Church's Mission

1. On the role and meaning of religious ideas, activities, and organizations among Russia's urban working class, see Herrlinger, "Class, Piety, and Politics," 85–95, 134–38, and 328–92; Zelnik, "Religion and Irreligion"; Steinberg, "Workers on the Cross"; and Steinberg, *Moral Communities*.

2. *Otchet o deiatel'nosti Obshchestva za pervyi god ego sushchestvovaniia 1881–1882*, 1–2.

3. After the Synod launched an intensive campaign to suppress this evangelism in the mid-1880s it came to be considered a sectarian movement, generally called *"Pashkovism."*

4. The sons of clergymen were educated in the diocesan pre-seminaries and seminaries regardless of whether they planned to join the clergy themselves; the daughters of the clergy could attend diocesan girls' schools through the secondary level. As a result, many people who were not members of the clergy but who came from clerical families received their education through the church's schools before entering lay professions.

5. The charter is in *Obshchestvo, 1881–1891*, appendix 3 to the report for 1883–1884, p. 52.

6. Although lay people dominated the society's membership, the clergy controlled the organization's governing council, which consisted of nine or ten clergymen and two or three laymen who usually worked in the church. Archpriest Filosof Ornatskii served as the society's president from 1891 until his death at the hands of the Bolsheviks in 1918.

7. *Otchet o deiatel'nosti Obshchestva za 1881–1882*, 21. Most members on the society's lists were not identified by estate or profession, with the exception of members of the clergy and graduates of the ecclesiastical academies.

8. See, for example, the remarks made by one of the society's founders, the archpriest Dmitrii Nikitin: *Otchet o deiatel'nosti Obshchestva za 1885*, 7; and *Otchet o deiatel'nosti Obshchestva za 1887–1888*, 23.

9. RGIA, f. 906, op. 1, d. 55, "Vozzvanie soveta Obshchestva rasprostraneniia religiozno-nravstvennogo prosveshcheniia," l. 1.

10. [Iakov (Domskii)], *Russkoe propovednichestvo*, 5.

11. Antonii (Khrapovitskii), "Ucheni o bozhestvennogo otkroveniia obozhestvennom znachenii slova Bozhiia," *Otchet o deiatel'nosti Obshchestva za 1889–1890*, 20–21.

12. *SPBDV* 46 (1895): 1043. Father Ioann, an honorary member of the society, made this remark in a speech he gave to the society in November of 1895. A similar comment was recorded at a meeting of the society's preachers in 1899: *Otchet o deiatel'nosti Obshchestva za 1899*, 102–3.

13. *Otchet o deiatel'nosti Obshchestva za 1881–1882*, 6–21. There were also gatherings at private homes, but no further information on these meetings is available.

14. The students who were responsible for lectures at several factories in the Nevskii district said that their audiences especially enjoyed the saints' lives and stories from the Gospels. *Otchet o deiatel'nosti Obshchestva za 1894–1895*, 26.

15. *Otchet o deiatel'nosti Obshchestva za 1883–1884*, 15–16.

16. Ibid., 6–18.

17. The reasons for the appeal of Lord Radstock's teachings were assessed in a pamphlet by the archpriest Filosof Ornatski, *Sekta pashkovtsev i otvet'e na pashkovtsie voprosy*, 2nd ed. (Spb, 1903).

18. The society never completely abandoned this cause, continuing to produce publications and sermons against Pashkovism at least through the 1890s, though in my view this was not their primary concern after the late 1880s. However, Herrlinger believes the sectarian threat remained the focus of the society's work even as they expanded and diversified their activities. Herrlinger, "Class, Piety, and Politics," 98–103.

19. A. P. Lopukhin, "Zaokeanskii zapad v religiozno-nravstvennom otnoshenii," *Khristianskoe chtenie* (1886): Part 2, 618–58. Lopukhin taught comparative theology at the academy and was an expert on religion in America.

20. *Otchet o deiatel'nosti Obshchestva za 1887–1888*, 95.

21. Ibid.

22. *Otchet o deiatel'nosti Obshchestva za 1889–1890*.

23. RGIA, f. 906, op. 1, d. 55, "Vozzvanie soveta Obshchestva," 5.

24. RGIA, f. 796, op. 176 (1895), otd. II st. II, No. 1516 "Ob utverzhdenii novogo ustava Obshchestva rasprostranenii religiozno-nravstvennogo prosveshcheniia" and RGIA, f. 797, op. 65, otd. II stol III, No. 413, "Ob utverzhdenii novogo ustava Obshchestva rasprostranenii religiozno-nravstvennogo prosveshcheniia."

25. *Otchet o deiatel'nosti Obshchestva za 1881–1882*, 9.

26. *Otchet o deiatel'nosti Obshchestva za 1894–1895*, 24–25.

27. *Otchet o deiatel'nosti Obshchestva za 1899*, 59–88.

28. Ibid., 89–103.

29. See George L. Kline, *Religious and Anti-Religious Thought in Russia* (Chicago, 1968); Leonid Sabaneeff, "Religious and Mystical Trends in Russia," *Russian Review* 24, no. 4 (1965): 354–68; Harold Bedford, *The Seeker: D. S. Merezhkovskiy* (Lawrence, 1975); Martha Bohachevsky-Chomiak, "'Christian' vs. 'Neophyte': Opposition to the Formation of a Christian Party in Russia," *Russian History* 4, no. 2 (1977): 105–21; Jutta Scherrer, "Intelligentsia, Réligion, Révolution: Premières manifestations d'un socialisme chrétien en Russie, 1905–1907," *Cahiers du monde russe et soviétique* 17, no. 4 (1976): 427–66 and 18, no. 1 (1977): 5–32. Also useful is *Russian Religious Thought,* ed. Judith Deutsch Kornblatt and Richard F. Gustafson (Madison, 1996).

30. The scholarly work that has been done on the Religious-Philosophical Society has focused on the concerns and contributions of the lay participants rather than on those of the clergy. Representative works include Scherrer, "Intelligentsia, religion, revolution"; Christopher Read, *Religion, Revolution, and the Russian Intelligentsia, 1900–1912: The Vekhi Debate and its Intellectual Background* (London, 1979); Sabaneeff, "Religious and Mystical Trends."

31. *Otchet o deiatel'nosti Obshchestva za 1903*, 31–34.

32. "Vozzvanie soveta Obshchestva," 3; *Otchet o deiatel'nosti Obshchestva za 1899*, 123; RGIA, f. 796, op. 442, d. 1986, "Otchet o sostoianii Peterburgskoi eparkhii za 1903," l. 65 ob. The reports of the diocesan consistory contain a lot of information about the activities of the ORRP between 1900 and 1905, some of it not found in the society's own published reports. This was probably because Father A. I. Ispolatov, one of the society's founding members and an early temperance activist, became the head of the consistory in 1900.

33. *Otchet o deiatel'nosti Obshchestva za 1906–1907*, 42. Herrlinger observes that workers had their own reasons for attending such church-sponsored activities: while some had a genuine interest in religious issues, others wanted to escape the noise and dirt of factory life or socialize with other workers outside of the dormitories and taverns; still others attended out of nostalgia for activities associated with the family or village community or an appreciation for the aesthetic appeal of religious music and services. Herrlinger, "Class, Piety, and Politics," 133–38.

34. *Otchet o deiatel'nosti Obshchestva za 1899*, 192; *Otchet o deiatel'nosti Obshchestva za 1904*, 158 and 274; *Otchet o deiatel'nosti Obshchestva za 1905*, 146–47; RGIA, f. 796, op. 442, d. 1986, "Otchet o sostoianii Peterburgskoi eparkhii za 1903," l. 55.

35. *Otchet o deiatel'nosti Obshchestva za 1899*, 7. The tsar donated five thousand rubles to the society in 1899. In the succeeding years, membership returned to "normal" levels: 1,330 members in 1901, 1,528 in 1903, and 1,311 in 1905. *Otchet o deiatel'nosti Obshchestva za 1901*, 7; *Otchet o deiatel'nosti Obshchestva za 1903*, 11; *Otchet o deiatel'nosti Obshchestva za 1905*, 5.

36. For the chronology of the temperance movement, see Patricia Herlihy, "Strategies of Sobriety: Temperance Movements in Russia, 1880–1914," Occasional Papers, no. 238 (Washington, D.C., 1990) and Herlihy, *The Alcoholic Empire: Vodka and Politics in Late Imperial Russia* (New York, 2002).

37. A. Zav'ialov, *Tsirkuliarnye ukazy Sviateishego Pravitel'stvuiushchego Sinoda, 1867–1895* (Spb, 1896), 217–18.

38. RGIA, f. 796, op. 442, d. 1948, "Otchet o sostoianii S. Peterburgskoi eparkhii za 1890," l. 12ob.

39. Herrlinger also noted that many of the lectures and activities the ORRP organized (including those related to temperance) were in response to worker requests. Herrlinger, "Class, Piety, and Politics," 93–94. One author has suggested that in Russian Finland, temperance societies were the first type of independent worker organization and should be viewed as part of the history of the labor movement: Irma Sulkunen, *History of the Finnish Temperance Movement: Temperance as a Civic Religion,* Interdisciplinary Studies in Alcohol and Drug Use and Abuse, vol. 3 (Lewiston, ME, 1990).

40. *Otchet o deiatel'nosti Obshchestva za 1894–1895*, 62–64.

41. RGIA, f. 796. op. 442, d. 1407, "Otchet o sostoianii Peterburgskoi eparkhii za 1892," ll. 40–41ob. and d. 1577, "Otchet o sostoianii Peterburgskoi eparkhii za 1895," ll. 78–78ob. However, an 1894 publication by a secular activist for temperance names only one church-based temperance society in St. Petersburg. N. Grigoriev, "Russkiia obshchestva trezvosti, ikh organizatsiia i deiatel'nost' v 1892–1893 gg." (Spb, 1894).

42. This was also the decade during which an independent, popular temperance movement developed among the city's working classes. Church authorities viewed these *trezvenniki* (from the Russian word for temperance, *trezvost'*), as sectarians. However, one historian has argued that the *trezvenniki* merely adapted elements of traditional peasant Orthodox culture to the conditions of urban life, as they made the transition from the village to the city. Arthur McKee, "Sobering up the Soul of the People: The Politics of Popular Temperance in Late Imperial Russia," *Russian Review* 58, no. 2 (April 1999): 212–34. Herlihy also discusses the group: *Alcoholic Empire*, 79–81.

43. Herlihy, *Alcoholic Empire*, 119. Temperance societies had existed earlier in Russian-controlled Finland and Estonia; during the 1880s and 1890s, membership in

those temperance societies increased dramatically, perhaps influenced by the growth of nationalism in those regions. See n. 50 on p. 203 and pp. 118–19.

44. Herlihy, *Alcoholic Empire*, 6–7.

45. Ibid., 15–17. In 1900 there were 364 committees in the empire with an average of about 40 members each for a total of about 15,000 members. Herlihy points out that many members were required to join the guardianship as part of their official duties. Of the more than 15,000 members only 5,600 were "taking an active role in the activity of the guardianships" in 1911. Herlihy concludes, "the guardianships could not easily tap into whatever local zeal there may have been for the temperance cause" (p. 17).

46. There is a published history of the St. Petersburg guardianship: S. Peterburgskoe gorodskoe popechitel'stvo o narodnoi trezvosti, *Kratkii ocherk deiatel'nosti S. Peterburgskogo gorodskogo popechitel'stva narodnoi trezvosti, 1898–1912* (Spb, 1913).

47. *SPBDV* 13 (1898): 254–55, and *SPBDV* 17 (1898): 327–30. The clergy's meetings were held on 23 March and 20 April of 1898.

48. P. Kul'bush, "Uchastvie dukhovenstva v deiatel'nosti popechitel'stv o narodnoi trezvosti," *SPBDV* 13 (1898): 244–49.

49. The guardianship's approach had many critics, including doctors, psychiatrists, zemstvo workers, and other members of the lay intelligentsia. See Herlihy, *Alcoholic Empire*, passim, but especially 29–35.

50. Herrlinger suggests that the clergy saw alcohol abuse as both a cause and a consequence of the tendency toward irreligion that they perceived among urban factory workers: Herrlinger, "Class, Piety, and Politics," 53–61. Although alcohol abuse was rampant in the villages as well, the church tended to worry much more about the cities, reflecting its belief that the most serious threats to popular piety came from the city: Freeze, "Going to the Intelligentsia," 219–20; and Herrlinger, "Class, Piety, and Politics," 1–5. The church's concern may also have reflected its perception of the differences between "traditional" and "modern" drinking cultures. Traditional drinking patterns associated alcohol use (and abuse) with ceremonial events celebrated by members of a community according to a ritual calendar; modern drinking patterns allowed more individual control over the time, place and context for alcohol consumption. See David Christian, *Living Water: Vodka and Russian Society on the Eve of Emancipation* (Oxford, 1990).

51. McKee argues that the church's temperance organizations were successful because they adopted elements of popular Orthodox culture, such as the use of oaths, prayers, and pilgrimages; he focuses on the period following 1905, but St. Petersburg's temperance societies incorporated these elements of popular Orthodoxy from the beginning. McKee, "Sobering Up," 214–15.

52. *Otchet o deiatel'nosti Obshchestva za 1905*, 3–4. The biography was included in the society's annual report as part of the commemoration of his early death.

53. A. V. Rozhdestvenskii, *Pamiatnaia knizhka trezvennika*, 2nd ed. (Spb, 1900), 5.

54. D. G. Bulgakovskii, *Rol' pravoslavnogo dukhovenstva v bor'be s narodnym p'ianstvom* (Spb, 1900), 19.

55. Rozhdestvenskii, *Pamiatnaia knizhka*, 10.

56. A. V. Rozhdestvenskii, "P'ianstvo i bor'be s nim," *SPBDV* 38 (1898): 686–88, and "Kto vinovat?" *SPBDV* 8 (1899): 93–94.

57. Rozhdestvenskii, *Pamiatnaia knizhka*, 23–24.

58. Herilhy, *Alcoholic Empire*, 75–76.

59. *Otchet o deiatel'nosti Obshchestva za 1901*, 80. In 1901, only 6,824 of the 41,262 members (16.6 percent) had taken pledges of a year or less. Compare this to the record of the temperance society of the Pokrovsko-Kolomenskoe church in St. Petersburg, which had 1,949 members in 1910, 93 percent of whom were peasants working in construction, artisanry, day labor, or street peddling. Only 12 percent took the pledge for a year, while 39 percent took it for 3 months and 27 percent for six months. Men constituted more than 98 percent of the pledge-takers. Most (76 percent) were between the ages of 20 and 40, married (79 percent) and fathers (50 percent). Herlihy, *Alcoholic Empire*, 77–78.

60. Rozhdestvenskii, *Pamiatnaia knizhka*, 13.

61. *Otchet o deiatel'nosti Obshchestva za 1906–1907*, 74.

62. Rozhdestvenskii, *Pamiatnaia knizhka*, 7. A moving description of one of Rozhdestvenskii's services for the members of the Nevskii Society was offered by Professor P. V. Nikol'skii of Warsaw University in *Otchet o deiatel'nosti Obshchestva za 1905*, 7–8. The five-hour long service included a sermon, the singing of prayers by the congregation, and the swearing in of new members.

63. Rozhdestvenskii, *Pamiatnaia knizhka*, 13–17. The attitude and activities promoted by the Nevskii Society resembled those the church considered to be characteristic of sectarian groups, whose modest and sober lifestyles appealed to many workers seeking to establish control over their lives. Herrlinger, "Class, Piety, and Politics," 313–19.

64. *Otchet o deiatel'nosti Obshchestva za 1906–1907*, 75.

65. Ibid., 74–87.

66. The temperance movement appealed to those living outside the capital as well. Between 1889 and 1891, the Orthodox clergy founded 205 temperance societies in the empire, the largest of which had a membership of six hundred. By 1900, one lay temperance expert estimated there were 890 clergy-run temperance societies in the empire. Another temperance worker asserted that there were 150 church temperance societies in Tambov province alone and that many churches had more than one thousand pledge-takers who had sworn to long-term commitments of more than one year. Herlihy, *Alcoholic Empire*, 82.

67. Membership numbers and sales numbers are all found in "Godovshchina Aleksandr-Nevskogo Obshchestva Trezvosti," *SPBDV* 39 (1899): 460; *Otchet o deiatel'nosti Obshchestva za 1899*, 120–21.

68. *Otchet o deiatel'nosti Obshchestva za 1901*, 87.

69. Bulgakovskii, "Rol' pravoslavnogo dukhovenstva," 26–27.

70. "Godovshchina Aleksandr-Nevskogo Obshchestva Trezvosti," 460.

71. *Otchet o deiatel'nosti Obshchestva za 1901*, 80. The Temperance Fraternity at the church of St. John the Baptist also experienced a growth surge in the years before 1905: it expanded from over 6,000 members in 1901 to 11,657 members in 1903: RGIA, f. 796, op. 442, d. 1966, "Otchet o sostoianii eparkhii za 1902," ll. 55ob., 56.

72. RGIA, f. 796, op 442, d. 2105, "Otchet o sostoianii S. Peterburgskoi eparkhii za 1905," l. 63. This report contains an obituary for Father Alexander and several memorial essays.

73. On attendance at the Nevskii Society's lectures and the pilgrimage, see RGIA, f. 796, op. 442, d. 2086, "Otchet o sostoianii S. Peterburgskoi eparkhii za 1904," ll. 122 and 56. On visitors to the church, see Antonov and Kobak, *Sviatyni Sankt-Peterburga*, 170.

74. Father Alexander contracted the fatal disease from drinking a glass of cold (presumably unboiled) *kvass* after the journey back. On the public response to his death, see E. Poselianin, *Sviashchennik Aleksandr Vasilievich Rozhdestvenskii* (Spb, 1905); and Obshchestvo rasprostraneniia religiozno-nravstvennago prosveshcheniia v dukhe pravoslavnoi tserkvi, *Narodnyi pechal'nik, otets A. V. Rozhdestvenskii* (Spb, 1905).

75. The ethic of service to the people demonstrated by the St. Petersburg clergy in the late imperial period resembles in many respects the service ethic of members of the professional intelligentsia, such as teachers, doctors, and lawyers. For example, see Ruane, *Gender*, 196–97.

6—IN THE FOOTSTEPS OF CHRIST

1. On Petrov as a model pastor, see A. Uspenskii, "Lishenie sana sv. G. Petrov," *Krasnyi zvon* (January 1908): 17; and T. Asov, "Otritsateli zhizni," *Tserkovnoe obnovlenie 8* (25 February 1907): 57–58. Strong expressions of support for Petrov were published during the years 1907–1908 in response to what many of his advocates viewed as his

persecution by church authorities. The students of the St. Petersburg Ecclesiastical Academy wrote a public letter of support for Petrov in which they expressed their admiration for him and assured him that the best clergy of the city also supported him; those who signed the letter were expelled from the academy. See "Otkrytoe pis'mo studentov S. Peterburgskoi Dukhovnoi Akademii sv. G. S. Petrovu," *Vek* 5 (4 February 1907): 66. There were numerous other articles in defense of Petrov in the journals of the St. Petersburg clergy in 1907 and 1908; see especially the Renovationist publications *Zvonar', Krasnyi zvon,* and *Vek,* and *Tserkovnoe obnovlenie.*

2. Petrov, *Pis'mo,* 7.

3. Petrov was a member of the ORRP from 1887 to 1904; he served on the council from 1894–1902. Petrov's name appears regularly in the annual reports of the society. He lectured primarily at the cathedral of St. Sergei and at the society's Trinity church.

4. On the theology of the archimandrite Feodor and the philosopher Solov'ev, see Valliere, *Modern Russian Theology.* Also of interest is Mikhail Sergeev, "Liberal Orthodoxy: From Vladimir Solov'ev to Fr. Alexander Men'" *Religion in Eastern Europe* 23, no. 4 (August 2003): 43–50.

5. Given that Father Grigorii was more of a popularizer than an academic, it can be difficult to know exactly whether or how these authors might have influenced him. His works do not show any particular familiarity with the work of the archimandrite Feodor or Pavel Svetlov. Father Grigorii did know Antonii (Vadkovskii), who had been rector of the St. Petersburg academy while Petrov was a student there. During that time, Antonii delivered at least two published addresses to the student body that called students to see their service in the church as a contribution to building the Kingdom of God: Antonii (Vadkovskii), *Rechi,* pp. 40–41 and 249–51. Petrov may well have known Father Mikhail Sokolov, a priest at the Kazan cathedral who was active in the ORRP until his death in 1895. Finally, Father Grigorii makes references to the writings of Solov'ev in essays collected in *Lampa Aladina,* 3rd ed. (Spb, 1906) and *Voina i mir G. S. Petrova* (Spb, 1904).

6. G. S. Petrov, *Evangelie, kak osnova zhizni,* 17th ed. (New York, 1921). A chapter from this work was separately published: G. Petrov, "Tsarstvo Bozhiia," *SPBDV* 19 (8 May 1898): 355–63 and 20 (15 May 1898): 373–82.

7. Petrov, *Evangelie,* 17–22.

8. According to a contemporary theologian, Orthodox believers commonly equated the Kingdom of God with the rewards of the afterlife. P. Ia. Svetlov, *Ideia Tsarstva Bozhiia v eia znacheniia dlia khristianskogo mirosozertsaniia* (Sergiev Posad, 1905), 26–27.

9. Petrov, *Evangelie,* 81.

10. Ibid., 23.

11. Svetlov's explanation of what he considered to be the full Orthodox interpretation of the Kingdom of God is similar: Svetlov, *Ideia Tsarstva Bozhiia,* 112–32. Father Grigorii's interpretation was also comparable to that of the archimandrite Feodor: Archimandrite Feodor (Bukharev), *O pravoslavii,* 259–74. See also John Meyendorff, "The Christian Gospel and Social Responsibility: The Eastern Orthodox Tradition in History," in *Continuity and Discontinuity in Church History,* ed. F. Forrester Church and Timothy George (Leiden, 1979): 119–22.

12. Antonii (Vadkovskii), *Rechi,* 40.

13. Ibid., 251. This idea was expressed in the speech that academy rector Antonii (Vadkovskii) gave to the graduating class of 1889.

14. This was a strong theme in many of Sokolov's published sermons. Sokolov, *Pastyrskie zavety.* See specifically the sermons "Miloserdie, serdtse khristianskoi zhizni," 96–104, and "Tsennost' miloserdiia," 144–54. Father Mikhail, who graduated from the academy in 1867 and began his service in 1872, was well known in the capital for his charitable work. The ORRP published this collection of sermons on the tenth anniversary of Father Mikhail's death.

15. Sokolov, *Pastyrskie zavety,* 88–90.

16. Ibid., 23. The philosopher Vladimir Solov'ev also emphasized the establishment of "right relations" among humans as a feature of the Kingdom of God. He discusses the meaning of the kingdom in his essay "O poddelkakh" in *Sobranie sochinenii Vladimira Sergeevicha Solove'va,* t. 6 (Spb, 1911), 301–9, and in V. S. Solovyof, *The Justification of the Good: An Essay on Moral Philosophy,* tr. Nathalie A. Duddington, ed. and annotated by Boris Jakim (1918; reprint, Grand Rapids, MI, 2005), 170–74 and 409–69. I am grateful to Greg Gaut for pointing me toward these writings. Professor Gaut's work is recommended: "A Christian Westernizer: Vladimir Solovyov and Russian Conservative Nationalism" (Ph.D. diss., University of Minnesota, 1992). See also his published article "Christian Politics: Vladimir Solovyov's Social Gospel Theology," *Modern Greek Studies Yearbook* 10/11 (1994–1995): 653–74.

17. Petrov, *Lampa Aladina,* 111.

18. G. S. Petrov, *K svetu,* 4th ed. (Moscow, 1904), 4.

19. Petrov, *Evangelie,* 37–78.

20. Father Grigorii believed that the clergy's primary responsibility was to offer individuals guidance and support in their efforts and to serve as role models. G. S. Petrov, *Ne s togo kontsa* (Spb, 1905).

21. Petrov, "Tsarstvo Bozhiia," 357–60.

22. G. S. Petrov, *Besedy o Boge i bozhei pravde,* 2nd ed. (Moscow, 1904), 51.

23. The importance of reading the Bible was one of the themes of the collection of essays in *K svetu* and was the subject of several stories in another collection. See G. S. Petrov, *Bozhii put',* 3rd ed. (Moscow, 1903). Petrov comments explicitly on the importance of the Gospels in his novel *Zateinik:* first, when the brother of the novel's main character, Ivan Postnikov, advises him to study the Gospels and pray as a means of keeping up his Christian spirit while at the seminary; and second, when an energetic new inspector at the seminary urges his students to read the Gospels themselves rather than commentaries on them. See G. S. Petrov, *Zateinik,* 3 vols. in 1 (Spb, 1904), 1:31 and 1:151.

24. This fear was implicit in the accusations of *"beztserkovnost'"* that were leveled against Petrov in 1903. See especially the article by E. Voronets, "Itogi polemiki po povodu propovednichestva sv. G. Petrova i istoricheskaia spravka," *Missionerskoe obozrenie* 3 (1903): 329–31. Individual reading of the Bible was one of the practices the Orthodox church associated most strongly with sectarianism, even as the spread of literacy in Russia enabled more members of the laity to read the Scriptures for themselves. Chulos argues there was a connection between the acquisition of literacy, the desire of newly literate peasant believers to interpret the teachings of Christianity for themselves, and the growing pressure from below for parish autonomy. Chulos, *Converging Worlds,* 5, 82–83, and 96.

25. Petrov, *Bozhii put',* 7–11 and 56–58.

26. In Petrov, *Bozhii put'.*

27. Deuteronomy 6:5.

28. The theme of repentance is strongly developed in Petrov's *Bozhii put'* in the stories "Inok Naum," "Provedeniia pokaianiia," "Pokaianie," "Govenie," "Sovest' zagovorila," and "Kamni." In the same collection, see the essay "Tsena vremeni" for Petrov's warning about the moral danger of idleness.

29. G. S. Petrov, *Po stopam Khrista,* 2 vols. (Spb, 1903). The original novel, written by Charles Monroe Sheldon, was first published in 1896, then reprinted in 1900, 1935, 1967, 1970, and 1980.

30. For examples of the theme in Petrov's own work, see the stories "Khrista spasitel'" and "Pervye shagi" in the collection *Besedy o Boge* or "Krestianin Veselov" in *Bozhii put'.*

31. Matthew 25:40; Matthew 21:26–28. The second verse continues, "and he who would be first must be a slave, just as the Son of Man did not come to be served, but to serve, and to give his life as a ransom for many." The parable of the Good Samaritan is in Luke 10:33.

32. See the stories "Chistaia radost'," "Priatnaia neozhidennost'," and "Krestianin Veselov" in the collection *Bozhii put'*.

33. Petrov, "Lepta vdovitsy," *K svetu*, 82–94. The parable of the widow's mite is found in Luke 21:1–4.

34. "Krestianin Veselov," in *Bozhii put,'* 83–91. Russian speakers will note the significance of the main character's name, derived from the root for "happiness," *veselost'*.

35. Another scholar has discussed this work: Valliere, "Modes of Social Action," 142–58. The novel was published in 1904, a year after Petrov's translation of the Sheldon work.

36. The surname of the main character is based on the Russian word *"post,"* which means "the fast" in the sense of abstinence from food. Fasting is an important part of Orthodox religious observance. Although Postnikov is very much a "new-style" clergyman such as that described in Sir Donald Mackenzie Wallace, *Russia on the Eve of War and Revolution* (Princeton, 1961), 390–91, the name links him to the saints and martyrs of the traditional church. The contrast between "old" and "new" clergymen that Wallace describes and Valliere refers to was a common theme in contemporary literature. See Rozov, *Sviashchennik*, 207–10. One western scholar has suggested that the assassination of Alexander II in 1881 marks the divide between the generations; in his view, the older generation was not necessarily more supportive of the existing order, but was perhaps more likely to regard it as something to be stoically endured rather than changed. See Argyrios Pisiotis, "Orthodoxy versus Autocracy: The Orthodox Church and Clerical Political Dissent in Late Imperial Russia, 1905–1914" (Ph.D. diss., Georgetown University, 2000), 439.

37. Petrov, *Zateinik*, 1:31 and 1:151.

38. Ibid., 1:66 and 1:177–78.

39. Ibid., 1:167–74.

40. Father Grigorii's former classmate at the St. Petersburg academy, Father Georgii Shavel'skii, initially refused entrance into the academy in order to serve at the low rank of psalmist in a rural parish. He entered the St. Petersburg academy only after seven years of rural service following the death of his wife. Shavel'skii eventually became the highest-ranking member of the parish clergy when he was appointed chief chaplain of the armed forces in 1911. See G. I. Shavel'skii, *Vospominaniia poslednego protopresvitera russkoi armii i flota*, 2 vols. (New York, 1954), 3–5.

41. *"Zateinik,"* the label applied to Postnikov by his critics in the novel, may mean trickster (as Paul Valliere suggested in his article), but also suggests one who organizes something (a business, a game) in an especially intricate and ingenious fashion. The events summarized here are in *Zateinik*, 2:51–78.

42. Petrov, *Zateinik*, 2:78–80. As a chaplain, he would have had no parish and thus no parishioners to influence.

43. Ibid., 3:102–11.

44. Such a death seems melodramatic, but it might well have reminded St. Petersburg clergymen of the early death of Father Alexander Gumilevskii, who died after contracting typhus during a visit to a hospital for the poor; likewise, Postnikov's sacrifice prefigured the death of the temperance activitist Father Alexander Rozhdestvenskii in 1905, which occurred after he became sick with typhoid during the Nevskii Society's annual pilgrimage.

45. Petrov, *Zateinik*, 2:58.

46. Ibid., 2:51 and 2:121–24.

47. This theme of the struggle between the well-intentioned individual and the hostile forces that prevent him from carrying out his good work is apparent also in other Russian works focusing on individual clergymen and their work. Most famous, of course, is the case of Father Savely in N. S. Leskov's novel *Soboriane;* see also the novel originally published in 1890 by I. N. Potapenko, *A Russian Priest*, with an intro. by James Adderly (New York, 1916). The same theme emerges in the touching memoir by the former priest Mikhail M——ski, *Ot bursy do sniatiia sana* (Spb, 1908).

48. Only the first period of Father Petrov's difficulties with the authorities will be discussed here. The second and more serious period of persecution that took place in 1907 and 1908 will be discussed in chap. 9.

49. P. Kozitskii, "O literaturnoi propovedi sv. Grigoriia Petrova," *Missionerskoe obozrenie* 7 (1903): 936–55.

50. [I. V. Preobrazhenskii], *Novye i traditsionnye dukhovnye oratory, Oo. G. Petrov i Ioann Sergiev (Kronshtadtskii). Kriticheskii etiud* (Spb, 1902); N. Griniakin, "Nedobraia 'prisposobliaemost'," *Missionerskoe obozrenie* 3 (1903): 331–33.

51. Ieromonakh Aleksandr, "O literaturnoi propovede sv. o. Grigoriia Petrova," *Missionerskoe obozrenie* 6 (1903): 753–69.

52. Voronets, "Itogi polemiki," 315–31. This article gives a brief history of the controversy over Petrov's teaching. On neglect of church teachings, see also Kozitskii, "O literaturnoi propovedi," 952–55; and [Preobrazhenskii], *Novye i traditsionnye dukhovnye oratory,* 8.

53. The articles attacking Father Grigorii contain a grab bag of criticisms, including correction of minor errors in his written works, comments about his personal comportment, derogatory remarks about the nature of his audiences, sneering asides, and mean-spirited innuendo. The view that Father Grigorii was inclined to grandstanding was echoed many years later in the autobiography of Metropolitan Evlogii, who was then a bishop and a Duma deputy. See Evlogii (Georgievskii), *Put' moei zhizni. Vospominaniia Mitropolita Evlogii,* comp. T. Manukhin (Paris, 1947): 178–79.

54. Petrov, "Tsarstvo Bozhiia," *SPBDV* 20 (15 May 1898): 373–80.

55. The call to renew the ORRP's mission to the intelligentsia came in the keynote speech delivered at the twentieth-anniversary meeting of the society by the archpriest Peter Lakhotskii, head priest at the society's main church and editor of the society's journal, *The Spiritual Messenger (Dukhovnyi vestnik).* Lakhotskii had been in Father Grigorii's class at the academy and had served on the ORRP's governing council with him.

56. See the comments included on the report of the society's lectures for educated audiences, which were intended to supplement the meetings of the Religious-Philosophical Society, *Otchet o deiatel'nosti Obshchestva za 1903,* 31–34; also N. Rozanov, "Chto delat' dlia privlecheniia intelligentsy k tserkvi?" *Pravoslavno-Russkoe Slovo (PRS)* 15 (September 1902): 330–48; and Ieromonakh Mikhail, "Zhiva-li tserkov'?" *PRS* 4 (February 1903): 291–309.

57. See the society's reports for those years: *Otchet o deiatel'nosti Obshchestva za 1902* (also for 1903 and 1904), and "Tekushchiia sobytiia tserkovno-obshchestvennoi zhizni," *PRS* 1 (January 1903): 13–14. This article numbers the workers' association headed by Father Gapon (and initially sponsored by the society) as one of its efforts at outreach. For other interpretations of the church's outreach work at this time, see Freeze, "Going to the Intelligentsia," 215–32; and Dixon, "Church, State, and Society," 11.

58. "Stolichnaia bogoslovskiia chtenie o khristianskoi nravstvennosti," *Missionerskoe obozrenie* 2 (1900): 840–41. The first lecture, given by the rector of the St. Petersburg seminary Archimandrite Sergei (Tikhomirov), who later became the archbishop of North America, attracted an audience of 300 people. An additional eight lectures were given, drawing a total audience of about 2,000. Academy professors gave most of the lectures. RGIA, f. 796, op. 442, d. 1913, "Otchet o sostoianii Peterburgskoi eparkhii za 1901," ll. 596–97.

59. RGIA, f. 796, op. 442, d. 1966, "Otchet o sostoianii Peterburgskoi eparkhii za 1902," l. 66; "Bogoslovskiia chteniia v stolitse," *Missionerskoe obozrenie* 2 (1902): 910. Bishop Sergii (Stragorodskii), rector of the St. Petersburg academy and later patriarch of the Russian Orthodox Church, presided over these lectures. Attendance was open to members of the laity, but most of the speakers seem to have belonged to the clergy or to the faculty at the St. Petersburg academy. The first lecture of this series was published: Ieromonakh Mikhail, "Otkliki na voprosy ishchushchei intelligentsia," *Missionerskoe obozrenie* 2 (1902): 911–27. The series continued even after the Religious-Philosophical

Society had been shut down; the titles of some lectures and the names of the lecturers are listed in the diocesan report of 1904: RGIA, f. 796, op. 442, d. 2086, "Otchet o sostoianii Peterburgskoi eparkhii za 1904," l. 52; others are noted in the society's annual report: *Otchet o deiatel'nosti Obshchestva za 1904*; 67–79.

60. On the decision to establish a youth group, see RGIA, f. 796, op. 442, d. 1966, "Otchet o sostoianii Peterburgskoi eparkhii za 1902," ll. 67–67 ob. On the group's organization, see P. Verkhovskii, "Khronika. Khristiansko sodruzhestvo uchashcheisia molodezhi," *Missionerskoe obozrenie* 1 (1904): 149–51; and RGIA, f. 796, op. 442, d. 1986, "Otchet o sostoianii Peterburgskoi eparkhii za 1903," l. 53–54. In its first year, the group enrolled 9 students or graduates from the ecclesiastical academy, 21 students from St. Petersburg University, 5 from the Military Medical Academy, 1 from the Mining Institute and 1 art student. Comments on the group's work can be found in *Otchet o deiatel'nosti Obshchestva za 1904*, 99–101; a partial list of the subjects the students addressed in 1906 can be found in *Otchet o deiatel'nosti Obshchestva za 1906–1907*, 106–8. The topics included "Christianity and the Land," "Christianity and Socialism," and "The Moral Obligations of the Clergy and Laymen in the Matter of the Spiritual Rebirth of Russia."

61. The fullest report on the REU's (Religious Educational Union) activities as well as a brief history, a list of members, and a register of the institutions where they carried out their work is found in *Otchet o deiatel'nosti Obshchestva za 1906–1907*, 101–6. By 1904, the REU had 86 members: RGIA, f. 796, op. 442, d. 1986, "Otchet o sostoianii Peterburgskoi eparkhii za 1904," l. 48. In 1910 it reached its peak with more than 200 members: *Otchet o deiatel'nosti Obshchestva za 1910*, 3. Most of the members were women of the educated classes.

62. "Ot redaktsii," *PRS* 1 (January 1902): 3–5. The other editors were A. Dernov and A. Nadezhdin. The journal published 20 issues a year, collected in two volumes, from 1902 to 1905. It was replaced in 1906 by *The Church's Voice (Tserkovnyi golos)*.

63. Petrov, *Zateinik*, 1:6.

64. Ibid., 3:104.

65. G. S. Petrov, *Tserkov' i obshchestvo* (Spb, 1906), 3–19.

66. Ibid., 22–24.

67. Petrov, *Zateinik*, 1:66.

68. Petrov, *Lampa Aladina*, 3–24.

69. Ibid., 86–88.

70. Ibid., 40–42.

71. Petrov, *Tserkov' i obshchestvo*, 26–27.

72. Ibid.

73. Ibid.

74. These liberals were initially associated with the Liberation movement headed by Peter Struve; they eventually formed the Constitutional Democrats party (known as the Kadet party from their initials K-D in Russian). Father Grigorii himself joined the Kadet party and was elected as one of their deputies to the Second Duma in 1906.

75. Petrov, *Tserkov' i obshchestvo*, 29–41.

76. Ibid., 57–63.

77. G. S. Petrov, *Velikii pastyr* (Spb, 1905), 33.

78. G. S. Petrov, *Zaprosy sovremennoi tserkvi* (Spb, 1906), 75.

79. Ibid., 3–36. This argument is made in an essay entitled "The Church and the Government" ("Tserkov' i gosudarstvo"). During the 1905 revolution, Father Grigorii came to support the dis-establishment of the church, an unusual position for a member of the Orthodox clergy to adopt.

80. Petrov, *Zaprosy*, 85–98. This was the argument made in the essay "What's to be Done for the Clergy?" ("Chto delat' dukhovenstvu").

81. Petrov, *Zaprosy*, 101.

82. Ibid., 102. It seems likely that the specific reference to the pious and well-intentioned bureaucrat was directed at Konstantin Pobedonostsev.

7—FROM RELIGION TO POLITICS

1. Although Gapon figures in many studies of the revolution of 1905, the only scholarly monographs that focus on him and his work are Walter Sablinsky, *The Road to Bloody Sunday* (Princeton, 1976); and Gerald D. Surh, *1905 in St. Petersburg* (Stanford, 1989).

2. Richard Pipes, *The Russian Revolution* (New York, 1991), 20–21.

3. Gapon's autobiography was first published serially in the London periodical *The Strand* between July and November of 1905 and then as a book in 1906. Gapon dictated his memoirs in Russian between January and late October of 1905. They were then rapidly translated into English and published as part of Gapon's effort to win international support for the revolution in Russia and to gain the cooperation of radical Russian émigrés. Father George Gapon, *The Story* (New York, 1906). The autobiography was partially translated back into Russian and published in Russia in 1918. A full translation with notes and commentary by a Bolshevik scholar was published in 1925: G. A. Gapon, *Istoriia moei zhizni*, ed. A. A. Shilov (Leningrad, 1925). The autobiography must be read with a critical eye because it was strongly influenced by Gapon's political agenda and his desire to appeal to an audience of secular revolutionaries.

4. Gapon, *Story*, 8–11.

5. Ibid., 8.

6. Ibid., 14.

7. Ibid., 12.

8. Ibid., 16–17.

9. Ibid., 18.

10. For discussion on Tolstoy and the Orthodox church, see Pal Kolsto, "Leo Tolstoy: A Church Critic Influenced by Orthodox Thought," in *Church, Nation, and State*, ed. Hosking, 148–166, and Kolsto, "A Mass for a Heretic? The Controversy over Leo Tolstoi's Burial," *Slavic Review* 60, no. 1 (Spring 2001): 75–95.

11. Gapon, *Story*, 19–20.

12. Gapon, *Story*, 20.

13. Ibid, 20–21. In his autobiography, Gapon accused the school authorities of being jealous of his intellectual gifts and of deliberately seeking to prevent him from pursuing a career outside the church that would prove his talents. However, a document from the Synod's archives published after the Bolshevik Revolution suggests that Gapon himself was responsible for the black mark on his record. Fearing that he would fail his exam in dogmatic theology, Gapon refused to take it. He threatened the professor and the professor's family and then claimed to be sick on the day of the exam. He was allowed to graduate anyway, and when the bishop of Poltava later wrote Gapon a recommendation for admission to the St. Petersburg Ecclesiastical Academy he blamed the teacher for not being more sympathetic to the "high-strung" and "overwrought" young man, whose academic record was otherwise excellent. Gapon's belief that the authorities were thwarting him when in fact they were protecting and helping him manifested itself on many other occasions later. On the bishop's letter of recommendation, see M. F. Paozerskii, "Gapon i Sinod," *Zvezda* 6 (1924): 160–61.

14. Gapon, *Story*, 21.

15. Bishop Ilarion's own background and interests perhaps made him particularly sympathetic to Father Georgii. Son of a poor village priest, Yushenov was an exceptional student whose desire to continue his studies after seminary was denied by his superiors. He served as a priest for more than forty years before taking monastic vows in 1873. After becoming bishop of Poltava in 1887, he promoted the development of charitable societies, missionary organizations, and associations for extra-liturgical religious education in his diocese. A noted preacher himself, he encouraged the parish clergy of the diocese to preach and helped them develop their sermons. Biographical information on Ilarion found at "Biografiia: Ilarion (Yushenov)," *Russkoe Pravoslavie,*

n.d., http://www.ortho-rus/ru/cgi-bin/ps_file.cgi?2_7905 (6 June 2006). My thanks to the Slavic Reference Service at the University of Illinois at Urbana-Champaign for assistance in locating this information.

16. Paozerskii, "Gapon i Sinod," 161.

17. Gapon, *Story,* 25.

18. Ibid., 39–46.

19. Ibid., 54. Gapon's criticisms of the monastic life were typical of the white clergy, but recent scholarship has demonstrated that many monasteries were actively engaged in education and charity work, as a result of which they enjoyed the respect and support of local populations. See Jennifer Jean Wynot, *Keeping the Faith: Russian Orthodox Monasticism in the Soviet Union, 1917–1939* (College Station, TX, 2004); William Wagner, "Paradoxes of Piety: The Nizhegorod Convent of the Exaltation of the Cross, 1807–1935," in *Orthodox Russia,* ed. Valerie Kivelson and Robert H. Greene (University Park, PA, 2003), 211–38.

20. A dozen of Gapon's private letters to an unnamed lay correspondent in the Crimea were published after the revolution of 1905: "Pis'ma Gapona," *Russkaia mysl'* 5 (1907): 104–16. Gapon discussed his career plans in the second and third letters, dated 7 November and 30 November 1899. The quotation is from the third letter, p. 107. See also Gapon, *Story,* 55–57.

21. "Pis'ma Gapona," 108 (third letter).

22. Gapon, *Story,* 59. In his autobiography, Gapon does not mention his indecision about continuing his clerical career, but says only that he returned to St. Petersburg refreshed and resolved to finish his studies at the academy in the hope of obtaining a position in the city after graduation.

23. The diocesan missionary fraternity was founded in 1884 to supervise the church's parish schools. The Pokrovskaia church (on Borovaia street, near Obvodnyi canal) served as the fraternity's first center, becoming one of the centers of Orthodox proselytism in the city in the 1890s. The students of the St. Petersburg academy did most of the work, which included extra-liturgical lectures, debates with Old Believers, thrice-weekly services in Church Slavonic, German, English, and Lettish, and direction of a large temperance society. For a short history and a good photograph of the church, see Antonov and Kobak, *Sviatyni Sankt-Peterburga,* 211–13. The church still stands today after undergoing extensive alterations in the 1930s. Ironically, in 1989 it was claimed by a Baptist group.

24. Gapon, *Story,* 46–47.

25. Ibid., 59. The church was part of the military-naval administration. Its official name was Tserkov' vo imia Miluiushchei Bozh'ei Materi. It was located on the far end of Bolshoi Prospekt on Vasilievskii Island near the Baltic Shipbuilding Works.

26. In Pobedonostsev's thinking, religion was the foundation of the social community and charity was especially important. A recent analysis of Pobedonostsev's world view is given in John Basil, "K. P. Pobedonostsev and the Harmonious Society," *Canadian-American Slavic Studies* 37, no. 4 (Winter 2003): 415–26; also Polunov, "Konstantin Petrovich Pobedonostsev," 17. In 1878, Pobedonostsev and other prominent government officials had established a charity at the church in order to counteract widespread public begging in the docks area. Pobedonostsev personally donated one thousand rubles to the charity upon its establishment. This church was the first site at which students from the academy were allowed to preach for the ORRP on a regular basis, starting in 1887. See Runkevich, *Prikhodskaia blagotvoritel'nost',* 294–96.

27. "Pis'ma Gapona," 109 (fourth letter).

28. Gapon, *Story,* 60. Gapon claimed to have had as many as two thousand people in attendance at some of his sermons.

29. "Pis'ma Gapona," 112 (sixth letter, dated 7 March 1900).

30. "Pis'ma Gapona," 109 (fourth letter).

31. "Pis'ma Gapona," 112 (sixth letter).

32. "Pis'ma Gapona," 112–13 (seventh letter, dated 24 May 1900).

33. Gapon, *Story*, 60–61.

34. "Pis'ma Gapona," 112–13 (seventh letter). In his autobiography, Father Georgii says that he resigned from his position at the Haven church and from the ORRP after his project was turned down because he no longer believed in the church's approach to the working-class mission. Gapon, *Story*, 61–62.

35. N. A. Bukhbinder, "Iz zhizni G. Gapona," *Krasnaia letopis'* 1 (1922): 102. This document is a short memoir about Gapon's work between 1900 and 1903 written by a classmate at the academy, Father M. S. Popov.

36. Gapon, *Story*, 63–65. City prefect Kleigels heard of Father Georgii's visits to the shelters and inquired into his work. He approved of what he discovered and gave Gapon permission to continue. Gapon's extra-curricular activities had a disastrous effect on his career at the academy. At the end of his repeated first year (spring 1900), he was ranked number 25 out of 65 in his class; by the end of his second year (spring 1901) he had dropped to number 47 out of 59. Paozerskii, "Gapon i Sinod," 163.

37. Gapon, *Story*, 67–71.

38. Pavlov mentioned this plan in his memoirs: I. Pavlov, "Iz vospominaniia o Rabochem Soiuze i sv. Gapone," *Minuvshie gody*, no. 2 (April 1908): 103.

39. Gapon sent copies of the proposal to the city prefect, General Kleigels; the director of the workhouses of the Institutions of the Empress Marie, General Maksimovich; and the vice president of the committee on workhouses and chief of the tsar's chancellery, General Taneev. In an undated letter that internal evidence suggests is from the fall of 1902, Gapon mentions that his "project" was then before the Council of Ministers. This may have been the workhouse project. "Pis'ma Gapona" (eleventh letter, undated).

40. In his memoirs, Gapon specifically named Madame Khitrovo, wife of the ambassador to Japan; Princess Eliazabeth Naryshkina, first lady-in-waiting to the empress; and Duchess Lobanov-Rostovskaia among the patrons he attracted at this time.

41. Pavlov, "Iz vospominaniia," 102–3.

42. Paozerskii, "Gapon i Sinod," 163; and N. Avidonov, "Gapon v dukhovnoi akademii," *Byloe* 1 (1925): 46–50. Father Georgii protested the expulsion, claiming he missed the exams because he was sick and that he had a medical certificate to prove it. He believed they had decided to expel him because he was involved in a personal feud with city council member N. Anichkov, who was also in charge of the city's poorhouses. This recalls Gapon's earlier experience at the Poltava seminary.

43. Father Georgii declared his wish to marry the young woman, Aleksandra K. Uzdaleva, but priests were not allowed to remarry. He could have married her only if he had resigned from the clergy. Some priests did request defrocking so that they could remarry after a spouse's death (particularly if they had young children to care for), but a defrocked priest lost all social status, a ramification that would have been particularly severe for Father Georgii given his humble background and the importance his family placed on his being a priest: Sablinsky, *Road*, 45. After Gapon was punitively defrocked by the Synod in 1905, Uzdaleva was regarded as his common-law wife; she bore him a son and after Gapon's death she referred to Gapon as her husband. Sablinsky discusses the details in *Road*, 51–53. The incident at the poorhouse is mentioned in Bukhbinder, "Iz zhizni," 104, and in the introduction to "Pis'ma Gapona," 104. See also the annotated Russian translation of Gapon's memoirs, *Istoriia moei zhizni*, 133–34; and V. I. Maksimov, "Pravda i lozh' o Georgii Gapone," *Russkii vestnik* 1 (3 January 1992): 10. The details of the confrontation come from the memoir of one of Gapon's classmates: Bukhbinder, "Iz zhizni," 104–5.

44. Gapon, *Istoriia moei zhizni*, 133–34. In his autobiography, Gapon said that it was his decision to leave the Olga poorhouse. He claimed that its directors did not want him to go because his large congregation would follow him to his new church. Gapon, *Story*, 77–78.

45. Gapon, *Story,* 74–78.

46. Zubatov had recently been promoted to the position after serving in Moscow. He arrived in St. Petersburg in the second half of August 1902. Father Georgii believed that the initial encounter with the police agent was the result of his being denounced as a revolutionary to the police by city councilor N. Anichkov. The most recent work on Zubatov, which presents a positive assessment of his innovations in the conception and implementation of security measures, is Jonathan W. Daly, *Autocracy under Siege: Security Police and Opposition in Russia, 1866–1905* (DeKalb, 1998).

47. Dmitry Pospielovsky, *Russian Police Trade Unionism: Experiment or Provocation?* (London, 1971), 79–80.

48. Ibid., 77. In Moscow, Zubatov first asked professors from the university to conduct lectures for his organization, but after they withdrew from the project in late 1902 he turned to the church and recruited Parfenii, bishop of Mozhaisk, Lev Tikhomirov, a conservative lay publicist with a strong interest in the church, and the Moscow priest Ioann Fudel', 81–83 and 151.

49. On Zubatov's skill in identifying and using particular individuals for his own agency's purposes, see Jonathan Daly, "The Security Police and Politics in Late Imperial Russia" in *Russia Under the Last Tsar: Opposition and Subversion, 1894–1917,* ed. Anna Geifman (London, 1999), 217–40.

50. Gapon, *Story,* 80–82. Specifically, Gapon criticized the demonstration that had been put on in February of 1902 to honor Alexander II for the emancipation of the serfs in 1861. The Moscow society had brought out 50,000 workers to lay a wreath at the tsar's monument.

51. Ibid., 81–91.

52. For a detailed account, see Jeremiah Schneiderman, *Sergei Zubatov and Revolutionary Marxism: The Struggle for the Working Class in Tsarist Russia* (Ithaca, NY, 1976), 174–80.

53. N. A. Bukhbinder, "K istorii 'Sobraniia russkikh fabrichno-zavodskikh rabochikh g. S. Peterburga.' Arkhivnye dokumenty," *Krasnaia letopis'* 1 (1922): 322–25 (Document 20, deposition given to the Department of Police on 27 January 1905 by the worker S. V. Kladovnikov). This collection of documents (pp. 288–329) is an important source for developments of 1902–1903, but it is essential to observe they are not presented in chronological order. They seem to be deliberately organized so as to influence the reader to conflate Zubatov's organization of late 1902 with the one that Gapon formed in mid–1903.

54. Bukhbinder, "K istorii 'Sobraniia,'" 291 (Document 4, an undated draft of a report from the Department of Police to the emperor).

55. "Tekushchiia sobytiia tserkovno-obshchestvennoi zhizni," *PRS* 1 (January 1903): 13–14. Gapon says that the professors of the St. Petersburg Ecclesiastical Academy took part in the organization at first: Gapon, *Story,* 82. The professors were more likely involved in a separate organization—the Society for Friends of Mercy and Charity, which held its first meeting in late November 1901. Although the society's original intent was to provide theological lectures for the educated classes, the titles of the lectures given in December of 1902 suggest a popular audience. See RGIA, f. 796, op. 442, d. 1913, "Otchet o sostoianii Peterburgskoi eparkhii," ll. 596–97.

56. "Tekushchiia sobytiia tserkovno-obshchestvennoi zhizni," *PRS* 3 (February 1903): 193–95. Gapon attended this meeting and said that the workers were disappointed with the tone of the metropolitan's speech. He was extremely critical of both Ornatskii and Antonii in his memoirs. Gapon, *Story,* 95–96. His harsh attitude toward Antonii is particularly surprising in view of the metropolitan's assistance to him in 1902 and 1903.

57. Schneiderman, *Sergei Zubatov,* 176–79.

58. Bukhbinder, "K istorii 'Sobranii,'" 292–98. The documents detailing this dispute are nos. 5–7: a report from the factory inspectorate to the director of industries at the Ministry of Finance, dated 11 January 1903; a secret note from Minister of Finance

S. Iu. Witte to Minister of the Interior V. K. Pleve, dated 14 January 1903; a note from Witte to Pleve, dated 2 February 1903.

59. Schneiderman says that Witte helped to persuade the ORRP to withdraw its support from the association in the spring of 1903 by informing Ornatskii of the involvement of the police in the organization. Schneiderman, *Sergei Zubatov*, 180. Gapon, on the other hand, believed that Ornatskii had close connections with the director of the police department, A. A. Lopukhin, and knew about the police involvement with the association when he offered the support of the ORRP. Gapon, *Story*, 95.

60. Schneiderman, *Sergei Zubatov*, 179–80.

61. Bukhbinder, "K istorii 'Sobraniia,'" 288 (Document 1).

62. Ibid., 288–89 (Document 2).

63. A. E. Karelin, "Deviatoe ianvaria i Gapon," *Krasnaia letopis'* 1 (1922): 106. Like others who knew Gapon at this time, Karelin described him as young, energetic, and attractive, with a mesmerizing gaze. Other descriptions of the priest also emphasize the effect of his gaze on observers: see Sablinsky, *Road*, 47–48. Several other figures revered as charismatic spiritual leaders at this time were also described by contemporaries as having a powerful, entrancing, or mesmerizing gaze: for example, the famous priest Father Ioann of Kronstadt; Grigorii Rasputin, the notorious intimate of the emperor's family; and the "mad monk" Iliodor (Trufanov), a fiery critic of Rasputin. In our own day, Russians often remark on the power of President Vladimir Putin's eyes.

64. Bukhbinder, "K istorii 'Sobraniia,'" 323–24 (Document 20, Kladovnikov's deposition).

65. Gapon, *Story*, 99–105.

66. Ibid., 105–6. Zubatov offered to pay Gapon two hundred rubles for the report. He accepted half of that sum. Gapon said that the workers of the deputation told him that Witte responded coldly to their presentation.

67. Sablinsky, *Road*, 76–78. Father Georgii's superiors suggested that he take monastic orders or accept a post as a seminary teacher in the provinces, but he refused. Gapon, *Story*, 96–99. After the events of Bloody Sunday, the metropolitan Antonii reported to a meeting of the capital's clergy that he had hesitated to appoint Gapon to a position in the capital because of his bad reputation. RGIA, f. 796, op. 442, d. 2105, "Otchet o sostoianii S. Peterburgskoi eparkhii za 1905," l. 55. As of 1903, this bad reputation was not the result of "revolutionism," as Gapon implied in his autobiography, but his own frequent conflicts with his immediate superiors, his behavior at the Olga poorhouse, and his poor performance at the academy.

68. Bukhbinder, "K istorii 'Sobraniia,'" 323–24 (Document 20, Kladovnikov's deposition). This worker said that Gapon became an active leader among the workers only after Zubatov's dismissal in August 1903, when the group became closer to the revolutionary parties. Kladovnikov presented himself as a reluctant member of the assembly who was suspicious of Gapon and his inner council; he would have quit the assembly but for the good job that Gapon had arranged for him and Gapon's persistent efforts to recruit him to his council.

69. Bukhbinder, "K istorii 'Sobraniia,'" 298–99 (Document 9, summary of an undated report by secret police agent Kremlevskii, possibly written in the summer of 1903).

70. Bukhbinder, "K istorii 'Sobraniia,'" 290–91 (Document 3, incomplete report of a police agent, dated 7 September 1903).

71. Sablinsky, *Road*, 87; Gapon, *Story*, 111.

72. Gapon, *Story*, 117.

73. There is a translation of the assembly's statute in Sablinsky, *Road*, 323–43. Sablinsky follows Gapon's autobiography in dating the statute to early November, but the date on the memo that was submitted with the statute to the director of the police department was 14 October 1903. P. Kobiakov, "Gapon i okhrannoe otdelenie do 1905 g.," *Krasnaia letopis'* 1 (1922): 28–45.

74. Sablinsky, *Road,* 85–88. The police agent who visited the group in early September observed that it had distanced itself from Zubatov and his agents: Bukhbinder, "K istorii 'Sobraniia,'" 291. Gapon said, "at the beginning of November all the men who had been formerly employed by Zubatoff were unanimously excluded from the society and forbidden to enter the premises." Gapon, *Story,* 112.

75. The city prefect was to approve the assembly's financial reports, the agenda of its meetings, its annual reports, and its elected leadership. The city prefect could audit the assembly's records at any time and could assign policemen to attend the assembly's meetings. The city prefect could also request the Ministry of the Interior to close the assembly. See paragraphs 10, 37, 41, 43, 48, 50, 56, and 62 for examples of the prefect's role: Sablinsky, *Road,* 323–43. Unlike Gapon's earlier projects, which were all connected in some way to the churches in which he served and thus had to be approved by the Synod, the assembly was not a church-based organization and consequently fell under the authority of the Ministry of the Interior.

76. Sablinsky, *Road,* 329, paragraphs 17 and 18 of the statute.

77. Sablinsky, *Road,* 323, paragraphs 1 and 2 of the statute; Kobiakov, "Gapon i okhrannoe otdelenie," 38–39.

78. Sablinsky, *Road,* 323, paragraphs 1 and 2 of the statute; also Kobiakov, "Gapon i okhrannoe otdelenie," 33. Herrlinger emphasizes that the religious elements of Gapon's organization—which both he and most of the assembly's members took very seriously—contributed strongly to its appeal. Herrlinger, "Class, Piety, and Politics," 328–31 and 350–87.

79. Sablinsky, *Road,* 330 and 334, paragraphs 21 and 34.

80. Kobiakov, "Gapon i okhrannoe otdelenie," 36.

81. Gapon, *Story,* 111–12.

82. Kobiakov, "Gapon i okhrannoe otdelenie," 42. Aspects of this argument do resemble that made by Zubatov in favor of unions organized under the supervision of the secret police, despite the fact that Gapon's organization was distinct and separate from that of Zubatov.

83. Ibid., 42–45. Gapon's reference to the parish system is rather incoherent, but it reflected his interest in the subject, about which he had written his candidate's dissertation at the academy, entitled "Sovremennoe polozhenie prikhoda v pravoslavnykh tserkvakh grecheskikh i russkikh." Professor Arkhimandrite Mikhail (Semenov) reviewed the thesis critically, noting that it was short and lacked originality in both its research and conception, but gave it a passing grade. Paozerskii, "Gapon i Sinod," 164.

84. Kobiakov, "Gapon i okhrannoe otdelenie," 45. The verse is Acts 5:38–39.

85. The charter was approved by the city prefect and the local police department in November and then submitted to the Ministry of the Interior, which made only minor changes before approving it in February 1904.

86. Sablinsky has studied the numerous sources for this period thoroughly and presents a detailed narrative of events in *Road,* 85 ff. A more analytical approach with a broader view of other important events in the year 1904 is given in Surh, *1905 in St. Petersburg,* 99–199. A very detailed and objective description of the January strike and the events of Bloody Sunday is that by V. Nevskii, "Ianvarskie dni v Peterburge v 1905 g.," *Krasnaia letopis'* 1 (1922): 13–74. A particularly dramatic account of the events of 8–13 January is given in a pamphlet written by Lev Gurevich, *Narodnoe dvizhenie v Peterburge 9-oe ianvaria 1905* (Berlin, 1906). There are many published memoirs and documents relating to the strike and Bloody Sunday: see the complete annotated bibliography in Sablinsky, *Road,* 351–404.

87. Gapon, *Story,* 118–19.

88. Karelin, "Deviatoe ianvaria," 106–8.

89. Ibid., 106; Pavlov, "Iz vospominanii," 2 (April 1908): 90–91. The program is given in Sablinsky, *Road,* 103, with the author's comments on pp. 102 and 104.

90. Gapon, *Story,* 123–25. A secret police report on the assembly's activity around

this time praised the good order of the assembly's meetings and its beneficial influence on the workers: Bukhbinder, "K istorii 'Sobraniia,'" 298–99 (Document 9, undated summary of report filed by Okhrana agent Kremenetskii). Gapon considered expanding the assembly to other cities and undertook a journey to the south to assess conditions in Moscow, Kiev, Kharkov, and Poltava: *Story*, 126–28. The governor-general of Moscow complained to the Ministry of the Interior about Gapon's visit: Bukhbinder, "K istorii 'Sobraniia,'" 300–301 (Document 10, secret memo from the office of the Moscow governor-general to the Ministry of the Interior dated 6 July 1904).

91. Pavlov, "Iz vospominanii," *Minuvshie gody* 1 (March 1908): 50–53; Karelin, "Deviatoe ianvaria," 107; Gapon, *Story*, 129–32.

92. On contacts with the underground parties, see Gapon, *Story*, 132–33. On contact with the Union of Liberation, see Gurevich, *Narodnoe dvizhenie*, 19. Richard Pipes identifies the specific individuals as E. Kuskova, S. N. Prokopovich, and V. Ia. Bogucharskii (Iakovlev): Pipes, *Russian Revolution*, 21. On the journalists, see Bukhbinder, "K istorii 'Sobraniia,'" 325–28 (Document 21, deposition by S. Ia. Stechkin, a journalist for the workers' newspaper *Russkaia gazeta*, dated 3 February 1905).

93. Gapon, *Story*, 133–36; Karelin, "Deviatoe ianvaria," 108–10; Bukhbinder, "K istorii 'Sobraniia,'" 314–15 (Document 19, second deposition of V. A. Ianov, a member of the assembly's general staff, dated 18 January 1905).

94. Gapon said that he began to consider something like a petition to the tsar at the beginning of 1904 and then discussed the idea of a "Tsar's Charter" with members of his secret council: Gapon, *Story*, 135. Members of Gapon's inner circle stated that a draft of the petition was first presented to them in the spring of 1904 in the form of the "Program of the Five." See Sablinsky, *Road*, 103–4. Karelin said that discussion of the petition was renewed in November on the initiative of the council: Karelin, "Deviatoe ianvariia," 110–11. Gapon discussed his thoughts about the political situation of the fall of 1904 in Gapon, *Story*, 136. Pipes has argued that both the idea for the petition and its content originated entirely with members of the Union of Liberation: see Pipes, *Russian Revolution*, 22–24. For a more complex account of the assembly and the Liberation movement, see Surh, *1905 in St. Petersburg*, 120–21 and 131–46. Sablinsky rightly emphasizes the differences between the liberals and Gapon in *Road*, 132–34.

95. Bukhbinder, "K istorii 'Sobraniia,'" 314–17 (Document 19, second deposition of Ianov) and 309–10 (Document 17, deposition of V. A. Inozemtsov, member of the council of the Narva branch, dated 20 January 1905). Gapon and several others worked on the petition on 5–7 January and sent copies of it to all the asssembly's branches (and to the Ministry of Justice, the Ministry of the Interior, Count Witte, and the emperor) on 8 January.

96. This was suggested by the author of a report on the workers' movement made by the Ministry of Finance's Division of Industries in 1906: RGIA, f. 23, op. 20 (1905–1906), d. 1, "Raznye svedeniia i perepiski o rabochem dvizhenii," l. 129ob. The successful strikes were at the leather manufacturers on 3 December 1904 and at the New Sampson textile plant on 17 December. The Ministry of Finance was generally inclined to connect any type of worker organization with strike activity: see Bukhbinder, "K istorii 'Sobraniia,'" 292–96 (Document 6, report of factory inspector A. P. Iakimov to the director of the Division of Industries, dated 11 January 1903).

97. Gapon, *Story*, 138–54; Bukhbinder, "K istorii 'Sobraniia,'" 307–11 (Document 17, deposition of Inozemtsov), 316–22 (Document 19, second deposition of Ianov); Nevskii, "Ianvarskie dni," 15–19.

98. Details on how many workers from which factories went on strike on which days are in RGIA, f. 23, op. 20 (1905–1906), d. 1, "Raznye svedeniia," ll. 130–31ob. A convenient summary, based on a different source, is available in Surh, *1905 in St. Petersburg*, 156.

99. For a full list of the demands, see Nevskii, "Ianvarskie dni," 19–20 and Sablinsky, *Road*, 161–63.

100. On the response of government officials at various levels, see "Doklad direktora departmenta politsii Lopukhina Ministerstvu vnutrennykh del o sobytiiakh 9–go ianvaria," *Krasnaia letopis'* 1 (1922): 330–38; S. Valk, "Peterburgskoe gradonachal'stvo i 9–oe ianvariia," *Krasnaia letopis'* 1 (1925): 37–46; and "9–oe ianvaria 1905," *Krasnyi arkhiv* 4–5 (1925): 1–25 (reports of Minister of Finance V. N. Kokovstev to the tsar for 5, 6, 16, and 19 January 1905). Since most of the army was fighting in the Far East, the forces the government had available for maintaining domestic order were limited. The government feared that too forceful a response could worsen the strike and fatally compromise the war effort.

101. On Gapon's popular status as a prophet, see "K istorii Krovavogo Voskresen'ia v Peterburge, *Krasnyi arkhiv* 1 (1935): 48–51; and Pavlov, "Iz vospominanii," 2 (April 1908): 99–100.

102. Copies of the petition and the accompanying letter of explanation sent to Count Witte on 8 January are located in RGIA, f. 1622, op. 1, d. 724, "Pis'mo sviashchennika Gapona Ministerstvu vnutrennykh del s vsepoddaneishim adresom rabochikh goroda S. Peterburga." A translation of the petition is given in an appendix to Sablinsky, *Road*, 344–49. The petition followed the Program of the Five closely with only four new demands: the separation of church and state, the performance of draft service at home and not abroad, an end to the war with Japan, and the elimination of the factory inspectorate. The demands for amnesty, civil rights, equality before the law for all, accountability of the bureaucracy, and state-supported universal education, as well as for changes in the tax system, the transfer of all land to the people, legalization of unions, an eight-hour day and limits on overtime, a minimum wage, state insurance for workers, and worker participation in factory administration were all part of the program as written in the spring of 1904.

103. Nevskii, "Ianvarskie dni," 36.

104. V. P. Sidorov, *Khristianskii sotsializm v Rossii v kontse XIX–nachale XX veka* (Chernopovets, 1995), 153. In 1905 and 1906, Father Grigorii Petrov and the Group of 32 also associated political activism with building the Kingdom of God on earth.

105. Bukhbinder, "K istorii 'Sobraniia,'" 311–13 (Document 18, first deposition of Ianov, dated 13 January 1905); Gapon, *Story*, 172–76; D. Gimer, "9–oe ianvaria 1905 g. v S. Peterburge," *Byloe* 1 (1925): 5; Nevskii, "Ianvarskie dni," 36–37; Maksimov, "Pravda i lozh'," 10.

106. Gapon, *Story*, 160–61.

107. Ibid., 172.

108. There is a detailed description of that morning in Gurevich, *Narodnoe dvizhenie*, 30–83.

109. Gapon claimed that 100,000 people signed the petition in *Story*, 169.

110. For the disposition of the military forces and the encounters between them and the crowds, see "9 ianvaria v Peterburge," *Krasnyi arkhiv* 1 (1930): 3–19; "K istorii 9 ianvariia 1905 goda," *Krasnyi arkhiv* 4–5 (1925): 444–48. For a detailed account, see Sablinsky, *Road*, 229–70.

111. Gapon's account ends with his escape from Russia: Gapon, *Story*, 206–46.

112. Revolutionary sources claimed thousands of casualties while officials estimated less than one hundred killed: "K istorii Krovavogo Voskresen'ia," 51. Nevskii estimated 150–200 dead and 450–800 wounded, pointing out that in many cases soldiers fired over the heads of the crowds. Around the Winter Palace, this tactic had a disastrous result: children who had climbed up into the trees around the Square to watch the spectacle were hit by bullets fired over the crowds on the ground. Nevskii, "Ianvarskie dni," 56. Sablinsky discusses the various figures and the problem of estimating the number of casualties in *Road*, 261–68.

113. Gapon, *Story*, 116–17.

114. Yet, perhaps not untypical. Pisiotis found that hierarchs frequently protected the parish clergy under their authority from punishment by the secular authorities during the 1905 revolution. Pisiotis, "Orthodoxy versus Autocracy," 236–63.

115. On Antonii's financial support and Gapon's appointment to the church of the transport prison, see Gapon, *Story*, 111, and on Gapon's work at the prison, 121. The metropolitan had a special concern for the prisons of the capital.

116. Gapon, *Story*, 116. Such an objection was wholly in keeping with the church's criticisms of how secular temperance societies and charities operated. Father Georgii's love of music and dancing (and his personal indulgence in both pleasures) were described by his contemporaries: Bukhbinder, "Iz zhizni," 102–3; and Pavlov, "Iz vospominanii," 1 (March 1908) 29–33.

117. N. Avidonov, "9 ianvaria 1905 goda i Sinod," *Byloe* 1 (1925): 55.

118. Gapon, *Story*, 162. Gapon mentions only one summons, which he refused.

119. The church was not alone in its hesitation to act. The confused response of the city and central authorities to the strike may well have encouraged its spread: "9-oe ianvaria 1905 g.," *Voprosy zhizni* 1 (1905): 331–33. Orders for Gapon's arrest were not issued until 8 January and even then were not vigorously enforced: Valk, "Peterburgskoe gradonachal'tsvo," 38–40 Although the city prefect posted warnings against large public gatherings on 8 January, the fact that the police did not interfere with the assembly's meetings or take down announcements about the march led many participants to believe that the march was permitted: Gapon, *Story*, 176–77. In fact, two policemen accompanied the marchers from the Narva branch and cleared the road for them, 181. The commander of the military units guarding the bridge connecting the Schlusselberg highway to the city center refused to let the marchers pass over the bridge but permitted them to cross the ice on foot without interference. At the points in the city where the use of weapons was threatened, the crowds believed that the soldiers would not fire or would use blank rounds, 188–205; see also "9 ianvaria v Peterburge," 3–10.

120. While the clergy have typically been associated with the forces of order under the old regime, Pisiotis has demonstrated that the clergy, like most other groups in Russian society, did speak and act out against the government during the 1905 revolution: Pisiotis, "Orthodoxy versus Autocracy," 119, 155, 194–95, 290, 327, and 432–39.

121. RGIA, f. 796, op. 442, d. 2105, "Otchet o sostoianii Peterburgskoi eparkhii za 1905," ll. 55ob.–57.

122. RGIA, f. 796, op. 442, d. 2105, "Otchet o sostoianii Peterburgskoi eparkhii za 1905," ll. 58 59.

123. Herrlinger characterizes these responses as essentially conservative in "Class, Piety, and Politics," 431–41.

124. A. V. Kartashev, "Russkaia tserkov' v 1905 g.," (Spb, 1906), 2. Kartashev was not present but had close contacts with some of the individuals who advocated this position. He had resigned from his position as professor at the St. Petersburg academy after the Religious-Philosophical Society was closed and had gone to the United States, where he was officially attached to the Orthodox diocese of North America. After returning to Russia in late 1905, he joined the Renovationist party and wrote for their publications.

125. Kartashev, "Russkaia tserkov'," 10.

126. Avidonov, "9 ianvaria," 51. The first prayer had originally been decreed in 1895, the second in 1904. The text of the Synod's message is on pp. 52–54.

127. Pisiotis found that dissident clergy often expressed their opposition in this way. Pisiotis, "Orthodoxy versus Autocracy," 142–44.

128. Ibid., 52–54.The statement was to be published in all the newspapers and read aloud by the clergy after Sunday services.

129. "Smutnaia nedelia v Peterburge," *PRS* 1 (1905): 27–33. Private funeral services (sing., *otpevanie*) had to be allowed for the victims; memorial services (sing. *panikhida*) were to be allowed only when requested by the victims' family members and were not to be open to the public at large.

130. RGIA, f. 796, op. 442, d. 2105, "Otchet o sostoianii Peterburgskoi eparkhi za 1905," ll. 55–55 ob. Portions of this document have been published by the editor of the

Russian translation of Gapon's memoirs. See A. Shilov, "Peterburgskoe dukhovenstvo i 9 ianvaria," *Krasnyi arkhiv* 5 (1929): 192–99.

131. Immediately after January 9, Father Georgii went abroad to raise support for the revolution among the émigrés. He returned after the October Manifesto. On 26 November 1905 the assembly was reopened, but its meetings were suspended in early February 1906 after the secret police reported that most of its members were Social Democrats. Requests to reopen it were denied and it was permanently closed at the end of March. Concerning the assembly during this period, see Bukhbinder, "K istorii 'Sobraniia,'" 301–3 (Documents 11–14 and document 16); and N. Petrov, "Gapon i graf Witte," *Byloe* 1 (1925): 15–27. Gapon tried to develop closer relations with revolutionary groups after his return, but they suspected he was a government spy. Members of a Socialist Revolutionary cell assassinated him some time in April 1906. Police discovered his body hanging in a small, isolated cottage near the Finnish border on 30 April. See A. Milovidov, "Dva dokumenty ob ubiistve Gapona," *Byloe* 1 (1925): 63–65.

132. RGIA, f. 796, op. 186 (1905), otd. 5, stol 2, No. 5618, "O sviashchennike S. Peterburgskoi eparkhii Georgii Gapon, obviniaemem v uchastii v zabastovskikh rabochikh." One of the documents from this file was published by Avidonov, "9 ianvaria 1905," 56–57. The grounds for defrocking were all related to insubordination. Pisiotis postulates that hierarchs were most likely to support punishing dissident clergymen who had defied episcopal authority in addition to or in connection with challenging the socioeconomic order or the political system. Pisiotis, "Orthodoxy versus Autocracy," 280–85.

133. Avidonov, "9 ianvaria 1905," 54. Nicholas II met with "representatives" from the workers who had been chosen by the police and approved by the city prefect's office. The meeting took place on 21 January; the Synod's message was published on 26 January. See also Gapon, *Story,* 216–18.

134. Kartashev, "Russkaia tserkov'," 3.

8—Renewing the Church

1. On the clergy's exclusion from politics by the Russian state, see A. Iu. Polunov, *Pod vlast'iu ober-prokurora. Gosudarstvo i tserkov' v epokhu Aleksandra III-ego* (Moscow, 1996), 79; Freeze, "Orthodox Church and Serfdom," 371 and 375–77, and "Handmaiden," 93 and 98.

2. Gruppa peterburgskikh sviashchennikov. *K tserkovnomu soboru. Sbornik* (Spb, 1906), i–ii.

3. Kartashev, "Russkaia tserkov'," 6.

4. A. I. Vvedenskii, *Tserkov' i gosudarstvo* (Moscow, 1923), 24. Kremlevskii graduated from the St. Petersburg academy in 1895 with a candidate's degree and later received a master's degree from the school. After becoming a priest at one of the capital's institutional churches he became active in the ORRP.

5. Gruppa peterburgskikh sviashchennikov, *Sbornik*, ii.

6. Ibid., ii. The group made their request for the meeting on February 9. The meeting was described briefly in the preface to the group's first collection of articles published one year later.

7. Ibid., iii. Quote is from the letter the members of the circle wrote to Metropolitan Antonii several weeks after this meeting to accompany the group's first essay on the need for a church council, which was published 15 March 1905. This letter was separately published on 5 April 1905.

8. Ibid.

9. Ibid., iii–iv.

10. Ibid., v.

11. The background to the movement for church reform is discussed in James Cunningham, *A Vanquished Hope: The Movement for Church Renewal in Russia, 1905–1906* (Crestwood, NY, 1981): 58–59 and 70–78; see also the more recent work,

Firsov, *Russkaia tserkov'*, 126–50. The subject of church reform was introduced to the Religious-Philosophical Society by two lay professors from the St. Petersburg academy: Alexander Brilliantov and Alexander Kartashev.

12. Two articles were especially influential in the reform discussions of 1902–1903: A. A. Papkov, *Neobkhodymost' obnovleniia pravoslavnogo tserkovno-obshchestvennaia stroia* (Spb, 1902), first published in the secular thick journal *Russkii vestnik* in June, 1902; and L. Tikhomirov, *Zaprosy zhizni i nashe tserkovnoe upravlenie* (Moscow, 1903), first published in the conservative newspaper that Tikhomirov edited, *Moskovskie vedomosti*.

13. On the widespread and growing unrest that had been developing since 1899, see Pipes, *Russian Revolution*, 1–10.

14. A. Iu. Polunov, "The State and Religious Heterodoxy in Russia, 1880s–1890s," *Russian Studies in History* 39, no. 4 (Spring 2001): 54–65. On tolerance as one of the causes of tension between the state and the church, see Gregory L. Freeze, "Subversive Piety: Religion and Political Crisis in Late Imperial Russia." *Journal of Modern History* 68 (1996): 308–50. Firsov also examines this issue, focusing specifically on the state's decision to extend religious tolerance to the Old Believers, in *Russkaia tserkov'*, 255–75.

15. For further discussion of how the state often used the church to promote its own agenda in the late imperial period despite frequent resistance from the clergy, see the following: Freeze, "Subversive Piety;" Freeze, "Tserkov', religiia, i politicheskaia kul'tura na zakate staroi Rossii," *Istoriia SSSR* 1 (1991): 107–19; Robert L. Nichols, "Church and State in Imperial Russia," The Donald W. Treadgold Papers, no. 102 (Seattle, 1995); and Polunov, *Pod vlast'iu ober-prokurora*, 11–18, 81–83, and 125–29. On the state's efforts to use the church to suppress political dissent among the clergy and the bishops' resistance to the state's pressure during the 1905 revolution, see Pisiotis, "Orthodoxy versus Autocracy," especially chap. 3, pp. 224–90. Concerning the ways in which Nicholas II in particular used religion as an element of his political scenario, see Wortman, *Scenarios of Power*, 2:344–53; 364–90; 440–68; and Firsov, *Russkaia tserkov'*, 53–66.

16. Cunningham, *Vanquished Hope*, 78–81.

17. The text of Antonii's memo is in A. R. [A. S. Rodosskii, ed., *Istoricheskaia perepiska o sudbakh pravoslavnoi tserkvi* (Moscow, 1912), 26–31, along with the texts of a number of other primary sources related to the debate on church reform. The memo is also summarized in detail in A. A. Bogolepov, "Church Reforms in Russia, 1905–1918," *St. Vladimir's Seminary Quarterly* 10, no. 1 (1966): 13–14.

18. A. R., *Istoricheskaia perepiska*, 8–17. Witte was strongly influenced by Papkov, who envisioned the pre-Petrine parish as a strong and stable community united by a sense of religious brotherhood that overcame social and economic differences. In Papkov's view, the clergy's role in the parish was not one of leadership but subservience to the needs and demands of the laity. Not surprisingly, few of the St. Petersburg clergy were sympathetic to Papkov's ideas, though many lay people supported them.

19. Cunningham notes that Pobedonostsev had been sick in January of 1905 when the discussions on reform began: *Vanquished Hope*, 95. Pobedonostsev and Witte had a long history of mutual hostility, so the differences between them on church reform are not surprising. Pobedonostsev seems to have been more angered by Antonii's support of reform than Witte's, judging from the self-justifying letters Antonii sent to Pobedonostsev. See RGIA, f. 1579, op. 1, d. 36, "Doklady i pis'ma," ll. 2–2ob. Firsov emphasizes Pobedonostsev's strong opposition to church reform and the role he played in obstructing the reform process, despite the fact that by 1905 he had long since lost his ability to exert a positive influence on Nicholas II. See Firsov, *Russkaia tserkov'*, 65–83; on Pobedonostsev's loss of influence, see Polunov, "Konstantin Petrovich Pobedonostsev," 27–28.

20. A. R., *Istoricheskaia perepiska*, 33–44.

21. One of Pobedonostsev's letters to the tsar was published later: "Iz chernovykh bumag K. P. Pobedonostseva," *Krasnyi arkhiv* 18 (1926): 203–7. Further details are available in Cunningham, *Vanquished Hope*, 95–107.

22. I. V. Preobrazhenskii, *Tserkovnaia reforma. Sbornik statei dukhovnoi i svetskoi periodicheskoi pechati po voprosu o reforme* (Spb, 1905), 1–8.

23. Ibid., 4.

24. Ibid., 2.

25. Ibid., 4 and 5.

26. Preobrazhenskii, *Tserkovnaia reforma*, 3. The author of the preface to the collected articles said that the number was not quite correct—only thirty clergymen signed the letter to Antonii. See Gruppa peterburgskikh sviashchennikov, *Sbornik*, vi. Their names were not published, though the signers had wanted and expected their names to appear with the article.

27. Cunningham, *Vanquished Hope*, 108.

28. Nicholas II's response is quoted in Cunningham, *Vanquished Hope*, 125–26.

29. Gregory Freeze has contrasted "clerical liberalism" with "episcopal conciliarism," arguing that clerical liberals, among whom he includes the Renovationists, were focused on improving the status of the clerical estate and the conditions of clerical service rather than on larger ecclesiastical, social, or political problems. Freeze, *Parish Clergy*, 389–97 and 440–59. This interpretation is embraced by Edward Roslof, *Red Priests: Renovationism, Russian Orthodoxy, and Revolution, 1905–1946* (Bloomington, 2002), 4–8; and by Firsov, *Russkaia tserkov'*, 331–42. Scott Kenworthy acknowledges the presence of estate-based interests in the group's program but emphasizes the importance of the group's religious agenda. See Scott M. Kenworthy, "Russian Reformation? The Program for Religious Renovation in the Orthodox Church, 1922–25." *Modern Greek Studies Yearbook* 16/17 (2000/2001): 89–91.

30. Gruppa Peterburgskikh sviashchennikov, *Sbornik*, 9–15. Nearly all reform proposals provoked heated debate and often scathing criticism. The different positions on major issues are thoroughly reviewed in Cunningham, *Vanquished Hope*. On the role that divisions in the church played in the failure of church reform, see Freeze, *Parish Clergy*, 462–68.

31. According to Firsov, Pobedonostsev believed most bishops would oppose church reform, for he was convinced that reform was something "dreamed up" in the capital. Pobedonostsev was wrong: the bishops' replies demonstrated near-universal support for a wide range of reforms. Firsov argues that the detail and sophistication of most of the responses also proves the bishops had already thought long and hard about what needed to be reformed and how, thus supporting his more general argument that the hierarchy was not the main obstacle to church reform. Firsov, *Russkaia tserkov'*, 183.

32. Reprinted in Gruppa Peterburgskikh sviashchennikov, *Sbornik*, 24–36.

33. Gregory Freeze has commented on the church's "supraclass" attitude toward politics in "Going to the Intelligentsia," 230–31. This attitude was reflected in the sources Pisiotis examined as well: "Orthodoxy versus Autocracy," 335–30 and 405–420.

34. The Duma was proposed in August 1905 in the document known as the "Bulygin constitution." The body was to have been elected on a restricted franchise favorable to well-off individuals and Russian peasants, and unfavorable to urban industrial workers and national minorities. This Duma was to have had only a limited consultative role. See Pipes, *Russian Revolution*, 34.

35. See John S. Curtiss, *Church and State in Russia: The Last Years of the Empire, 1900–1917* (New York, 1940), 196–211 and 237–70. Pisiotis has published an article on clerical dissent, based on his dissertation research: "The Unknown Dissident: The Prosopography of Clerical Anti-Tsarist Activism in Late Imperial Russia," *Modern Greek Studies Yearbook* 18/19 (2002/2003): 63–94.

36. Pisiotis emphasizes that the clergy felt it was part of their professional responsibility to offer the people guidance and leadership: "Orthodoxy versus Autocracy," 157–65, 195–96, 305–7, 315–21, 327.

37. Gruppa Peterburgskikh sviashchennikov, *Sbornik*, 25.

38. Ibid., 27.

39. Ibid., 29.
40. Ibid., 30.
41. Ibid. Both their ideals and their language recall Belliustin's 1858 polemic.
42. Gruppa Peterburgskikh sviashchennikov, *Sbornik,* 31.
43. Ibid., 32. They cited Jesus' words as given in John 27:15 and 18, "I do not pray that You take them away from the world, but that You preserve them from evil . . . As You sent me into this world, so I send them into the world."
44. Ibid., 33. The allusion is to Matthew 9:10–14.
45. Gruppa Peterburgskikh sviashchennikov, *Sbornik.*
46. Ibid.
47. Pisiotis shares this observation in "Orthodoxy versus Autocracy," 333–35, 359–60, 403, and 580. Pat Herlihy makes a similar argument with regard to the evolution of political activism among temperance workers, both lay and secular, in *Alcoholic Empire,* 3–12 and 147–50. Herrlinger, however, believes that the parish clergy of the capital maintained a clear sense of the distance between moral-religious and political concerns: Herrlinger, "Raising Lazarus," 348.
48. Kartashev, "Russkaia tserkov'," 3–6.
49. E. G. Kopenkin, "Sotsial'no-politicheskaia i ideologicheskaia pereorientatsia Russkoi pravoslavnoi tserkvi v predrevoliutsionnoi Rossii kak faktor evolutsiia pravoslaviia" (Kand. diss., Gosudarstvennyi Pedagogicheskii institut im. Gertsena, 1973); and V. M. Andreev, "Liberal'no-obnovlencheskoe dvizhenie v russkom pravoslavie nachale XX v. i ego ideologiia" (Kand. diss., Gosudarstvennyi Pedagogicheskii institut im. Gertsena, 1972). The best Soviet study is that of N. S. Gordienko and P. K. Kurochkin, "Liberal'no-obnovlencheskoe dvizhenie v russkom pravoslavii nachale XX v.," *Voprosy nauchnogo ateizma* 7 (1969): 313–40. More recently, the Renovationists have been discussed in chap. 2 of O. V. Ostanina, "Obnovlenchestvo i reformatorstvo v russkoi pravoslavnoi tserkvi v nachale XX veka" (Kand. diss., Leningradskii gosudarstvennyi universitet, 1991). Recent western works on the Renovationists have concentrated on the post-1917 period, describing the 1905 group only briefly or not at all. See Roslof, *Red Priests;* Gregory L. Freeze, "Counter-reformation in Russian Orthodoxy: Popular Response to Religious Innovation, 1922–1925," *Slavic Review* 64, no. 2 (1995): 305–39; Kenworthy, "Russian Reformation?"
50. Gruppa Peterburgskikh sviashchennikov, *Sbornik,* vii. Pisiotis emphasizes the close connections between clerical political dissent and lay political opposition in "Orthodoxy versus Autocracy," 130–66, 194–214, 300–327, and 551–84.
51. Gruppa Peterburgskikh sviashchennikov, *Sbornik,* vii.
52. Ibid., viii.
53. Ibid., xi.
54. Soiuz revnitelei tserkovnogo obnovleniia, *Ob otnoshenii Tserkvi i sviashchenstva k sovremennoi obshchestvenno-politicheskoi zhizni* (Spb, 1906), 5.
55. Ibid., 6.
56. Ibid., 18.
57. Mikhail Pavlovich Chel'tsov (1870–1931) was from a clerical family of Riazan' province. He attended the ecclesiastical academy at Kazan (1890–1894), where he became involved in missionary work. He was transferred to St. Petersburg in 1898 after his exemplary work was praised at the Third Missionary Congress of 1897. He established a missionary course for lay proselytizers and served as assistant editor of *Missionerskoe obozrenie* and co-editor of the journal *Pravoslavnyi putevoditel'* while working in the synodal bureaucracy. He was arrested five times between 1917 and 1922 and was sentenced to death in the 1922 trial of the St. Petersburg churchmen. The sentence was commuted and he was given five years in prison instead. He was released in 1923, only to be arrested again in 1930 and shot in 1931. See "Protoierei Mikhail Pavlovich Chel'tsov. Zhizn' i deiatel'nosti," *Zhurnal Moskovskogo Patriarshestva* 10 (1993): 36–48.

58. M. Chel'tsov, "Khristianstvo i politika," *Khristianskoe chtenie* (March 1906): 415–36, and "Pravoslavnoe pastyrstvo i obshchestvennaia deiatel'nost'," *Khristianskoe chtenie* (May 1906): 735–46 and (June 1906): 878–88. The publication of these Renovationist pieces in the academy journal is significant because it demonstrates Chel'tsov was not part of a lunatic fringe but an individual whose ideas found a sympathetic response among some of the most well-educated minds in the church.

59. Chel'tsov, "Khristianstvo i politika," 418.

60. Ibid., 428.

61. Ibid., 426.

62. Ibid., 430.

63. Chel'tsov, "Pravoslavnoe pastyrstvo," 735–38.

64. Ibid., 745–46.

65. S. S. Broiarskii, "Tserkovno-prikhodskaia zhizn' na novykh nachalakh," *Zvonar'* (May–June 1906): 236.

66. The Renovationists relied exclusively on the term "pastor" in their writings, preferring it over "priest" because it was positively associated with the clergy's work of social outreach. In the above-cited article, "Gosudarstvennyi Duma i pastyr' tserkvi," the authors repeatedly use the phrase "we pastors" and address their audience as "fellow brother pastors" *(sobrat'ia pastyri)*.

67. "Bratstvo revnitelei tserkovnogo obnovleniia," *Zvonar'* (September 1906): 307–9. Also in *Tserkovnoe obnovlenie* 1 (12 November 1906): 13–16.

68. "Ot redaktsiia," *Zvonar'* (April 1906): 1–2.

69. The bishops' replies were published by the Synod as soon as they had all been received: *Otzyvy eparkhial'nykh arkhiereev po voprosu o tserkovnoi reforme*, 3 vols. (Spb, 1906). Analyses of these replies have been published by Father John Meyendorff, "Russian Bishops and Church Reform in 1905," in *Russian Orthodoxy under the Old Regime*, ed. Theofanis Stavrou and Robert Nichols (Minneapolis, 1978) pp. 170–82; and Nicholas Zernov, "The Reform of the Church and the Pre-Revolutionary Russian Episcopate," *St. Vladimir's Seminary Quarterly* 6, no. 3 (1962): 128–38. Both of these authors emphasized the role of the bishops in formulating the reform program. Cunningham's very detailed discussion of the replies pays close attention to the opinions that the laity and the parish clergy expressed at the pre-council convention: Cunningham, *Vanquished Hope*, 127–205.

70. The chief advocates of a council were Witte, serving as chair of the Council of Ministers; the new director general of the Synod, Prince Andrei Obolenskii; and the metropolitan of St. Petersburg, Antonii (Vadkovskii). Cunningham, *Vanquished Hope*, 205–6. Obolenskii served for only a few months before being replaced by Peter Izvol'skii.

71. Quoted in part by Metropolitan Antonii in his opening address to the pre-council conference: *Zhurnaly i protokoly zasedanii, vysochaishe uchrezhdennago Predsobornogo Prisutstviia*, 4 vols. (Spb, 1906–1907), 1: vi.

72. "Podgotovlenie k Soboru," *Tserkovnyi golos* 5 (3 February 1906): 131–32; untitled notice, *Tserkovnyi golos* 10 (10 March 1906): 388. The list of members appointed by the beginning of March is in N. D. Kuznetsov, *Po voprosam tserkovnykh preobrazovanii* (Moscow, 1907), 6–7. It is incomplete and must be supplemented by the list given in the *Zhurnaly i protokoly*, 1: vi. The members included the three metropolitans, the archbishops of Kherson, Litovsk, Iaroslavl, and Finland, and the bishops of Volynia, Pskov, and Mogilev. The professors chosen from the St. Petersburg academy were Father A. Rozhdestvenskii, N. N. Glubokovskii, I. Sokolov, and A. Brilliantov. Father P. Ia. Svetlov of St. Vladimir's University was also a member of the conference. The only St. Petersburg clergyman initially appointed was archpriest A. Lebedev, supervisor of the church of the Ascension. On 10 March, archpriest P. Sokolov, the president of the Synod's Schools Commission, was invited to the conference. Among the laymen were D. A. Khomiakov, D. F. Samarin, Prince E. Trubetskoi, A. A. Papkov, and N. P. Aksakov. The laymen were added on 27 February and the clergymen just days before the conference opened.

73. For example, see the series of articles by the bishop of Mogilev, Stefan (Arkhangelskii), "K kanonicheskomu ustroistvu Rossiiskoi pomestnoi Tserkvi," continued under the title "Navstrechu soboru Russkoi Tserkvi," published as lead articles in the January 1906 issues of *Tserkovnyi golos*. This weekly newspaper, published by the ORRP, tended toward pro-reformist views. Various articles on the conference agenda also appeared in the first issue of the Renovationist monthly *Zvonar'*, which began publication in April of 1906: for example, X. Belkov, "V chem dolzhno sostoit upravlenie tserkov'iu?" 178–86; and S. S. Broiarskii, "Navstrechu Rossiiskomu Soboru," 187–208.

74. *Zhurnaly i protokoly* 1: vii–xiii.

75. The decisions are discussed at length in Cunningham, *Vanquished Hope*, 213–312, and summarized in Curtiss, *Church and State*, 224–26. The proceedings were published by the Synod in four large volumes, the first two in the summer of 1906 and the second two in January of 1907.

76. *Zhurnaly i protokoly*, 3:1.

77. Cunningham, *Vanquished Hope*, 304–6.

78. *Zhurnaly i protokoly*, 3:3.

79. Untitled notice, *Tserkovnyi golos* 19 (11 May 1907): 501.

80. Cunningham, *Vanquished Hope*, 267–77. The emperor was not to be allowed to preside over the meetings of the council nor was he to participate in the council's discussions. Firsov argues that the church's dependence on the state was the primary reason reform failed in the pre-revolutionary period: Firsov, *Russkaia tserkov'*, 220–50 and 396–425.

81. The group published an article on the council in October of 1905 in the secular journal *Rus.'* It was critical of the government's interference with the council project and of some hierarchs' efforts to prevent the participation of lay people and non-monastic clergymen. The article prompted a polemical exchange between Archbishop Antonii (Khrapovitskii), chief defender of episcopal power and privilege, and Nikolai P. Aksakov, a pro-democratizing professor of canon law at the Moscow Ecclesiastical Academy, in the pages of the Moscow academy's journal *Bogoslovskii vestnik* in December of 1905.

82. "Navstrechu soboru Russkoi Tserkvi," *Tserkovnyi golos* 2 (13 January 1906): 33–36. The paper also ran two articles criticizing the conference for its initial exclusion of non-monastic clergy and lay people: "Podgotovlenie k Soboru," *Tserkovnyi golos* 5 (3 February 1906): 131–32 and "K voprosu o Sobore," 133–35.

83. There were many articles critical of the work of the conference, including: X. Belkov, "V chem dolzhno sostoit upravlenie tserkov'iu," *Zvonar'* (April 1906): 178–86; S. S. Broiarskii, "Navstrechu Rossiiskomu Soboru," *Zvonar'* (April 1906): 187–208; Broiarskii, "Tserkovno-prikhodskaia zhizn' v novykh nachalakh," *Zvonar'* (April 1906): 209–20; X. Belkov, "Slepota dukhovnoi biurokratii," *Zvonar'* (May–June 1906): 218–27; X. Belkov, "Obnovlenie tserkovnoi zhizn'," *Zvonar'* (August 1906): 213–24.

84. Renovationist periodicals flourished briefly in 1906 and 1907. In addition to the new monthly *Zvonar'*, there was the weekly newspaper *Vek*, edited by the archimandrite Mikhail and Professor Alexander Kartashev, which began publication in November 1906. *Tserkovnoe obnovelenie* was a weekly supplement edited by V. A. Nikol'skii.

85. A. Rozhdestvenskii, "V edinenii——sila," *Tserkovnoe obnovlenie* 1 (12 November 1906): 4–6; a similar article is A. Iasnev, "S narodom ili bez naroda," *Tserkovnoe obnovlenie* 4 (3 December 1906): 49–53.

86. Untitled and unattributed comment on the Synod's new rules for church-based associations, *Tserkovnoe obnovlenie* 4 (3 December 1906): 49–53.

87. Pisiotis argues that while the bishops often tolerated political dissent, they responded decisively to challenges to their own authority: Pisiotis, "Orthodoxy versus Autocracy," 236–47, 267–71, and 280–86.

88. This emphasis on the influence of estate-based interests on the Renovationists' program is preserved in Roslof, *Red Priests*, 4–8.

89. Arkhimandrit Mikhail, "Novogo neba i novoi zemli zhdem," *Tserkovnoe obnovlenie* 1 (12 November 1906): 1–3.

90. V. Ilinskii, "Est' li u nas tserkov'?" *Tserkovnoe obnovlenie* 5 (10 December 1906): 69–72, and "Tserkov' i narodnyia bedstviia," *Vek* 3 (26 November 1906): 32–34. According to Pisiotis, the rural parish clergy needed little urging; village priests not only supported peasant demands for social and economic justice but even led communal political actions: "Orthodoxy versus Autocracy," 130–55.

91. "Pered novoi zadachei," *Tserkovnoe obnovlenie* 3 (26 November 1906): 38–41. Pisiotis discusses several examples of clerical political dissidents from outside the capitals who shared these ideas in "Orthodoxy versus Autocracy," 157–66. He argues that such ideas were not restricted to a few urban intellectuals but were widespread among parish priests throughout the empire, including in provincial towns and rural areas, 155; see also Argyrios Pisiotis, "Unknown Dissident."

92. E. Belkov, "Letopis' tserkovno-obshchestvennoi zhizni," *Zvonar'* (January 1907): 89–91; "Stolichnye pastyri o partiiakh i vyborakh," *Tserkovnoe obnovelenie* 2 (13 January 1907): 16–17.

93. L. Tamarenko, "Za kem idti?" *Tserkovnoe obnovelenie* 3 (21 January 1907): 17–19. Pisiotis concludes that while clerical party affiliations were fluid in the 1905–1914 period, urban priests tended to be liberals, supportive of the Constitutional Democrats, while rural priests tended to be populists who preferred the non-party All-Russian Peasant Union over the extremist Socialist Revolutionary party. See Pisiotis, "Orthodoxy versus Autocracy," 156–57 and 335–59, and on the relation of the Orthodox clergy to parties of the radical right, 515–547. See also Pisiotis, "The Orthodox Clergy and the Radical Right at the Beginning of the Twentieth Century: Ideological Mentor or Strange Bedfellow?" *Konservatizm v Rossii i v mire*, n.d. http://conservatism.narod.ru/oktober/pisiotis.doc (2/26/05); and Firsov in *Russkaia tserkov'*, 294–317. Both scholars emphasize that church support for and clerical involvement in the extremist parties of the Right was limited, often nominal, and frequently driven by non-political motivations.

94. T. Asov, "Svoboda vyborov i dukhovenstvo," *Tserkovnoe obnovlenie* 5 (4 February 1907): 34–35.

95. T. Asov, "V kakuiu partiiu 'zapisano' dukhovenstva," *Tserkovnoe obnovelenie* 4 (28 January 1907): 25–27.

96. For example, "Tserkovnaia programma partii narodnoi svobody," *Vek* 1 (7 January 1907): 10–11; Tamarenko, "Za kem idti?" 19; "Khronika," *Tserkovnoe obnovlenie* 9 (4 March 1907): 71; T. Asov, "Pastyr i zhizn'," *Vek* 13 (1 April 1907): 156–57.

97. "Presviterianstvo v Russkoi Tserkvi," *Tserkovnyi golos* 24 (15 June 1907): 605–7.

98. M. Pospelov, "Obshchestvo i dukhovenstvo," *Zvonar'* (February 1907): 1–3; D. Filosofov, "Russkaia Tserkov' v 1908," *Krasnyi zvon* (January 1909): 281–85. Critics feared the Renovationists sought to increase the church's share of the state budget by demanding a state salary for all members of the clergy and state money for church schools. There were also concerns that the clergy wanted to increase their power in matters of family law, particularly with regard to marriage and divorce.

99. After 1906, Metropolitan Antonii cut off contacts with the group. RGIA, f. 1569, op.1, d. 34 (1906–1909), "Perepiska s Mitropolitom Antoniim," ll. 18–19, letter of 10 March 1907 to director general of the Synod Izvol'skii concerning the Renovationists.

9—THE DECADE OF DESPAIR

1. Gregory L. Freeze, "Church and Politics in Late Imperial Russia: Crisis and Radicalization of the Clergy," in *Russia under the Last Tsar: Opposition and Subversion, 1894–1917*, ed. Anna Geifman (New York, 1999), 269–97.

2. Among the issues dividing the government from the church in this period: the questions of liberalizing laws on marriage and divorce, reducing the number of officially observed religious holidays, adopting the western calendar, and expanding religious tolerance. Freeze, "Church and Politics," 272. On state-church conflicts over family law, see William G. Wagner, *Marriage, Property, and Law in Late Imperial Russia* (Oxford, 1994).

3. See Freeze, "Subversive Piety," 308–50; Robert L. Nichols, "Friends of God: Nicholas II and Alexandra at the Canonization of Serafim of Sarov, July 1903," in *Religious and Secular Forces in Late Tsarist Russia*, ed. Charles E. Timberlake (Seattle, 1992), 206–43; Wortman, *Scenarios of Power*, 2:383–90.

4. Challenges to the socioeconomic order, the political system, and the ecclesiastical authorities often went together, representing a "comprehensive challenge to autocratic authority:" Pisiotis, "Orthodoxy versus Autocracy," 119. My generalization about Renovationist concerns is based on my survey of the movement's journals for 1906 and 1907.

5. Pisiotis, "Orthodoxy versus Autocracy," 230–32.

6. Ibid., 236–59.

7. Ibid., 280. Pisiotis's work has led me to change my description and explanation of the events discussed in this section from what they were in the original dissertation. See 567, and 582 n. 28.

8. Arkhimandrite Mikhail was born Pavel Semenov in Simbirsk province in 1874, the son of a Jewish peasant military recruit who converted to Orthodoxy and educated his son at the local church schools. Semenov entered the Moscow Ecclesiastical Academy on a scholarship in 1895, later transferring to the Kazan Ecclesiastical Academy in order to follow his mentor, the arkhimandrite Antonii (Khrapovitskii). Semenov took monastic vows in 1899. He completed his master's dissertation on the rights and privileges of the church under the Roman and Byzantine emperors in 1901, after which he was offered the position at the St. Petersburg Ecclesiastical Academy. My thanks to William J. Comer for sharing his work on the archimandrite Mikhail, which includes these details, "The Evolution of a Cleric: The Path of Archimandrite Mikhail from Orthodoxy to the Christianity of Golgotha" (paper presented at the annual meeting of the American Association for the Advancement of Slavic Studies, Seattle, 1997), 1–2.

9. Archimandrite Mikhail wrote many pamphlets during the revolution, some original, some adapted from foreign works. Many of them were published in the series "Khristianstvo i svoboda," which appeared during the year 1906. My characterization of Mikhail's views is based on reviewing a number of Mikhail's works, including: "Aktivno ili passivno khristianstvo?" *Khristianskoe chtenie* (March 1903): Part 1, 423–42; *Tserkov', literatura, i zhizn'* (Moscow, 1905); *Pochemu nam ne veriat?* (Spb, 1906); *Sviashchennik-sotsialist i ego sotsial'nyi roman* (Spb, 1906); *Khristianstvo i sotsial'-demokratiia*, 2nd ed. (Spb, 1907). Mikhail's most famous work was *Kak ia stal narodnym sotsialistom*. The memoir *Ot bursy do sniatiia sana* (Spb, 1908) has been *mistakenly* attributed to Mikhail; he did not write it. A good study of Mikhail's thought is Ostanina, "Obnovlenchestvo i reformatorstvo," 106 ff.

10. Untitled memo from the editor, *Vek* 5 (10 December 1906): 58. The following issue carried a letter from a group of academy students protesting the repression of Father Mikhail for his political views: *Vek* 6 (17 December 1906): 73–74.

11. Mikhail, *Kak ia stal narodnym sotsialistom*, 1–12 and 25–32. Internal evidence indicates this pamphlet was written early in 1907.

12. "Smes'," *Zvonar'* (September 1907): 33–34. This short article did not go into further details about what conditions would be like for Mikhail at the monastery, but the outraged author clearly considered the confinement to be a hardship for Mikhail. Pisiotis has suggested that at least in some cases such confinement was not particularly onerous and was sometimes used to protect clergymen rather than to punish them. Pisiotis, "Orthodoxy versus Autocracy," 262.

13. RGIA, f. 1569, op.1, d. 93, "Pismo arkhimandrita Mikhaila P. P. Isvol'skomu." The letter itself is undated but logically must have been written in the fall of 1907, though the file is dated 1908.

14. Comer reports that Mikhail provided three reasons for his conversion to the Old Belief: his respect for the suffering that Old Believers had endured for their faith; his recognition that their rituals were more ancient; and his conviction that the synodal administration of the church was uncanonical. Comer, "Evolution of a Cleric," 7.

The Renovationist press continued to be interested in Mikhail after his defection from the synodal church (for which he was defrocked): "U staroobriadcheskogo episkopa Mikhaila," *Krasnyi zvon* (July 1909): 306–10; "Sobornyi sud nad staroobriadcheskom episkopom Mikhailom," *Krasnyi zvon* (September 1909): 193–98. Mikhail's departure from Russia on 14 November was noted in "Letopis' tserkovnyi zhizni," *Zvonar'* (October 1907): p. 64. (Although this volume of the journal was scheduled for publication in October, it did not actually come out until late November, so its chronicle contained events for the later month.)

15. For an overview and summary, see Uspenskii, "Lishenie sana," 17–33. The case was followed closely by *Peterburgskii listok,* and numerous articles from that journal were reprinted in *Zvonar'.* See especially the group reprinted in the August 1907 issue, pp. 115–81.

16. Pisiotis asserts that the parish clergy were well advanced in developing a sense of civic consciousness by 1905: "Orthodoxy versus Autocracy," 554. He attributes this to their involvement in programs of church outreach to society in the pre-revolutionary period, 157 and 301–4. He also suggests that the bishops were considerably more likely to follow the "rule of law" in dealing with alleged dissidents than the state, 236–55.

17. The accusation against Metropolitan Vladimir was made in a pro-Petrov pamphlet: N. G. Vysotskii, *Delo sv. Grigoriia Petrova* (Moscow, 1907).

18. Pisiotis, "Orthodoxy versus Autocracy," 267.

19. "Khronika," *Tserkovnoe obnovlenie* 9 (4 March 1907): 71. This Renovationist journal suggested that the timing of the charges against both Father Mikhail and Father Grigorii indicated that the Synod was deliberately trying to exclude these popular clergymen from the Duma.

20. "Obzor pechati," *Tserkovnyi golos* 10 (9 March 1907): 295–99.

21. Petrov, *Pis'mo.*

22. Metropolitan Antonii wrote that he saw no harm in Petrov's teachings and believed that he might even be good for the church because his work was so widely known and respected. He said that he would not oppose the Synod's final decision, but he did want to make sure that the case was handled fairly and that any punishments would be intended to reform Petrov rather than to destroy him. RGIA, f. 1569, op. 1, d. 35 (1906–1909), "Perepiska s Mitropolitom Antoniim," ll. 15–16. Pisiotis found that it was common for hierarchs to defend dissident priests under their supervision from the central authorities: "Orthodoxy versus Autocracy," 243–45 and 255–59.

23. Petrov, *Pis'mo,* 9.

24. Ibid., 18.

25. Ibid., 11.

26. Ibid., 23.

27. "Khronika," *Krasnyi zvon* (February 1908): 41.

28. "Tserkovno-obshchestvennaia zhizn'," *Krasnyi zvon* (June 1909): 208–9.

29. Evlogii, *Put' moei zhizni,* 178.

30. For example, see the untitled, unsigned letter to the editor, *Tserkovnyi golos* 4 (26 January 1907): 125–26. This newspaper was associated with the Society for Moral-Religious Enlightenment, which supported church reform but tended to be conservative on political issues. For articles specifically blaming the hierarchy for Petrov's repression, see "Mneniia i otzyvy," *Tserkovnyi vestnik* 4 (25 January 1907): 114–15; also T. Asov, "Otritsateli zhizni," *Tserkovnoe obnovlenie* 8 (25 February 1907): 57–58; and the untitled notice, *Tserkovnyi golos* 22 (1 June 1907): 574–75. The Renovationist periodicals had a very strong anti-episcopal bent: every issue of each publication carried articles criticizing the Synod, the hierarchy in general, or particular bishops for actions deemed to be aimed at repressing or abusing the parish clergy.

31. Untitled letter, *Vek* 6 (10 December 1906): 58. Mikhail was dismissed on 29 November along with two other young professors who were members of the Renovationist Union, Alexander Kartashev and Vladimir V. Uspenskii. The All-Russian Con-

gress of Seminary Students, which met in Moscow at the end of December 1906, also published a letter of support for Father Mikhail: *Tserkovnoe obnovlenie* 1 (7 January 1907): 8.

32. The council's response is in *Zhurnaly zasedanii soveta S. Peterburgskoi dukhovnoi akademii za 1906–1907*, 126. The assembly was held on 20 December. The Synod's decree, issued 31 December, is referred to on 187–89.

33. Ibid., 212–15. The Synod's first decree was issued on 20 January 1907, the second on 22 January. The faculty council did not review these decrees until the meeting of 28 February.

34. The students held their meeting on 25 January. "Otkrytoe pis'mo studentov S. Peterburgskoi Akademii sv. G. S. Petrovu," *Vek* 5 (4 February 1907): 66; "Letopis' tserkovno-obshchestvennoi zhizni," *Zvonar'* (February 1907): 172.

35. Some of the students who signed the second letter (most were in the first and second years of study) were readmitted the following year on the decision of the faculty council. The discussion about readmitting one of these students is summarized in *Zhurnaly zasedanii soveta S. Peterburgskoi dukhovnoi akademii za 1908–1909*, 120–21. A year after the expulsions, the faculty council reported to the Synod that all signatories to both letters had revoked their signatures: "Khronika," *Krasnyi zvon* (February 1908): 40. The faculty council's compliance with the Synod's policies was slow and grudging at best; they seem to have done their best to protect the students from punitive action in the beginning and to reduce the impact of the penalties that were imposed afterward.

36. A. Popov, "Nezrimiya tragediia," *Tserkovnoe obnovlenie* 9 (4 March 1907): 67–68.

37. Father Mikhail intervened on behalf of the defrocked deputies, agreeing in August of 1907 to accept his sentence of imprisonment in the Zadonsk monastery on the condition that the Synod restore the other men to their clerical status and rank. If the Synod refused, Mikhail threatened to reject the Synod's authority publicly and leave the church without renouncing his clerical orders, since "a priest unjustly defrocked is still a priest." "Smes'," *Zvonar'* (August 1907): pp.23–24. This compendium contains a description of Father Mikhail and several articles on the cases of Mikhail and Father Grigorii.

38. I know of these cases solely from the notices given of them in the Renovationist press, which often had incomplete or biased information. From this source, we can see how the Renovationist clergy perceived their situation, but we cannot determine how accurate this perception was without archival research on actual cases. Pisiotis's dissertation is based on such research in the synodal archive. He concluded that while many parish clergymen (he suggests as many as half of those of priestly rank) sympathized with, expressed, and even acted on dissident views, relatively few were seriously disciplined by church authorities, at least at the synodal level. For his views on the number of clerical dissidents, see Pisiotis, "Orthodoxy versus Autocracy," 432–39.

39. "Khronika," *Vek* 2 (13 January 1907): 7.

40. "Letopis' tserkovno-obshchestvennoi zhizni," *Zvonar'* (October 1907): 73–74; "Khronika," *Zvonar'* (February 1908): 42. Father Orlov may well have been assigned to another position in the diocese, but this was not reported. Such a transfer might have led to an improved situation or a diminished one, depending on how the metropolitan judged his case. Pisiotis found that state and church authorities often disagreed on whether and how dissident clergy should be punished, with bishops tending to keep priests who had not challenged episcopal authority or the church's laws, despite pressure on the bishops in such cases from central and local authorities to demote or defrock these priests. Pisiotis, "Orthodoxy versus Autocracy," 271–85.

41. "Russkaia tserkov' v 1906," *Tserkovnyi vestnik* 2 (11 January 1907): 43.

42. *Tserkovnyi vestnik* 7 (15 February 1907): 218.

43. Untitled notice, *Vek* 18 (13 May 1907): 267.

44. P. Ternigorev, "Svobodna tserkov' ili krepostnoe pravo," *Zvonar'* (September 1907): 1–8.

45. Notice in *Vek* (17 June 1907): 367.

46. Disorders at the church's schools, widespread and sometimes violent during the revolution, were a significant cause of concern for church authorities. Most of this unrest was displayed at the seminaries, with some incidents at the pre-seminaries. See Leont'eva, "Vera i bunt"; Pisiotis, "Orthodoxy versus Autocracy," 121–29; Freeze, "Crisis and Radicalization," 278–79, and "Between Reform and Reaction: Church, State, and Society on the Eve of Revolution," in *Church, State, and Opposition,* ed. Simon, 10–11.

47. Izvol'skii communicated the goals of the investigation to three of his allies in the hierarchy in letters preserved in: RGIA, f. 797, op. 96, d. 223, "O revizii Peterburgskoi dukhovnoi akademii," ll. 18–23, letters from P. P. Izvol'skii to the archbishop Dmitrii and bishops Germogen and Serafim.

48. There were numerous notices and articles on the school in *Zvonar'/Krasnyi zvon* in 1908 and 1909, many in the current events columns "Khronika" and "Tserkovno-obshchestvennaia zhizn'." Among the more important long articles were "Nauka ili tserkovnost'?" *Krasnyi zvon* (May 1908): 270–72; and A. Gorain, "Bor'ba za akademicheskuiu avtonomiiu," *Krasnyi zvon* (June 1908): 161–75.

49. The repression of the school is described at length in my dissertation: Jennifer Hedda, "Good Shepherds: The St. Petersburg Pastorate and the Emergence of Social Activism in the Russian Orthodox Church" (Ph.D. diss., Harvard University, 1998), 123–46. On the fear that the measures taken against the school would compromise the church's future, see A. Popov, "Nezrimyia tragediia," *Tserkovnoe obnovlenie* 9 (4 March 1907): 67–68. The following critical articles appeared in *Krasnyi zvon:* "O tserkovnoi propovedi" (November 1908): 245–48; "Tserkovnoe obnovlenie" (April 1909): 249–56; D. Filosofov, "Mech' dukhovenstva" (September 1909): 288–92; "Universitety i dukhovnye akademii" (December 1909): 274–77. The journal *Tserkovno-obshchestvennyi vestnik* published: "K voprosu o polozhenii akademicheskikh nastavikov," 16 (25 April 1913): 5–7; V. P. "Pod gnetom novogo ustava," 17 (2 May 1913): 10–11; "Novye akademicheskie professora," 20 (16 May 1914): 6–8; "Nashi bogoslovy," 42 (15 October 1914): 1–2. See also F. B. "Upadok dukhovnoi shkoly," *Prikhodskii sviashchennik* 1 (8 January 1911): 5–6.

50. "S novym godom," *Tserkovnyi vestnik* 1 (4 January 1907): 3–4; "Tserkovnaia platforma pravitel'stva," *Tserkovnyi vestnik* 5 (1 February 1907): 154–56.

51. "Sinod i sobor," *Tserkovnoe obnovlenie* 9 (4 March 1907): 69–70. Firsov emphasizes that the large majority of the bishops strongly supported church reform. Firsov, *Russkaia tserkov',* 183. However, the bishops and the parish clergy generally supported different types of reform, particularly with regard to ecclesiastical administration.

52. "K Soboru," *Vek* 13 (1 April 1907): 154–56; "Letopis' tserkovno-obshchestvennoi zhizni," *Zvonar'* (November 1907): 101; "Khronika," *Krasnyi zvon* (February 1908): 31.

53. "Khronika," 31.

54. "Khronika," *Krasnyi zvon* (January 1909): 191; Grigorii Petrov, "Krugom i okolo," *Krasnyi zvon* (September 1909): 282–84; "Tserkovnoe obnovlenie," *Krasnyi zvon* (August 1909): 236–41.

55. "Sozyv tserkovnogo sobora," *Prikhodskii sviashchennik* 9 (4 March 1912): 1–3.

56. "Nashi zadachi," *Tserkovno-obshchestvennyi vestnik* 1 (1 July 1912): 3–5.

57. "Pravoslavnaia tserkov' v 1912 godu," *Prikhdoskii sviashchennik 1* (January 1913): 4–8. See the following articles from *Tserkovno-obshchestvennyi vestnik:* "K budushchemu soboru," 2 (12 July 1912): 1–3; "Bezsil'noe tvorchestvo," 12 (20 September 1912): 1–2; "Shirokie zamysli i skromnaia deiatel'nost'," 5 (31 January 1913): 1–2; "Tserkovnaia zhizn' v 1913 godu," 1 (2 January 1914): 3–7; "Tserkovnye reformatory," 16 (17 April 1914): 11–13.

58. Gregory Freeze noted that this conference "should be regarded more as an alibi" than a real effort at advancing the cause of church reform. Freeze, "Between Reform and Reaction," 15.

59. Pisiotis found that many clergy were reluctant to express direct criticism of the emperor, though it is difficult to know to what extent this reflected naïve monarchism as opposed to simple pragmatism. "Orthodoxy versus Autocracy," 137–46 and 196–98.

60. Their readiness to reform the church was further demonstrated by how quickly they convened a council once the monarchy had fallen. The long-awaited council finally opened in August of 1917, not quite six months after the revolution that toppled Nicholas II from the throne. Firsov discusses the work of the council in *Russkaia tserkov'*, 536–65. Significant portions of the transcript of the council's discussions are available in James Cunningham, *The Gates of Hell: The Great Sobor of the Russian Orthodox Church, 1917–1918* (Minneapolis, 2002).

61. This question has been the subject of some research: E. V. Fominykh, "Samoderzhavie i vopros o preobrazovanie tserkovnogo prikhoda v 1905–1917 godakh," *Vestnik Leningradskogo universiteta*, seriia 2, *Istoriia, Iazykoznanie, Literaturnovedenie* 4 (October 1986): 86–88; and Freeze, "All Power to the Parish?"

62. Papkov, *Neobkhodymost' obnovleniia*.

63. The most comprehensive source on the fate of parish reform is the enormous file located in RGIA, f. 797, op. 84 (1914), otd. 2, stol 3, No. 396, "O pravoslavnom prikhode." The role of the clergy in the third Duma has been the subject of two articles in Russian: I. Z. Kadson, "Deputaty iz dukhovenstva v III-ei Gosudarstvennoi Dume," *Istoricheskie zapiski* 106 (1981): 302–22; and E. Zamakhova, "Vnedumskaia deiatel'nost' deputatov-sviashchennosluzhitelei III Gosudarstvennoi Dumy," *Vestnik Moskovskogo universiteta*, seriia 8, *Istoriia* 4 (1993): 13–23. Firsov discusses the role of the clerical deputies in the Duma and the relation of the church to the Duma in *Russkaia tserkov'*, 343–88.

64. For the clerical press's view of the prospects for parish reform, see the following articles in *Prikhodskii sviashchennik:* "Proekt prikhoda," 12 (26 March 1911): 1–2; untitled notice, 46 (4 December 1911): 13; and "Reforma prikhoda," 47 (11 December 1911): 1–3. There were numerous articles on the subject in *Tserkovno-obshchestvennyi vestnik*. See A. Sovetov, "O prikhodskoi reforme v sviazi s mysl'iu o neobkhodimosti Sobora," 18 (9 May 1913): 7–9; V. Pravdin, "Sud'by prikhodskoi reformy," 30 (1 August 1913): 1–3; A. Papkov, "Neudachnye sinodal'nye zakonoproekty i meropriiatiia," 46 (21 November 1913): 3–5; N. Zaozerskii, "Sredotochie okolo khrama," 47 (28 November 1913): 1–3; "Prichiny zaderzhki prikhodskoi reformy," 2 (9 January 1914): 5–7; "Preobrazovanie prikhoda," 6 (6 February 1914): 1–3; "Prikhodskaia reforma," 29 (15 July 1914): 2–4.

65. Soiuz 17 oktiabria, *Prikhodskii vopros v chetvertoi gosudarstvennoi Dume* (Spb, 1914); *Zakonodatel'nyi otdel Kantseliariia Gosudarstvennoi Dumy, Spravka po voprosu o preobrazovanii pravoslavnogo prikhoda* (Petrograd, 1915).

66. In the spring of 1917 the Synod approved a new temporary rule for the parishes that was remarkably simple and straightforward: Sviateishii Pravitel'stvuiushchii Sinod, *Vremennoe polozhenie o pravoslavnom prikhode* (Petrograd, 1917). Also of interest is A. A. Papkov, *Besedy o pravoslavnom prikhode* (Petrograd, 1917). However, preliminary discussions of the parish issue at the all-Russian church council that was finally convened in August of 1917 indicate that significant controversy on this issue continued to exist.

67. Although support for the autocracy was frequently associated in the public mind (and the traditional historiography) with the episcopate, further study has disproved this connection. See Michael Agursky, "Caught in a Cross Fire: The Russian Church between Holy Sinod and Radical Right," *Orientalia christiana periodica* 50 (1984): 163–96; Freeze, "Crisis and Radicalization," 270–78; Pisiotis, "The Orthodox Clergy and the Radical Right." Moreover, some clergymen famously associated with the Right were not bishops: Father Ioann of Kronstadt and Father Ioann Vostorgov of Moscow were both priests; the arkhimandrite Iliodor (Trufanov) was a member of the monastic clergy, but not a bishop. Pisiotis argues persuasively that clergy who became active in the Right after the revolution had concerns and motivations similar to those who were active in the Left during the revolution, "Orthodoxy versus Autocracy," 545–47.

68. *Otchet o deiatel'nosti Obshchestva za 1912*, 216. The ORRP's records do not indicate why donations fell off so precipitously. The decline might have reflected the economic impact of the revolution, or perhaps donations were directed to more localized church-based organizations or to secular voluntary societies.

69. *Otchet o deiatel'nosti Obshchestva za 1910*, 30; see also the appendix to the report, which lists the members.

70. Ibid.

71. *Otchet o deiatel'nosti Obshchestva za 1912*, 34.

72. *Otchet o deiatel'nosti Obshchestva za 1910*, 126; *Otchet o deiatel'nosti Obshchestva za 1912*, 173. Recall that pre-revolutionary attendance had numbered more than two million over the course of a year at dozens of locations.

73. This development challenges Herrlinger's claim that St. Petersburg workers became alienated from the church after the revolution because the ORRP failed to address their class-based concerns. Herrlinger, "Class, Piety, and Politics," 441–59.

74. *Otchet o deiatel'nosti Obshchestva za 1912*, 176.

75. *Otchet o deiatel'nosti Obshchestva za 1912*, 83.

76. Herlihy explains these divisions with insight and sympathy in *Alcoholic Empire*, especially chaps. 3, 5, and 7.

77. Patricia Herlihy, "Strategies of Sobriety," 14–15.

78. Arkhimandrit Mikhail, "Religiozno-filosofskoe dvizhenie poslednego goda i blizhaishchego budushchego," *Krasnyi zvon* (February 1908): 1–6.

79. The most successful of these short-lived publications was *Prikhodskii sviashchennik*, which supported itself through advertising everything from guns to rat poison to hair-growth products to its clerical audience. It still lasted barely two years, even after shifting from a weekly to a monthly publishing schedule.

80. M. Pospelov, "Obshchestvo i dukhovenstvo," *Zvonar'* (February 1907): 1–17; Filosofov, "Russkaia Tserkov' v 1908 g.," 281–82.

81. "Reformy v tserkvi," *Tserkovno-obshchestvennyi vestnik* 7 (16 August 1912): 1–2; "Gosudarstvennaia Duma i tserkovnye voprosy," *Tserkovno-obshchestvennyi vestnik* 41 (17 October 1913): 9–10.

82. "Khronika," *Krasnyi zvon* (September 1908): 201. The journal worried about the apathy of the clergy: "Tserkovno-obshchestvennaia zhizn'," *Krasnyi zvon* (April 1909): 220–21.

83. Mikhail was secretly ordained in November of 1908 by Innokentii, the Old Believer bishop of Nizhnii Novgorod, who had converted Mikhail. The ordination was uncanonical, and after it became known he and bishop Innokentii were both suspended from their duties in 1909. Innokentii was restored to his position a few months later, but Mikhail was not because he refused to accept the conditions the Old Believer council imposed on him. The suspension remained in force until Mikhail's death in 1916, when it was lifted in order to permit his burial as a bishop in the main Old Believer cemetery in Moscow. Comer, "Evolution," 8–9.

84. G. M. Karabinovich, ed., *Sobranie statei po delu episkopa Mikhaila Kanadskogo* (Moscow, 1914), 96–98.

85. Ibid., 101–3.

86. Ibid., 65–66.

87. Vladimir, mitropolit Moskovskii i Kolomenskii, *O rabochem voprose* (Moscow, 1909). This was a published version of a speech the metropolitan gave on 3 June 1907 for the Commission on Readings for the Workers at the Moscow Historical Museum; see also his work *Nasha pastyrskaia zadacha v bor'be s sotsial-demokraticheskoi propagandoiu* (Moscow, 1909).

88. Episkop Mikhail, "Besedy s chitatel'iami," *Staroobriadcheskaia mysl'* 7 (July 1910): 415–19; Karabinovich, *Sobranie statei*, 70. Mikhail explicitly rejected the claim that human suffering had a redemptive function, either for those who endured it or for others around them.

89. Episkop Mikhail, "Kopeika Davida Leizera," *Staroobriadcheskaia mysl'* 1 (January 1910): 6–8.

90. Karabinovich, *Sobranie statei*, 93.

91. Ibid. Mikhail's belief in the redemptive power of the voluntary suffering of innocents for the sins of others and in collective salvation echo the views of Feodor Dostoevsky, particularly as expressed in *The Brothers Karamazov*.

92. Episkop Mikhail, "Khristianstvo ne moral'," *Staroobriadcheskaia mysl'* 6 (June 1910): 321–25. The title of this article stated his response to Leo Tolstoy, who rejected the theological content of Christianity while embracing its moral teachings.

93. Karabinovich, *Sobranie statei*, 2–20.

94. In the course of a journey to the capital for treatment, he wandered away from his caretaker into a stable used by a group of Moscow cabdrivers, who beat him severely in the mistaken belief that he was a thief. He was taken to a local hospital, where he died of blood poisoning. Ostanina, "Obnovlenchestvo," 130; Comer, "Evolution," 11–12.

95. Daniel Peris found that a significant number of anti-religious activists under the Bolsheviks were former priests, many of whom had been dissidents during the tsarist period. See Peris, "Commissars in Red Cassocks: Former Priests in the League of the Militant Godless," *Slavic Review* 64, no. 2 (1995): 340–44. Roslof argues more specifically that there was a strong connection between frustration with the failure of church reform in the pre-1917 period and the conversion of some clergymen to Renovationism after 1917: Roslof, *Red Priests*, 10.

96. B. V. Titlinov, *Pravoslavie na sluzhbe samoderzhaviia* (Leningrad, 1924).

97. Father Alexander also wrote a scathingly critical history of the established church: A. I. Vvedenskii, *Tserkov' i gosudarstvo* (Moscow, 1923).

98. Some of his writings suggest that he was familiar with the ideas of the Golgotha Christians: M. V. Galkin, "Dumy o pastyrstve," *Prikhodskii sviashchennik* 3 (22 January 1911): 5–6, and "Tragediia pastyrstve," *Prikhodskii sviashchennik* 39 (30 September 1911): 3–4. For details on Galkin's career as a Bolshevik, see Peris, "Commissars," 345–48. Galkin wrote under the revolutionary pseudonym of M. Gorev, authoring the polemical work *Poslednii sviatoi. Poslednie dni Romanovskoi tserkvi, kanonizatsionnyi protsess Ioanna Tobol'skogo* (Moscow-Leningrad, 1928), which strongly criticized the synodal church, though not Orthodoxy more generally.

99. "Mnenie i otzyvy," *Tserkovnyi vestnik* 1 (4 January 1907): 11–14.

100. P. S., "Nepravil'nost' polozheniia," *Tserkovnyi golos* 11 (16 March 1907): 305–8; P. L——skii, "Rol' pastyria v sovremennoi obshchestvennoi zhizni," *Zvonar'* (October 1907): ch. 2, pp. 7–10.

101. "O krestianskikh kreditnykh tovarishchestvakh i ob uchastii dukhovenstva v delakh ikh," *Krasnyi zvon* (January 1908): 155–57.

102. B. N., "Sovremenniia zadachi dukhovenstva," *Krasnyi zvon* (January 1908): 137–40.

103. "Chto nuzhno dlia sovremennykh pastyrei?" *Krasnyi zvon* (January 1908): 116–19; "Stesnitel'nyia usloviia pastyrskogo sluzheniia," *Krasnyi zvon* (January 1908): 158–60.

104. "Pastyrskaia obshitel'nost' i samodeiatel'nost dukhovenstva," *Krasnyi zvon* (November 1908): 241–45.

105. "Pravoslavnaia Tserkov' v 1912 godu," *Prikhodskii sviashchennik* 1 (January 1913): 7–8. This journal also published two articles by the younger Galkin in which he argued that reform would be achieved by the clergy working in their parishes. M. Galkin, "Ot liubvi" (January 1913): 13–21, and "K chemu nas ob"iazyvaet tekushchii moment" (April 1913): 599–612.

106. M. Kliatskii, "K voprosu o tserkovnykh reformakh," *Tserkovno-obshchestvennyi vestnik* 31 (31 July 1914): 11–14.

107. Freeze, "Crisis and Radicalization," 269–71.

CONCLUSION

1. For a striking example, see the press report on the 10th World Council of Russian People, held in April 2006: Victor Yasmann, "The Orthodox Church and the Kremlin's New Mission," Radio Free Europe/Radio Liberty, 10 April 2006, accessed 15 January 2007 at http://www.rferl.org/featuresarticle/2006/04/9768f306-a076-429f-802c-07f591fc6417.html.

2. "Introduction of Religious Curriculum Studied," Radio Free Europe/Radio Liberty, 7 September 2006, accessed on 15 January 2007 at http://www.rferl.org/featuresarticle/2006/09/e021de9a-947a-424d-ad46-0f825a39a8c3.html.

3. Yakov Krotov, "Interpretative biography of Alexander Men'," accessed on 14 January 2007 at Alan Carmack's website, http://www.krotov.info/engl/Myen.html. Krotov is a church historian and journalist living in Moscow who was baptized by Father Alexander and knew him for seventeen years. Krotov lists a number of individuals who carry on Father Alexander's work and the names of their publications and organizations. See also Father Michael Meerson, "The Life and Work of Father Aleksandr Men'," in *Seeking God: The Recovery of Religious Identity in Orthodox Russia, Ukraine, and Georgia,* ed. Stephen K. Batalden (DeKalb, 1993), 13–27.

WORKS CITED

UNPUBLISHED SOURCES

Rossiskii gosudarstvennyi istoricheskii arkhiv (RGIA), St. Petersburg, Russia
Fond 7d 796, Kantseliariia Sv. Sinoda
Opisi 161–195
Opisi 204–205
Opis' 440
Opis' 442
Fond 797, Kantseliariia Ober-prokurora
Opisi 51–86
Fond 799, Khoziastvennye upravleniia Sv. Sinoda
Opis' 19
Fond 802, Uchebnyi komitet Sv. Sinoda
Opis' 10
Fond 834, Rukopisi Sv. Sinoda
Fond 835, Plany i fotografii Sv. Sinoda
Fond 1569, Lichnyi fond Ober-Prokurora P. P. Izvol'skogo
Fond 1574, Lichnyi fond Ober-Prokurora K. P. Pobedonostseva
Fond 1622, Lichnyi fond S. Iu. Vitta

Bakhmeteff Collection, Rare Books and Manuscripts Room, Columbia University Library, New York City, New York
Papers of *protopresvyter* G. I. Shavel'skii, boxes 4–6.

PUBLISHED WORKS

"9–e ianvaria 1905." *Krasnyi arkhiv* 4–5 (1925): 1–25.
"9–e ianvaria 1905." *Voprosy zhizni* 1 (1905): 329–38.
"9 ianvaria v Peterburge." *Krasnyi arkhiv* 1 (1930): 3–19.
250 let Sankt-Peterburgskoi eparkhii. Spb: Tip. S. Peterburgskogo mitropolita, 1992.
Aggeev, K. *Istoricheskii grekh.* Biblioteka *Vek*, no. 4. Spb: [n.p.], 1907
Agursky, Michael. "Caught in a Cross Fire: The Russian Church between Holy Sinod and Radical Right." *Orientalia christiana periodica* 50 (1984): 163–96.
Aivazov, I. G. *Obnovlentsy i starotserkovniki. V nedrakh tserkovno-obshchestvennykh nastroenii nashego vremeni.* Moscow: Russkaia pechatnia, 1909.
Aksakov, A. P., ed. *Bratskaia zhizn'. Sbornik statei o vozrozhdenii russkoi zhizni.* 6 vols. Spb: M. P. Frolov, 1910–1911.
Akvilonov, E. *Khristianstvo i sotsial-demokratiia v otnoshenii k sovremennym sobytiiam.* Spb: M. Merkushev, 1906.
Aleksandr, ieromonakh. "O literaturnoi propovedi sv. Grigoriia Petrova." *Missionerskoe obozrenie* 6 (1903): 753–69.
Alfavitnyi ukazatel' k zhurnalam i protokolam zasedanii Vysochaishie uchrezhdennogo predsobornogo prisutstviia. Spb: Sinodal'naia Tipografiia, 1909.
Alston, Patrick L. *Education and the State in Tsarist Russia.* Stanford: Stanford University Press, 1969.
Anderson, Margaret Lavinia. "The Limits of Secularization: On the Problem of Catholic Revival in Nineteenth-Century Germany." *The Historical Journal* 38, no. 3 (1995): 647–80.

Andreev, V. M. "Liberal'no-obnovlencheskoe dvizhenie v russkom pravoslavii nachala XX veka i ego ideologiia." Kand. diss., Gosudarstvennyi pedagogicheskii institut im. Gertsena, 1972. Avtoreferat.

Antonii (Amfiteatrov). *Pastyrskoe bogoslovie.* Kiev: Tip. Kievsko-Pecherskoi Lavry, 1851.

Antonii (Khrapovitskii), mitropolit Kievskii i Galitskii. *Nravstvennie idei vazhneishikh khristianskikh pravoslavnykh dogmatov.* Edited by Bishop Nikon (Rklitskii). New York: Izd. Severo-Amerikanskoi i kanadskoi eparkhii, 1963.

———. "Prikhodskii sovet i vybornoe dukhovenstvo." *Vera i tserkov'* 1: no. 2 (1906): 316–26.

———. *Uchenie o pastyre, pastyrstve, i ob ispovedi.* Edited by Bishop Nikon (Rklitskii). New York: Izd. Severo-Amerikanskoi i kanadskoi eparkhii, 1966.

Antonii (Vadkovskii), mitropolit S. Peterburgskii i Ladozhskii. *Iz istorii khristianskoi propovedi. Ocherki i issledovaniia.* 2nd ed. Spb: A. L. Katanskii, 1895.

———. *Rechi, slova, i poucheniia.* 2nd ed. Spb: Sinodal'naia Tipografiia, 1901.

Antonov, V. V., and A. V. Kobak. *Sviatyni Sankt-Peterburga. Khristianskaia istoriko-tserkovnaia entsiklopediia.* Spb: Liki Rossii, 2003.

Asov, T. "Otritsateli zhizni." *Tserkovnoe obnovlenie* 8 (25 February 1907): 57–58.

Avidonov, N. "9 ianvaria 1905 i Sinod." *Byloe* 1 (1925): 51–57.

———. "Gapon v dukhovnoi akademii." *Byloe* 1 (1925): 46–50.

Barnes, Andrew. "The Social Transformation of the French Parish Clergy, 1500–1800." In *Culture and Identity in Early Modern Europe (1500–1800): Essays in Honor of Natalie Zemon Davis,* edited by Barbara B. Diefendorf and Carla Hesse, 139–58. Ann Arbor: University of Michigan Press, 1993.

Barsov, N. I. *Istoriia pervobytnoi khristianskoi propovedi do IV-ogo veka.* Spb: S. Dobrodeev, 1885.

———. "O vozmozhnykh ulushcheniiakh v sovremennoi nashei tserkovnoi propovedi." *Khristianskoe chtenie* (1894): pt. 1, 174–75.

Barsov, N. V. *Neskol'ko issledovanii istoricheskikh i razsuzhdenii o voprosakh sovremennykh.* Spb: M. M. Stasiulevich, 1899.

Barsov, T. V. *Iz sbornika deistvuiushchikh i rukovodstvennykh tserkovnykh i tserkovno-grazhdanskikh postanovlenii po vedomstvu pravoslavnogo ispovedeniia. Glava 40, O prikhodskikh popechitel'stvakh pri pravoslavnykh tserkvakh.* Moscow: N. I. Kumanin, 1896.

Basil, John D. "Imperial Russia's Canonists and the Issue of Church and State." In *New Perspectives in Modern Russian History: Selected Papers from the Fourth World Congress for Soviet and East European Studies, Harrowgate, 1990,* edited by Robert B. McKean, 65–79. New York: St. Martin's Press, 1992.

———. "K. P. Pobedonostsev and the Harmonious Society." *Canadian-American Slavic Studies* 37, no. 4 (Winter 2003): 415–26.

———. "Konstantin Petrovich Pobedonostsev: An Argument for a Russian State Church." *Church History* 64, no. 1 (1995): 44–61.

———. "Revolutionary Leadership and the Russian Orthodox Church in 1917." *Church History* 48, no. 2 (1979): 189–203.

Batalden, Stephen K. "The British and Foreign Bible Society's St. Petersburg Agency and Russian Biblical Translation, 1856–1875." In *Sowing the Word: The Cultural Impact of the British and Foreign Bible Society, 1804–2004,* edited by Stephen K. Batalden, Kathleen Cann, and John Dean, 169–96. Sheffield, England: Phoenix Press, 2004.

———, ed. *Seeking God: The Recovery of Religious Identity in Orthodox Russia, Ukraine, and Georgia.* DeKalb: Northern Illinois University Press, 1993.

Bater, James. *St. Petersburg: Industrialization and Change.* Montreal: McGill-Queen's University Press, 1976.

Bauberot, Jean. *Un Christianisme Profan? Royaume de Dieu, Socialisme, et Modernité Culturelle dans le périodique 'chrétian-social' L'Avant-Garde (1899–1911).* Paris: Presses universitaires de France, 1978.

Bazarov, I. I. "Vospominaniia protoiereia." *Russkaia starina* 105 (1901): 283–304, 521–28; 106 (1901): 53–75, 277–306, 497–522; 107 (1901): 77–96, 241–66, 531–44; 108 (1901): 85–100, 271–91, 533–60.

Bedford, Harold. *The Seeker: D. S. Merezhkovskiy.* Wichita: University of Kansas Press, 1975.

Belliustin, I. S. *Description of the Clergy in Rural Russia: The Memoir of a Nineteenth-Century Parish Priest.* Translated with an interpretive essay by Gregory L. Freeze. Ithaca, NY: Cornell University Press, 1985.

Benzin, V. M. *Tserkovno-prikhodskaia blagotvoritel'nost' na Rusi.* Spb: Gosudarstvennaia Tipografiia, 1907.

Berdiaev, N. *Dukhovnyi krizis intelligentsiia. Stat'i po obshchestvennoi i religioznoi psikhologii, 1907–1909.* Spb: Obshchestvennaia pol'za, 1910.

———. *Novoe religioznoe soznanie i obshchestvennost'.* Spb: M. V. Pirozhkov, 1907.

Berdnikov, I. *Chto nuzhno dlia obnovleniia pravoslavnogo russkogo prikhoda?* Spb: Sinodal'-naia Tipografiia, 1907.

Biograficheskii slovar' studentov Imperatorskoi Petrogradskoi Dukhovnoi Akademii, nachinaia s XXIX kurs vypuska 1871 goda. Prilozhenie, *Pamiatnaia knizhka za 1915 god Obshchestva dukhovnoi i material'noi vzaimopomoshchi byvshikh pitomtsev Imperatorskoi Petrogradskoi Dukhovnoi Akademii.* Petrograd: M. Merkushev, 1916.

Biriukov, E. *Nazidatel'nye rasskazy iz zhizni pravoslavnykh russkikh arkhipastyrei i pastyrei.* Kamylov [Elizavetograd province]: Tip. N. P. Bushevoi, 1905.

Blagorazumov, N. *K voprosu o vozrozhdenii pravoslavnogo russkogo prikhoda i obnovleniia tserkovno-obshchestvennoi zhizni v nem.* Moscow: M. Borisenko, 1904.

Blagovidov, F. V. *K rabote obshchestvennoi mysli o tserkovnom reforme.* Kazan: Tsentral'naia Tipografiia, 1905.

Bogolepov, A. A. "Church Reforms in Russia, 1905–1918." *St. Vladimir's Seminary Quarterly* 10, no. 1 (1966): 12–66.

Bogoliubov, D. I. *Religiozno-obshchestvennye techeniia v sovremennoi russkoi zhizni i nashe pravoslavno-khristianskaia missiia.* Spb: I. V. Leont'ev, 1909.

Bogoslovskie trudy. Sbornik, posviashchennyi 175–letno Leningradskoi Dukhovnoi Akademii. Moscow: Moskovskaia Patriarkhiia, 1986.

Bohachevsky-Chomiak, Martha. "'Christian' vs. 'Neophyte': Opposition to the Formation of a Christian Party in Russia." *Russian History* 4, no. 2 (1977): 105–21.

Boldovskii, A. V. *Vozrozhdenie tserkovnogo prikhoda.* Spb: Sinodal'naia tipografiia, 1903.

Bowen, Desmond. *The Idea of the Victorian Church: A Study of the Church of England, 1833–1889.* Montreal: McGill University Press, 1968.

Bozherianov, I. N. *Lavry, monastyrii, i khramy na Sviatoi Rusi, S. Peterburgskoi eparkhii.* Spb: Tip. Uchilishcha Glukhovemykh Vedomstva Uchrezhdenii Imperatritsy Marii, 1908.

Brackett, Jeffrey R. *Social Service through the Parish.* New York: The National Council, 1923.

Bradley, Joseph. "Subjects into Citizens: Societies, Civil Society, and Autocracy in Tsarist Russia." *American Historical Review* Vol. 107 (October 2002): 1094–123.

Broiarskii, S. S. "Tserkovno-prikhodskaia zhizni na novykh nachalakh." *Zvonar'* (May-June 1906): 234–37.

Bronzov, A. A. "Vospominaniia. Protopresviter Ioann Leont'evich Ianyshev." *Trezvye vskhody,* nos. 7–10 (1910): 1–108.

Brooks, Jeffrey. *When Russia Learned to Read: Literacy and Popular Literature, 1861–1917.* Princeton: Princeton University Press, 1985.

Brower, Daniel R. *The Russian City between Tradition and Modernity, 1850–1900.* Berkeley: University of California Press, 1990.

Bukhbinder, N. A. "Iz zhizni G. A. Gapona." *Krasnaia letopis'* 1 (1922): 101–5.

———."K istorii 'Sobraniia russkikh fabrichno-zavodskikh rabochikh goroda S. Peterburga.' Arkhivnye dokumenty." *Krasnaia letopis'* 1 (1922): 288–329.

Bulgakov, Sergii N. *Avtobiograficheskie zametki.* Edited by A. A. Zander. Paris: YMCA Press, 1946.

———. *The Orthodox Church.* Translation revised by Lydia Kesich. Crestwood, NY: St. Vladimir's Seminary Press, 1988.

———. "Social Teaching in Modern Russian Orthodox Theology." Twentieth Annual Hale Memorial Sermon, 7 November 1934. Evanston, IL: Seabury-Western Theological Seminary, 1934.

Bulgakovskii, D. G. *Rol' pravoslavnogo dukhovenstva v bor'be s narodnym p'ianstvom.* Spb: P. I. Soikin, 1900.

Byrnes, Robert F. *Pobedonostsev: His Life and Thought.* Bloomington: Indiana University Press, 1968.

Carlson, Maria. *No Religion Higher Than Truth: A History of the Theosophical Movement in Russia, 1875–1922.* Princeton: Princeton University Press, 1993.

Chadwick, Owen. *The Victorian Church.* 2 vols. London: Adam and Charles Black, 1970.

Chel'tsov, M. P. "Khristianstvo i politika." *Khristianskoe chtenie* (March 1906): 415–36.

———. "Pravoslavnoe pastyrstvo i obshchestvennaia deiatel'nost'." *Khristianskoe chtenie* (May 1906): 735–46 and (June 1906): 878–88.

———. *Sushchnost' tserkovnogo obnovleniia.* Biblioteka *Vek,* no. 3. Spb: [n.p.], 1907.

Chetyrkin, F. V. *Minuvshiia sud'by Peterburgskogo kraia.* Spb: P. P. Soikin, 1903.

Chistovich, I. S. *Istoriia S. Peterburgskoi Dukhovnoi Akademii.* Spb: Iakov Trei, 1857.

———. *Peterburgskaia Dukhovnaia Akademiia za posledniia 30 let (1858–1888).* Spb: Sinodal'naia Tipografiia, 1889.

Christian, David. *Living Water: Vodka and Russian Society on the Eve of Emancipation.* Oxford: Clarendon Press, 1990.

Chrysostomus, Johannes. "Die russische Orthodoxie angesichts der zeitgenossichen sozialen Stromungen am Vorabend der Revolution von 1917." *Ostkirchliche Studien* 17, no. 4 (1968): 297–314.

Chulos, Chris. *Converging Worlds: Religion and Community in Peasant Russia, 1861–1917.* DeKalb: Northern Illinois University Press, 2003.

———. "Myths of the Pious or Pagan Peasant in Post-Emancipation Russia (Voronezh Province)." *Russian History* 22, no. 2 (Summer 1995): 181–216.

———. "Peasant Perspectives on Clerical Debauchery in Post-Emancipation Russia." *Studia Slavica Finlandensia* (1995): 33–53.

———. "Peasant Religion in Post-Emancipation Russia: Voronezh Province, 1880–1917." Ph.D. diss., University of Chicago, 1994.

———. "Revolution and Grass-Roots Re-evaluations of Russian Orthodoxy: Parish Clergy and Peasants of Voronezh Province, 1905–1917." In *Transforming Peasants: State, Society, and the Peasantry, 1860–1930. Selected Papers from the Fifth World Congress of Central and East European Studies,* edited by Judith Pallott, 113–29. New York: St. Martin's Press, 1998.

Clark, Katerina. *Petersburg: Crucible of Cultural Revolution.* Cambridge: Harvard University Press, 1995.

Clay, Eugene. "The Theological Origins of the Christ-Faith." *Russian History* 15, no. 1 (1988): 21–41.

Clayton, Dennis R. "Parish or Publish: The Kiev Ecclesiastical Academy, 1819–1869." Ph.D. diss., University of Minnesota, 1978.

Clendenin, Daniel B. *Eastern Orthodox Christianity: A Western Perspective.* Grand Rapids, MI: Baker Books, 1994.

Coleman, Heather J. "Defining Heresy: The Fourth Missionary Congress and Cultural Power after 1905 in Russia." *Jahrbucher für Geschichte Osteuropas* 52, no. 1 (2004): 70–91.

Confino, Michael. "Present Events and the Representation of the Past: Some Current Problems in Russian Historical Writing." *Cahiers du monde russe* 35, no. 4 (1994): 839–68.

Cracraft, James. *The Ecclesiastical Reforms of Peter the Great.* Stanford: Stanford University Press, 1971.

Crowther, M. A. *The Church Embattled: Religious Controversy in Mid-Victorian England.* Hamden: Archon Books, 1970.

Crummey, R. O. "Old Belief as Popular Religion: New Approaches." *Slavic Review* 52, no. 4 (1993): 700–712.

Cunningham, James W. *The Gates of Hell: The Great Sobor of the Russian Orthodox Church.* Minneapolis: University of Minnesota Press, 2002.

———. "Reform Projects of the Russian Orthodox Church at the Beginning of the Twentieth Century." In *The Legacy of St. Vladimir,* edited by J. Breck, J. Meyendorff, and E. Silk, 107–138. Crestwood, NY: St. Vladimir's Seminary Press, 1990.

———. *A Vanquished Hope: The Movement for Church Renewal in Russia, 1905–1906.* Crestwood, NY: St. Vladimir's Seminary Press, 1981.

Curtiss, John S. *Church and State in Russia: The Last Years of the Empire, 1900–1917.* New York: Columbia University Press, 1940.

D—n, I. "Prikhodskaia zhizn' pri Blagoveshchenskoi Vasileostrovskoi tserkvi s 1862 do 1912 goda." Spb: Obshchestvennaia pol'za, 1912.

Daly, Jonathan W. *Autocracy Under Siege: Security Police and Opposition in Russia, 1866–1905.* DeKalb: Northern Illinois University Press, 1998.

Davis, Robert H. "Nineteenth-Century Russian Religious-Theological Journals: Structure and Access." *St. Vladimir's Seminary Quarterly* 33, no. 3 (1989): 235–59.

Derzhavin, N. "Pastyrskoe sluzhenie v russkoi pravoslavnoi tserkvi v XX veke." Kandidatskoe sochinenie, Leningradskaia Dukhovnaia Akademiia, Leningrad, 1988.

Direction générale de l'économie locale du Ministère de l'intérieur. *L'assistance publique et privée en Russie.* St. Petersburg: Académie Impériale des Sciences, 1906.

Dixon, Simon. "Church, State, and Society in Late Imperial Russia: The Diocese of St. Petersburg, 1880–1914." Ph.D. diss., University of London, 1990.

———. "How Holy was Holy Russia? Rediscovering Russian Religion." In *Reinterpreting Russia,* edited by Geoffrey Hosking and Robert Service, 21–39. New York: Oxford University Press, 1999.

———. "The Orthodox Church and the Workers of St. Petersburg, 1880–1914." In *European Religion in the Age of Great Cities, 1830–1930,* edited by Hugh McLeod, 119–41. London: Routledge, 1995.

Dmitriev, D. "Kak ia stal sviashchennikom." Sergiev Posad: Tip. Sviato-Troitskoi Lavry, 1908.

Dmitriev, P. M. *Obshchestvo vspomozheniia bednym prikhoda tserkvi Pokrova Presviatiia Bogoroditsy, chto v Bolshoi Kolomne v gorode S. Peterburge, 1871–1911.* Spb: A. M. Medelevich, 1912.

Dmitrievskii, A. *Lichnye vospominaniia o mitropolite Peterburgskom Antonii kak uchitele i sosluzhivetse.* Petrograd: Obshchestva rasprostraneniia religiozno-nravstvennogo prosveshcheniia, 1916.

Dobroklonskii, A. *Rukovodstvo po istorii russkoi tserkvi.* 4 vols. Moscow: Universitetskaia Tipografiia, 1893.

Dobronravov, I. *Sobesednik pastyria. Pastyrskiia stat'i i zametki po voprosam poslednego vremeni.* Saransk [Penza province]: Tip. Brat'ev Syromiatnikovykh, 1906.

Dobrovol'skii, G. *Znachenie kreditnykh tovarishchestva v dele otrezvleniia naroda i uchastie v nem dukhovenstva.* Spb: Tip. Aleksandr-Nevskogo Obshchestva, 1910.

Dobrovol'skii, I. *Spravochnaia kniga dlia pravoslavnogo dukhovenstva.* Spb: I. L. Sytin, 1898.

The Doctrine of the Russian Church, Being the Primer or Spelling Book, the Shorter and Longer Catechisms, and a Treatise on the Duty of Parish Priests. Translated by the Rev. R. W. Blackmore. London: Joseph Masters, 1845.

"Doklad direktora departmenta politsii Lopukhina Ministry Vnutrennykh Del o sobytiiakh 9–ogo ianvaria." *Krasnaia letopis'* 1 (1922): 330–38.

Dolling, Robert R. *Ten Years in a Portsmouth Slum*. London: Swan Sonnenschein and Co., 1896.

Durnovo, N. N. *Kak dolzhen byt' ustroen prikhod*. Moscow: Tip. Shtaba Moskovskogo voennogo okruga, 1906.

Edwards, David W. "Orthodoxy during the Reign of Tsar Nicholas I: A Study in Church-State Relations." Ph.D. diss., Kansas State University, 1967.

Eklof, Ben. *Russian Peasant Schools: Officialdom, Village Culture, and Popular Pedagogy, 1861–1914*. Berkeley: University of California Press, 1986.

———. *School and Society in Tsarist and Soviet Russia: Selected Papers from the Fourth World Congress for Soviet and East European Studies, Harrowgate, 1990*. New York: St. Martin's Press, 1993.

Ekzempliarskii, V. *Evangelie i obshchestvennaia zhizn'*. Kiev: I. N. Kushnerov, 1913.

Elashevich, I. Ia. "Iz istorii kontrrevoliutsionnoi deiatel'nosti pravoslavnoi tserkvi na Putilovskom zavode." *Antireligioznik* 6 (1933): 7–11.

Ellis, Jane. *The Russian Orthodox Church: A Contemporary History*. London: Croom Helm, 1986.

Engelstein, Laura. "The Dream of a Civil Society in Tsarist Russia: Law, State, and Religion." In *Civil Society before Democracy*, edited by Nancy Bermeo and Philip Nord, 23–41. Lanham, MD: Rowman and Littlefield, 2000.

———. "Holy Russia in Modern Times: An Essay on Orthodoxy and Cultural Change." *Past and Present* 17, no. 3 (November 2001): 129–56.

———. "Paradigms, Pathologies, and Other Clues to Russian Spiritual Culture: Some Post-Soviet Thoughts." *Slavic Review* 57, no. 4 (Winter 1998): 864–77.

———. "Rebels of the Soul: Peasant Self-Fashioning in a Religious Key." *Russian History* 23 (1996): 197–213.

Eparkhial'noe bratstvo vo imia Preosviashchennoi Bogoroditsy. *Vnebogosluzhebniia besedy pastyria s pasomymi*. 3 vols. bound in 1. Spb: P. I. Shmidt, 1890–1894.

Evdokim, ([Meshcherskii] archbishop of the Aleutian Islands and North America) arkhiepiskop. "Pastyrsko-prosvetitel'noe bratstvo pri Akademii." In *Po tserkovno-obshchestvennym voprosam*. Vol. 3, *Dobroe proshloe imperatorskoi Moskovskoi Dukhovnoi Akademii*, 268–319. Sergiev Posad: Tip. Sviato-Troitskoi Lavry, 1915.

Evlogii (Georgievskii), mitropolit zapadno-evropeiskii. *Put' moei zhizni. Vospominaniia Mitropolita Evlogii*. Compiled by T. Manukhin. Paris: YMCA Press, 1947.

Evtuhov, Catherine. "Voices from the Provinces: Living and Writing in Nizhnii Novgorod, 1870–1905." *Journal of Popular Culture* 31, no. 4 (Spring 1998): 33–48.

Fedorov, V. A. *Russkaia pravoslavnaia tserkov' i gosudarstvo: sinodal'nyi period, 1700–1917*. Moscow: Russkaia panorama, 2003.

Feodor (Bukharev). *O pravoslavii v otnoshenii k sovremennosti*. Spb: Obshchestvo rasprostraneniia religiozno-nravstvennago prosveshcheniia v dukhe pravoslavnoi tserkvi, 1906.

Fil', A. *Vinoven li sviashchennik G. S. Petrov? Tragediia pravoslavnogo dukhovenstva*. Moscow: I. I. Pashkov, 1907.

Firsov, Sergei. *Russkaia tserkov' nakanune peremen konets 1890x-1918 gg*. Spb: Kruglyi stol po religioznomu obrazovaniiu i diakonii, 2002.

Flindall, R. P. "The Parish Priest in Victorian England." *Church Quarterly Review* 168 (1967): 296–306.

Florovsky, Georges. *Puti russkogo bogosloviia*. Paris: 1937; reprint, Ann Arbor: University Microfilms, 1971.

———. "The Social Problem in the Eastern Orthodox Church." *Journal of Religious Thought* 8, no. 1 (1950–1951): 41–51.

Flynn, James T. *The University Reform of Tsar Alexander I, 1802–1835*. Washington, D. C.: Catholic University of America Press, 1988.

Fominykh, E. V. "Samoderzhavie i vopros o preobrazovanie tserkovnogo prikhoda v 1905–1917 godakh." *Vestnik Leningradskogo Universiteta*. Seriia 2, *Istoriia, Iazykovanie, Literaturnovedenie* 4 (October 1986): 86–88.

Freeze, Gregory L. "All Power to the Parish? The Problems and Politics of Reform in Late Imperial Russia." In *Social Identities in Revolutionary Russia*, edited by Madhavan K. Palat, 174–208. New York: Palgrave, 2001.

———. "A Case of Stunted Anticlericalism: Clergy and Society in Imperial Russia." *European Studies Review* 13 (1983): 177–200.

———. "Counter-reformation in Russian Orthodoxy: Popular Response to Religious Innovation, 1922–1925." *Slavic Review* 64, no, 2 (1995): 305–39.

———. "Family Crisis in Late Imperial Russia: Divorce, Reform, and Institutional Crisis." Paper delivered at the Historians' Seminar, Russian Research Center, Harvard University, on 17 March 1994.

———. "Going to the Intelligentsia: The Church and its Urban Mission in Post-Reform Russia." In *Between Tsar and People: Educated Society and the Quest for Public Identity in Late Imperial Russia*, edited by Edith W. Clowes, Samuel D. Kassow, and James L. West, 215–32. Princeton: Princeton University Press, 1991.

———. "Handmaiden of the State? The Church in Imperial Russia Reconsidered." *Journal of Ecclesiastic History* 36, no. 1 (1985), 82–102.

———. "The Orthodox Church and Serfdom in Prereform Russia." *Slavic Review* 43, no. 3 (1989): 361–87.

———. *The Parish Clergy in Nineteenth-Century Russia*. Princeton: Princeton University Press, 1983

———. "A Pious Folk? Religious Observance in Vladimir Diocese, 1900–1914." *Jahrbucher für Geschichte Osteuropas* 54, no. 3 (2004): 323–40.

———. "The Rechristianization of Russia: The Church and Popular Religion, 1750–1850." *Studia Slavica Finlandensia* 7 (1990): 101–36.

———. *The Russian Levites*. Cambridge: Harvard University Press, 1977.

———. "A Social Mission for Russian Orthodoxy: The Kazan Requiem of 1861 for the Peasants in Bezdna." In *Imperial Russia, 1700–1917: State, Society, Opposition*, edited by Ezra Mendelsohn and Marshall S. Shatz, 113–35. Dekalb: Northern Illinois University Press, 1988.

———. "The Stalinist Assault on the Parish, 1929–1941." In *Stalinismus vor dem Zweiten Weltkrieg. Neue Wege der Forschung*, edited by Manfred Hildermeier. pp. 209–32. Schriften des Historischen Kollegs, Kolloquien 43. Munich: Oldernbourg, 1996.

———. "Subversive Piety: Religion and Political Crisis in Late Imperial Russia." *Journal of Modern History* 68 (1996): 308–50.

———. "Tserkov', religiia, i politicheskaia kul'tura na zakate staroi Rossii." *Istoriia SSSR* 1 (1991): 107–19.

Frieden, Nancy Mandelker. *Russian Physicians in an Era of Reform and Revolution, 1856–1905*. Princeton: Princeton University Press, 1981.

Fudel', I. *K reforme prikhodskikh popechitel'stv*. Moscow: Universitetskaia tipografiia, 1894.

———. *Osnovy tserkovno-prikhodskoi zhizni*. 2nd ed. Moscow: Universitetskaia tipografiia, 1894.

Gagarin, I. S. *The Russian Clergy*. Translated by Ch. du Gard Makepeace. London, 1872. With a new introduction and bibliography by Gregory Freeze. Newtonville, MA: Oriental Research Partners, 1976.

[Galkin], M. V. *Antonii, Mitropolit S. Peterburgskii i Ladozhskii*. Spb: Obshchestvo rasprostraneniia religiozno-nravstvennogo prosveshcheniia, 1915.

Gapon, George. *Istoriia moei zhizni*. Edited by A. A. Shilov. Leningrad: Rabochee izdatel'stvo Priboi, 1925.

———. *Ot sv. Georgiia Gapona ko vsemu krestianskomu liudu vozzvanie*. [St. Petersburg? 1905].

———. *Poslanie k russkomu krestianskomu i rabochemu narodu ot Georgiia Gapona*. [St. Petersburg?]: Gruppa Russkikh Anarkho-Kommunistov, 1905.

———. *The Story of My Life*. New York: E. P. Dutton, 1906.

Gaut, Greg. "Christian Politics: Vladimir Solovyov's Social Gospel Theology." *Modern Greek Studies Yearbook* 10/11 (1994–1995): 653–74.

———. "A Christian Westernizer: Vladimir Solovyov and Russian Conservative Nationalism." Ph.D. diss., University of Minnesota, 1992.

Geekie, John H. M. "The Church and Politics in Russia, 1905–1917: A Study of the Political Behavior of the Russian Orthodox Clergy in the Reign of Nicholas II." Ph.D. diss., University of East Anglia, 1976.

Geifman, Anna, ed. *Russia under the Last Tsar: Opposition and Subversion, 1894–1917.* New York: Blackwell Publishers, 1999.

Geno, A. *K 200–letiiu S. Peterburga. Danniia o Peterburgskoi eparkhii.* Spb: Suvorin, 1901.

Giliarov-Platonov, N. P. *Sbornik sochinenii.* 2 vols. [Published by K. P. Pobedonostsev] Moscow: Sinodal'naia tipografiia, 1899–1900.

———. *Voprosy very i tserkvi. Sbornik statei (1868–1886).* 2 vols. [Published by K. P. Pobedonostsev] Moscow: Sinodal'naia Tipografiia, 1905–1906.

Gimer, D. "9–e ianvaria goda v S. Peterburge." *Byloe* 1 (1925): 3–14.

Gleason, William. "Public Health, Politics, and Cities in Late Imperial Russia." *Journal of Urban History* 16,no. 4 (1990): 341–65.

Glubokovskii, N. N. *Po voprosam dukhovnoi shkoly (srednei i vysshei) i ob Uchebnom Komitete pri Sviateishem Sinode.* Spb: Sinodal'naia Tipografiia, 1907.

———. *Pravoslavnoe russkoe beloe dukhovenstvo po ego polozheniiu i znacheniiu v istorii.* Petrograd: Sinodal'naia tipografiia, 1917.

———. *Russkaia bogoslovskaia nauka v eia istoricheskom razvitii i noveishem sostoianii.* Warsaw: Sinodal'naia tipografiia, 1928.

Golos spasitelia k pastyriu khristianskoi tserkvi. Translated by protoierei A. Koval'nitskii. 2nd ed. St. Petersburg: I. L. Tuzov, 1905.

Gordienko, N. S., and P. K. Kurochkin. "Liberal'noe-obnovlencheskoe dvizhenie v russkoi pravoslavii nachala XX v." *Voprosy nauchnogo ateizma* 7 (1969): 313–40.

Gorev, M. [M. V. Galkin]. *Poslednii sviatoi. Poslednie dni Romanovskoi tserkvi, kanonizatsionnyi protsess Ioanna Tobol'skogo.* Moscow-Leningrad: Gosudarstvennoe izdatel'stvo, 1928.

Gorodetsky, N. *Saint Tikhon of Zadonsk: Inspirer of Dostoevsky.* Crestwood, NY: St. Vladimir's Seminary Press, 1976.

Gorodtsev, P. *Kratkie ocherki pravoslavnogo khristianskogo nravoucheniia.* 2nd ed. Spb: S. Dobrodeev, 1892.

Grigoriev, N. I. *Russkiia obshchestva trezvosti, ikh organizatsiia i deiatel'nost v 1892–1893.* Spb: P. P. Soikin, 1894.

Griniakin, N. "Nedobraia prisposobliaemost'." *Missionerskoe obozrenie* 3 (1903): 331–33.

Grisiuk, N. "Evangelie, kapital, trud." Spb: Montvida, 1906.

Gruppa peterburgskikh sviashchennikov. *K tserkovnomu soboru. Sbornik.* Spb: M. Merkushev, 1906.

Gruppa stolichnykh sviashchennikov. *O neobkhodimosti peremen' v russkom tserkovnom upravlenii.* Spb: M. Merkushev, 1905.

Gurevich, L. *Narodnoe dvizhenie v Peterburge 9–ogo ianvaria 1905.* Berlin: Hugo Steinitz, 1906.

Haig, Alan. *The Victorian Clergy.* London: Croom Helm, 1984.

Hamm, Michael F., ed. *The City in Late Imperial Russia.* Bloomington: University of Indiana Press, 1983.

Hammond, Peter C. *The Parson and the Victorian Parish.* London: Hodder and Stoughton, 1977.

Harrison, Brian. *Drink and the Victorians: The Temperance Question in England, 1815–1872.* London: Faber and Faber, 1971.

Hedda, Jennifer. "Good Shepherds: The St. Petersburg Pastorate and the Emergence of Social Activism in the Russian Orthodox Church." Ph.D. diss., Harvard University, 1998.

————. "The Russo-Japanese War and the Delegitimation of the Autocracy." *Modern Greek Studies Yearbook* 18/19 (2002/2003): 49–62.

Heeney, Brian. *A Different Kind of Gentleman: The Parish Clergy as Professional Man in Early and Mid-Victorian England.* Studies in British History and Culture, vol. 5. Hamden: Archon Books, 1976.

Heier, Edmund. *Religious Schism in the Russian Aristocracy, 1860–1900: Radstockism and Pashkovism.* The Hague: Martinus Nijhoff, 1970.

Helmstadter, Richard J., and Paul T. Phillips, eds. *Religion in Victorian Society: A Sourcebook of Documents.* New York: University Press of America, 1985.

Herlihy, Patricia. *The Alcoholic Empire: Vodka and Politics in Late Imperial Russia.* Oxford and New York: Oxford University Press, 2002.

————. "Strategies of Sobriety: Temperance Movements in Russia, 1880–1914." Occasional Papers Series, no. 238. Washington, D.C.: Woodrow Wilson International Center for Scholars, 1990.

Herrlinger, Kimberly Page. "Class, Piety, and Politics: Workers, Orthodoxy, and the Problem of Religious Identity in Russia, 1881–1914." Ph.D. diss., University of California at Berkeley, 1996.

————. "Raising Lazarus: Orthodoxy and the Factory *Narod* in St. Petersburg, 1905–1914." *Jahrbucher für Geschichte Osteuropas* 52, no. 3 (2004): 341–54.

Hole, Robert. *Pulpits, Politics, and Public Order in England, 1760–1832.* Cambridge: Cambridge University Press, 1989.

Hopkins, Charles Howard. *The Rise of the Social Gospel in American Protestantism, 1865–1915.* New Haven: Yale University Press, 1940; reprint, New York: AMS Press, 1982.

Hosking, Geoffrey A., ed. *Church, Nation, and State in Russia and Ukraine.* London: Macmillan. 1991.

[Iakov, arkhimandrit (Ieronym Petrovich Domskii)]. *Pastyr' v otnoshenii k sebe i pastve.* Spb: N. A. Lebedev, 1880.

————. *Russkoe propovednichestvo. Istoricheskii ego obzor i vzgliad na sovremennoe ego napravlenie.* Spb: Strannik, 1871.

Ianyshev, I. L. *Pravoslavnoe khristianskoe uchenie o nravstvennosti.* 2nd ed. Spb: M. Merkushev, 1906.

————. *Slova i rechi.* Petrograd: M. Merkushev, 1916.

Il'icheva, T. I., ed. *Khramy Peterburga. Spravochnik-Putevoditel'.* Spb: Informatsionno-izdatel'skoe agentstvo LIK, 1992.

Imennyi spisok rektoram i inspektoram dukhovnykh akademii i seminarii, prepodavateliam dukhovnykh akademii, smotriteliam dukhovnykh uchilshch i ikh pomoshchnikam, monashestvuiushchim prepodavteliam dukhovnykh seminarii i uchilishch, i sviashchenno-sluzhiteliam pri russkikh tserkvakh zagranitsei na 1904 god. [Spb: Sinodal'naia tipografiia, 1904].

Inglis, K. S. *Churches and the Working Classes in Victorian England.* London: Routledge and Kegan Paul, 1963.

Innokenti, arkhimandrit. *Pastyrskoe bogoslovie v Rossii za XIX vek.* Sergiev Posad: Tip. Sviato-Troitskoi Lavry, 1899.

Ioann (Snychev), mitropolit Sankt-Peterburgskii i Ladozhskii, ed. *Ocherki istorii Sankt-Peterburgskoi eparkhii.* Spb: Izd. Andreev i synov'ia, 1994.

Isakov, P. N. *Spravochnaia kniga o blagotvoritel'nykh uchrezhdeniiakh i zavedeniiakh v S. Peterburge.* Spb: Iakor', 1911.

Jefferys, W. H. *The City Mission Idea.* New York: Department of Christian Social Service, 1922.

"K istorii 9 ianvaria 1905 goda." *Krasnyi arkhiv* 4–5 (1925): 444–48.

Kadson, I. Z. "Deputaty iz dukhovenstva v III-ei Gosudarstvennoi Dume." *Istoricheskie zapiski* 106 (1981): 302–22.

Kandidov, B. "Religioznaia rabota sredi zhenshchin v poslednie dni tsarisma." *Antireligioznik* 8 (1926): 8–23.

Kantseliariia po uchrezhdeniiam Imperatritsy Marii. *Sbornik svedenii o blagotvoritel'nosti v Rossii, s kratkimi ocherkami blagotvoritel'nykh uchrezhdenii v S. Peterburge i Moskve.* Spb: M. D. Lomkovskii, 1899.

Karabinovich, G. M. *Sobranie statei po delu episkopa Mikhaila Kanadskogo.* Moscow: I. M. Mashistov, 1914.

Karelin, A. E. "Deviatoe ianvaria i Gapon." *Krasnaia letopis'* 1 (1922): 106–16.

Kartashev, A. *Reforma, reformatsiia, i ispolneniia tserkvi.* Petrograd: Korabl', 1916.

———. *Russkaia tserkov' v 1905 godu.* Spb: M. Merkushev, 1906.

———. *Tserkov' i gosudarstvo.* Supplement to *Put'.* Paris: YMCA Press, 1932.

Kassow, Samuel D. *Students, Professors, and the State in Tsarist Russia.* Berkeley: University of California Press, 1989.

Katanskii, A. L. "Vospominaniia starogo professora, 1847–1913." *Khristianskoe chtenie* (1914): 54–77, 328–51, 500–522, 581–613, 755–91, 867–91, 1067–90, 1217–33, 1346–62; (1916): pt. 1 45–67, 283–308, 394–419, 499–515. Separately published under same title in 2 volumes. Spb: Sinodal'naia tipografiia, 1914; Petrograd: Sinodal'naia tipografiia, 1918.

Kenworthy, Scott. "The Role of the Russian Orthodox Military Clergy before 1914: Associations and Connotations." *Jahrbucher für Geschichte Osteuropas* 52, no. 3 (2004): 388–401.

———. "Russian Reformation? The Program for Religious Renovation in the Orthodox Church, 1922–1925." *Modern Greek Studies Yearbook* 16/17 (2000/2001): 89–130.

Khristianskoe chtenie. Monthly. Spb: St. Petersburg Ecclesiastical Academy, 1821–1917.

Kil'chevksii, V. *Bogatstvo i dokhody dukhovenstva.* Spb: Rabotnik, 1906.

Kirill (Naumov), arkhimandrit. *Pastyrskoe bogoslovie.* Spb: Tip. Opekunskogo soveta, 1853.

Kivelson, Valerie, and Robert H. Greene, eds. *Orthodox Russia: Belief and Practice under the Tsars.* University Park, PA: Pennsylvania University Press, 2003.

Kizenko, Nadieszda. "Ioann of Kronstadt and the Reception of Sanctity, 1850–1988." *Russian Review* 57, no. 3 (July 1998): 325–45.

———. "The Making of a Modern Saint: Ioann of Kronstadt and the Russian People, 1855–1917." Ph.D. diss., Columbia University, 1995.

———. *A Prodigal Saint: Father John of Kronstadt and the Russian People.* University Park, PA: Pennsylvania State University Press, 2000.

Kline, George L. *Religious and Anti-Religious Thought in Russia.* Chicago: University of Chicago Press, 1968.

Kniaginitsii, I. "Poezdka v Kronshtadt." *Istoricheskii vestnik* 80 (1900): 632–44.

Kobiakov, R. "Gapon i okhrannoe otdelenie do 1905 g." *Krasnaia letopis'* 1 (1922): 28–45.

Koehler-Bauer, Maria. *Die Geistlichen Akademien in Russland im 19. Jahrhundert.* Wiesbaden: Harrassowitz Verlag, 1997.

Kolsto, Pal. "A Mass for a Heretic? The Controversy over Leo Tolstoi's Burial." *Slavic Review* 60, no. 1 (September 2001): 75–95.

Kopenkin, E. G. "Sotsial'no-politicheskaia i ideologicheskaia pereorientatsia russkoi pravoslavnoi tserkvi v predrevoliutsionnoi Rossii kak faktor evoliutsiia pravoslaviia." Kand. diss., Gosudarstvennyi pedagogicheskii institut im. Gertsena, 1973. Avtoreferat.

Kornblatt, Judith Deutsch, and Richard F. Gustafson, eds. *Russian Religious Thought.* Madison: University of Wisconsin Press, 1996.

Korol'kov, I. *Pamiati vysokopreosviashchennogo Antoniia, Mitropolit Petrogradksogo i Ladozhskogo.* Kiev: [n.p.], 1916.

Kozitskii, P. "O literaturnoi propovedi sv. G. Petrova." *Missionerskoe obozrenie* 7 (1903): 936–55.

Kozlovskii, I. I. "Ocherk zhilishchnykh uslovii zhizni studentov Imperatorskoi S. Peterburgskoi dukhovnoi akademii." *Khristianskoe chtenie* (1914): 975–1004.

Krasnikov, N. P. "Evoliutsiia sotsial'noi kontseptsii russkogo pravoslaviia." *Voprosy istorii* 9 (1970): 16–33.

———. *Pravoslavnaia etika. Proshloe i nastoiashchee*. Moscow: Politizdat', 1981.

———. "Sotsial'no-eticheskie aspekty religioznogo reformatorstva kontsa XIX–nachala XX veka." *Voprosy nauchnogo ateizma* 26 (1980): 206–22.

———. "Sotsial'no-politicheskaia pozitsiia pravoslavnoi tserkvi v 1905–1916 godakh." *Voprosy istorii* 9 (1982): 30–41.

Krasnyi zvon. Monthly. Spb, 1908–1909. Continuation of the Renovationist journal *Zvonar'*.

Kratkaia zapiska o S. Peterburgksoi dukhovnoi seminarii za sto let, 1809–1909. Spb: M. I. Akinfiev, 1909.

Kratkii spisok litsam sluzhashchim po vedomstvu pravoslavnogo ispovednaiia na 1906 god. Spb: Sinodal'naia Tipografiia, 1906.

Kratkiia svedeniia o tserkvakh i sviashchenno-tserkovno-sluzhiteliakh S. Peterburga. Spb: Ia. Krovitskaia, 1895.

Kremlevskii, P. M. *Opravdanie pastyrstva*. Spb: M. Merkushev, 1907.

Krylov, I. I. *Protoierei Vasilii Feofilaktovich Nikitin. Nekrolog*. Spb: M. P. Frolova, 1904.

Kudelli, P. *Rabotnitsa v 1905 godu v Peterburge*. Leningrad: Priboi, 1926.

Kuliukin, S. "Ideia pastyrskogo dushepopecheniia." *Khristianskoe chtenie* (1901): pt. 2, 341 69 and 467 81.

Kutepov, N. M. *Pamiatnaia kniga po S. Peterburgskoi eparkhii*. Spb: Tip. Otdel'nogo Korpusa Pogranichnoi strazhi, 1899.

Kuznetsov, N. D. *Po voprosam tserkovnykh preobrazovanii. Doklady, osobiia mneniia, i rechi v Osobom Prisutsvii uchrezhdennom v Sv. Sinode*. Moscow: Pravovedenie, 1907.

———. *Tserkov', dukhovenstvo, i obshchestvo*. Supplement to *Russkii den'*, no. 20. General editor S. Sharapov. Moscow: I. M. Mashistov, 1905.

Labutin, I. K. *Kharakter khristianskoi blagotvoritel'nosti*. Spb: Tip. V. D. Smirnov, 1899.

———. *Propovedi*. 2 vols. Spb: Tip. V. A. Smirnov, 1900–1905.

Latimer, R. S. *Dr. Baedecker and His Apostolic Work in Russia*. London: Morgan and Scott: 1907.

Lebedev, I. *Tserkovno-prikhodskie popechitel'stva*. Chernigov: Tip. Gubernskogo pravleniia, 1902.

Leont'eva, T. G. "The Peasantry and the Rural Clergy in Russia, 1900–1920." *The Soviet and Post-Soviet Review* 27, nos. 2–3 (2000): 143–62.

———. "Vera i bunt. Dukhovenstvo v revoliutsionnom obshchestve Rossii nachala XX veka." *Voprosy istorii* 1 (2001): 29–43.

Lindenmeyr, Adele. "Charity and the Problem of Unemployment: Industrial Homes in Late Imperial Russia." *The Russian Review* 45, no. 1 (1986): 1–22.

———. "The Ethos of Charity in Imperial Russia." *Journal of Social History* 23, no. 4 (1990): 679–94.

———. *Poverty Is Not A Vice: Charity, Society, and the State in Imperial Russia*. Princeton: Princeton University Press, 1996.

———. "A Russian Experiment in Voluntarism: The Municipal Guardianships of the Poor, 1894–1914." *Jahrbucher für Geschichte Osteuropas* 30, no. 3 (1982): 429–51.

———. *Voluntary Associations and the Russian Autocracy: The Case of Private Charity*. The Carl Beck Papers in Russian and East European Studies, no. 807. Pittsburgh: University of Pittsburgh Center for Russian and East European Studies, June 1990.

Lopukhin, A. "Semidesiatipiatiletie *Khristianskogo chteniia*." *Khristianskoe chtenie* (January-February 1896): 3–25.

———. "Zaokeanskii zapad v religiozno-nravstvennom otnoshenii." *Khristianskoe chtenie* (1886): pt. 2, 618–58.

Luch sveta. Edited by E. Belkov. Weekly. Spb: January-March 1908. Supplement to *Tserkovnaia reforma*.

M——ckii, Mikhail. *Ot bursy do sniatiia sana*. Spb: Sever, 1908.

Makkaveiskii, N. "Ieromonakh Innokenti. Pastyrskoe bogoslovie v Rossii na XIX v." *Trudy Kievskoi Dukhovnoi Akademii* 3 (1899): 604–6.

Maksimov, V. I. "Pravda i lozh' o Georgii Gapone." *Russkii vestnik* 1 (3 January 1992): 9–12.

Maloney, George A. *A History of Orthodox Theology Since 1453.* Belmont, MA: Nordland Publishing Company, 1976.

Manchester, Laurie. "Harbingers of Modernity, Bearers of Tradition: *Popovichi* as a Model Intelligentsia Self in Revolutionary Russia." *Jahrbucher für Geschichte Osteuropas* 50, no. 3 (2002): 321–44.

———. "Secular Ascetics: The Mentality of Orthodox Clergymen's Sons in Late Imperial Russia." Ph.D. diss., Columbia University, 1995.

———. "The Secularization of the Search for Salvation: The Self-Fashioning of Orthodox Clergymen's Sons in Late Imperial Russia." *Slavic Review* 57, no. 1 (1998): 50–76.

Martov, L., P. Maslov, and A. Potresov. *Obshchestvennoe dvizhenie v Rossii v nachale XX veka.* Vol. 2, pt. 1. Spb: Obshchestvennaia pol'za, 1909.

Mavritskii, V. A. *Voskresenyia i prazdnichnyia vnebogosluzhebnyia sobesedovanyia kak osnovyi vid tserkovno-narodnoi propovedi.* 4th ed. Moscow: V. V. Chicherin, 1890.

McCarthy, Mark. "Religious Conflict and Social Order in Nineteenth-Century Russia: Orthodoxy and the Protestant Challenge, 1812–1905." Ph.D. diss., University of Notre Dame, 2004.

McClelland, James C. *Autocrats and Academics: Education, Culture, and Society in Tsarist Russia.* Chicago: University of Chicago Press, 1979.

McKee, Arthur W. "Sobering up the Soul of the People: The Politics of Popular Temperance in Late Imperial Russia." *Russian Review* 58, no. 2 (April 1999): 212–34.

McLeod, Hugh. *Class and Religion in the Late Victorian City.* Hamden: Archon Books, 1974.

———. "Protestantism and the Working Class in Imperial Germany." *European Studies Review* 12 (1982): 323–44.

Meehan, Brenda. *Holy Women of Russia.* Harper Collins: San Francisco, 1993.

——— [Meehan-Waters, Brenda]. "To Save Oneself: Russian Peasant Women and the Development of Women's Religious Communities in Pre-revolutionary Russia." In *Russian Peasant Women,* edited by Beatrice Farnsworth and Lynne Viola, 121–33. New York: Oxford University Press, 1992.

Meyendorff, John. "The Christian Gospel and Social Responsibility: The Eastern Orthodox Tradition in History." In *Continuity and Discontinuity in Church History,* edited by F. F. Church and Timothy George, 118–30. Leiden: E. J. Brill, 1979.

Mikhail, arkhimandrit. "Besedy s chitateliami." *Staroobriadcheskaia mysl'* 7 (1910): 415–19.

———. *Kak ia stal narodnym sviashchennikom.* Moscow: I. D. Sytin, 1908.

———. *Khristiane li my?* Spb: Montvida, 1906.

———. *Khristianstvo i sotsial'-demokratiia.* 2nd ed. Spb: Berezhlivost', 1907.

———. "Khristianstvo ne moral'." *Staroobriadcheskaia mysl'* 6 (1910): 321–25.

———. *Khristos v veke mashin.* Spb: Berezhlivost', 1907.

———. "Kopeika Davida Leizera." *Staroobriadcheskaia mysl'* 1 (1910): 6–8.

———. *Novaia tserkov'. Sviashchennik i prikhozhan.* Spb: Vera i znanie, 1905.

———. *Otets Ioann Kronshtadtskii.* Spb: Slovo, 1904.

———. *Pastyr', vybory, Duma.* Spb: Obshchestvo rasprostraneniia religiozno-nravstvennago prosveshcheniia v dukhe pravoslavnoi tserkvi, 1906.

———. *Pochemu nam ne veriat?* Spb: I. D. Tuzov, 1906.

———. *Prokliatnye voprosy i khristianstvo.* Spb: Montvida, 1906.

———. *Prorok khristianskoi svobody i svobodnogo khristianstva.* Spb: Montvida, 1906.

———. "Proshloe i sovremennyia zadachi staroobriadchestva." *Staroobriadcheskaia mysl'* 2 (1910): 65–67; 3 (1910): 137–40.

————. *Sviashchennik-sotsialist i ego sotsial'nyi roman.* Spb: Montvida, 1906.

————. *Tserkov', literatura i zhizn'.* Moscow: I. D. Sytin, 1905.

————. *Zhenshchina-rabotnitsa.* Spb: Montvida, 1906.

Mikhailov, S. "Khramy S. Peterburga, 1912 g." Spb: V. V. Valdin, 1994.

Miliukov, Paul. *Outlines of Russian Culture.* Part 1, *Religion and the Church.* Edited by Michael Karpovich. Translated by Valentine Ughet and Eleanor Davis. Philadelphia: University of Pennsylvania Press, 1942.

Milovidov, A. "Dva dokumenty ob ubiistve Gapona." *Byloe* 1 (1925): 63–65.

Mirtov, P. A. *Vera i zhizn.* Spb: Vera i znanie, 1905.

Missionerskoe obozrenie. Editor V. M. Skvortsov. Spb, 1896–1916, monthly after 1900.

Mudie-Smith, Richard, ed. *The Religious Life of London.* London: Hodder and Stoughton, 1904.

Mukhin, Vyacheslav. *The Church Culture of St. Petersburg.* Spb: Ivan Fyodorov, 1994.

Muller, Alexander V. *The Spiritual Regulation of Peter the Great.* Seattle: University of Washington Press, 1972.

Murchland, Bernard. *The Dream of Christian Socialism: An Essay on its European Origins.* Washington: American Enterprise Institute for Public Policy Research, 1982.

Myshtyn, Vasilii. *Po tserkovno-obshchestvennym voprosam. Sbornik statei.* Sergiev Posad: Tip. Sviato-Troitskoi Lavry, 1905.

Nadezhdin, A. "Istoricheskaia zapiska o S. Peterburgskoi dukhovnoi seminarii." *Khristianskoe chtenie* (1884): pt. 1, 818–50.

————. *Istoriia S. Peterburgskoi pravoslavnoi dukhovnoi seminarii, 1809–1884.* Spb: Sinodal'naia tipografiia, 1885.

Nechaev, P. I. *Uchebnik po prakticheskomu rukovodstvu dlia pastyrei.* 2 vols. 3rd ed. Spb: I. N. Skorokhodov, 1889.

Neuberger, Joan. *Hooliganism: Crime, Culture, and Power in St. Petersburg, 1900–1914.* Berkeley: University of California Press, 1993.

Nevskii, V. "Ianvarskie dni v Peterburge v 1905 goda." *Krasnaia letopis'* 1 (1922): 13–74.

Nichols, Robert L. "Church and State in Imperial Russia." The Donald W. Treadgold Papers, no. 102. Seattle: Henry M. Jackson School of International Studies, University of Washington, 1995.

————. "The Icon and the Machine in Russia's Religious Renaissance, 1900–1909." In *Christianity and the Arts in Russia,* edited by William C. Blumfield and Milos C. Velimirovic, 131–44. Cambridge: Cambridge University Press, 1991.

————. "Metropolitan Filaret of Moscow and the Awakening of Orthodoxy." Ph.D. dissertation, University of Washington, 1972.

Nikol'skii, P. V. *Tserkov' i obshchestvennaia zhizn', 1905 g.* Spb: I. V. Leont'ev, 1906.

Nikon (Rklitskii), bishop of Florida. *Zhizneopisanie blazhneishego Antoniia, mitropolita Kievskogo i Galitskogo.* 10 vols. New York: Diocese of North America and Canada, 1956.

O blagoustroenii prikhoda. Svod mnenii eparkhial'nykh preosviashchennykh. Spb: Sinodal'naia tipografiia, 1906.

Obshchestvo rasprostraneniia religiozno-nravstvennago prosveshcheniia v dukhe pravoslavnoi tserkvi. *Narodnyi pechal'nik. Otets A. V. Rozhdestvenskii.* Spb: M. P. Frolov, 1905.

————. *Obsheshchtvo rasprostraneniia religiozno-nravstvennogo prosveshcheniia v dukhe pravoslavnoi tserkvi, 1881–1891.* Spb: A. Katanskii, 1891.

————. *Otchet o deiatel'nosti Obshchestva rasprostraneniia religiozno-nravstvennogo prosveshcheniia v dukhe pravoslavnoi tserkvi za [1881–1912].* Spb: ORRP, 1882–1913.

————. *Sekta pashkovtsev i razgovor pravoslavnogo s pashkovtsem.* Spb: Tip. tovarishchestva Pechatnia S. P. Iakoviva, 1895.

Olesnitskii, M. *Nravstvennoe bogoslovie.* 4th ed. Spb: I. L. Tuzov, 1907.

Olezewski, Mieczyslaw. "Die Pastoraltheologie in der orthodoxen Kirche Russlands des 19 Jahrhunderts." *Ostkirchliche Studien* 38, no. 4 (1989): 311–28.

Ornatskii, F. N. *Sekta pashkovtsev i otvet'e na pashkovskie voprosy.* 2nd ed. Spb: M. P. Frolov, 1903.

Osinskii, A. *Sotsializatsiia khristianstva pri svete Evangel'skogo ucheniia.* Novgorod-Seversk: Kh. I. Bokrimov, 1911.

Ostanina, O. V. "Obnovlenchestvo i reformatorstvo v russkoi pravoslavnoi tserkvi v nachale XX veka." Kand. diss., Leningradskii gosudarstvennyi universitet, 1991.

"Otkrytoe pis'mo studentov S. Peterburgskoi Dukhovnoi Akademii sv. G. S. Petrovu." *Vek* 5 (4 February 1907): 66.

Otzyvy eparkhial'nykh arkhiereev po voprosu o tserkovnoi reforme. 3 vols. Spb: Sinodal'naia Tipografiia, 1906.

Ovchinnikov, V. G. "Pravoslavnaia tserkov' v istorii nashei strany." *Voprosy istorii* 5 (1988): 111–21.

Pamiati professora A. P. Lopukhina. Spb: M. Merkushev, 1904.

Pamiatnaia knizhka S. Peterburgskoi Dukhovnoi Akademiia na 1900–01 uchebnyi god. Spb: Tip. Glavnogo upravleniia udelov, 1902.

Papkov, A. A. *Besedy o pravoslavnom prikhode.* Petrograd: Izdatel'skii sovet pri Sv. Sinode, 1917.

———. *Nachalo vozrozhdeniia tserkovno-prikhodskoi zhizni v Rossii.* Moscow: V. Chicherin, 1900.

———. *Neobkhodymost' obnovleniia pravoslavnogo tserkovno-obshchestvennogo stroia.* Spb: V. V. Komarov, 1902.

———. *O blagoustroistve pravoslavnogo prikhoda.* Spb: Sinodal'naia tipografiia, 1907.

———. *Tserkovnyia bratstva. Kratkii statisticheskii ocherk o polozhenii tserkovnykh bratstv k nachalu 1893 goda.* Spb: Sinodal'naia tipografiia, 1893.

———. *Upadok pravoslavnogo prikhoda (XVIII-XIX veka). Istoricheskaia spravka.* Moscow: V. Chicherin, 1899.

Paozerskii, M. F. "Gapon i Sinod." *Zvezda* 6 (1924): 159–73.

Parsons, Gerald, ed. *Religion in Victorian Britain.* 3 vols. Manchester: Manchester University Press, 1988.

Pavlov, I. "Iz vospominanii o Rabochem Soiuze i sv. Gapone." *Minuvshie gody* 1 (March 1908): 22–57 and 2 (April 1908): 79–107.

Peris, Daniel. "Commissars in Red Cassocks: Former Priests in the League of the Militant Godless." *Slavic Review* 64, no. 2 (1995): 340–64.

Petrov, G. S. *Apostoli trezvosti.* 9th ed. Spb: V. Mil'shtein, 1903.

———. *Besedy o Boge i Bozhiei put'.* Moscow: I. D. Sytin, 1904.

———. *Bozhii put'.* 3rd ed. Moscow: I. D. Sytin, 1903.

———. *Doloi p'ianstvo!* 5th ed. Moscow: I. D. Sytin, 1904.

———. *Evangelie, kak osnova zhizni.* 17th ed. New York: Obshchestvo Vsemirnoe Bratstvo, 1921.

———. *K svetu.* 4th ed. Moscow: I. D. Sytin, 1904.

———. *Lampa Aladina.* 3rd ed. Spb: P. Voshchinskaia, 1906.

———. *Liudi-bratia.* Spb: P. Voshchinskaia, 1903.

———. *Ne s togo kontsa.* Spb: P. Voshchinskaia, 1905.

———. *Pis'mo sviashchennika Grigoriia Petrova Mitopolitu Antoniiu.* Berlin: Rosenthal, [n.d.].

———. *Po stopam Khrista.* 2 vols. Spb: P. Voshchinskaia, 1903.

———. *Tserkov' i obshchestvo.* Spb: P. Voshchinskaia, 1906.

———. *Veliki pastyr.* Spb: P. Voshchinskaia, 1905.

———. *Voina i mir G. S. Petrova.* Spb: P. Voshchinskaia, 1904.

———. *Zaprosy sovremennoi tserkvi.* Spb: P. Voshchinskaia, 1906.

———. *Zateinik.* 3 vols. in 1. Spb: P. Voshchinskaia, 1904.

Petrov, L. *Vospominaniia protoiereiia Leonida Petrova.* Spb: Tip. Glavnogo upravleniia udelov, 1909.

Petrov, N. "Gapon i graf Vitte." *Byloe* 1 (1925): 15–27.

Petrov, V. *Dobryi pastyr'. Pastyrskaia khrestomatiia.* Vol. 1. Sergiev Posad: Tip. Sviato-Troitskoi lavry, 1915.

Pevnitskii, V. F. *Iz istorii gomiletiki: Gomiletika v novoe vremia, posle reformatsii Liutera.* Kiev: I. I. Gorbunov, 1899.

———. *Ob otnoshenii k tserkvi nashego obrazovannogo obshchestva.* Kiev: Tip. Imperatorskogo universiteta Sv. Vladimira, 1902.

———. *Sluzhenie sviashchennika v kachestve dukhovnogo rukovoditelia prikhozhan.* Kiev: S. V. Kulzhenko, 1890.

———. *Sviashchennik. Prigotovlenie k sviashchenstvu i zhizn' sviashchennika.* 2nd ed. Kiev: A. N. Ivanov, 1886.

———. *Sviashchenstvo. Osnovye punkty v uchenii o pastyrskom sluzhenii.* Kiev: S. V. Kulzhenko, 1885.

Pipes, Richard. *The Russian Revolution.* New York: Alfred Knopf, 1991.

Pisiotis, Argyrios. "The Orthodox Clergy and the Radical Right at the Beginning of the Twentieth Century: Ideological Mentor or Strange Bedfellow?" Located at http://conservatism.narod.ru/oktober/pisiotis.doc. Accessed 2/26/05.

———. "Orthodoxy versus Autocracy: The Orthodox Church and Clerical Political Dissent in Late Imperial Russia, 1905–1914." Ph.D. diss., Georgetown University, 2000.

———. "The Unknown Dissident: The Prosopography of Clerical Anti-Tsarist Activism in Late Imperial Russia." *Modern Greek Studies Yearbook* 18/19 (2002/2003): 63–94.

"Pis'mo Gapona." *Krasnyi arkhiv* 2 (1925): 294–97.

Plamper, Jan. "The Russian Orthodox Episcopate, 1721–1917: A Prosopography." *Journal of Social History* 34, no. 1 (Fall 2000): 5–30.

Pobedonostsev, K. P. "Iz chernovyk bumag K. P. Pobedonostseva." *Krasnyi arkhiv* 18 (1926): 203–7.

———. *Reflections of a Russian Statesman.* Translated by R. C. Long. Ann Arbor: University of Michigan Press, 1965.

Pokrovskii, S. *Kurs prakticheskogo rukovodstva dlia pastyrei.* 2nd ed. Spb: I. L. Tuzov, 1898.

Polisadov, Grigorii. *Iz vospominanii o vremeni prebyvaniia moego v S. Peterburgskoi Akademii (1857–1861).* Spb: M. Merkushev, 1912.

Polnyi pravoslavnyi bogoslovskii entsiklopedicheskii slovar'. 2 vols. Spb: P. P. Soikin [1913]; reprint, London: Variorum, 1971.

Polunov, A. Iu. "Church, Regime, and Society in Russia (1880–1895)." *Russian Studies in History* 39, no. 4 (Spring 2001): 33–53. Originally published in *Voprosy istorii* 11 (1997): 125–36.

———. "Konstantin Petrovich Pobedonostsev—Man and Politician." *Russian Studies in History* 39, no. 4 (Spring 2001): 8–32. Originally published in *Otechestvennaia istoriia* 1 (1998): 42–55.

———. *Pod vlast'iu ober-prokurora. Gosudarstvo i tserkov' v epokhu Aleksandra III-ego.* Moscow: Airo-xx, 1996.

———. "The State and Religious Heterodoxy in Russia, 1880s–1890s." *Russian Studies in History* 39, no. 4 (Spring 2001): 54–65. Originally published in *Rossiia i reformy.* *Sbornik statei,* no. 3, compiled by M. A. Kolerov, 126–41. Moscow: Medved, 1991.

Pomyalovsky, N. G. *Seminary Sketches.* Translated by Alfred Kuhn. Ithaca, NY: Cornell University Press, 1973.

Popov, D. *Zametki prikhodskogo sviashchennika o vozrozhdenii tserkovnogo prikhoda.* Kharkov: Tip. Gubernskogo pravleniia, 1904.

Popov, E. *Pis'ma po pravoslavno-pastyrskomu pastyrstvu.* 4 vols. 2nd ed. Perm: Tip. gubernogo upravleniia, 1877.

Poselianin, E. *Russkie podvizhniki 19–ogo veka.* Spb: I. D. Tuzov, 1901.

———. *Sviashchennik Aleksandr Vasilevich Rozhdestvennskii.* Spb: Sinodal'naia Tipografiia, 1905.

Pospielovsky, Dmitry. *Russian Police Trade Unionism: Experiment or Provocation?* London: London School of Economics and Political Science, 1971.

Potapenko, I. N. *A Russian Priest.* With an introduction by James Adderly. New York: Dodd, Mead, 1916.

Potorzhinskii, M. A. *Obraztsy russkoi tserkovnoi propovedi XIX veka.* Kiev: K. M. Milevskii, 1882.

———. *Russkaia gomileticheskaia khrestomatiia, XVII–XIX vv.* Kiev: K. M. Milevskii, 1887.

Pravila o pravoslavnykh tserkovnykh bratstvakh i polozhenie o prikhodskikh popechitel'stvakh pri pravoslavnykh tserkvakh. Spb: Sinodal'naia Tipografiia, 1881.

Pravoslavnaia bogoslovskaia entsiklopediia. Edited by A. P. Lopukhin. 12 vols. Spb: Strannik, 1900–1911.

Pravoslavno-russkoe slovo. Spb: ORRP, 1902–1905. Twice-monthly.

Preobrazhenskii, I. *Otechestvennaia tserkov' po statisticheskim dannam s 1840/41–1890/91.* Spb: E. Arngol'd, 1897.

Preobrazhenskii, I. V. *Konstantin Petrovich Pobedonostsev, ego lichnost' i deiatel'nost'.* Spb: Kolokol', 1912.

———. *Novye i traditsionnye dukhovnye oratory, Oo. Grigorii Petrov i Ioann Sergeev (Kronshtadtskii). Kriticheskii etiud.* Spb: Slovo, 1902.

———. *Periodicheskaia pechat' po voprosu o prikhodskoi reforme.* Spb: Montvida, 1908.

———. *Tserkovnaia reforma. Sbornik statei dukhovnoi i svetskoi periodicheskoi pechati po voprosu o reforme.* Spb: E. Arngol'd, 1905.

Preston, W. C. "The Bitter Cry of Outcast London." Boston: Cupples, Upham and Co., 1883.

Prestwich, Patricia E. *Drink and the Politics of Social Reform: Antialcoholism in France since 1870.* Palo Alto, CA: The Society for the Promotion of Science and Scholarship, 1988.

Prikhodskii sviashchennik. Editors M. V. and V. P. Galkin. Spb. Weekly, 1911–1912; monthly January–April 1913.

Problemy russkogo religioznogo soznaniia. Berlin: YMCA Press, 1924.

Programma pastyrskikh sobranii po voprosu o prikhode, byvshikh v 1904 i 1905 godakh. Spb: M. Frolov, 1906.

"Protoierei Mikhail Pavlovich Chel'tsov. Zhizn' i deiatel'nosti," *Zhurnal Moskovskogo Patriarshestva* 10 (1993): 36–48.

Protopov, D. I., ed. *S tserkovnogo ambona. Sbornik obrazovykh propovedei.* 2nd ed. 12 vols. bound in 3. Moscow: Tip. Russkogo knizhnogo magazina, 1890–1891.

Putnam, George F. *Russian Alternatives to Marxism: Christian Socialism and Idealistic Liberalism in Twentieth-Century Russia.* Knoxville: University of Tennessee Press, 1977.

R. S. T. *Neshto o russkoi tserkvi v Ober-Prokurorstve K. P. Pobedonostseva.* Leipzig: Brockhaus, 1887.

Racheotes, N. S. "Values in Collision: The Byzantine Tradition, Scholasticism, and the Birth of the Russian Intelligentsia." *Canadian-American Slavic Studies* 34, no. 3 (Fall, 2000): 311–35.

Raninskii, N. *Pastyrenachal'nik Gospod Iisus Khristos i ego sviatye apostoly.* Spb: S. E. Dobrodeev, 1891.

Raspisanie prikhodov eparkhial'nogo vedomstva v gorode St. Peterburge. Spb: Tip. Glavnogo upravleniia udelov, 1900.

Read, Christopher. *Religion, Revolution, and the Russian Intelligentsia, 1900–1912: The Vekhi Debate and Its Intellectual Background.* London: Macmillan Press, 1979.

Riabchenko, A. E. *Otkrytoe pis'mo ober-prokuroru Sv. Sinoda o nuzhdakh tserkovnoi zhizni.* Spb: P. P. Soikin, 1916.

Rieber, Alfred J. *Merchants and Entrepreneurs in Imperial Russia.* Chapel Hill: University of North Carolina Press, 1982.

Rimskii, S. V. "Tserkovnaia reforma 60–70-x godov XIX veka." *Otechestvennaia tserkov'* 2 (1995): 166–81.

Robson, Roy. "Liturgy and Community among Old Believers." *Slavic Review* 52, no. 4 (1993): 713–24.

———. *Old Believers in Modern Russia.* Dekalb: Northern Illinois University Press, 1995.

Rodosskii, A. S. [A. R.]. *Istoricheskaia perepiska o sudbakh pravoslavnoi tserkvi.* Moscow: I. D. Sytin, 1912.

Roslof, Edward E. "The Heresy of 'Bolshevik' Christianity: Orthodox Rejection of Religious Reform During NEP." *Slavic Review* 55, no. 3 (Fall 1996): 615–35.

———. *Red Priests: Renovationism, Russian Orthodoxy, and Revolution, 1905–1946*. Bloomington: University of Indiana Press, 2002.

———. "The Renovationist Movement in the Russian Orthodox Church, 1922–1946." Ph.D. diss., University of North Carolina at Chapel Hill, 1994.

Rozanov, N. P. *Deiatel'nosti dukhovenstva v bor'be s narodnym p'ianstvom*. Moscow: A. I. Snegirov, 1912.

Rozanov, V. V. *Russkaia tserkov'*. Paris: D. Zhukovskii, 1906.

Rozhdestvenskii, A. K. *Odin iz bol'nykh voprosov prikhodskikh zhizni*. Sergiev Posad: Tip. Sviato-Troitskoi Sergeevskoi Lavry, 1907.

Rozhdestvenskii, A. V. *Chto sdelalo pravoslavnoe dukhovenstvo v bor'be za trezvosti*. Spb: P. P. Soikin, 1900.

———. *Pamiatnaia knizhka trezvennika*. 2nd ed. Spb: V. D. Smirnov, 1900.

Rozov, A. N. *Sviashchennik v dukhovnoi zhizne russkoi derevne*. Spb: Aleteiia, 2003.

Ruane, Christine. *Gender, Class, and the Professionalization of Russian City Teachers, 1860–1914*. Pittsburgh: University of Pittsburgh Press, 1994.

Runkevich, S. G. *Prikhodskaia blagotvoritel'nost' v Peterburge. Istoricheskie ocherki*. Spb: Tip. Glav. upravleniia udelov, 1900.

———. *Russkaia tserkov' v XIX v*. Spb: Tip. A. P. Lopukhina, 1901.

———. *Studenty-propovedniki. Ocherki peterburgskoi religiozno-prosvetitel'noi blagotvoritel'nosti*. Spb: Department Udelov, 1892.

Runovskii, P. *Znachenie khristianstva v dukhovno-nravstvennom razvitii i otnoshenie ego k blagoustroistvu zemnoi zhizni chelovechestva*. Spb: I. L. Tuzov, 1889.

Russkaia mysl'. Editor P. B. Struve. Spb. Monthly, 1905–1918.

Sabaneeff, Leonid. "Religious and Mystical Trends in Russia." *Russian Review* 24, no. 4 (1965): 354–68.

Sabler, V. K. *O mirnoi bor'be s sotsializmom*. 2 vols. Sergiev Posad: Tip. Sviato-Troitskoi Lavry, 1911.

Sablinsky, Walter. *The Road to Bloody Sunday: Father Gapon and the St. Petersburg Massacre of 1905*. Princeton: Princeton University Press, 1976.

S. Peterburg. Putevoditel' po stolitse s istoriko-statisticheskim ocherkom i opisaniem eia dostoprimachatel'nostei i uchrezhdenii. Spb: S. Peterburgskii obshchestvennyi upravlenie, 1903.

S. Peterburgskaia Dukhovnaia Akademiia. *Otchet o sostoianii S. Peterburgskoi dukhovnoi akademii za 1881–1916*. Spb: M. Merkushev, 1882–1917.

———. *Zhurnaly zasedanii soveta S. Peterburgskoi dukhovnoi akademii za 1881–1913*. Spb: A. P. Lopukhin, 1882–1914.

S. Peterburgskaia gorodskaia uprava po statisticheskomu otdeleniiu. *S. Peterburg po perepisi 15–ogo dekabria 1881 g*. Spb: A. Petrov, 1883.

———. *Sbornik spravochnykh i statisticheskikh svedenii o blagotvoritel'nosti v S. Peterburge za 1884 g*. Spb: Shreder, 1886.

———. *Sbornik svedenii o blagotvoritel'nosti v S. Peterburge za 1889*. Spb: Shreder, 1891.

S. Peterburgskii dukhovnyi vestnik. Weekly. Spb: ORRP, 1895–1901. Twice-monthly supplement *Izvestiia po S. Peterburgskoi eparkhii*.

S. Peterburgskii eparkhial'nyi istoriko-statisticheskii komitet. *Istoriko-statisticheskiia svedeniia o S. Peterburgskoi eparkhii*. 10 vols. Spb: Department Udelov, 1869–1885.

S. Peterburgskoe gorodskoe obshchestvennoe upravlenie. *Spravochnik o blagotvoritel'nykh upravleniiakh, deistvuiushchikh v gorode S. Peterburge*. Spb: A. F. Dresler, 1913.

S. Peterburgskoe gorodskoe popechitel'stvo o narodnoi trezvosti. *Kratkii ocherk deiatel'nosti S. Peterburgskogo gorodskogo popechitel'stva o narodnoi trezvosti*. Spb: D. Dreiden, 1913.

Savva (Tikhomirov), arkhiepiskop Tverskii and Kashinskii. *Khronika moei zhizni*. 9 vols. Sergiev Posad: Tip. Sviato-Troitskoi Lavry, 1897–1911.

Scherrer, Jutta. "Intelligentsia, Réligion, Révolution: Premières manifestations d'un socialisme chrétien en Russie, 1905–1907. *Cahiers du monde russe et soviétique* 17, no. 4 (1976): 427–66 and 18, no. 1 (1977): 5–32.

Schneiderman, Jeremiah. *Sergei Zubatov and Revolutionary Marxism: The Struggle for the Working Class in Tsarist Russia.* Ithaca, NY: Cornell University Press, 1976.

Schulkin, Marc Lee. "The Politics of Temperance: Nicholas II's Campaign against Alcohol Abuse." Ph.D. diss., Harvard University, 1985.

Seregny, Scott J. *Russian Teachers and Peasant Revolution: The Politics of Education in 1905.* Bloomington: Indiana University Press, 1989.

Sergeev, Mikhail. "Liberal Orthodoxy: From Vladimir Solov'ev to Fr. Alexander Men." *Religion in Eastern Europe* 23,4 (Aug. 2003): 43–50.

Sergii (Stragorodskii), arkhimandrit. *Pravoslavnoe uchenie o spasenii.* 2nd ed. Kazan: Tip. Imperatorskogo universiteta, 1898.

Shavel'skii, Georgii Ivanovich. *Pravoslavnoe pastyrstvo. Osnovy, zadachi, i dukh pravoslavnogo pastyrskogo sluzheniia.* Sofiia: Tip. Iunion, 1930.

———. *Sluzhenie sviashchennika na voine.* Spb: Sel'skii Vestnik, 1912.

———. *Vospominaniia poslednego protopresvitera russkoi armii i flota.* 2 vols. New York: Chekhov Publishing House, 1954.

Sheinman, M. M. *Khristianskii sotsializm. Istoriia i ideologiia.* Moscow: Nauka, 1969.

Shevzov, Vera. "Chapels and the Ecclesial World of Prerevolutionary Russian Peasants." *Slavic Review* 55, no. 3 (Fall 1996): 585–613.

———. "Icons, Miracles, and the Ecclesial Identity of Laity in Late Imperial Russian Orthodoxy." *Church History* 69, no. 3 (September 2000): 610–32.

———. *Russian Orthodoxy on the Eve of Revolution.* New York: Oxford University Press, 2000.

Shilov, A. "Peterburgskoe dukhovenstvo i 9 ianvaria." *Krasnyi arkhiv* 5 (1929): 192–99.

Shishkin, A. A. *Sushchnost' i kriticheskaia otsenna 'obnovlencheskogo' raskola russkoi pravoslavnoi tserkvi.* Kazan: Izd. Kazanskogo Universiteta, 1970.

Shishkin, I. T. *Krasota spaset mir. Vpechatleniia ot lektsii G. S. Petrova.* Kharkov: Tip. R. Radomyshel'skogo, 1914.

Sidorov, V. P. *Khristianskii sotsializm v Rossii v kontse XIX–nachale XX veka.* Chernopovets: Izd. ChGPI im. Lunacherskogo, 1995.

Simon, Gerhard. *Church, State, and Opposition in the USSR.* Translated by K. Matchett. London: C. Hurst, 1974.

Skrobotov, N. A. *Pamiatnaia knizhka okonchivshchikh kurs v S. Peterburgskoi dukhovnoi seminarii s 1811 po 1895 g.* Spb: I. A. Frolov, 1896.

———. *Prikhodskii sviashchennik A. V. Gumilevskii. Podrobnyi biograficheskii ocherk.* Spb: I. O. Ettinger, 1871.

Smirnov, N. A., ed. *Tserkov' v istorii rossii (IX v.–1917 g.). Kriticheskie ocherki.* Moscow: Nauka, 1967.

Smolitsch, Igor. *Geschichte der russischen Kirche, 1700–1917.* Leiden: E. J. Brill, 1964.

Soiuz 17 oktiabria. *Prikhodskii vopros v chetvertoi gosudarstvennoi Dume.* Spb: A. S. Suvorin, 1914.

Soiuz revnitelei tserkovnogo obnovleniia. *Ob otnoshenii Tserkvi i sviashchenstva k sovremennoi obshchestvo-politicheskoi zhizni.* Spb: M. Merkushev, 1906.

Sokolov, A. R. "Rossiskaia blagovoritel'nost' v XVIII–XIX vekakh (k voprosu o periodizatsii i poniatom apparats)." *Otechestvennaia istoriia* 6 (2003): 147–58.

Sokolov, M. I. *Pastyrskie zavety.* Spb: M. P. Frolov, 1905.

Sokolov, N. M. *Ob ideiakh i idealakh russkoi intelligentsy.* Spb: M. M. Stasiulevich, 1904.

Sollertinskii, S. A. *Pastyrstvo Khrista Spasitelia.* Spb: F. G. Eleonskii, 1887.

———. *Propovedi na nekotorye prazdnichnye i voskresenye dni.* Spb: Tip. artillereiskogo zhurnala, 1903.

Solov'ev, Vladimir S. *The Justification of the Good: An Essay on Moral Philosophy.* Translated by Nathalie A. Duddington. Edited and annotated by Boris Jakim. 1918; reprint, Grand Rapids, MI: William B. Eerdmans, 2005.

————. "O poddelkakh." In *Sobranie sochineniia Vladimira Sergeevicha Solov'eva*. Vol. 6. Spb: Izdanie Tovarishchestva "Obshchestvennaia Pol'za," 1911.

Spinka, Matthew. *The Church and the Russian Revolution*. New York: Macmillan, 1927.

Spisok litsam, sostoiashchim v vedomstve imperatorskogo chelovekoliubivogo obshchestva. Spb: Gosudarstvennaia tipografiia, 1894.

Stavrou, Theophanis G., and Robert L. Nichols, eds. *Russian Orthodoxy under the Old Regime*. Minneapolis: University of Minnesota Press, 1978.

Stead, W. T. *The Truth about Russia*. New York: Cassell, 1888.

Steinberg, Mark. *Moral Communities: The Culture of Class Relations in the Russian Printing Industry, 1867–1907*. Berkeley: University of California Press, 1992.

————. "Workers on the Cross: Religious Imagination in the Writings of Russian Workers, 1910–1924." *Russian Review* 53, no. 2 (1994): 213–39.

Stites, Richard. *Russian Popular Culture: Entertainment and Society since 1900*. Cambridge: Cambridge University Press, 1992.

Sulkunen, Irma. *History of the Finnish Temperance Movement: Temperance as a Civic Religion*. Interdisciplinary Studies in Alcohol and Drug Use and Abuse, vol. 3. Lewiston: The Edwin Mellen Press, 1990.

Surh, Gerald D. *1905 in St. Petersburg: Labor, Society, and Revolution*. Stanford: Stanford University Press, 1989.

————. "Petersburg's First Mass Labor Association: The Assembly of Russian Workers and Father Gapon." *Russian Review* 40, no. 3 (1981): 241–62 and no. 4 (1981): 412–41.

Svetlov, P. Ia. *Ideia Tsarstva Bozhiia v eia znacheniia dlia khristianskogo mirosozertsaniia*. Sergiev Posad: Tip. Sviato-Troitskoi Lavry, 1905.

————. *Obrazovannoe obshchestvo i sovremennoe bogoslovie*. Sergiev Posad: Tip. Sviato-Troitskoi Lavry, 1904.

Sviateishii Pravitel'stvuiushchii Sinod. *Obzor deiatel'nosti dukhovnogo vedomstva za 1911 g*. Spb: Sinodal'naia Tipografiia, 1913.

————. *Obzor deiatel'nosti neskol'kikh storon dukhovnogo vedomstva za 1910 g*. Spb: Sinodal'naia tipografiia, 1911.

————. *Ustav dukhovnykh konsistorii*. Spb: Sinodal'naia Tipografiia, 1883.

————. *Vremennoe polozhenie o pravoslavnom prikhode*. Petrograd: Gosudarstvennaia tipografiia, 1917.

————. *Vsepoddaneishii otchet ober-prokurora sviateishego sinoda za 1884 g*. Spb: Sinodal'naia tipografiia, 1885.

————. *Vsepoddaneishii otchet ober-prokurora sviateishego sinoda K. Pobedonostseva po vedomstvu pravoslavnogo ispovedaniia za 1892 i 1893 gody*. Spb: Sinodal'naia Tipografiia, 1895.

————. *Vsepoddaneishii otchet ober-prokurora sviateishego sinoda K. Pobedonostseva po vedomstvu pravoslavnogo ispovedaniia za 1898 god*. Spb: Sinodal'naia Tipografiia, 1901.

————. Uchilishchnyi sovet. *Istoricheskii ocherk razvitiia tserkovnykh shkol za istekshee dvadtsatipiatiletie (1884–1909)*. Spb: Sinodal'naia tipografiia, 1909.

Sviderskii, M. *Vopros o tserkovnom prikhode v Predsobornom prisutsvii i v russkoi literature XX veke*. Kiev: Tip. Imperatorskogo Universiteta Sv. Vladimira, 1913.

Tareev, M. "Arkhimandrit Feodor (Bukharev)." *Khristianin* 10 (1907): 301–23.

Teodorovich, T. *Sovremennyia zadachi tserkovnogo prikhoda*. Warsaw: Tip. Varshavskogo uchebnogo okruga, 1907.

Teplov, A. *Zapiski putilovtsa. Vospominaniia, 1891–1905*. Spb: A. E. Vineke, 1908.

Thompson, Kenneth A. *Bureaucracy and Church Reform: The Organizational Response of the Church of England to Social Change, 1800–1965*. Oxford: Clarendon Press, 1970.

Tikhomirov, Lev. *Russia, Political and Social*. Translated by Edward Aveling. London: Swan Sonnenschein, Lowrey and Co., 1888.

————. *Zaprosy zhizni i nashe tserkovnoe upravlenie*. Moscow: Universitetskaia tipografiia, 1903.

Tikhomirov, N. A. *Putevoditel' po tserkvam goroda S. Peterbuga i blizhaishikh ego okrestnostei*. Spb: Vera i Znanie, 1906.

Tikhomirov, T. S. *Na prikhode. Sviashchennicheskaia entsiklopediia po vsem storonam pastyrskoi deiatel'nosti.* 2 vols. Moscow: I. D. Sytin, 1915.

Timberlake, Charles E. *Religious and Secular Forces in Late Tsarist Russia: Essays in Honor of Donald W. Treadgold.* Seattle: University of Washington Press, 1992.

Titlinov, B. V. *Dukhovnaia shkola v Rossii v XIX stoletii.* 2 volumes. Vil'na: Russkii pochin, 1908.

———. *Novaia tserkov'.* Petrograd: Izdatel'stvo "Petrograd," [1923].

———. *Pravoslavie na sluzhbe samoderzhaviia.* Leningrad: Gosudarstvennoe izdatel'stvo imena Bukharina, 1924.

———. *Tserkov' vo vremia revoliutsii.* Petrograd: Byloe, 1924.

——— *Vopros o prikhodskoi reforme v tsarstvovanie imperatora Aleksandra II.* Petrograd: Sinodal'naia tipografiia, 1917.

Titov, F. I. *Preobrazovaniia dukhovnykh akademii v Rossii v XIX v.* Kiev: I. I. Gorbunov, 1906.

Titov, G. *Polemika po voprosu o vetkhozavetnom sviashchennstve i sushchnosti sviashchennicheskogo sluzheniia voobshche.* Spb: Glazunov, 1882.

Trufanoff, Sergei Michailovich. *The Mad Monk of Russia, Iliodor.* New York: The Century Co., 1918.

Tsentral'nyi statisticheskii komitet Ministra vnutrennykh del. *Raspredelenie naseleniia po glavnym ispovedeniiam.* Spb [n.p.], 1901.

Tserkov' i obshchestvo. Spb. Weekly. January-February 1916. Faculty of the St. Petersburg Ecclesiastical Academy.

Tserkov' i zhizn'. Petrograd. Weekly. 1916–1917.

Tserkovnaia rech'. Spb. Single issue, 9 February 1903. Intended as a daily, to be edited by Father A. V. Rozhdestvenskii, focused on questions raised by meetings of the Religious-Philosophical Society.

Tserkovno-obshchestvennyi vestnik. Spb. Weekly. 1912–1915.

Tserkovnoe obnovlenie. Spb. Weekly. 1906 (1–7) and 1907 (1–12). Supplement to *Vek.*

Tserkovnyi golos. Spb. Weekly. January 1906–June 1907. ORRP.

Tserkovnyi vestnik. Spb. Weekly. 1875–1917. St. Petersburg Ecclesiastical Academy.

Tsimbaev, K. N. "Pravoslavnaia tserkov' i gosudarstvennye iubelei imperatorskoi Rossii." *Otechestvennaia istoriia* 6 (November-December 2005): 42–51.

Tsvetkov, M. V. "O prikhode." Biblioteka *Vek,* no. 2. Spb [n.p.], 1907.

Turenskii, I. D. *Tserkov' presviatyia Bogoroditsy, chto v Bolshoi Kolomne v S. Peterburge. Eia istoriia i opisanie.* Spb: A. M. Mendelevich, 1912.

Tverdokhlebov, L. *Pamiati v boze pochivshego Vysokopreosviashchennogo Arseniia (Briantsev), Arkhiepiskop Kharkovskogo i Akhtyrskogo.* Kharkov: Eparkhial'naia Tipografiia, 1914.

U Troitsy v Akademii, 1814–1914. Iubileinyi sbornik. Moscow: I. D. Sytin, 1914.

Urban, Linwood. *A Short History of Christian Thought.* Rev. ed. New York: Oxford University Press, 1995.

Uspenskii, A. "Lishenie sana sv. G. Petrov." *Krasnyi zvon* (January 1908): 17.

Ustav Obshchestva v pamiati otsa Ioanna Kronstadtskogo s predvaritel'nymi kratkimi svedeniami o samom obshchestve. Spb: I. V. Leont'ev, 1914.

V. M. *Dva dnia v Kronshtadte. Iz dnevnika studenta.* 2nd ed. Sergiev Posad: Tip. Sviato-Troitskoi Lavry, 1902.

Vadkovskii, M. "Prilozhenie k *Vospominaniam o mitropolite Antonii.*" *Istoricheskii vestnik* 147 (1917): 162–72.

Valk, S. "Peterburgskoe gradonachalstvo i 9–e ianvaria." *Krasnaia letopis'* 1 (1925): 37–46.

Valliere, Paul. "The Humanity of God in Liberal Orthodox Theology." *Modern Theology* 9, no. 1(1993): 55–65.

———. "The Liberal Tradition in Russian Orthodox Theology." In *The Legacy of St. Vladimir,* edited by J. Breck, J. Meyendorff, and E. Silk, 93–108. Crestwood, NY: St. Vladimir's Seminary Press, 1990.

————. *Modern Russian Theology: Bukharev, Solov'ev, Bul'gakov, Orthodox Theology in a New Key.* Grand Rapids, MI: Eerdmans, 2000.

————. "Modes of Social Action in Russian Orthodoxy: The Case of Father Petrov's *Zateinik.*" *Russian History* 4, no. 2 (1977): 142–58.

Vartagav, N. P. *Istinnyi pastyr'. Sviatootecheskii ideal khristianskogo pastyria.* Simferopol: Tavricheskaia gubernskaia tipografiia, 1906.

Vek. Spb. Weekly. 12 November 1906–8 July 1907. Editors Archimandrite Mikhail (Semenov) and A. V. Kartashev. Supplements *Tserkovnoe obnovlenie* (weekly) and *Biblioteka "Vek"* (monthly).

Vissarion, episkop. ([Nechaev] bishop of Kostroma from 1891–1905) *Uteshenie i sovety liudiam, zhivushchim v bednosti.* 5th ed. Moscow: G. I. Prostakov, 1898.

Vladimir, mitropolit Moskovskii i Kolomenskii. *Nasha pastyrskaia zadacha v bor'be s sotsial-demokraticheskoi propagandoiu.* Moscow: I. D. Sytin, 1909.

————. *O rabochem voprose.* Moscow: Russkaia pechatnia, 1909.

Voprosy religii. Moscow: Vil'de, 1908.

Voprosy very i tserkvi v III-ei gosudarstvennoi Dume. Otchet gruppy progressivnykh sviashchennikov Gosudarstvennoi Dumy. Spb: V. F. Kirshbaum, 1912.

Voprosy zhizni. Moscow: Sinodal'naia Tipografiia, 1904.

Voronets, E. "Itogi polemiki po povodu propovednichestva sv. G. Petrova i istoricheskaia spravka." *Missionerskoe obozrenie* 3 (1903): 315–31.

Voronova, E. A. *Neskol'ko lepestkov. Pamiati pochivshego mitropolita Antoniia.* Spb: Tip. Aleksandr-Nevskogo obshchestva trezvosti, 1913.

Vostokov, E. *Tserkovniki Isaakievskogo sobora v bor'be protiv naroda.* 2nd ed. Leningrad: Gosudarstvennyi anti-religioznyi muzei, 1940.

Vvedenskii, A. I. *'Religioznoe obnovlenie' nashikh dnei.* 2 vols. Moscow: Universitetskaia tipografiia., 1903–1904.

Vvedenskii, Aleksandr Ivanovich *Tserkov' i gosudarstvo.* Moscow: Mospoligraf, 1923.

Vysotskii, N. G. *Delo sviashchennika Grigoriia Petrova.* Moscow: I. M. Elov, 1907.

Wallace, Donald Mackenzie. *Russia on the Eve of War and Revolution.* Edited by Cyril E. Black. Princeton: Princeton University Press, 1961.

Ware, Timothy. *The Orthodox Church.* New York: Penguin Books, 1963; reprint, 1987.

Wortman, Richard. *Scenarios of Power: Myth and Ceremony in Russian Monarchy.* Vol. 2, *From Alexander II to the Abdication of Nicholas II.* Princeton: Princeton University Press, 2000.

Wynot, Jennifer Jean. *Keeping the Faith: Russian Orthodox Monasticism in the Soviet Union, 1917–1939.* College Station, TX: Texas A & M University Press, 2004.

Young, Glennys. "'Into Church Matters:' Lay Identity, Rural Parish Life, and Popular Politics in Late Imperial and Early Soviet Russia, 1864–1928." *Russian History* 23 (1996): 367–84.

Zakonodatel'nyi otdel Kantseliariia Gosudarstvennoi Dumy. *Spravka po voprosu o preobrazhenii pravoslavnogo prikhoda.* Petrograd: Gosudarstvennaia tipografiia, 1915.

Zamakhova, E. "Vnedumskaia deiatel'nost' deputatov-sviashchennosluzhitelei III Gosudarstvennoi Dumy." *Vestnik Moskovskogo universiteta.* Seriia 8, *Istoriia* 4 (1993): 13–23.

Zaozerskii, N. *Chto est' pravoslavnyi prikhod i chem on dolzhen byt'?* Sergiev Posad: M. S. Elov, 1912.

————. *O nuzhdakh tserkovnoi zhizni nastoiashchego vremia.* Sergiev Posad: N. N. Elov, 1909.

Zarnitskii, Ia. I. *Sbornik propovednicheskikh obraztsov. Opyt gomiletcheskoi khrestomatii.* Spb: P. F. Voshchinskaia, 1891.

Zav'ialov, A. *Tsirkuliarnye ukazy Sviateishego Pravitel'stvuiushchego Sinoda, 1867–1895.* Spb: I. A. Frolov, 1896.

Zelnik, R. E. *A Radical Worker in Tsarist Russia: The Autobiography of Semen Ivanovich Kanatchikov.* Stanford: Stanford University Press, 1986.

————. "Religion and Irreligion in the Experience of St. Petersburg Workers in the 1870s." *Russian History* 16, no. 2 (1989): 297–326.

Zernov, N. M. "The Reform of the Church." *St. Vladimir's Seminary Quarterly* 6, no. 3 (1964): 128–38.

————. *The Russian Religious Renaissance of the Twentieth Century.* New York: Harper & Row, 1963.

Zhivotova, N. N. *Propovednichestvo Ioanna Il'icha Sergieva Kronshtadtskogo.* Moscow: I. D. Sytin, 1892.

Zhurnaly i protokoly zasedanii, vysochaishe uchrezhdennago Predsobornogo Prisutstviia. 4 vols. Spb: Sinodal'naia tipografiia, 1906–1907.

Zhurnaly zasedanii s"ezda deputatov dukhovenstva S. Peterburgskoi eparkhii, 20–29 sentiabria 1905. Spb: I. V. Leont'ev, 1905.

Zhurnaly zasedanii s"ezda deputatov dukhovenstva S. Peterburgskoi eparkhii, 10–19 oktiabria 1906. Spb: I. V. Leont'ev, 1906.

Znamenskii, P. V. *Istoriia Kazanskoi dukhovnoi akademii.* 2 vols. Kazan: Tip. Imperatorskogo Universiteta, 1891–1892.

————. *Pravoslavie i sovremennaia zhizn'. Polemika 60–kh godov otnoshenii pravoslavii k sovremennoi zhizni.* Moscow: I. D. Sytin, 1906.

————. *Uchebnoe rukovodstvo po istorii russkoi tserkvi.* Spb: Sinodal'naia tipografiia, 1896.

Zolotarev, A. M. *Zapiski voennoi statistiki Rossii.* Spb, 1885.

Zvonar'. Spb. Monthly. April 1906–December 1907. Editor Kh. Belkov. Continued as *Krasnyi zvon.*

INDEX